D1201959

The Nature of Love

3
The Modern World

Books by Irving Singer

The Nature of Love
  1. Plato to Luther
  2. Courtly and Romantic
  3. The Modern World
Mozart and Beethoven: The Concept of Love in Their Operas
The Goals of Human Sexuality
Santayana's Aesthetics
Essays in Literary Criticism by George Santayana (Editor)

The
NATURE
of LOVE

3
The Modern World

Irving Singer

The University of Chicago Press
Chicago and London

The University of Chicago Press, Chicago 60637
The University of Chicago Press, Ltd., London

Library of Congress Cataloging-in-Publication Data

Singer, Irving.
  The nature of love.

  Vol. 1, 2nd ed.
  Includes bibliographies and indexes.
  Contents: 1. Plato to Luther—2. Courtly and
romantic—3. The modern world.
  1. Love.   I. Title.
BD436.S5   1984   128   84-2554
ISBN 0-226-76094-4 (cl. : v. 1)
      0-226-76095-2 (pbk. : v. 1)
      0-226-76096-0 (cl. : v. 2)
      0-226-76097-9 (pbk. : v. 2)
      0-226-76098-7 (cl. : v. 3)

To
Emily

*

Contents

Preface   ix

PART I: Love in the Modern World
  1. Our Present Condition   3
  2. Traditions That Survive   8
  3. Anti-Romantic Romantics: Kierkegaard,
        Tolstoy, Nietzsche   38

PART II: The Twentieth Century
  4. Freud   97
  5. Proust   159
  6. Twentieth-Century Puritanism: D. H. Lawrence
        and G. B. Shaw   219
  7. Santayana   254
  8. Sartre and the Varieties of Existentialism   281

PART III. The Future without Illusion
  9. Scientific Intimations   345
 10. Toward a Modern Theory of Love   369

Conclusion
  The Search for Harmonization   438

Notes   441
Index   467

Preface

I$_N$ W$_{RITING}$ T$_{HIS}$ B$_{OOK}$, I H$_{AVE}$
tried to make it a self-contained entity, more or less independent of
volumes 1 and 2. The title that I use for one of its parts—*Love in the
Modern World*—could have served as the title of the entire book.
Readers who have not finished (or begun) the preceding volumes
will find that they can follow the reasoning in this one without
much difficulty.

At the same time the present book is more than just a supplement to the others. As the final segment of a single work, it knits
together the threads of history and analysis left dangling by the
volumes that concentrate on centuries prior to our own. Since the
present is both a completion of the past and an anticipation of the
future, the "modern" must always locate itself within a continuity
of time. There are several ways in which a philosophical historian
may cope with this necessity. Like Hegel he can acknowledge that
he has inherited from earlier concepts his ability to think about the
world he lives in. He may then conclude that his own ideas reveal
what the past has been seeking to achieve. This approach always
runs the risk of egotism and megalomania. For how can one know
that one's own vision is objective and peculiarly valid? How can one
be sure that time has been moving on a trolley that leads it to
oneself and then goes onward predictably?

A second approach avoids such hazardous assumptions by reporting faithfully what has happened in the past but leaving the

future open, like uncharted terrain that can be known only as it is traversed. Though this methodology is sane and teachable, whereas the other kind may not be, it generally lacks imaginative scope. Even when its contributions are helpful, they must always seem to be unadventuresome.

Throughout my trilogy I have wished to follow a middle path between these extremes. My approach to the history of philosophy and literature has been guided by a personal perspective. I have not hidden it, and by the end of this book it should be evident. It represents what I have learned from past ideas as they have filtered through the contemporary modes of philosophizing in which I have been trained. The trilogy focuses on writers (almost entirely Western) who have influenced my thinking about problems that spoke to my own sense of reality. I have no doubt that others, coming from intellectual milieux not wholly congruent with mine, will create comparable histories that are very different in their conception of what is either sayable or worth saying. My effort can possibly be useful to them. It does not claim to be definitive.

In keeping with this basic pluralism, I have sought to avoid the tendentiousness of those who think that future as well as past occurrences in history must carry out the dictates of some thesis that has fixed itself within their intellect. But since my writing is consciously motivated by my own philosophical point of view, I would be disingenuous if I denied that my critical analyses have served as projections in that respect. This admission does not relieve me of the obligation to study both past and present authors with scrupulous fidelity to detail. It only means that even if my achievement is persuasive or acceptable, it cannot aspire to objective certitude. Its genre approximates conceptual art, and its success or failure must be determined accordingly.

In Part I of this volume, I relate the conclusions of the first and second volumes to our present condition in the post-Romantic era that we inhabit. The concepts of courtly and Romantic love cannot be meaningful to us in the way they formerly were. In the chapter on traditions that survive, I show why the problems inherent in both courtly and Romantic ideologies caused thinkers of the nineteenth century to reject them while also prolonging their influence.

In Kierkegaard, Tolstoy, and Nietzsche I find alternate expressions of this ambivalence.

In Part II, I address myself to writers who have contributed most to the analysis of love in the twentieth century: Freud, Proust (and Bergson), Lawrence, Shaw, Santayana, Sartre, and existentialists such as Beauvoir, Buber, and Marcel. Since my presentation is always interpretive and partial, I do not give an exhaustive account of their philosophical thought. Moreover, as in the other two volumes, I study explicit theories offered by literary figures such as Proust, Lawrence, and Shaw without regard to the fact that their major achievements are those of creative artists and not of speculative philosophers. Though my approach gives a limited view of their total genius, it puts us in touch with ideas that they themselves valued very highly. On the other hand, I have bypassed great authors who wrote about love in the context of their fictional work but chose to avoid theorization or conceptual analysis. (Henry James is a case in point, and others could also be mentioned.) In general I felt no obligation to discuss everyone in the twentieth century who had something important to say about the nature of love.

The same also applies to the material in Part III. The chapter on scientific intimations deals with recent work in psychoanalytic theory, ethology, sociobiology, and other specialized areas of the life sciences. I mainly consider problems in these fields that have philosophical or quasi-philosophical relevance. As a result, empirical studies—for instance, those devoted to case histories or data about mating choices—tend to be neglected. I did not need them for the theory construction that I present in the last chapter. There and in the Conclusion I sketch the outlines of my philosophy of love as it presently exists. I offer a series of conceptual distinctions and try to answer actual or possible objections to them. I also examine the work of several recent writers, and touch on issues in both feminist theory and theology, in order to test the parameters of my anti-reductivist approach. Readers who are looking for a resounding solution to life's problems will be disappointed by what I have to say. If, however, they can put my distinctions to a use that they find significant for themselves, they will have initiated or advanced their own philosophy and my efforts will have succeeded to that extent.

Since this volume is designed to be somewhat autonomous, there is no need to summarize the contents of volumes 1 and 2. Nevertheless there are a few reminders that I wish to make. First, the reader should know that in all three volumes the word "idealization" functions in different ways at different times. In the first volume, I distinguished my own use of that term from Freud's and Santayana's, which also differ from each other. None of them is exactly the same as the meaning in ordinary language. That implies distortion based upon a mistaken belief that something is perfect. The ramifications of Freud's and Santayana's concepts will appear in the relevant chapters. Here I want to make sure the reader remembers that when I employ the term "idealization" for my own purposes it refers to the making of ideals through the bestowing of value. As I argue, this is not necessarily a distortion and it need not be a search for perfection. It is just the having of an affirmative response that orients us toward some chosen object, or type of object, which then seems uniquely real and desirable. By the "bestowing of value" I refer to the fact that lovers create a value in one another that exceeds the individual or objective value each may also be appraised to have. The nature of idealization and the differences between bestowal and appraisal were originally analyzed in Part I of the first volume. I return to the details of that analysis in this volume's final chapter, where I amplify my distinction and defend it against its critics.

I must also remind the reader that I capitalize "Romantic" wherever it refers to the appropriate cluster of concepts developed in the eighteenth or nineteenth century. When the word occurs in its contemporary and colloquial usage, "romantic" appears in lower case.

Finally, the reader should recognize that I think of love as a pervasive attitude and not as merely a feeling. The loving response will certainly include feelings, the most obvious of which is the feeling of tenderness or warm-hearted affection. But love cannot be reduced to any particular feeling, even if there are feelings that count as a sine qua non for love. In being an attitude, love involves a disposition to act in diverse ways that ultimately conduce to another's benefit and, ideally, to one's own.

This book investigates attempts by thinkers in the modern world to elucidate the attitude or state of mind which is love. Some of them are philosophers, some are writers of literature, and some are scientists. The future of mankind may depend on our ability to synthesize the best in all three.

❊

Like most of my recent publications, this book was written in virtual collaboration with Josephine Fisk Singer. Her ideas and editorial criticism are deeply embedded in it, though at various points her opinions differ from my own. I am also grateful to Herbert Engelhardt, Jean H. Hagstrum, Richard A. Macksey, Moreland Perkins, and Robert C. Solomon for very useful comments on parts or all of the book. Katherine Matasy and Mimi Starr helped me by typing the manuscript and by assembling the references that appear at the end of this volume. The Provost's Fund for the Humanities, Arts, and Social Sciences at M.I.T., where I have taught for almost three decades, has enabled me to do some last-minute research.

In the years that have gone into the writing of my trilogy, many people have given me moral support. Some of them will not have realized how important their casual remarks were (to me), and others would be embarrassed to be named in this place. Nevertheless, I mention two whose encouragement and faith have endured throughout: Walter Jackson Bate and Richard Macksey.

I. S.

Part 1
Love in the Modern World

1

Our Present Condition

T HIS IS A BOOK IN PHILOSO-
phy and the history of ideas. But I wish to begin with a simple
question about contemporary attitudes. Does anyone still believe in
romantic love? The enormous number of romance novels con-
sumed by American women would seem to indicate that the faith
lives on. In many respects this type of literature closely resembles
romances that enthralled readers (or listeners) in the Hellenistic
period, in the Middle Ages, and continuously from the seventeenth
through the nineteenth centuries. By and large, it is fiction based
upon wish-fulfillment, enabling the reader to escape the unpleas-
antness of ordinary life. Moralists have often condemned, and critics concerned about aesthetic standards have always scorned, such
literature on the grounds that it distorts the realities of human existence. Ever since Freud there has been general agreement that sexual instinct is one of those realities, that it is usually present in
affections between men and women, and that wish-fulfillments are
falsifications if they fail to recognize its pervasive importance.
While the romances glorify love between the sexes—what is clearly
understood to be sexual love—they make considerable efforts to
avoid graphic details. In their moments of ecstasy the lovers are
carried away by powerful emotions, but they do not have orgasms.
Or at least, the authors do not *tell* us that they do. The lush and
breathless descriptions do not portray genital behavior and libidinal need.

3

This being the nature of most romance fiction nowadays, one may wonder whether it really manifests a belief in sexual love. Theorists of the nineteenth century who thought that love between man and woman provided the only means by which human beings could be happy, or satisfy their human nature, frequently insisted that it involved the fullest sexuality. Writers such as Keats, Shelley, Stendhal, or Schlegel were not permitted to describe the physiological dimension of sexual completeness, but in various ways they managed to convey its desirability. In our age, literature and even conversation have been liberated from restraints upon explicit acknowledgment of sexual reality. In the process, however, the importance of love has often been neglected or denied. Many people who believe in the giving and taking of sensuous pleasure seem to have lost all interest in sexual love. Side by side with romance literature, or in some dialectical interaction with it, we were flooded in the 1970s by how-to-do-it manuals and best sellers that depicted coital positions with all the glossy detachment of an Audubon print. Far from manifesting the joyful consequences of sexual love, this orientation generally belongs to an alternative attitude. It is an expression of the contemporary acceptance not of love but of the goodness in gratifying the senses.

As formulated by nineteenth-century Romantics, themselves the product of courtly, Christian, and Neoplatonic traditions in the Western world, the concept of sexual love provided an erotic goal for which all men and women could strive. It involved oneness with an alter ego, one's other self, a man or woman who would make up one's deficiencies, respond to one's deepest inclinations, and serve as possibly the only person with whom one could communicate fully. If the world were properly attuned to the value of love, this would be the person one married, establishing a bond that was permanent as well as ecstatically consummatory. The sexual bond would participate in a social order constructed out of loving relationships that united all people to one another and mankind to nature as a whole. Since love was God, romantic lovers would be carrying out the dictates of divinity throughout their mutual intimacy—in their sexual as well as nonsexual oneness. It is this faith, this extensive ideology, that has waned in our century. To many

you... ...olly foreign to the world they have grown
...istoric."

...1e 1950s many sociologists believed that
...an any that preceded it, was character-
...)nize love and marriage. Girls and boys
...1to loveless marriages arranged by the
...1ic reasons; they were free not only to
...but also to terminate their marriage
...t least as far back as John Milton in the
...ential strand of Protestant thinking
...this mode of integrating love and
...eriment was undertaken with great
...xual love to bring about happy and

...sociologists have evaluated this phenomenon
... while some have defended love as the only factor
that can prevent modern marriage from turning into an impersonal
offshoot of socioeconomic determinants, most investigators have
linked the increasing divorce rate and frequency of family disinte-
gration to the unrealistic assumption that romantic love can last
beyond a brief period of discovery and initial excitement. If
marriage were devoted to the beauty of love, the sociologists maintained, it could hardly cope with the ugly realities that confront
family life within a difficult environment. Once the romantic couple
got to know each other's shortcomings, they would naturally lose
heart and discontinue their relationship. In a similar vein, some
anthropologists interpret the modern idea that marriage should be
predicated upon love as an expression of bourgeois values inherited
from eighteenth- and nineteenth-century capitalism. They think
that belief in the exclusiveness, even sanctity, of the marital bond
symbolizes adoration of personal property acquired through free
enterprise. As succeeding generations become increasingly dis-
enchanted with capitalist attitudes, it is presumed that they will
lose faith in monogamy, romantic love, and any suggestion that
these can buttress one another.

As a mere philosopher I leave this debate to the sociologists and
anthropologists. In the last two decades developments within the

5

women's liberation movement have contributed to further complexities. I deal with these in later chapters, though only from the point of view of conceptual analysis. I am primarily interested in studying the evolution of Western ideals as they show forth the human capacity to create a world that is meaningful. Concepts that belong to the "idealist" tradition are obviously relevant, but so are the "realist" critiques of it, as well as diverse attempts to reconcile the two extremes. As an example of the latter, consider the approach of Bertrand Russell. He defends a modified or revisionist version of the belief in romantic love. In *Marriage and Morals* Russell repeatedly claims that it is one of the great goods that human beings rightly cherish and naturally wish to enjoy. Romantic love is, he says, "the source of the most intense delights that life has to offer . . . something of inestimable value, to be ignorant of which is a great misfortune to any human being." But, contrary to many Romantics, Russell denies that this is the kind of love that underlies happy or stable marriages. They depend upon "affectionate intimacy quite unmixed with illusion" whereas, Russell believes, romantic love inevitably involves a "glamorous mist" that prevents the lovers from truly understanding each other's being. Also Russell sees marriage as an institutional device for the rearing of children. Romantic love has no such concern, he says, and therefore it must be subordinated for the sake of parental duties once the lovers have finally married each other.

While there is much wisdom in what Russell claims, it nevertheless perpetuates an unwholesome dichotomy between romantic and married love. Unlike Montaigne, or any number of cynics in the past, Russell does not advise against marrying the object of one's romantic interest. But he too magnifies the differences between the two types of love, treating them as if they could have virtually no effect upon one another.

In opposition to that approach, I shall be arguing that romantic love is part of the search for a long-term relationship such as married love, and that married love not only completes the aspirations of romantic love but also permits some vestige of its continuance within the new context of marriage. In the second volume of this trilogy, I tried to show how nineteenth-century concepts of Romantic love arose as a response to the thinking of seventeenth- and eighteenth-century Rationalists who followed Montaigne's lead and asserted that passionate love was incompatible with the demands of a happy marriage. Romantics, Shelley in England and Schlegel in Germany, for example, sought to unify passionate and married love. They believed that feeling and reason, nature and society, were ultimately united, organically interrelated, jointly requisite for a good life that human beings could ideally attain. Writing in the post-Romantic twentieth century, Russell reflects contemporary doubts about the feasibility of such utopian harmony. I share his skepticism and applaud his desire to get beyond the benign optimism of nineteenth-century romanticism, as well as the antithetical pessimism to which it often led. I nevertheless believe that the Romantic dream was a wholesome one. We who have gone through reactions for and against its many excesses may now be able to reconstitute it in a saving remnant, a viable and realistic conception of what is humanly possible.

2
Traditions That Survive

In Previous Volumes Of This trilogy, I suggested that philosophies of love in the West could be categorized as either "idealist" or "realist." The idealist approach I analyzed in terms of magic, metaphysical import, and the concept of merging. Despite the great diversity among themselves, the idealists agree in denying that love can be explained merely by reference to biological, physiological, or sociopsychological coordinates. The realists seek that kind of explanation, generally relying on the latest science available at their moment in history. When Lucretius states that passionate love is the product of erotic images resulting from sexual frustration, when Zola approaches human intimacy in the way that a physicist studies the friction of colliding objects in a laboratory, when Schopenhauer describes the varieties of love as so many examples of a will to reproduce the species, they are speaking as realists who consciously attack any idea that love involves merging of a special metaphysical sort. The idealist tradition does not doubt that there are physiological components in sexual or even religious love, but it rejects the idea that such components define what love is and may become. It claims that they are neither necessary conditions for love nor sufficient to understand its elusive essence. In seeking to delineate the relationship between love and sex, however, the different schools of idealism follow different paths and sometimes reach utterly different conclusions.

Analyzing sexual love in his own way, Plato treats it with his char-

8

acteristic ambiguity. At times, he sounds as if sex and love were largely incompatible: since love is directed toward absolute beauty beyond the empirical world, the enlightened philosopher must renounce physical interests that tie him to mundane sense experience. When self-indulgent Alcibiades depicts the sexual continence of Socrates and remarks that between them there can never be peace, Plato seems to be saying that the very presence of carnal appetite interferes with the philosophical attitude in which true love consists. At other times, however, Socrates is shown to have erotic interests in young men. In several places we are told that only a god could live a life of pure contemplation: since the philosopher is human like everyone else, he cannot eradicate his material nature but must satisfy it while possibly conforming to the spiritual principles in which he believes. A similar ambiguity arises in medieval thought. Some theologians in the Middle Ages considered sexual impulse sinful, irreconcilable with the love of God even when directed toward one's spouse. Other theologians, Aquinas for instance, maintained that desire becomes evil only if it subdues man's higher faculty of reason. Dante argued that, once it has been rendered subservient, sexual inclination may even further the love of God. But though Aquinas and Dante recognize the need to harmonize sexual and religious interests, they reinstate the Platonic ambiguity by portraying the former as forever problematic and certainly unworthy of being idealized in itself.

In courtly love a great effort is made to eliminate the traditional ambiguity. The courtly attitude accepts sexual love and idealizes cultivated means of furthering it. While distinguishing between "pure" and "mixed" (i.e. consummatory) types of intimacy, the concept of courtly love generally locates evil in the betrayal of ethical standards. It sees no sinfulness in the fact that love between man and woman is sexual and involves another human being instead of God. To that degree ideas about courtly love humanized, and thereby challenged, theological orthodoxy. In the idealism of courtliness, love and sexuality are both good as long as their object is morally or aesthetically suitable. Though continence was often advocated, sexual love that merged bodies as well as souls was frequently defended as the norm.

The enemies of courtly love attacked it as a cunning glorification of sex. To say this, however, is to misunderstand it completely. The delights of physical contact, the joyful magnetism of erotic feeling, were important to the courtly lover, and they were sometimes treated as if they proved that love must have transcendent significance. But sex itself was generally relegated to secondary importance, subordinate to the quest for values that effect an honorific union between a man and a woman. Among courtly lovers sexual desire was expected to arise as a consequence of true love, a sign and even guarantee that it exists, rather than being the cause of love. The medieval romances assume that lovers will have sexual relations if circumstances permit. Yet their actual lovemaking is not described in detail or taken to indicate the nature of love. When courtly literature mentions carnal feelings that accompany love, it depicts them as epiphenomena, by-products of a noble dedication to elevated ideals.

Romantic love deviates from courtly love by interpreting beauty or goodness in terms of the erotic experience itself, with the result that sexuality takes on greater significance. To the Romantic, sexual desire is usually more than just a vehicle or concomitant of love: it is a prerequisite, even when it appears in a somewhat attenuated form. Without the emotions that belong to our sexual being, how could the striving in love achieve the explosive dynamism that the Romantics found so definitive? Only sex can generate the intensity of impulse that both symbolizes and incorporates the mystical merging idealized by romanticism. Only sexual drive, which may be satisfied in ways that are infinitely varied, can explain the frequently undirected, unobjectified character of Romantic love. At the same time, the lover was thought to experience what no physical mechanism could ever instill. For his love is never *equated* with sex. Instead, Romantic love elevates sexuality into something super-physical, metaphysical, something transcendental and more than merely biological. The bond between man and woman ceases to be an animal trait; it becomes a divine agency by which human beings rise above their material nature. Though the sexual ingredient in this transformation was sometimes denied or prudishly condemned, romanticism generally returned to that much of the ancient world which still retained primitive beliefs about orgasmic ecstasy leading to identification with a deity. Much of romanticism explicitly seeks to harmonize human and religious love by accentuating the element of sexuality they have in common.

That Romantic love goes beyond courtly love in idealizing sexual experience can readily be seen by comparing, once again, Wagner's *Tristan and Isolde* with the medieval legend. In the opera most of the heroic adventures that adorn the original tale have been dropped. Their place is taken by a succession of passionate love scenes, each consisting of little action but great emotion. Throughout the lengthy second act, Tristan and Isolde make love in magnificently inarticulate exclamations that show us the force of erotic destiny better than if the singers had enacted intercourse on the stage. The music is itself sexual—ardent, chaotic, swollen with yearning and the mutual joy of penetration. Even though the libretto gives no information about consummatory sex that the lovers may have had with one another, Wagner's music makes this aspect of their relationship more vivid to us than all the medieval versions that depict their prolonged adultery.

Romantic philosophers often speak of music as the most metaphysical of the arts. For in being nonobjective, a sheer sequence of expressive sounds, does it not reveal passion and the nature of human emotion more profoundly than any other medium? Needless to say, it is primarily Romantic music they had in mind. Music such as Wagner's is thoroughly and blatantly sexual, erotic in a way that medieval music was only rarely, and classical music not infrequently but always with greater restraint. While music of the Middle Ages presents sound patterns similar to visual designs— beautiful objects to be contemplated as a courtly lover contemplates perfection in the person he loves—Romantic music deters us from turning sounds into objects of any sort. It employs an apparent formlessness that stimulates enjoyment of life as it is immediately felt, just as the Romantic lover cultivates the affective potentialities in mere experience. In medieval music one listens with the eye; in Romantic music one listens with the entire body, sexual organs included. Courtly love derives from a world that idealized the visual as that which perceives external reality in an objective manner no other sense possesses. All of Platonism is based on the metaphorical identification of sight and philosophic intuition, and all medieval Christianity aspires to that seeing of divinity which Dante records in the final cantos of the *Divine Comedy*. As opposed to this, Romantic love dignifies the nonvisual faculties. For they convey the sense of lived experience as a fusion of moments in time, and that reveals the magical metaphysics of merging. In Wagner's operas the music expresses this Romantic philosophy as much as, or even more than, the words that any character utters.

✸

In the development of the idealist tradition, ideas about possible oneness between men and women altered as much as attitudes toward sex. When courtly love transmuted religious reverence into human devotion, it gave womankind an inherent value that had not existed in the ancient world. Within the Judaeo-Christian-Moslem tradition, religious love had generally been predicated upon the supremacy of the male. God, Christ, and most of the saints were masculine; in heaven as on earth men asserted cosmic authority by means of the same hierarchy of gender dominance. It seems obvious to us that one sex has received preferential treatment when we recall the Mohammedan conception of paradise as a sumptuous bordello. But until recently, Western scholars failed to see that a similar attitude prevailed in religions closer to home. By the eleventh or twelfth century, however, the glorification of the female begins. In medieval religion it turns into the adoration of the Virgin, sometimes even into Mariolatry, with all its overtones of what we would call momism. In various concepts of courtly love it appears as a comparable dedication to aristocratic women. Instead of worshipping the Lord of Hosts and serving the lord of the manor, the courtly male could worship female beauty and serve that noble lady of his heart who perfectly embodied it. She, in turn, would love only a man who revered her, thereby acknowledging her rightful dominance and eliminating any necessity for her to love an odious spouse. Courtly love was originally created for women in the ruling classes who felt themselves dispossessed by all-powerful husbands. They found ready allies in men, younger brothers of the lord, for instance, who had given up the hope of attaining power through normal channels.

In its own way, Platonic philosophy contributed to this medieval outburst of feminism. There are no women in the *Symposium* other than the flute-girls. The speeches are delivered at a stag party, in what primitive societies sometimes call the House of Men. The dialogue seeks to define the highest values usually associated with male homosexuality. Scholars may debate about Plato's own beliefs about erotic choice, but it is clear that everything in Socrates' final statement tends toward the idea that true friendship can exist only among men, as Aristotle was also to say. And yet, there is much in Socrates' speculations that could buttress the medieval lady's struggle for recognition. Though Plato elsewhere describes the causal efficacy that the highest form has in the actual world, his doctrine of love concentrates upon beauty rather than power. He defines love as a longing for the very idea of perfection, which may or may not prevail against the material order in things. The philosophical leap from this to courtly love is gentle enough. In orthodox Christianity, God's omnipotence is fundamental, and therefore medieval theologians spent much time trying to prove his existence. To Plato, and the courtly tradition that caught his hint, only the Beautiful was worthy of adoration. The feudal lady, a pawn of local politics, a bartered bride regardless of her rank, could hardly hope to exercise much power; but she might well attain beauty. For such as she, what could be more attractive than a doctrine that idealized the male's submission to values she embodied to the extent that she made herself more beautiful?

In Neoplatonism of the Renaissance, Platonic and courtly concepts mingle through an overt synthesis that also tries to include religious idealization in general and the love of God in particular. The glorified female now becomes a stairway to divinity, and even a manifestation of Christian agapē. While this conception of woman recurs in the nineteenth century, when she is often treated as an angel in the bourgeois home, there also develops a typically Romantic idealization of the male. In courtly love a man's devotion to a woman's beauty of person and of soul enabled him to express his virtue. The medieval knight found honor in fighting for the greater glory of his lady. He had to be a great warrior on his own, but his ferocity could further justify itself as dedication to the perfect woman he loved. In Romantic love, the elevation of the male occurred through an idealization that often had nothing to do with the beauty of women. This new ideal was the modern conception of heroism: self-sacrifice in the interest of humanity, the nation, a revolutionary cause, the demands of one or another art. Through heroism men could not only become worthy of love but also an embodiment of value comparable to the medieval lady. The Romantic male, when he succeeds in this endeavor, uses heroism as a way of regaining whatever dominance he may have lost when women began to emancipate themselves in the Middle Ages.

Like everything else that reached fruition in the nineteenth century, Romantic love is largely a blending of history, a mixture of elements from the past. In it, exaltation of the heroic male exists side by side with exaltation of the beautiful female. In some romances of the period, women dream of giving themselves to a man who is dedicated to his own heroic potentialities rather than to female beauty; in others, men continue to revere women as if perfection could only originate with them. Sometimes it is the idealized women who become heroic, thus earning their domi-nance through love by taking action in a noble cause as a man would do. This is the theme of Beethoven's *Fidelio,* and much of nineteenth-century culture concerned itself with questions about woman's capacity for attaining the highest love by means of both heroism and fidelity, or else fidelity which is itself heroic. Some-times this meant subservience to a dominant male; but often Romantic love presents itself as a search for equality between the sexes, each having access, jointly and reciprocally, to its own type of heroic action. On many occasions the realist tradition also advo-cates equality, while denying, of course, that it can be achieved through anything as idealistic as Romantic love.

Discussing religious concepts of merging, I distinguished in pre-vious volumes between medieval mysticism that sought oneness with an external deity and later forms of mysticism that placed the greatest emphasis upon the experience of merging itself. A similar distinction applies to the differences between courtly and Romantic love with respect to the idea of perfection. The concept of courtly love assumes that a man loves a woman because she is "perfect" as a lady. In return she loves the man because, in principle at least, he is perfect as her courtier. For both, the object of devotion is a superlative example of its type—an idealization of what men and women are able to become. The man is an outstanding knight, an incomparable doer of deeds that benefit other people—thereby revealing his purity of heart as well as the fact that he is not his own master. Lancelot's name bespeaks the fact of military prowess; Tristan's the sense of sadness that results from subservience and dispossession. The lady is always beautiful in body and soul, of high rank and often of the highest, endowed with every virtue though somehow unsatisfied with the life she leads. To the subjects of a Guinevere or an Iseult the question must always be: how can so perfect a creature, one who has everything valued in society, fail to be happy? The courtly lover provides, by means of love, the happiness the lady objectively deserves. He does so by dedicating himself to her sheer perfection, her astounding proximity to the ideal. His effort can succeed because her perfection is undeniably real. It is in no sense illusory. It exists for all to see, though only the lover can fully appreciate it. The lady's beauty is prior to love, which does not bring it into being. If anything, her beauty brings love into being— not literally, perhaps, since a philter or some other form of magic may be needed for that, but symbolically. As a perfection, the lady *should* be loved: love for her is demanded by the craving for objective goodness that everyone feels innately.

The perfectionism in courtly love comes ultimately from Plato. But Romantic love often turned to other philosophers for inspiration. Platonism sees love as an intermediary between the aspiring soul and the perfect object it naturally desires. Romanticism focuses upon the inherent creativity of love. Medieval theology had always insisted upon the creative character of agapē, God's love, but no one dared suggest that anything comparable originated with human beings. For theorists of Romantic love, however, the erotic underlies everything in man that is creative. Far from uniting persons who are antecedently perfect, the experience of love *makes* their ideality. From merging and the return to wholeness there accrue values that the lovers could not have had previously or in isolation. In addition to the notion of merging, the Romantics introduced organic and genetic metaphors. As a child is an organism that results from the fusing of male and female biology, so too Romantic lovers become in their totality a new and higher form of life. The use of such metaphors stems from post-Kantian German thinkers who tried to explain all reality by means of them. The emergent-perfectionism in Romantic love displaces the prior-perfectionism in courtly love, just as the idealism of Hegel supplants the idealism of Plato.

Given its faith in the creative powers of merging, Romantic love idealized men and women who were far from perfect before they loved. In fact, the worse they were, the better could their experience reveal the infinite power of love. El amor brujo—Love the Magician—could turn sinners into saints. This would have been impossible if they were saintly, or close to perfection in any other way, from the start. In the Romantic period one begins to hear about the "woman behind every great man." Which is to say, the heroism for which a woman loves a great man results paradoxically from her love itself. The woman develops the man's capacity for heroic action by getting him to love her, thereby infusing him with her faith in his eventual achievement. This much resembles courtly attitudes since it provides women with the power to elicit love, and it is not surprising that Goethe's notion of the eternal feminine leading men on to spiritual heights should have been taken as a medieval element in his work. Actually, however, Goethe's concept is purely Romantic. For it is not the perfection of the woman, whether Gretchen or another, that motivates the Faustian man. He does not act in her service; he acts for the sake of masculine ideals that are mainly independent of her. The woman does not make the Romantic lover a hero by being perfect, but only by giving him an opportunity to love. In order to further his greatness, the woman may sometimes sacrifice herself, a fairly common occurrence in operas and novels of the Romantic period that is rarely found in the courtly tradition. But even so, her moral perfection results from love instead of being that which occasions it. Though Romantic versions of medieval legends often tried to retain the prior eminence of the original courtly lovers, the major idealization generally pertains to their all-transforming union rather than any independent excellence they may have had in themselves.

In that passage from the *Symposium* I have quoted more than once, Aristophanes spoke of the other self, really a part of one's own self, into which each lover wished to melt. But though merging is basic to all idealist theorizing about love, the "other" with which one merges varies considerably in that tradition. Religious love, like Platonic love, unites the soul with its "ultimate reality." For Plato this is the cosmic order presided over by the Good or the Beautiful, which is present in all humanity but usually in a distorted fashion; for the Christian mystic the most real Being is a God whose spirituality turns out to be an infinite though unknowable magnification of the mystic's. In the *Republic* Plato says that "the philosopher, in constant companionship with the divine order of the world, will reproduce that order in his soul and, so far as man may, become godlike." The mystic uses similar means in a similar attempt to approximate divinity. His effort was often condemned by orthodox theologians as arrogance or presumption. But in the Renaissance, Ficino's Neoplatonism synthesized the interests of the church with man's desire to become perfect and immortal.

In a sense, this is what the courtly lover also sought, though he chose a different kind of love-object. Identifying his own reality with what was noblest in himself, his love was an attempt to merge it with the goodness in a perfect woman. That is why courtly lovers, being each other's alter ego, had to belong to the same high level of social and human distinction. Courtly love could not occur between members of the lower orders, just as it could not exist among animals. Love required the courtesy and cultivation that was limited to the upper classes, who therefore laid claim to all the other perfections on which love depended. This usually meant that courtly lovers would have a similar station in society, though Andreas Capellanus is much concerned about the possibility of men and women changing ranks by means of love. When such changes did occur, they were highly circumscribed. Only in medieval fairy tales does the prince fall in love with a commoner. Even then, she is often a princess in disguise. Aristotle had taught the courtly tradition that "like attracts like."

The Romantic lover also merged with his alter ego and thus attained the completion of his own reality. But now the other self could, in principle, be found in almost any individual. Like attracts like only in a world of symmetry and order. When they disappear, as began to happen by the end of the Middle Ages, Aristotle's truth yields to the idea of like attracting unlike, and even the notion of opposites gravitating toward one another. By the nineteenth century every scullery maid could dream of dancing her way into some Prince Charming's heart, and every young aristocrat could yearn for the vampish woman of the streets who would elicit his true virility. Within the ideal of Romantic love, biological as well as social barriers crumble. Just as a person could love anyone else regardless of rank, so might human beings enjoy a quasi-romantic love for animals. In the medieval legend Tristan had a great sense of attachment to Hodain, his dog, but his feeling is mainly military—the affection of a commanding officer towards a devoted underling. There is none of the egalitarian sentimentality evinced by Walt Whitman when he speaks of wanting to live among the animals or by Albert Schweitzer when he throws food to ants under the table. It is largely with the advent of romanticism that one encounters in the West pleas for compassion toward creatures that suffer on the lower rungs of evolution. St. Francis could express a loving kinship with all other animate beings because they too were the offspring of a perfect God whose goodness appeared in whatever he chose to make. Everything was to be loved as a way of loving God. Only with nineteenth-century philosophers such as Schopenhauer does one find, in a fully developed form, the idea that nonhumans should be loved as fellow sufferers within a world that has no perfection to it.

Seeing in everyone and everything the ability to become love's alter ego, romanticism develops a segment in the theme of magic that had previously been neglected. By its very nature, magic transcends the limits of ordinary life and established convention. That is why love need not unite only aristocrats to one another. There is nothing in a love philter that requires it to be drunk by social and moral equals. Relying upon love's transforming magic, romanticism attests to the supernatural efficacy of merging, as well as to its unlimited goodness. At the same time, however, accounts of Romantic love had to treat magic realistically. Courtly love flourished in a superstitious age that accepted the possibility of miraculous potions and wondrous charms. The courtly tales often treat magic as a literal fact, frequently asserting that it alone causes the occurrence of true love. In Romantic love, magic becomes the symbol for everything that makes erotic merging so different from the rest of life. Magic no longer brings love into existence: love itself is now magical. Here again, it is the experience of love that interests the Romantic most of all.

This reliance upon experience explains the abundance of psychological detail in all modern romances. Where the medieval storyteller recounts perilous events that befall the lovers, thereby showing that love is always dangerous, the Romantic novelist describes their feelings at various stages within the relationship. Where the courtly poet depicts the outer trappings of his lady's beauty as well as her manifest virtue, his Romantic counterpart speculates about the woman's sentiments and tries to determine whether they correspond to his own.

Since Romantic love endows the amatory experience with supreme importance and permits the choice of a beloved who is not perfect or even beautiful, its critics have often claimed that it is "a love of love" more than anything else. If by this they mean that the Romantic lover is not concerned about the welfare of the beloved or is incapable of loving anyone as just the person he or she happens to be, I find little in the history of ideas to justify their criticism. It reduces to a cliché that writers like Babbitt and de Rougemont glibly assert without proving that it applies in general. One can say, however, that Romantic love—the eighteenth- and nineteenth-century concept that we are here investigating—is usually an affirmation of *love for love's sake*, love being accepted as perfect in itself, which means something quite different from saying that it is merely a love of love and not of another person. There is some significance in the fact that Romantic love developed in the same period as art for art's sake, knowledge for knowledge's sake, and business for business' sake.

This point is worth accentuating. The entire tradition of idealism glorifies the existence of love and gives it transempirical meaning. But the formulations that preceded theories about Romantic love placed the marvellous occurrence within a system of realities external to itself. For Plato true love was man attaining a realm of forms logically prior to everything in the universe. The love of God served the same function for a medieval Christian; and in humanizing religious love, courtly concepts remained similarly objectivistic. The courtier and his lady could love each other in the approved manner only to the extent that their behavior was commendable apart from love. Though Iseult's conduct is blameworthy in some respects, the courtly poets do not question her residual virtue, since it was posited as that which enabled her to love and be loved. Her turpitude was generally blamed upon corrupt society (the felon knights) or else upon the poisonous philter. Even when she uses deceit in her sworn oath during the ordeal by fire, Iseult does not lose her moral excellence as the foundation of her suitability for love. So long as they continue to love one another, the courtly lovers are thought to embody perfections that cannot be altered by anything they do. In Romantic love none of this applies any longer. For now the mere occurrence of love itself creates a new objectivity that mediates with no preceding reality and needs nothing but its own intrinsic value to be justified. For the Romantic, the experience of merging is so obviously desirable as to require no other validation for love. In that sense, he accepts love for love's sake, as its own self-justification.

The absence of prior and objective perfections in the concept of Romantic love might be explained by its derivation from mentalistic philosophies that originate with Descartes' doubts about the external world. Within the structure of courtly love, however, there were sufficient tensions to account for the massive change that was to occur. Like all thinking directly or indirectly Platonistic, ideas about courtly love had to clarify the relation between a particular and its universal, between an individual alter ego and the general perfection embodied in it. The two being quite different, which of them is really the object of love? Does the courtly lover yearn for a specific person or does he merely wish to serve an ideal? Does he love a woman who lives and dies like everyone else, or is she just a symbol for that abstract beauty that he desires most of all?

Plato raises but does not resolve questions of this sort. He defines true love as the rational search for the highest form, but he does not explicitly limit love to the striving of philosophers. That would have involved too flagrant a distortion of ordinary language. Plato leaves open the possibility that persons who have not been purified by philosophical training can undergo love in some sense of that word. Only the philosopher could love all things properly, for only he would know how to perceive them as symbols of absolute beauty. At the opposite extreme, a sensualist could hardly be said to love since his infatuation with one material object or another would prevent him from abstracting its essential form. But in between, might there not be an approximate kind of love in which nonphilosophers loved one another as particulars and yet also as symbols of perfection? Though Plato does not deny that this too is love, he ignores important problems about it that confronted the courtly tradition. The in-between, ambiguous, unphilosophical love was the love it cultivated. It sought, with great difficulty, to show how such love might actually be the best that human beings can hope to attain.

As might have been expected, advocates of courtly love dealt with the issue in different ways. Petrarch's Laura sounds more like a particular woman than like the embodiment of an ideal; Dante's Beatrice may actually have existed but she is mainly presented to us as an abstract symbol. In the poetry of the troubadours, of Neoplatonists in the Renaissance, and of many others in the courtly tradition, one can never be sure whether and to what extent the beloved is real or imagined, an actual person or an idealized possibility. In either event, the situation is philosophically unsatisfactory. If the beloved is just an individual, the erotic relationship lacks the search for perfection upon which the concept of courtly love insists. If the lady is nothing but a representation of absolute beauty, one's love is really directed toward the ideal and not toward her. The exponents of courtly love rarely allow their devotion to be limited to one or another of these alternatives, but neither do they find it easy to show how the two may be reconciled. As an individual, the woman belongs to the empirical world, which is radically imperfect since immersed in matter and removed from the realm of ideals. As a purified symbol, however, the beloved can have no personal identity since she is then just a manifestation of the universal. I am not suggesting that there is a logical impossibility in treating a person both as an individual and as a symbol, even simultaneously. But courtly love, as it developed in the Middle Ages and in the Renaissance, could not work that feat because of a basic flaw in its thinking about individuals whom one loves.

This flaw appears most clearly when we consider courtly love in relation to promiscuity and frustration. In principle, courtly love requires absolute fidelity. The knight swears to love no one but his lady, and she is expected to love no one but him. Such at least is the ideal relationship. In all their utterances to one another, the lovers claim there is no one else they can love. That is why they die so readily when something in the outside world destroys their union. As the troubadours lament in poem after poem, what is there to live for if the lover is deprived of the irreplaceable beloved to whom he truly belongs?

This conception of fidelity devolves from that aspect in courtliness which treats the loved one as a unique individual. It hardly comports with the idea that love is directed toward someone who merely symbolizes perfection. For if the woman deserves to be loved because of her beauty or moral superiority, a devotee may rightly turn to others whom he subsequently finds to be admirable in a similar manner and therefore equally deserving. Indeed, the Platonic influence would seem to *require* promiscuity, for only by moving from one beautiful object to another can we ever be liberated from the particularity of each in our attempt to discover the eternal form that is present in them all. Putting the two sides of courtly love together, we find those ingenious poets who sing to one lady after another that she is the only person he can possibly love and that he loves her because of his dedication to beauty itself.

As a means of paying for this deceit or contradiction, courtly love often issues into a characteristic type of frustration, as in the trou-

badour concept of "fin' amors." Theoretically, the lovers reach the
ultimate in human achievement by virtue of their oneness with
each other. That is what the poets tell us, and we are expected to
blame their difficulties upon hostility from the environment,
including ecclesiastic condemnation of extramarital love. On closer
inspection, however, we find that the frustrating of oneness is often
indigenous to the relationship itself. If the lovers try to accept each
other as individuals who hope to attain perfection, they cannot be
satisfied. For no human beings can ever live up to the ideal. It is
only a matter of time before the lover realizes the imperfection of
his lady. He may move on to love someone else and he may
honestly believe that now he will finally reach the goal he is seeking.
But we, who observe the spectacle impartially, know that he is
striving for the unattainable and is sure to be disappointed.

Perhaps the ladies themselves were somewhat aware of this.
Their haughty disdain, that cruelty of the beloved which the troubadours so often lament, may not signify the excruciating remoteness of perfection—as the poets wish us to believe—but
rather the understandable desire to hide the fact of imperfection
while also showing scorn for anyone who is foolish enough to think
that a perfect woman can exist. Though troubadour love differs
from other types of courtly love inasmuch as it frequently uses
sexual incompleteness to express love's inherent contradiction, the
logical problem remains the same throughout.

There are various ways in which medieval philosophy sought to
resolve this difficulty. Manicheans despised the world of sense in
order to assure the fidelity of their love for God. Since God was the
only individual whose being comprises all perfection, nothing else
could be worthy of devotion. This solution was considered heretical,
the church preferring the "caritas-synthesis" with its emphasis
upon the partial though derivative goodness of everything God
creates. In the seventeenth century, Spinoza provided an alternative
that was no less extreme than Manicheanism but better suited to
the needs of his time. By identifying God with nature taken as a
whole, Spinoza made it possible to conceive of loving all things in the
world. For everything was a mode of the ultimate Being—God
or Nature—which was eminently lovable. Romantic philosophers

took this to mean that *any* love showed forth divinity. It was the only true individual and the only true perfection. But since a totality belongs to all its parts, God was present in whatever one loved.

This move enabled romanticism to go beyond the courtly approach and to sidestep many of its difficulties. Nevertheless the conflict between individual and symbol reappeared in the new context, though much disguised. If the Romantic lover really loved someone as just the individual she happened to be, he would accept her with all her imperfections. He would seek an ideal good in her exactly as she is. Yet most of the Romantic theorists, Rousseau for example and even Shelley (who is otherwise so different from him), defined love as part of a search for perfection. The beloved did not have to embody beauty or goodness prior to the experience of love, but in the lover's imagination she was to symbolize unrealized perfections for which everyone yearns. To this extent, however, she has not been accepted as just the reality she is in herself.

Problems about promiscuity and frustration were also left unsolved. If we really believed in love as its own justification, we could and should move freely from one beloved to another once our affection diminishes or turns stale. Among the Romantics, Stendhal does accept this as a valid outcome. He was not representative, however: most others thought that fidelity was an essential part of love. If the Romantic lover were a libertine, there would have been no need to expect much constancy in his love life, particularly in a world where feelings are so notoriously inconstant. But romanticism differs from libertinism in its belief that love forges an eternal bond. This could not happen if each relationship were merely a variable episode within a series.

As in other versions of the idealist approach, the Romantic affirms that men and women truly love each other only if they are somehow made for one another, permanently and to their mutual benefit as human beings. But the Romantic also thinks that the experience of love *creates* their attunement. These two beliefs are inconsistent and sure to lead to failure or frustration. Pursuing an unknown, seeking no objective goodness that he can recognize, the Romantic lover must depend upon the felt quality of his own emotion, and there is no guarantee that this will be what is needed to live successfully with another human being. Courtly love runs the risk of Tantalus, who strives for a known and desired good that he can never reach; the peril in Romantic love is symbolized by Sisyphus or the Flying Dutchman, who wanders endlessly with neither hope for nor awareness of a final consummation. How then can a Romantic lover enjoy the kind of experience romanticism idealizes?

If the object of love is unknowable, romanticism faces the further problem of determining how love can be reciprocal. The goodness of mutual love is affirmed by every version of the idealist tradition. The notion of magical merging virtually requires it. In religious love, reciprocity is illustrated by the Christian belief that God loves and can be loved in return. God so loved the world that he gave his own son in sacrifice; and salvation is reserved for those who love God either through an elevation in their nature or as a result of his gracious infusion into them. Greek religion had always insisted upon an insurmountable barrier between man and god. The gods might often mingle with men and women, but they did not seem to spend their time cultivating reciprocal love. The Greek gods rarely love human beings in the way that the Christian God constantly loves his creation. The gods could play favorites, as in Homer, and they were capable of having intense love affairs; but except in the mystery cults, which are not wholly representative of ancient re- ligion, they were not thought to merge with mortals. The associa- tion between a god and a human being derived its greatest import from the heroic offspring that resulted, rather than from a spir- itual attainment in the relationship itself. The mortal singled out for the honor of being loved by a god—Io, Alcmena, Europa, Leda, to name only sweethearts of Zeus—was not expected to give herself for the glory of love so much as for the aggrandizement of the community to whom she was providing a new hero. If the wom- en suffer by this intimacy, as they often do, it is the *distance* between humanity and the godhead that is symbolized by their pain rather than the joyful anguish of merging.

The enormous chasm between the finite and the infinite, be- tween the littleness of mortal beings and the grandeur of God, is also emphasized by Luther when he argues that man's sinful nature makes it impossible for him to love God on his own. At the same time, Luther provides a conception not only of man loving God reciprocally but also of their merging, becoming "one cake." Since man cannot love by his own nature, this holy bond results from a freely given bestowal of God's love, which descends in a burst of agapē and makes the unworthy recipient into its vehicle. Reciprocity exists insofar as God's love comes back to him after having descended to whatever creature has been chosen for its circuit. This trajectory discloses God's love for himself, love having originated with him and then returned through no efficacy other than his own. Whether that can be considered an authentic example of reciprocal love between God and man (who is only a conduit for God's love) remains an unresolved problem in Lutheran doctrine.

Comparable difficulties apply to the romanticization of Luther's thought. Since love or Romantic agapē infuses helpless human beings, invades them with awesome power, strikes for reasons of its own and not because the individuals have willed this for themselves, one can hardly see how the transaction genuinely includes reciprocity. If love is the search for an unknown, if it does not presuppose much knowledge about another person, if two people merge through an experience that reveals divinity but has no objective basis in what they are as a particular man and woman, it seems strange to say that they mutually or reciprocally love each other.

Courtly love did not encounter problems exactly of this sort, since it was a searching for prior perfections rooted in the order of being. But it too had difficulties with the notion of reciprocity. For it could not show how courtly lovers, who were still flesh and blood, might love one another while still being imperfect like all mortality. In a sense, the troubadours understood the dilemma best of all. For though they sought reciprocity and sometimes seem to have experienced it, they popularized the idea—not that they were limited to it or that all of them espoused it—of reciprocated love being generally unattainable, and even undesirable.

The realist tradition avoids these difficulties of courtly and Romantic love by arguing that they issue from an idealistic attitude that is simply false to the world we live in. Eliminate the assumption that love is a striving for an ideal, either directly as an external goal or indirectly through its embodiment in an idealized experience, and all these problems disappear. The realist may be right about this, and the life sciences of the future may enable us to construct a philosophy of love between human beings that can resolve the issues we have been considering. But no such eventuality will be acceptable if it fails to recognize that love includes valuation, and above all the creating of ideals, rather than a mere releasing of appetitive mechanisms. It is the typically human craving for values, for goods ideally relevant to our condition, that the theorists of courtly and Romantic love were primarily interested in. Though the twentieth century has moved beyond their limitations, both types of idealism are still important. They are essential for an adequate perspective, even in the present.

Nor should we pretend that realists of the past have ever attained reassuring uniformity of opinion among themselves. Some have claimed that the oneness of love is always an illusion, nonexistent as a matter of fact, since human beings can love only selfishly. But other realists have argued that without mutual and reciprocal love man could neither survive nor satisfy most of the needs that are basic to his nature. The controversy has not been eliminated by even the most recent research. In developing our own philosophy of love, we can wish to use science as much as possible, but we must not assume that the problems I have been discussing have only historical interest and may be disregarded by those who have access to empirical methods of investigation. For those methods inevitably employ, indeed rely upon, concepts furnished by the history of ideas. Even in science, there is no royal road to truth.

Although I make little attempt to exploit the findings of behavioral studies, it may be useful to develop a little further some of the sociological comments I previously offered. This will help us to see how modern thinking about love has often perpetuated courtly and Romantic concepts while also going beyond them. As we know, medieval marriages were made in the council chamber, not in heaven. Nobles entered into matrimony for reasons of statecraft or financial gain. A woman was not chosen for her personal charms so much as for her material worth. Annulments could easily be obtained, and were frequently granted when a wife was no longer politically useful. Arising as part of a feminine search for power in society, courtly love helped women resist the oppressiveness of medieval marriage. It dignified an alternate conception of sexual possibilities. A wife's resentment toward the status quo could be expressed by having devotees who would swear undying obedience to her. Whether or not a noblewoman practiced adultery, the mere fact that she had admirers would give her an avenue of escape from her husband. Particularly if there were little or no overt sexuality between the lovers, the woman could avoid public condemnation while also enjoying the benefits of a separate life. In some aspects of its varieties, Romantic love makes this new and separate life into an autonomous world. Love then becomes a haven away from social reality rather than a fortification within it, which is all that courtly love had generally wanted.

Having these different attitudes toward society, the courtly and Romantic approaches also differ in their views about the destructiveness of love. Throughout its history, the idealist tradition extols the joy and creative power of love while also recognizing how destructive it can be. As I have suggested, magic destroys by its very being. Through it, lovers break down many of the barriers that keep them apart from one another. In negating the influence of a hostile environment, however, magic can also isolate the lovers from the world outside. In Platonism and in all Western religion, there runs an ascetic imperative that uses the love of beauty or of God as an excuse for abolishing natural interests—the lusting of the senses, the lure of worldliness. Neither courtly nor Romantic love fits neatly into this pattern, but both occasionally borrow from it. The concept of courtly love belongs to a humanistic dimension in medieval thought which tries to civilize intimate relations rather than to expurgate them as a Manichean might. In their struggle with the institution of marriage, courtly lovers wish merely to avoid its limitations upon their freedom. They have no desire to lose the pleasures of feudal life; and even those who do consider love and marriage incompatible rarely condemn the matrimonial bond. When their passionate love brings them into conflict with society, they may choose the painful necessity of renouncing the goods that marriage provides. But such sacrifice is usually made with great reluctance. From this point of view, drinking the philter is a catastrophe that courtly lovers regret even though they accept it in the name of love.

In the world of Romantic love, conventional marriage can appear attractive, and its destruction calamitous, but now the lovers do not always *feel* the calamity. Their love can easily turn into a denial that the life others cherish, which they themselves may have valued before they became lovers, is really worth retaining. Reacting against evils in society, courtly love could sometimes displace the everyday world—as in those medieval fantasies of lovers who escape to fairyland. But that was just a better version of what they left behind. Romantic love was capable of going much further. It could renounce, as if to eradicate, the world as a whole, which it often considered vile and loathesome. This type of Romantic love renews the Manichean attempt to subjugate the empirical realm completely. As in Manicheanism, the Romantic then rejects ordinary life for the sake of rising through the spirit, though possibly immersing himself in carnal experience as a preliminary tactic that eventually leads to spiritual purification. To succeed in this, he must systematically destroy conventions and restraints needed for living in all but the most utopian of societies.

The destructiveness of idealist love was often directed inward as well as out. However blissful, love involved much pain, much agony, and not infrequently, the death of both participants. Since their oneness was magnificent but fragile, idealist lovers were infinitely sensitive to anything that might sully its perfection. Their constant concern about separation or disunity subjected them to the anguish of jealousy and the fear of being deceived. The more idealistic lovers were, the more they seemed to suffer—and sometimes, like the troubadours, they claimed to enjoy their suffering. The world, which does not understand the nature of love, was certainly unwilling to make life easier for them. But often their greatest punishment was self-inflicted and quasi-masochistic.

Here again, we may recognize vast differences between courtly and Romantic love. Courtly lovers suffer because society is against them and because their noble aspirations are so hard to satisfy. Sometimes it is the remoteness of the beloved, as a consequence of her disdain or the fact that she has been idealized, that causes the suffering. More often, however, it exists regardless of how completely she reciprocates. The misery of love is accepted not because the lovers desire it but because they have no other choice under the circumstances. Though courtly lovers may submit to hardships, and even welcome the opportunity to do so, they are attesting to the supreme value of their love: they give no other significance to the suffering. For the Romantics, on the other hand, the pain in love tends to become self-validating. It is idealized in its own right. It still indicates how hostile the world can be, and it still reveals the heroism of lovers who are prepared to sacrifice so much. But also it is treated as a crucial part of love itself. From having been a joyous experience painfully difficult to protect against weaknesses in the lovers and animosity in everyone else, love becomes an experience that is by definition more pain than joy. I do not mean to suggest that the Romantics introduced this idea. On the contrary, it is often found in ancient and medieval descriptions of "lovesickness." But to many Romantic theorists, this became their principal conception of love in general. The passionate suffering which is the merging with another person took on so central and predominant a role as to make all other aspects of love seem peripheral.

However far back in the history of mankind we may trace the concept of love as pain and destructiveness, sometimes including hatred or cruelty toward the beloved as a necessary element in its constitution, the fullest expression of this idea occurs in the latter half of the nineteenth century. Lucretius saw love as a possessiveness that drove men to violence, even insanity, and the Marquis de Sade reviled it as an aberration in the search for happiness. But these thinkers, like many of the intervening moralists who warned about the disease of passion, belonged to the realist tradition and therefore rejected any attempt to idealize suffering that comes from love. Though the Romantics also feared that love between the sexes includes a need to hurt and to be hurt, they did not repudiate the suffering of love. They joyously accepted it as an ideal condition even when it causes the annihilation of the lovers. The Romantic concept of Liebestod, love-death, carries this idealization of joyful suffering to a level previously unattained by the idealist tradition. Death becomes idealized as a desirable, though bitter, component within the love experience.

I call this part of modern thinking about love "Romantic pessimism." It is by no means the only type of Romantic love; and if I am right in suggesting that the different theories interweave within the philosophy of particular thinkers, Romantic pessimism must not be reified in total separation from more optimistic approaches to Romantic love (or even from the realist tradition). The optimistic attitude I have discussed under the heading of "benign romanticism." Romantic love is benign whenever it stresses the possibility of affective success in the world as we know it, or as it may well become. To this extent, Romantic love perpetuates that much of the courtly attitude which emphasizes the positive and joyful potency of sexual love, its ability to make life worth living here on earth.

Romantic love as a benign potentiality includes more than just an optimism about attaining erotic happiness and the harmonization of male and female values. It also links up with related concepts, some of which had been maturing for a long time, while others were just beginning. Among the first of these is the idealization of married love. Even when theorists of courtly love saw no incompatibility between love and marriage, they generally had little to say about the sexual love that might exist between husband and wife. In many medieval romances, which were often courtly, the lovers succeeded in marrying one another. But despite some interesting exceptions, their married love was usually left unexamined. The doctrinal authorities of the church, who advocated conjugal love, insisted that affection within marriage must not become too passionate and must always be rendered subordinate to the love of God. Few thinkers in the Middle Ages, and fewer still in the ancient world, explore the concept of married love as a moral achievement within human sexuality. Ideas of that sort start developing in the late Renaissance, particularly in Protestant countries pursuing the implications of Luther's denial that celibacy was sanctified or that priests should remain unmarried. Among the Puritans, married love became the foundation of the Christian commonwealth. It was a holy form of heterosexual friendship, a source of communion or righteous intimacy between husband and wife.

To this conception romanticism had only to add its belief in the metaphysical value of merging through passionate experience. Whether the wife was idealized as a domestic angel or as an equal participant in a worthy institution essential to society and organically related to the cosmos as a whole, a large portion of Romantic thought dealt with the beneficial consequences that married love entailed. Did this include sexual fulfillment? In principle, yes. But Romantic theory did not provide an adequate account of how married love could be compatible with, indeed predicated upon, the demands of sexuality.

As we shall see, the unrealistic attitude toward marriage that sometimes occurred in romanticism was attacked by Tolstoy, Nietzsche, Shaw, D. H. Lawrence, and many others. The need for a confluence between sexual interest and married love is best established by Freud's essay "The Most Prevalent Form of Degradation in Erotic Life." Freud there reports that many of his patients complain that while they have no sexual difficulties with their mistresses, they find themselves impotent in lovemaking with their wives. They claim to love their wives and to enjoy what otherwise would be a happy marriage. At the same time, they admit that they do not love their mistresses, although they derive a great deal of pleasure from them. After some analysis, Freud concludes that these men are suffering from a split within their erotic disposition: "Where such men love they have no desire and where they desire they cannot love." He explains this by noting that the wives have been chosen because they resembled the mothers and sisters of the men. These women all belong to the same socioeconomic class; they are all embodiments of respectability; they are all idealized as too elevated for anything as crude or vulgar as sexual enjoyment. Mother and sister being approved objects of love to whom total access is forbidden by the incest taboo, the wives are also perceived as women one must not demean through sex.

I introduce Freud's analysis here because of its relevance to various Romantic beliefs about conjugal love as a purified merging of souls. In effect, Freud was saying that any such dichotomous approach is false to the requirements of normal life between married people. Far from effecting a reconciliation between love and marriage, it encourages a husband to court someone other than the wife he loves (in one sense or another) while she remains unsatisfied throughout her married life with the man she may also love. In other words, the difficulties in courtly love have not been overcome, but only repeated in a pathology that hardly indicates a viable solution.

In working at the problem of married love, romanticism contributed to the idea—new in the nineteenth century—that love between man and woman can be an agency of health or healthy-mindedness. As such, love may be considered a wholesome symbiosis, in principle attainable through the satisfaction of natural needs, both social and biological. This aspect of benign romanticism brings the idealist approach close to a possible reconciliation with realists throughout the ages who have sought to analyze love in terms of natural phenomena. Questions about what is or is not "natural" may still separate the two traditions, and details of the ultimate synthesis remain to be clarified. But in one way or another, harmonization between idealist and realist now becomes possible.

Until a hundred years ago the life sciences were so backward they could hardly contribute much in this direction. Only in recent decades has unification of the different strands begun to appear feasible. The origins of this great achievement are to be found in benign romanticism, however primitive or naive its conceptions may seem today. For us in the modern world, it serves as a key to the future, as well as to the past. Its theories are to be cherished, though we can no longer accept them in their earlier formulation.

❋

In the West there have been several great legends (or myths) that have concentrated upon these problems about the nature of love. Since the problems overlap, it would be foolhardy to think that any legend deals exclusively with one and only one of them. Nevertheless, the story of Heloise and Abelard, mythic despite its origin in actual events, has served to express Western man's persistent desire to love a real person of the opposite sex while also loving God in the totalistic way demanded by Judaeo-Christian religion. I discussed this problem, in relation to the sorrows of Abelard and Heloise, in my chapter on "Medieval Romance" in volume 2. In that chapter I also examined the legend of Tristan and Iseult. There the drama results from the conflict between sexual love and marriage, not only because in loving each other the protagonists are both in love with someone to whom they are not married, but also because it is understood that they above all should rightfully be married to one another. In this respect the myth of Tristan and Iseult, far from being subversive to marriage, as de Rougemont has claimed, contributes to the idealization of married love. The legend manifests a desire not to separate but to harmonize passion and marriage.

In the myth of Don Juan, one encounters the greatest attempt to reduce all sexual love to hostility and aggression of a sort that realist philosophers have frequently treated as the substratum in human affect. This legend officially begins in the seventeenth century, but its mythic sources extend far into the past and throughout various cultures. The story is partly a secularization of mystical ideas about divinity (portrayed as masculine) violently taking possession of the human soul, which is seized like a captured female and overpowered in an act of raptus. In many pagan religions the gods behave like Don Juans, making love to women one after the other and often against their will, but also touching them with holiness as if they were nature being sanctified through the goodness of fructification. In the Don Juan legend male promiscuity is sometimes idealized as having a virtue comparable to this. But usually it is portrayed as vicious and harmful. In the nineteenth century the behavior of Don Juan was often contrasted with idealistic love considered more authentic, and occasionally the protagonist became a Romantic lover himself. Nevertheless the original versions of the legend—in Tirso, Molière, and even Mozart—use Don Juan to show how appetite and aggression masquerade as a noble ideal that actually has no basis in reality. By and large, the mythic Don Juan succeeds in his seductions by playing upon the pitiful human need to idealize sex. Idealization itself is generally depicted as an act of self-delusion.

Organizing this historical material, we could possibly suggest that there are temporal stages and even cycles through which the philosophy of love has progressed. Whether we accept Hegelian notions about the dialectical development of history or something akin to Toynbee's belief in challenge and response, we might imagine a systematic pattern through which the concept of love has evolved in the Western world. I myself find little reason to expect objectivity in any such enterprise since it inevitably depends upon the theorist's choice of what shall count as representative for one or another moment in the historical progression. But the venture is worth considering, however briefly.

For instance, we could speculate about five stages of conceptualization in the Middle Ages. The first might include ideas about love and the appropriate relationship between the sexes formulated by Carolingian literature of the ninth and tenth centuries, reflecting social customs of the Dark Ages as well as doctrines of the church at that time. In this stage male supremacy is dominant throughout, women are expected to look up to men as exemplars of the ideal rather than vice versa, and the role of courtship is minimized. In the next stage an antithetical idealization of the female occurs, as if to ease the dominant male's sense of guilt for having subdued women previously. The symbolic rectification is accomplished by ideas, as in troubadour poetry, about the importance of wooing ladies who embody transcendental values. The third stage envisages male and female attaining reciprocity in love, which happens in the Tristan legend (and in courtly romances as a whole). Where the earlier stages alternated between supremacy of the male and supremacy of the female, the third stage enacts an armistice within that struggle by uniting the sexes in a condition of equality and mutual love. This leveling of dominance is also an exaltation for both male and female, since it involves a supreme and final oneness between the lovers even though the outcome of their love may be tragic for other reasons. In the fourth stage the experience of love becomes a spiritual achievement congruent with the contemporary religion. The love between Dante and Beatrice, for instance, is an ultimate union similar to what Tristan and Iseult desired except that now all earthly and material elements have been removed. The fourth stage is, however, pitched so far above the everyday world of ordinary human beings that it engenders a deflationary reaction. It is followed by philosophies of love, as in the second part of *The Romance of the Rose,* that reduce love to a thoroughly naturalistic congress of men and women satisfying needs for sexual pleasure and the reproduction of the species.

With a little ingenuity, one could work out comparable patterns for the ancient world, for the Renaissance, and for more recent periods of history. The project is hardly worthwhile, I am convinced, because at any one time we can find aspects of all five stages existing simultaneously in literature, philosophy, and the relevant social mores. Consider the troubadours, who are usually depicted as idealizing the female in accordance with the second stage. These writers comprised a school of poetry that existed for two or three hundred years and voiced a wide gamut of differing attitudes toward love. Even in the works of a particular troubadour, we often find diverse and contradictory ideas that seem to have been evoked by a passing mood or momentary occasion, and at times by the need to say something the audience wanted to hear.

Moreover, it would be extremely difficult to demonstrate a causal sequence between any one of the stages and those that preceded or followed it. We know that the young Boccaccio greatly admired Dante, although Boccaccio's own beliefs were much more hedonistic than Dante's. We also know that Boccaccio's thinking about love became religiously orthodox, even repressive, as he got older and retreated from his youthful optimism. But to assume a causative connection in Boccaccio between his feelings about Dante and either his earlier naturalism or his later reversion to orthodoxy is to ask for more than history can yield.

We can certainly affirm that extreme ideas about male or female supremacy are likely to induce their contradictories. But more elaborate generalizations of the type I have mentioned are sure to be suspect. Even if we give up the search for cause and effect, even if we limit ourselves to stages that follow one another in a regular pattern without our pretending that causal truths are thereby revealed, we may well be imposing our own classification upon the facts. Different stages often occur at the same time throughout each epoch. Can we guarantee that we have not defined these stages by reference to authors who catch our attention because they are geniuses, or theorists who mattered to later generations, or else convenient exemplifications of what we are looking for? Though the effort can be stimulating to the imagination, we should not expect it to prove that there are discernible cycles in history.

On the other hand, the fivefold analysis that I have suggested may remind us that the different approaches to love do not occur in total isolation from one another. Thought does not exist apart from a context of inherited ideas. Greatness consists in the ability to redirect the present and the future in accordance with one's own sense of reality. No dialectic or deterministic program can reliably predict how individuals will change the course of historical development; and yet the conceptual structures that have been wrought by earlier thinkers reveal the human mind's creative powers, whether or not it employs intellectual components that are stages or parts of a causal network.

Studying contemporary concepts of love in this book, I shall approach them as organic growths rather than as schematic reenactments. The modern world, as it exists for us, defines itself in reaction to, and sometimes revulsion from, the romanticism of the nineteenth century. Throughout the struggle for emancipation, however, extensive roots remain. They provide a nourishing lifeline to the present. This cathexis with the past, as well as with the future, is what we must try to elucidate.

3

Anti-Romantic Romantics
Kierkegaard, Tolstoy,
Nietzsche

O<small>F</small> T<small>HESE</small> T<small>HREE</small> A<small>UTHORS</small>, Kierkegaard would seem to provide the most fertile opportunities for comment. He writes book after book about the nature of love, and he fills them with translucent, if not transparent, allusions to his own emotional state. At the same time, Kierkegaard's works are so richly dialectical, so greatly given to irony, and so often pseudonymous that everything he says lends itself to different interpretations. He wished to confront his readers with ambiguities in their own being, forcing them to make authentic decisions rather than submit to any external dogma. But Kierkegaard also felt that his mission in life, the reintroduction of Christianity into Christendom, was based upon unwavering truth. To that extent his philosophy presupposed the incontrovertible authority of religious belief. In his final books he writes under his own name, acknowledges his theological priorities, and explicitly announces that his *Works of Love* is to be taken as "Christian reflections."

One could very well approach Kierkegaard by studying *Works of Love* and showing how his earlier thought had really been tending in that direction, drawn to this terminus as if by magnetism. But it is easier to start with his first and most famous book, *Either/Or*, written while he was beginning the long process of convincing Regina Olsen that he could never marry her. Part I of *Either/Or* formulates the concept of what Kierkegaard calls the "immediately erotic." This is the life of pure sensuousness, devoted to the pleasures of a moment-by-moment existence. In Mozart's Don Giovanni, whom Kierkegaard considers to be the definitive embodiment of the Don Juan myth, the pursuit of the immediately sensuous is unreflective; in the character whose "Diary of the Seducer" ends the volume, reflection serves as a device for snaring the hedonic potential of each moment as it passes. In general, this is a way of life devoted to beauty, which Kierkegaard interprets as fundamentally erotic. It is a level or dimension in the being of everyone, a universal sensibility that he calls "the aesthetic" in contrast to "the ethical" and "the religious."

In later books, such as *Repetition* and *Stages on Life's Way*, Kierkegaard continues this analysis but develops the idea that the aesthetic is more than just an element in human nature. He uses the concept to characterize the entire being of men who refuse to consider alternative ways of living. In either event, the aesthetic appears as a possibility that Kierkegaard finds both attractive and frightening. It is what comes naturally to one's animal interests, providing sexual gratification with none of the encumbrances of responsibility or interpersonal commitment. Through "the rotation method" one escapes the dangers of boredom by constantly moving from one source of pleasure or type of beauty to another without expending energies that would be needed to preserve a relationship. But Kierkegaard implies that the aesthetic life is unsatisfactory: it is generally a thin veneer that hides infinite recesses of despair and self-loathing.

These negative attributes are not evident to the voices of immediacy that dominate Part I of *Either/Or*. In Part II, however, we encounter the views of a man, called Judge William, who defends marriage and the ethical against the aesthetic. Here again, Kierkegaard concentrates upon matters of love and sexuality. As the aesthetic showed itself most vividly in an appetite for physical beauty, so too does the ethical appear in the longing for married love. The aesthetic way of life may use the language of love, and the philanderer may seduce by pretending to experience love, but at this level of existence love can never be taken seriously. Only in marriage, Judge William argues, is love between persons really possible. Perhaps with Kant in mind, he claims that there is no incompatibility between "romantic love" and matrimony. On the contrary, he says that romantic love is itself merely the preliminary to married love, which fulfills it by providing constant and prolonged association between the lovers. Married love completes romantic love by allowing it to develop through time and in the creation of a family. Judge William claims that the benefits of the aesthetic recur in marriage, where they become transformed by the ability to enjoy pleasures that persist rather than being merely momentary. And finally, Judge William harmonizes the ethical with the religious, since he refuses to believe that there can be "a collision between love for God and love for the persons for whom love has been planted by Him in our hearts."

The philosophy of Judge William has sometimes been described as "ethical humanism"; and if Kierkegaard had allowed his thinking to remain permanently at this level, which he presents in sympathetic detail, his doctrine could be taken as an advance upon Hegelian conceptions of love. In Hegel the love of persons is ultimately jeopardized by the ontological need to submerge all individuals, indeed all particularities of being, into a larger pattern of spiritual development. As opposed to Hegel, Kierkegaard strenuously tries to salvage the love of particular persons. Throughout his books, and here in the voice of Judge William, he argues that persons can love each other only in their acceptance of the unique and unpredictable characteristics that all human beings acquire by living their own individual lives, by merely existing in time. Neither Hegelian Reason, Kierkegaard maintains, nor any other, can account for married love, since that involves the ability to respond continuously and affirmatively to another person as he or she happens to exist at each moment.

As an even more radical departure from Hegelian orthodoxy, Kierkegaard also attacks the idea that "the inward" is identical with "the outward." Hegel believed that spirit was not purely mentalistic or essentially closed to observation. Whether in man or in God, spirit showed itself in action and had its very being in the world it progressively created: spirit did not belong to a hidden realm of privacy. For Kierkegaard this tenet in all Hegelianism is antithetical to Christianity as he conceives it. The idea that the inward is the outward he interprets as a glorification of bourgeois conformism and muscular religiosity, turning the nineteenth century into a Christendom that betrays its original faith. Against Hegel and secular liberals alike, Kierkegaard proclaims the importance of recognizing the separateness of each individual soul and its inability to reach God through self-renunciation for the sake of a higher synthesis. He concludes that interpersonal love requires a commitment that is neither rational nor wholly explicable by reason. Every achievement of the spirit, and of love in particular, is for Kierkegaard an "existential leap" in which the inward becomes manifest through outward behavior without ever being fully revealed thereby.

Relying upon criticism of this sort, Kierkegaard frequently attacks, even ridicules, Hegelianism. Nevertheless his ideas are also compatible with an approach to love not wholly different from Hegel's. This mediating approach is present in the position Judge William defends. He claims that the outward fulfills itself in love which arises from total acceptance of another's ultimate separateness. The inward self thus retains its individuality while also achieving the love of other persons. By merging the ethical with the religious, Judge William optimistically affirms, man can—with God's help—overcome his sense of alienation. The methodology differs from Hegel's, and certainly the attitude toward Christianity is no longer the same, but the promise of a successful and even predictable attainment of love between persons remains constant in both philosophies.

From the very start, however, Kierkegaard was not satisfied with the wholesome if somewhat banal ideas of Judge William. He did continue to affirm the anti-Hegelian arguments, and as time went by they became more and more extreme. The emphasis upon commitment, choice, and in general the leap of faith he also retained from book to book. But through the years he was increasingly obsessed with the conflict, and possible inconsistency, between the ethical and the religious. In his *Concluding Unscientific Postscript,* in which he reviews his earlier pseudonymous writings, he says that *Stages on Life's Way* marks an advance upon *Either/Or* in its presentation of the final stage as a level of development that goes far beyond the ethico-religious conceptions of Judge William. *Either/Or* had posed the alternative of the aesthetic life on the one hand, and the ethico-religious on the other. That was the choice one had to make in deciding whether to live either for the beauties of erotic experience or for the rewards of married love as the embodiment of both the ethical and the religious. In *Stages on Life's Way,* however, Kierkegaard emphasizes the differences between the ethical and the religious.

The book begins with a section called "In Vino Veritas," which resembles Plato's *Symposium* in some respects. In it the aesthetic is presented through various voices that modify the first part of *Either/Or.* Johannes the Seducer speaks of women in ways that show him to be much more than just a scheming philanderer. He clearly likes women, enjoys their company, and even considers them a perfection that only an erotic sensualist like himself can fully appreciate. Judge William is given another opportunity to make observations about marital fidelity and the equality of man and woman. But Kierkegaard then introduces a long "passion narrative" entitled "'Guilty?'/'Not Guilty?'" in which the character Quidam provides an account of what is, in effect, the painful period during which Kierkegaard broke off his engagement to Regina Olsen. Though Quidam loves the woman he has been courting and in some sense wishes to marry her, he goes through contortions of the spirit that finally lead to separation. The question about guilt arises because Quidam, like Judge William, believes that married love belongs to the ethical category and therefore indicates a moral obligation that applies to all men and women. The marital condition is an ethical universal inasmuch as anyone who does not participate in it must be guilty of neglecting his human responsibilities. Since marriage transcends the merely aesthetic, it is not a possibility that one accepts or rejects in accordance with inclination and personal taste. Marriage is an obligation since God, as Kierkegaard conceives of him, commands human beings to love. If one does not even *try* to succeed in married love, one fails with respect to both the ethical and the religious.

At this point the paradoxical character of Kierkegaard's philosophy occurs in its most strident form. As a creative thinker who generalizes about human nature, Kierkegaard follows the Kantian tradition in arguing that what is morally right for a particular person can only be something that applies to everyone. Ethics cannot be determined by individual whim. Being an ethical universal, married love incorporates an ideal for which everyone ought to strive. To the extent that anyone does not approximate it, he is guilty, even sinful, in his mode of existence. At the same time, Kierkegaard feels that he himself is incapable of entering into marriage, above all with the woman he presumably loves. For him, as for his spokesmen in the pseudonymous writings, the great problem of life consists in determining what circumstances, if any, justify considering oneself an exception.

In his *Journals,* as well as in the books we have been discussing, Kierkegaard wonders whether he is disqualified from marriage by two things peculiar to himself: first, he mentions what he calls his "melancholy disposition"; second, there is his mission as one who must testify to the original truth of Christianity in order to make his contemporaries realize how far they have strayed. In neither event is he sure that such phenomena can validly classify a person as an exception. His melancholia he recognizes to be psychological illness—what we would call neurosis and what some commentators have not hesitated to describe as a pathological fear of sexual involvement. Kierkegaard sees no reason to think that marriage will cure him of his disability, but neither can he know that it frees him from the ethical obligation to get married. Similarly, he does not suggest that his self-imposed mission provides an objective warrant for celibacy. As much as he would like to think that God has chosen him for a religious destiny that sets him apart, and as much as he would welcome the experience of martyrdom, he is too honest to pretend that proof is at hand. He must resort, therefore, to an act of nonrational faith which does not eliminate the absurdity of his condition but possibly enables him to leap over it in fear and trembling.

In the book entitled *Fear and Trembling* Kierkegaard illustrates his own situation by analyzing the story of Abraham and Isaac in the Old Testament. For Abraham to kill his son, as God demands, would seem to be an act of murder. It is only through faith that

Abraham can justify this apparently immoral deed. Yet there is nothing in reason, or anything else other than the religious commitment itself, that can enable his leap of faith to escape the ethical category. The connection between Kierkegaard's personal problems and the biblical story of Abraham is heightened by the fact that Abraham really loves his son. In killing him, he would not merely be committing murder: he would also be destroying his own capacity for love. Only if there is a higher love that overrides human attachments can one justify such exceptional behavior.

In *Stages on Life's Way*, Quidam-Kierkegaard struggles with the problem by discussing the notion of a "teleological suspension of the ethical." In *Either/Or* Judge William too had discussed the possibility that some men might justifiably treat themselves as exceptions who need not live up to the universal obligation to marry and to strive for married love. Judge William rejects mysticism because he considers it a permanent evasion of the everyday world rather than a brief encounter with divinity which enables one to follow an ethical (and religious) life on earth. He concludes that the truly extraordinary man, the one who could best be treated as an exception, would really be the most *ordinary* of men. Though purified through inward acts of religious faith, this chosen one would live in the world like other men and make no pretense to any special sanctity. But then he too would have to seek for love in a marital context, just like everyone else.

In part at least, Kierkegaard desperately approved of the healthy-mindedness that Judge William's ethics and religion idealize. After Regina Olsen had eventually accepted his rejection of her and married another man, Kierkegaard wrote in his *Journals:* "Had I had faith I would have remained with Regina. Thank God, I know this now." He means that faith, if he truly had it, would not have ratified his claim to be an exception to the ethical but would rather have made him live up to the demands of universal obligation. He could then surmount neurotic shortcomings while also meeting the extraordinary requirements of his appointed mission. Far from being a suspension of the ethical, religious faith would serve as a compatible means by which ethical necessities were properly satisfied.

Despite his desire, and even yearning, for this solution, it is not the one that survives in Kierkegaard's development. After losing Regina definitively, his religious views reinforce and even magnify the feelings of worthlessness in himself. The unending pain of his existence, the sickness of the soul, recurs in Kierkegaard through all his writings. At times he resembles the part of Luther that transmutes self-hatred into a sense of sin so destructive as to create a barrier excluding the sensitive spirit from all hope of peace or happiness. There is not only the notion that, as Kierkegaard puts it, "before God we are always in the wrong," but also the firm conviction that suffering is the sole reliable approach to God. In the *Concluding Unscientific Postscript* Kierkegaard says that the aesthetic is characterized by "enjoyment-perdition" and the ethical by "action-victory," but the religious by "suffering alone." In his renewed attempt to clarify the circumstances under which one can rightly be considered exceptional, he ends up with the idea that only the torment of alienation, the horror of knowing one is cut off from all the conventional means of justifying one's existence, can provide the blissful suffering in which a religious leap occurs. The Christianity that issues from Hegel's philosophy is to Kierkegaard no Christianity at all precisely because it seeks to alleviate the sense of primordial sin, ultimate separation between persons, and the infinite distance between man and God. At times the mature Kierkegaard expresses distaste for the things of this world in a virulent manner reminiscent of Pascal. Occasionally he welcomes the monastic life as a flight into solitude that symbolizes and facilitates the awareness of metaphysical isolation without which a man cannot be religious. Kierkegaard does not deny that his thinking may be sick. He nevertheless insists that the healthiness he associates with salvation is predicated upon recognition that this kind of sickness is inescapable in our nature.

Kierkegaard's last books, often ignored nowadays because they tend to be doctrinal and discursive rather than dialectical, are mainly religious tracts that need not detain us long. In the *Works of Love*, however, Kierkegaard interprets the biblical commandments about love in a way that may throw light upon the conflict between sick and healthy aspects of his being. He argues that the love of

God and the love of one's neighbor are really inseparable. Far from being inconsistent, as they may have seemed to be in earlier theology, both enact a similar submission to God's will, an acceptance of him as the source of one's ability to love at all.

In this, Kierkegaard's final statement about love, there are several components worth noting. First, it duplicates Luther's belief that man is too sinful, too corrupt, too guilty in his sheer materiality to be able to love without outside assistance; second, it explains the possibility of love in terms of God's agapē, which descends in grace and raises human beings above their own nature; third, it interprets the biblical commandments to love God and to love one's neighbor as categorical imperatives of a Kantian sort and therefore dependent on appropriate action rather than feeling or inclination; and lastly, it ordains that when human beings succeed in following these injunctions, they do so by loving God as the principal object of devotion and then, through the supervening presence of God, their neighbor as another human being whom God is loving through them.

In saying that love reveals itself in action and not in special feelings, which ethical obligations may be unable to elicit, Kierkegaard is clearly rejecting all Romantic attempts to explain interpersonal love by reference to emotion, instinct, or erotic response. The idea of sexual love as such hardly enters into the program of his later theory. Married love belongs to it only in the sense that the word "neighbor" applies to any person we happen to encounter in the world, including a husband or wife. This means that marriage cannot be justified as a unique relationship consisting in the intimate bonds that unite men and women, but only as an instance of love for another human being. The Romantics wished to reach God through the sanctity of marital or sexual love. Some thought such love was too pure to survive on earth; others believed its inherent goodness already signified a sanctified presence. Both of these alternatives Kierkegaard ends up rejecting. The love of God must come first, he insists, and married love is merely derivative from it. Rather than being an ethical universal as he originally thought, married love is just one among other ways in which love for one's neighbor may occur. This is the only conception that Kierkegaard now finds coherent with religious love. To seek a beloved through impulse or desire, or to maintain that sexual and married love can be justified except as a way of loving our neighbor, is, he tells us, "very far from being Christian love."

I suggested earlier that Kierkegaard may have found a way of resolving the paradox within the sick and healthy aspects of his thinking. But probably it would be more accurate to say that the doctrine in *Works of Love* shows Kierkegaard giving up the struggle. For at this point he seems merely to eliminate the conflict instead of providing a resolution or culminating synthesis. Judge William had argued that romantic love completes itself in married love and that married love could not be inharmonious with the love of God. Kierkegaard's final statement satisfies these conditions but not as Judge William had intended. For now all idealizations of romantic love have been discounted. Though hallowed by religious love, marriage no longer functions as a vehicle toward the ideal. The ethical universal has been swallowed up by the love of God. All other values are to be subsumed under that alone.

At the center of Kierkegaard's religious teachings inwardness remains as his prime concern, and he still associates it with the private isolation of each person. He no longer feels the need to defend the unmarried state of the exceptional individual. At last the burden of that problem has been removed. For though he does not contribute to the world in the manner required by Judge William (which is to say, the segment within himself that Judge William represented), Kierkegaard frees himself of the idea that only through marriage and interpersonal commitment can God's commandments be fulfilled. The unmarried state justifies itself through its own participation in religious love. Whatever the nobility of its aspirations, Romantic idealism is thus an inflated form of pagan heresy.

In one respect Kierkegaard's final approach is superior to his previous one. That all men are guilty or ethically inferior if they do not marry is indefensible. In the pages given to Judge William, however, we did find many suggestive insights about the nature of married love, though not much about sexual love. All this no longer interests the older Kierkegaard: it has been superseded. Once his personal difficulties with Regina had been quieted by her marriage to someone else, Kierkegaard's thinking about the love of persons would seem to have atrophied. The doctrine in *Works of Love* extends and enriches the Protestant faith whose revitalization Kierkegaard took as his mission in life; but it scarcely helps us to understand the erotic problems of ordinary people seeking enlightenment about instincts, impulses, conflicting emotions in their daily existence. The early Kierkegaard wrote brilliantly about these aspects of human nature, albeit in a dialectical fashion that bespoke his inability to resolve the dilemmas they engender. The later Kierkegaard provides a kind of solution, but one that is too remote from human experience to be convincing.

As a result, Kierkegaard survives the vicissitudes of the nineteenth and twentieth centuries through his earlier rather than his later writings. As Johannes the Seducer says in his "Diary" that love seeks "infinitude" and fears "limitation" so too will Nietzsche remark that "all desire craves eternity." When we reach Sartre's philosophy of love, we shall see that it also originates in Kierkegaard. In the "Diary" Johannes claims that "the highest conceivable enjoyment lies in being loved." As a philosophical seducer he wishes for more than just the superficial pleasures of invading a woman's body or stealing a virginity that she prizes. Instead his erotic maneuvers are all directed toward creating in this other person the ability to love, and not just to love but to love passionately, and not just passionately but with him as the sole object of her infinite desire. "A pure, innocent femininity, transparent as the sea and as profound, with no clear idea of what love is! Now she is to learn its power. . . . But this must happen through me; and when she learns to love, she learns to love me; and as she extends her domain, the paradigm by which she herself is governed increasingly grows in power, and this is myself. When through love she becomes aware of her full significance, she expends this in loving me; and when she suspects that she has learned this from me, then her love for me is doubled. The thought of my joy so overwhelms me that I almost lose my senses."

While Johannes manipulates his amatory prey in this endeavor, he realizes that passionate love for him must arise in the woman as a free expression of herself. "She must owe me nothing; for she must be free; love exists only in freedom, only in freedom is there enjoyment and everlasting delight. Although I am aiming at her falling into my arms, as it were, by a natural necessity, yet I am striving to bring it about so that as she gravitates toward me, it will still not be like the falling of a heavy body, but as spirit seeking spirit."

In Sartre's works a hundred years later, all of this reappears. Kierkegaard obviously believes that Johannes' approach to love characterizes the stage of immediacy and therefore neglects the goals of ethical and religious love, married love and the love of God. Though Sartre introduces a different dialectic, his analysis of love renews Kierkegaard's idea that it begins with the desire to be loved as an absolute by one who bestows his or her love with apparent necessity which is really total freedom. Sartre's reasons for concluding that such love must be futile are not the same as Kierkegaard's. But it is from Kierkegaard that he derives the questions about love that he then tries to answer through his own ontology. Without the antecedence of Kierkegaard, Sartre's questioning might not have occurred exactly as it did.

Kierkegaard was born in 1813; Tolstoy was born only fifteen years later, though he died in 1910. There is no reason to think that either of them read anything the other wrote. They are nevertheless alike in many ways. They are kindred nineteenth-century spirits tormented by similar ambivalences and subject to similar paradoxes. Like Kierkegaard, Tolstoy was a Christian who rejected much of the traditional dogma and declared himself an enemy of official Christendom. Had he lived long enough, Kierkegaard like Tolstoy might have been excommunicated from his church on the grounds of heresy. In their personalities too Kierkegaard and Tolstoy resembled one another. Though Tolstoy received the adoration of millions of people throughout his literary career, he suffered from the same sense of personal worthlessness as Kierkegaard. And like Kierkegaard he could only assume that the evil he perceived in himself, and in everyone else, must derive from an original sinfulness in the human condition. It is not too surprising, therefore, that these two great post-Romantics eventually reached parallel conclusions about love, marriage, and sexuality.

In his *Recollections,* written when he was well over seventy, Tolstoy demarcates four stages in his life. If we put aside the first one—what he calls his "innocent, joyful, poetic childhood up to fourteen"—the remaining three duplicate Kierkegaard's categories of aesthetic, ethical, and religious. The second period Tolstoy describes as one of "vulgar profligacy, devoted to ambition, vanity, and, above all, lust." It lasted for the twenty years of his young manhood, until his marriage at the age of thirty-four. The characterization of this period is written from the hostile perspective of a later stage; but it is the Kierkegaardian "aesthetic life" Tolstoy has in mind. It was followed by the span of eighteen years that began with his marriage and culminated with a religious conversion in his fifties. Tolstoy asserts that "from a worldly point of view" this period could be called ethical: "That is, during those eighteen years I lived a correct, honest, family life, not practicing any vices condemned by social opinion." But since the activities of this third stage were devoted to the selfish interests of his family and, Tolstoy significantly adds, "pleasures of all kinds," he ultimately deemed it inferior to the religious stage that followed. Though the writing for which Tolstoy is most famous, notably *War and Peace* and *Anna Karenina,* belongs to the third period, it is only in his fourth stage that Tolstoy claims to have solved the human and erotic problems that beset him for so many years.

The works of Tolstoy's final period are often ignored and not infrequently dismissed as the utterances of an old fanatic. The crisis that led to Tolstoy's conversion has been described by one psychiatrist as "a perfect textbook case of involutional melancholia"—from which it is argued that the subsequent theorizing is merely evidence of emotional instability. Other critics have remarked that the contradictions between Tolstoy's beliefs in the third and fourth stages are already adumbrated by ambivalences within his earlier writings. On this view, his life as a whole manifests a continuing struggle between irreconcilable attitudes: on the one hand, loving appreciation of the physical, sensory, self-oriented desires that belong to each individual's existence in nature; on the other hand, fierce but unrealizable craving, motivated by disdain rather than love, to rise above the distractions of materiality. If this interpretation is right, Tolstoy's literary realism may be taken as an expression of the first inclination. The second would explain his theories about a cosmic force whose dynamic surge propels the course of history and whose spiritual meaning is to be found in the message of the gospels. From the one arises Tolstoy's acceptance of married love, indeed its idealization in the endings of *War and Peace* and *Family Happiness* and throughout the Levin-Kitty relationship in *Anna Karenina;* from the other comes his attack on marriage in *The Kreutzer Sonata,* whose condemnation of all marital relations was so extreme that the book was originally banned.

We are thus left with two ways of approaching Tolstoy. We may treat him as an inwardly divided soul, a man who suffered throughout his life from doubts and contradictory beliefs that can only be considered sick. Or else—as he himself suggests—we can read his succession of ideas as an intellectual and spiritual development that leapt from one stage to another, culminating in a world outlook that embodied everything this remarkable man had learned in a long life of intense experience. Perhaps we need not choose either interpretation to the exclusion of the other. If we disregarded or minimized the second, more flattering, approach, we would not be able to appreciate Tolstoy's final period. The ideas in *The Kreutzer Sonata* and *What is Art?*, to say nothing of all the religious and theological writings, would have to be cast aside as aberrations of an occasionally insane dogmatist who ought to have been writing realistic novels, at which he excelled, rather than pretentious philosophy. Tolstoy's wilder notions in this period may well be pathological. But, as often happens in men of genius, they are too challenging, too radical in their probing at the roots of human nature, to be rejected without thorough and sympathetic investigation.

Let us start with *The Kreutzer Sonata*. It is a novel about a man named Pozdnyshev who murders his wife in a fit of jealousy caused by fears about her fidelity that may or may not have been justified. Most of the story is narrated by the murderer himself, who recognizes that he may be insane but nevertheless propounds views about human relations with clarity as well as forcefulness. After the scandal that surrounded the publication of this work and possibly to defend himself against the sneering charges that the novel exhibited Tolstoy's quarrels with his own wife—his jealousies, his sudden outbursts, etc.—Tolstoy wrote an epilogue in which he explicitly spoke in his own voice. This epilogue, together with other statements of the same period, clearly indicates that Tolstoy is not to be identified with Pozdnyshev. To use the novel as proof that the older Tolstoy was not a true pacifist but really given to violence and possibly madness, as some critics have suggested, does him considerable injustice.

At the same time, there is an unmistakable similarity between much of Pozdnyshev's philosophy and what Tolstoy himself believed. Whatever else it may be, this novel is a vehicle for testing, within the framework of a realistic narrative, ideas that tempted and beguiled Tolstoy. By having a disturbed criminal as narrator, he creates a tension and sense of doubt that the reader must resolve by making up his own mind. Tolstoy shrewdly realized that this would be the most effective way of directing attention to his scandalous proposals.

The most shocking of these was the suggestion that marriage must not be idealized. *The Kreutzer Sonata* begins with the assertion, by people Pozdnyshev has met on a train, that marriage is sanctified through love and that love is a spiritual affinity that can be reciprocal as well as endless. Pozdnyshev tells his tragic story to refute such beliefs. Generalizing on the basis of his own experience, he insists that while it is *conceivable* for mutual love to exist throughout a lifetime of marriage, as a matter of fact that does not happen—"just as it cannot be that in a cartload of peas, two marked peas will lie side by side." This is reminiscent of Schopenhauer's ironic concession to the tenderhearted, when he says that love in marriage is not necessarily impossible though far too rare a phenomenon for any rational person to count on its occurrence. And like Schopenhauer, Pozdnyshev proves the futility of marriage by arguing that sexual instinct determines human behavior while also deluding its victims. The lover thinks he feels a spiritual longing for a pure and noble female but really he is driven by a need to possess her sexually. Social pressures, represented by the crass and commercial interests of the girl's mother, trap him into thinking that marriage will satisfy his romantic passion. Instead, as Pozdnyshev's narrative shows, marriage leads to satiety, hatred, and disgust. The novel looks like a case study, albeit a very lurid one, for Schopenhauer's teachings.

As we shall see, Tolstoy's epilogue reveals that his own thinking about marriage was more complex than this would indicate. Even so, the assertion that marriage must not be idealized pervades all his later thought. In a letter written towards the end of his life, he includes the following paragraph:

> The principal cause of family unhappiness is that people are brought up to think that marriage brings happiness. Sexual attraction leads to marriage and it takes the form of a promise, a hope, for happiness, which is supported by public opinion and literature. But marriage is not only not happiness. It is constant suffering, which is the price for sexual satisfaction; suffering in the form of lack of freedom, slavery, overindulgence, disgust with all kinds of spiritual and physical defects of the mate which one has to bear—maliciousness, stupidity, deception, vanity, drunkenness, laziness, miserliness, self-interest and corruption— all defects which are especially difficult to bear when they're not your own but somebody else's. And the same with physical defects—ugliness, uncleanliness, stench, sores, insanity, etc.—which are even more difficult to bear when not your own. All this, or at least something of this, will always be and to bear it will be difficult for everyone. But that which should compensate for it—concern, satisfaction, aid—all these things are taken as a matter of course . . . and one suffers the more from them the more one expects happiness. The principal cause of this suffering is that one expects what does not happen, and does not expect what always happens.

We are a long way from the final scenes of *War and Peace*. In that work only marriage could survive the absurd search for heroism, power, social distinction, or proud independence. Arguing that the ultimate purpose of history lies beyond human reason, that one begins to understand how and why things happen as they do only by intuitively identifying with the cosmic, volitional force that flows through life, Tolstoy then portrays the happy marriage Pierre and Natasha attain once they learn this fundamental truth. Far from trying to cultivate the sexual allurements she had used instinctively before marriage, Natasha now spurns them in order to experience the kind of domestic intimacy that she cares about most of all. "She felt that her unity with her husband was not maintained by the poetic feelings that had attracted him to her, but by something else—indefinite but firm as the bond between her own body and soul." This "something else" is a sense of the family as the purpose of marriage. The family, which includes property, friends, and relatives as well as children, results from a husband and wife directing their total energies toward serving one another reciprocally and beneficially.

When he wrote *Anna Karenina* a few years later, Tolstoy's views about family happiness had already changed. In the troubled searchings of Levin one can perceive Tolstoy's attempt to rectify the bland assurances of *War and Peace*. Nevertheless, throughout *Anna Karenina* the ideal of a monogamous marriage predicated upon the holiness of the family remains as the last great hope for men and women. By the time he had reached his fourth stage in life, however, after passing the age of fifty, after two decades of marriage with a wife eighteen years younger than himself, after his religious conversion—whether or not it was a pathological crisis— Tolstoy thought he could detect a higher ideal. The Epilogue to *The Kreutzer Sonata* is even more devastating than what Pozdnyshev had said inasmuch as Tolstoy now contrasts marriage with a condition of spirituality that lies far beyond its province. Married love was not to be condemned or eliminated, but it was firmly relegated to a lower rung on the ladder that leads to human well-being.

The theses that Tolstoy asserts as his own are easily enumerated: sexual activities are not necessary for health, and in fact abstinence is more hygienic than sexual intercourse; the "aim and justification" of marriage is procreation; acts of coitus are warranted only on occasions when the parents are trying to have children, the use of contraception being akin to murder; children are to be reared in such a way as to minimize the possibility of sensuality in them, and they are not to be treated as playthings for the parents; physical passion is not a noble achievement, and marital infidelity for reasons of love is merely sinful self-indulgence; in general, romantic love between men and women must not be "exalted into the highest poetical aim of human tendencies" but rather deplored as an unworthy expression of what is basically a subhuman instinct.

These are the essentials, Tolstoy tells us, that he wished to communicate in *The Kreutzer Sonata.* They do not deny the validity of marriage conceived as an institution for bringing the next generation into existence, and they are even protective of marriage in denouncing premarital sexuality or postmarital infidelities. But marriage itself becomes for Tolstoy a mere utility rather than an ideal. Above it he places total chastity as the end for which human beings should strive. Like everyone else, married people must overcome their animal impulses and thereby approximate the spiritual love that Tolstoy associates with the gospels. He distinguishes between an ideal and a precept, the latter providing a rule about attainable behavior while the former indicates a goal or direction that one cannot reach but should seek unendingly. According to Tolstoy, the Christian teaching does not concern itself with precepts about sexual behavior. Instead it proclaims the ideal of the greatest chastity, toward which one must continuously struggle despite frequent and inevitable failures.

In these later writings, Tolstoy is primarily interested in the *concept,* rather than the actuality, of love. That human beings will succumb to their carnal impulses he takes for granted. He even recommends marriage as a device for channeling and controlling the sexual appetites of those who have trouble living up to the ideal of abstinence. What he cannot tolerate is the Romantic belief in sexual love as either itself the highest attainment or else the manifestation of a superior cosmic love that sanctions and completes it. Above all, he rejects the notion that love is a way of *enjoying* another person. That idea, which permeates the writings of Christian as well as non-Christian humanists, seems to irritate Tolstoy most of all. He scornfully uses Diderot's term "jouissance" in his rejection of the belief that sexual intercourse may be considered a form of enjoyment. But also he attacks traditional church doctrine as an insidious glorification of sexuality within the confines of marriage. Under no circumstances should matrimony sanction the cultivating of appetites that ought to be renounced. Instead of encouraging the spouses to enjoy each other through physical intimacy, marriage must help them to overcome and possibly eradicate animal desires.

Tolstoy's ideal of marriage thus becomes synonymous with religious love as he interprets it in various places towards the end of his life. Discarding what he took to be the lies and fables of Christian dogma, he returned to that much of the gospels which centers about the two great commandments: to love God and to love one's neighbor as oneself. Since his conception of God is hardly orthodox and scarcely transcendental, however, the ideal effort toward which he thinks all men must direct themselves amounts to little more than a love of humanity. Husbands and wives are to love each other not as biological complementarities but only as pure-minded brothers and sisters jointly engaged in charitable work for the good of others. By destroying the need to unite through sexual love, they can achieve a spiritual union with all mankind.

If we ask Tolstoy what is meant by union of this sort and exactly *how* men and women can unite with all humanity, we may have difficulty getting clarification from him. In some respects his message is best presented not in his writings on marriage or religion but in the book *What is Art?* that has infuriated so many artists and aestheticians in the twentieth century. Tolstoy rejects the definition of art as beauty since beauty depends upon pleasure (and thus jouissance). He sees art as having the function of communicating emotion: the artist expresses some particular feeling in a work of art which then instills the same feeling in the audience. Through art human beings can surmount their solitude in creations that affectively link one person to another. Excellence in art is therefore a matter of infectiousness, and this requires sincerity in the feeling the artist conveys. But however sincere a feeling may be, it will contribute to the ideal of art only if it serves to unite mankind in one or the other of two dimensions that Tolstoy specifies. What he calls "religious art" evokes the feelings of brotherly love as well as the love of God, and what he calls "universal art" transmits feelings that all people share in their mere humanity: "Only two kinds of feeling unite all men: first, feelings flowing from a perception of our sonship to God and of the brotherhood of man; and next, the simple feelings of common life accessible to every one without exception—such as feelings of merriment, of pity, of cheerfulness, of tranquillity, and so forth." As Tolstoy then goes on to say, both kinds of feeling produce the "loving union" which is the goal of human existence. This end is not achieved through art alone, of course, but it suggests a blueprint for the work that men and women must do in life.

Whether or not we are satisfied with Tolstoy's radical aesthetics and utopian ethics, they reveal a longing in him that belongs as much to his early periods as to his final one. They derive from that region of his being which, incurably aristocratic though he was, idealized the mindless faith and crude simplicity of the Russian peasant. Being furthest from the civilized depravities of the upper classes, the peasants seemed to him much closer to the state of nature.

Many critics have pointed out Tolstoy's indebtedness to Rousseau, whose major ideas he often duplicates and whose violent and disturbed character he reincarnates. Even the title of his self-condemnatory *Confession* comes from Rousseau. In an interview late in life Tolstoy reveals that at the age of fifteen he worshipped Rousseau to the point of wearing a medallion with his portrait on it, that he had read all twenty volumes of his collected works, and that Rousseau's text was so familiar he felt as if he had written some of the passages himself. And indeed the Tolstoyan ideal of brotherly love as a union or communication of feeling preferable to any form of erotic and marital love reaches back to Rousseau's childhood memory of civic oneness described in the *Letter to M. d'Alembert*. *Emile* served as a newer gospel for Tolstoy's theories about sex as well as education. Tolstoy relives the eighteenth century to an uncanny degree in one so fully immersed, as he was, in the daily developments of the nineteenth. Renato Poggioli puts it very well when he says that many of the paradoxes in Tolstoy can be explained by the fact that he agreed with Voltaire in using reason to destroy ideas that were false or unreal while emulating Rousseau in denying that reason is capable of discovering the meaning of life. It was only feeling and the appropriate kind of humanitarian love that could perform that office. In this respect Tolstoy is typically post-Romantic, just one among many nineteenth-century thinkers who were swept along by the idealizations in Rousseau.

Referring to his literary origins, Tolstoy mentions Stendhal as the writer to whom, apart from Rousseau, he was most indebted. One can see how this may have been true with respect to Tolstoy's realistic technique in his novels, particularly in the battle scenes of *War and Peace* that are reminiscent of Stendhal's descriptions not only of Waterloo but also of all the other grand and glorious events that finally lead to the inevitable "Ce n'est que ça?" In other respects, however, Tolstoy's remark is baffling. For surely he could have felt nothing but disdain for the philosophy of love that Stendhal presents in *De l'Amour*. Tolstoy constantly reviled the idea of romantic passion as a dangerous delusion. The beauties of crystallization and the search for perfection in another person meant very little to him at any time. He never accepted them as justifications for erotic fervor of the sort that Stendhal extols. In listing the four stages in his life Tolstoy mentions one of purity, one of sensuality, one of family devotion, one of asceticism—but none that would include romantic love. In a letter written about the time of *The Kreutzer Sonata,* he says: "I have often thought of falling in love, and have never been able to find a place and meaning for it."

Nevertheless, we must also recognize that Tolstoy carefully studied and analyzed l'amour-passion, even portraying it favorably on occasion. Though in *War and Peace* it serves only to delude Pierre about Helene, and Natasha about Helene's brother Anatole, in *Anna Karenina* it shows itself as a feverish madness that can sometimes lead to a joyful outcome. This occurs in Levin's love for Kitty. At the beginning of his own marriage, Tolstoy himself seems to have experienced something similar; and immediately after the sentence I quoted in which Tolstoy says he has never found a meaning for erotic love, he goes on to provide one: it helps young people ("sixteen years until twenty and more") who cannot abstain from sex to avoid a hopeless struggle with chastity, thereby facilitating their entrance into matrimony. This is not what Stendhal meant, of course, but it is less than the total repudiation of passionate love that one might have expected from Tolstoy.

With respect to sexuality itself, his attitude was more consistent. For here he was dealing with something he knew from an early age. Throughout his writing, and presumably in his life, sex does not appear as an enjoyable part of human nature. Oblonsky in *Anna Karenina* may claim to find moments of happiness in his sexual adventures, but neither Tolstoy nor the characters he identifies with have reason to believe such reports. And even if these spurts of happiness do occur, Tolstoy was convinced they must always be purchased at a price that exceeds their value. Far from leading to permanent joy or fulfillment, they contribute to persistent suffering and moral degradation. Even without the sorrow depicted in *The Kreutzer Sonata*, we need only cite the shame that Levin and Kitty, like Pierre and Natasha, experience during their honeymoon. Happiness begins after these couples have *given up* the hope of finding pleasure through sexual activity with one another.

Whether or not sex is "the tragedy of the bedroom," to use Tolstoy's phrase, he considers it an inhuman instinct, an animalistic mechanism that cannot be cultivated without perversion. When Vronsky and Anna first make love, supposedly providing her with the "dream of happiness" for which she had hungered, their encounter is described as a murder and desecration. Vronsky begins to talk about their "bliss." " 'What bliss?' she said with disgust and horror, and the horror was involuntarily communicated to him. 'For heaven's sake, not another word!' " After this we are prepared not only for her eventual suicide but also for the portrayal of her love affair as itself a spiritual death. Nowhere in his writings does Tolstoy represent sex—even at its best—as a beneficial union or cause of harmony. When he finally insists that sexual love must not be pursued for the sake of enjoyment, he is reasoning from lifelong assumptions about its inherent unenjoyability. In his own experience, and in the experience of those whose judgment he respected, it was enmeshed in feelings of guilt that would effectively keep it from being enjoyed—except as a degenerate and criminal urge.

Neither Tolstoy's critique of sexual love nor his inability to enjoy sex resulted from a lack of vital impulse. On the contrary, Tolstoy himself, like all the critics who have found him so paradoxical, frequently mentions how powerful his appetite remained almost to the last months of his life. His desires were for him that raging beast which the character in Plato's *Republic* describes as the nature of sexuality. His own body was a fascination as well as a horror, causing him both vanity and revulsion. Thomas Mann quotes Tolstoy as having said "I am ashamed to speak of my disgusting body," although in his *Confession* he remarks that "he would have given anything he had for a handsome face." Mann does not tell us whether these attitudes existed at one and the same time, but they are not inconsistent and could well have occurred simultaneously throughout Tolstoy's life. His boundless interest in the body contributed to his particular genius as a novelist. Nor is it surprising that the greatest resistance to sexual inclinations should be found in one whose carnal drives were so powerful and pervasive. The real paradoxes in Tolstoy appear on the conceptual level, when he seeks to resolve his problems by constructing the system of ideal values that would justify a purified love of mankind.

The most prominent of these ideals, the one that stands out most clearly in all the years of Tolstoy's creative life, is the love of nature. Even after his conversion to primitive Christianity, he could worship only a God who showed himself in nature, in the simple and unrefined patterns of life experienced by the peasants Tolstoy idealized. But what are we to think about a love of nature that demeans the natural appetite for sexual enjoyment? Like Rousseau before him, Tolstoy insists that sex is really "unnatural," something fabricated by the artifices of civilization. He tells us to imagine how revolting sex is to an innocent young girl. He argues that animals seek intercourse only when reproduction is their motive. The facts about human sexuality do not enter into his thinking. His love of nature fails to encompass the psychobiological interests of men and women. One even wonders how much of nature he is willing to accept as congruent with humanity. Maxim Gorky recounts an occasion on which he and Tolstoy observed a chaffinch while they were strolling through the woods. With great precision and affec-

tion Tolstoy described the sexual behavior of this particular species. When Gorky remarked that in *The Kreutzer Sonata* he had
expressed a totally different view of sexuality, Tolstoy replied:
"But I am not a chaffinch."

It is to the glory of mankind that he was not, but can one truly
maintain the ideal of love for nature if one systematically denies
those aspects of oneself that are the same in human beings as in
other creatures, including birds? The power of denial itself made
Tolstoy different, and in that sense he was certainly not a chaffinch. But if his love of nature was genuine and complete, would he
have felt this need to set himself apart? To the degree that he did,
one must wonder about the authenticity of his ideal.

One also wonders about his religion. He may well be consistent in
his assessment of Romantic love as an irreligious idealization of sexual desire. But the love of God which he offers as a substitute, with
all its pantheistic overtones, is largely a creation of the nineteenth-
century idealism he thought he had superseded. It is the same faith
that pervades the thinking of Beethoven, who also sought religious
communion through a heightened love of mankind. Tolstoy's
repeated attacks on Beethoven therefore seem strange—until one
realizes that they may actually be the expression of self-doubt, a
hidden distrust for beliefs that Tolstoy shared with him. In *What is
Art?* Tolstoy criticizes Beethoven for arousing strong feelings in the
listener without communicating anything that can easily be assimilated by ordinary people. But aside from the fact that Beethoven's
vision in works like *Fidelio* and the Ninth Symphony is evident to
everyone who knows his life and thought, Tolstoy fails to recognize
that his own religious ideals are just as abstract as Beethovian
music. Neither is contagious in the way that Tolstoy's aesthetics
demands, for both are meaningful only to a sophisticated portion
of mankind familiar with one or another facet of Western romanticism. The peasants who could make so little out of Beethoven's
music, as Tolstoy observed, would hardly have understood how the
love of God required sexual abstinence, how Christianity did not
exist in the life of the church, or how the true gospels were to be
distinguished from the comforting dogmas handed down from
generation to generation.

Once we see Tolstoy as the product not only of Rousseau and the eighteenth century but also of cross-currents within nineteenth-century Romantic thought, his fusion of the healthy-minded and the diseased, the optimistic and the pessimistic, becomes more understandable. Despite his aversion to the philosophy of Hegel, whose teaching he considered "cloudy and mystical," Tolstoy shares his forward-looking, dynamic acceptance of action in the world as the manifestation of a spiritual force that realizes itself through history. Tolstoy does not think that spirit is embodied rationality, and he has few of Hegel's ontological beliefs about the Absolute. But he too yearns for a wholesome immersion in deeds that eliminate ills of the mind and tyrannies of the body.

In one place Tolstoy criticizes Dostoyevsky for not liking healthy people and for lacking the courage to make Mishkin in *The Idiot* one of them: "Since he [Dostoyevsky] was sick, then he wanted the whole universe to be sick with him." Whether or not this was true of Dostoyevsky, it cannot be applied to Tolstoy himself. If he paraded his sicknesses, what he called his sinfulness, it was always part of a moralistic and reformative effort to repair the damage in his soul. This trope, this almost sickly craving for health, enabled Tolstoy to become a political and religious cult figure. It explains his importance for Gandhi and the cause of nonviolence, for anarchism in Russia and the West, and even for theories of the élan vital. He served as a model of the all-too-human sinner who finds salvation by merging with the life force and then changes the world through acts of love.

In his own way Tolstoy also appropriates Hegel's vision of the end of things. Where Hegel saw history concluding at the moment that the Absolute realized itself in a world become totally transcendentalized, Tolstoy foresees a termination of the human race when the ideal of chastity is finally consummated. I do not mean to suggest that these are identical ideals, but only that they function in a similar fashion. They each provide an ultimate goal, a "meaning of life," that comprises the eventual disappearance of mankind as we know it—not through death or self-destruction, but through progressive and continuous ethical behavior.

At the same time, there is in Tolstoy a close kinship to the pessimistic side of romanticism. Behind his utopian ideals about the step-by-step advance toward purity and sexual abstinence there lurks a revulsion from the human condition that reminds one more of Schopenhauer than of Hegel. Tolstoy acknowledged his indebtedness to Schopenhauer. It shows itself in Tolstoy's comments about the pettiness of humanity, subject not only to self-deceit about romantic love and freedom of the will but also striving to preserve itself when really it would do best to welcome its own annihilation. "The human race will come to an end? . . . What a misfortune! . . . Let it come to an end. I am as little sorry for this two-legged animal as for the ichthyosauri and so forth."

In this place Tolstoy is talking about "the animal man," which must be supplanted by superior "beings capable of love." Possibly he is not condemning mankind as a whole. Yet one can almost smell the vehemence of his bile. Schopenhauer's pessimism was fueled by feelings of compassion for all who suffered through their subjugation to the cruel and merciless will of nature, but Tolstoy's religiosity takes him in a somewhat different direction. The biological oneness of humanity, the quasi-instinctual uniting into one totality "like a swarm of bees," inspires neither pity nor compassion in him. He feels hatred for the present state of mankind, satisfied as it is with its trivial interests and its life of sex and propagation, stupidly ignoring the ends that Tolstoy knows to be more rewarding.

Nor is there in him anything like the serene acceptance of personal dissolution that one finds in Schopenhauer. During the crisis that preceded his conversion, Tolstoy's fear of death convinced him that life was not worth living—not because, as Schopenhauer said, the sense of individuality is a delusion, but only because Tolstoy's defeated ego could not brook the idea that what it wanted and what it did would turn into nothingness sooner or later. With his usual perspicacity, Thomas Mann saw that Tolstoy's obsessiveness about death was not unrelated to his "fear of the love of nature." Some of this fear may have derived from, or duplicated, Schopenhauerian pessimism; but it occurs in a world outlook that would seem to be more thoroughly diseased than Schopenhauer's ever was.

In Tolstoy's writings one finds most of the misogyny for which Schopenhauer is renowned. But while Schopenhauer was trying to defeat bogus ideals of "the lady" inherited from the past and inflated by sentimentalists of his day, Tolstoy is mainly concerned to undermine tendencies that would encourage women to emulate the self-indulgent males who devote themselves to pleasure. Like Schopenhauer, Tolstoy believes that women are designed by nature for domestic and nurturant roles rather than intellectual or spiritual activities. But Tolstoy also insists that women are corrupted by men's desire for sexual freedom, which can be satisfied only by the debauching of females. At this point Tolstoy does evince a real sense of compassion. As one who suffers from feelings of guilt for the Don Juanism in himself, he sympathizes with the helplessness of women who are pushed by both nature and civilization into the clutches of the unscrupulous seducer. If in the long run women tyrannize over men, as Tolstoy repeatedly states, it is because oppression by the male has made them into relentless adversaries. "Just like the Jews: as they pay us back for their oppression by a financial domination, so it is with women. 'Ah, you want us to be traders only—all right, as traders we will dominate you!' say the Jews. 'Ah, you want us to be merely objects of sensuality—all right, as objects of sensuality we will enslave you,' say the women."

Tolstoy's solution to this problem is to give women equality in their sexual behavior. If men can be sexually liberated, so too should women be. But since Tolstoy wants everyone to abstain entirely, this is hardly a concession to feminism. He sees no advantage in giving women the vote or allowing them to assume the duties of public office. He does, however, complain about their lot as beasts of burden. He vehemently opposes any social order in which men can escape the physical labor that is forced upon women despite their lesser strength. He is truly horrified at the idea that husbands can so easily lead a life of idleness while their wives must perform domestic chores for which their muscular equipment is barely sufficient.

We need not reach a final conclusion about these tensions in Tolstoy. We do not have to decide whether his thinking is indeed paradoxical rather than a series of stages in his development. Like others at the end of the nineteenth century, he displays the fruitful though tortured conflict between different aspects of Romantic ideology as it had already existed for a hundred years in Europe. Tolstoy's creativity flourished by means of this conflict. At the time of his mid-life crisis, he writes that he is "struggling with all my soul and I am suffering, but I thank God for my suffering." This will to continue striving, however painfully, may have been the greatest of the Romantic influences upon Tolstoy. Even the ideal of asceticism was not to be attained by solutions, such as castration, that he deemed too mechanical or easy to accomplish. Instead of mutilating the flesh, Tolstoy says, man must learn how to master it. Only then would nature and spirit be harmonized in a love worth having. Only then could people in the future succeed where he himself had failed so badly.

In his *Journals* Kierkegaard records a momentous conversation with his personal physician about the "disproportion in my constitution between the physical and the psychic." Kierkegaard wished to know whether his neurotic affliction could be cured or the suffering of his isolation controlled. The doctor gives him little reason to hope and even cautions him against exerting willpower, since that might only destroy his precarious equilibrium. Kierkegaard tells us that he then made his fateful decision. He gave up his attempt to be like other people, to "realize the universal." He finally accepted his melancholy nature as the thorn in the flesh that makes Christian faith both possible and accessible. "With this thorn in my foot," he remarks, "I leap higher than anyone whose feet are whole."

I begin with this anecdote because it seems to me symbolic of something comparable that must have happened—pervasively, if not on a particular occasion—in the depths of Nietzsche's soul. For him the leap of faith did not culminate in anything like Christian belief. He would have admired much of Kierkegaard's attack upon the hypocrisy of official Christendom, but the alternatives he envisaged Kierkegaard could only have rejected as hideous perversions of a search for authenticity. At the same time Kierkegaard and Nietzsche, each independently of the other, accept (even cherish) their physical and psychological sufferings as a paradoxical boon that enabled them to achieve harmony with the totality of things. Though Nietzsche differs from Tolstoy as well as Kierkegaard in denying that asceticism or self-renunciation provide a solution to the search for faith, he resembles Tolstoy no less than Kierkegaard in believing that routine pleasures of existence are beneath contempt, that the Romantic bases of nineteenth-century idealism are illusory and debilitating, that human nature is doomed unless its future development becomes radically different from anything it has thus far achieved, and in general, that life is worth living only if one realizes that the world as we know it—the everyday pattern of purposive behavior, sexual desire, social aspiration, moral conformity, and religious adherence—is without value in itself and is justifiable only as the raw material an isolated individual molds in accordance with his own creative impulse.

These beliefs, or rather philosophical attitudes, that Nietzsche shares with Kierkegaard and Tolstoy made all three of them opponents not only of romanticism but also of eighteenth- and nineteenth-century naturalism, whether it be French materialism or English utilitarianism. But unlike Kierkegaard and Tolstoy, Nietzsche also preserves these naturalistic traditions. He does not wish to eliminate them completely. In his thoroughgoing atheism, in his attempt to analyze morals as a human phenomenon that cannot be explained through any transcendental reference, in his claim—tentatively asserted in *The Birth of Tragedy* and fully trumpeted in *The Will to Power*—that life is best understood as an aesthetic artifact, a tragic work of art, he contributes to the development of humanistic naturalism while also rejecting what he considers to be unnecessary compromises with edifying ideas retained from Christianity and its idealist offshoots.

Nietzsche prided himself on being a "free thinker," and indeed so free and speculative is his thought that it draws sustenance from every influence it can digest. That Nietzsche should favor Voltaire over Rousseau will not surprise us, even though his philosophy is often closer to the latter's than to the former's, but we are continually struck by his preference for religious thinkers like Pascal and Dostoyevsky rather than fellow naturalists like John Stuart Mill. He considers Mill a cultural leveler, a fatuous do-gooder, a sentimental optimist within the humanitarian camp. The tendentiousness of Pascal and Dostoyevsky, bordering on fanaticism as it sometimes does, he ignores because he is so thoroughly moved by their honest and utterly ruthless descriptions of the human condition when alienated from Christian faith. If that faith is no longer available, as Nietzsche believed, these misguided Christians could reveal the terrible truth more effectively than moralists whose concern for happiness blinded them to the horror of an ultimate nihilism which must permeate human existence once man recognizes that apart from natural processes there is no meaning, no permanence, and certainly no hope of redemption or immortality.

This aspect of Nietzsche's paradoxical vision is best seen by comparing him with left-wing followers of Hegel such as Feuerbach, Engels, and Marx. Feuerbach prepares us for Nietzsche by reducing religion to an agency of human imagination, to man projecting upon the external world symbols of his own moral aspiration. In explaining why he dedicated *The Art Work of the Future* to Feuerbach, Wagner describes in his autobiography the liberating effect that Feuerbach had upon him at the time. He was the only philosopher he had encountered, Wagner says, who rightly understood that spirit is just "an aesthetic perception of our senses" and therefore that philosophy, as opposed to art, was ultimately futile.

Whether or not Wagner's interpretation of Feuerbach is correct, Feuerbach did believe that his own philosophy would free man from delusions about the spiritual life in general, and religious love in particular. Both God's love and man's love of God made sense, he thought, as expressions of the human need to love humanity itself. Christianity falsified the nature of love by positing an extra-human divinity as first the source and then the recipient of such love. When men came to realize that no such being exists, they would understand that their ideal was really directed toward the human species itself. This awareness would eventually make them capable of loving other people. Christian dogma was for Feuerbach the greatest and most insidious deterrent to love. For it limited

God's love only to those who believed in his divinity, and it encouraged men to despise, even to murder, anyone who failed to accept the sectarian doctrines that always accompanied religious faith.

Christ being nothing but the symbol of mankind wanting to love itself, Feuerbach could then go on to enunciate a humanist creed beyond all religion: "Man is to be loved for man's sake. Man is an object of love because he is an end in himself, because he is a rational and loving being. This is the moral law of the species, the law of intelligence. This love should be immediate, and only if it is immediate, directed directly at my fellow man, is it love. But if I, who can realize and fulfill my human nature only through love, interpose between my fellow man and myself the idea of an individual in whom the ideal of the species is supposed to be already realized, I annihilate the very essence of love and disturb the unity between me and my fellow man by the idea of a third person external to us. My fellow man is then an object of love to me only on account of his resemblance or relation to this model, not for his own sake, not on account of his nature."

Engels and Marx redefine the concept of man in their critiques of Feuerbach. They deny it is mankind as an abstract essence that is loved or that expresses its self-love through religious symbols. Instead, they claim, it is society, mankind in its social and economic dimensions, that elicits the need for self-oriented love. The humanistic import of Feuerbach's analysis was retained by Engels and Marx; only his definition of humanity had to be changed. In various places, for instance in *The Holy Family* and the *Economic and Philosophical Manuscripts,* Marx seems to anticipate the kind of criticism that Martin Buber and others in the twentieth century leveled against Feuerbach. Marx insists that love must be reciprocal and that it must show itself in a concrete relationship between individuals responding directly to one another: "Love only can be exchanged for love, trust for trust, etc. . . . If you love without evoking love in return, i.e. if you are not able, by the *manifestation* of yourself as a loving person, to make yourself a *beloved person,* then your love is impotent and a misfortune." In a letter Marx wrote to his wife in 1856, he says: "But love, not the love of Feuerbach's

Man . . . nor again love of the Proletariat, but love of the beloved and more particularly of you, makes a man a man again . . . 'Buried in her arms, revived by her kisses'—yes, in your arms and by your kisses."

Apart from such vague utterances, neither Marx nor Engels contribute much to Feuerbach's ideas about love. In his book on the origins of the family, Engels does trace the development of "individual sex-love" and "love marriage" in the modern world. But his approach is mainly anthropological: he makes little attempt to clarify the concept of love. For all three of these writers, as for the English utilitarians and their counterparts among French positivists like Auguste Comte, what mattered most was the recognition that love—even, and especially, religious love—is ultimately reducible to mankind's persistent and wholly commendable love for itself, both as a species and as the collectivity of paired human beings reciprocally engaged with one another.

Nietzsche's thought derives from this humanistic (and obliquely Romantic) tradition, but only in part. For in him the love of mankind has soured and become problematic. Though he staunchly combats the pessimist philosophy of Schopenhauer, he scorns the oppressive optimism of Hegel's followers as well as the confident good will of those who merely wish to increase human happiness. And yet there is in Nietzsche an affirmative, even hopeful, acceptance of future possibilities that constantly indicates his affinity to edifying naturalists and idealists alike.

This ambivalence, with all the paradoxes it entails, resonates in Nietzsche as in no other philosopher of his period. It defines his particular genius. His greatest talents are those of a critic or analyst rather than a systematic thinker. When he examines the beliefs of Wagner, Schopenhauer, Rousseau, the dogmas of Christianity, the theories of philosophers who advocate socialism or democracy or German nationalism, his ambivalent insight issues into penetrating prose that has never been equalled in the German language. It radiates a clarity of perception that cuts like a laser beam. But this is generally true only of Nietzsche's negative side. When he presents his affirmative vision and reveals what to him makes life a great adventure, his ideas—about "amor fati" (the love of all reality), eternal recurrence, the superman, and the will to power—become muddy, obscure, incomplete, intellectually deficient, and sometimes crazy.

How then is the sympathetic reader to respond to Nietzsche? Our dilemma is most acute with respect to his pronouncements about love, sex, and the relations between men and women. Out of context, what he says in these areas is scarcely worth considering. Aside from some clever, occasionally brilliant, aperçus, he has much less to tell us about details of the erotic life than either Kierkegaard or Tolstoy. They seem to have suffered affectively in a way that Nietzsche did not, throughout their lives and in more intimate situations than he experienced. What makes Nietzsche's thinking about love and sexuality so important, however, is the fact that it arises from a personal philosophy that expresses much of what people at the end of the nineteenth century and the beginning of the twentieth could appropriate for themselves. Despite its unbalanced strength as criticism rather than creative innovation (or perhaps because of it), Nietzsche's philosophy embodies the malaise of his time and our own. He effectively shows us what is no longer tenable in beliefs about men, women, and their erotic being. If he cannot reach the new faith that might sustain a better and more authentic world, he nevertheless helps to clear the ground of concepts that are either infertile or overgrown. In various ways that I shall suggest, his philosophy serves as an indispensable link between romanticism and the naturalistic possibilities toward which we are struggling in the present.

I do not mean to deny that Nietzsche's affirmative ideas have great value in themselves, over and above their importance for succeeding generations. Behind his notions of amor fati or eternal recurrence, for instance, we find extremely fruitful explorations into human nature—new insights about health, about life as a creative phenomenon, and about moral achievement that results from the "spiritualization" of instinctual drives. As I shall try to show, these ideas are fundamental to the ambivalence within Nietzsche's approach to the nature of love. They also reveal why so much of his work has been able to survive. Though I myself distrust the concept of amor fati, I will return to it throughout this book. Like many others in the twentieth century, I will be working toward an acceptable reformulation.

❀

In one of the notes collected in *The Will to Power*, Nietzsche states: "The need for faith, for anything unconditional, in Yes and No, is a proof of weakness; all weakness is weakness of will. The man of faith, the believer, is necessarily a small type of man." This idea also appears in the context of Nietzsche's lengthy attack on Christianity in *The Antichrist*. But though Nietzsche explicitly maintains that the great man must be a doubter, even a skeptic, the bulk and brilliance of his inspiration consists in his attempt to create a new faith for contemporary man. Beginning with ideas about the inherent cruelty and meaninglessness of nature which he directly receives from Schopenhauer, Nietzsche strives throughout his philosophical career to overcome the nay-saying that Schopenhauer recommended as the only road to salvation. He develops "overcoming," and what he sometimes calls "self-overcoming," into a principle of moral growth that enables us to see the truth without being destroyed by our own vision. The search for this new perspective, this faith for the future, motivates book after book.

There is little detailed argumentation in Nietzsche's writing. Much of it is exhortation and shrieking revelation. *Thus Spake Zarathustra* is largely prophetizing, prose-poetry filled with quasi-biblical parables and epiphanies. Even in his critical works, Nietzsche shocks and startles in the hope of stimulating conversion to the faith that will, he thinks, save the coming world from decadence or total nihilism. At the same time, what Nietzsche says about weakness in the need for faith should not be taken as an inconsistency. For he is criticizing an "unconditional" need for Yes and No. The faith that Nietzsche tries to instill is *wholly* conditional, a combination of destructive as well as generative elements, and therefore a product of skepticism as well as affirmation.

As Schopenhauer shows the residual traces of Christianity in his advocacy of renunciation and asceticism, so too does Nietzsche continue the teachings of that same traditional faith, in which he did not believe. Nietzsche resembles the orthodox Christians in denying the goodness of pleasure or worldly comfort, and—as we shall see—in urging us to accept reality as a way of achieving power over a universe whose horror we recognize while also loving it. Since he is an atheist, Nietzsche's faith is directed not toward discovery of meaning but only toward the creating of it. By overcoming our own limitations, by transcending our justified nihilism, by triumphantly asserting the basic futility of man's life and the cosmos as a whole, our affirmative faith is rendered heroic, even godlike. On Nietzsche's view, we *make* the world meaningful, much as the Absolute in Hegel provided through spiritual development of human beings a meaningfulness that the world would not otherwise have. In this respect, Nietzsche's philosophy is Hegelianism without the Absolute.

The ties that link Nietzsche to Hegel have been pointed out and studied by various commentators. But Nietzsche differs from Hegel in never wishing to eliminate Schopenhauerian pessimism as the groundwork of his thinking. He merely wants to overcome it, to fit it into an approach that goes beyond it without denying its limited authenticity. This process is itself Hegelian, involving as it does a kind of "Aufhebung" or higher synthesis. Unlike Hegel, however, Nietzsche always denies that his final optimism or yea-saying is determined by the order of things or has any source other than an individual's need for faith. As a result, Nietzsche's philosophy is redolent with a kind of fin-de-siècle subjectivism teetering on anxiety that one never finds in Hegel. Nietzsche, oddly reminiscent of St. Augustine in this regard, is the spokesman of a will to believe despite absurdities. He knows he is not the voice of the Absolute using a philosopher to be the vehicle of its own self-revelation as Hegel thought, but neither will he repudiate this world of suffering as Schopenhauer claimed that every honest thinker must. In transcending Schopenhauer as well as Hegel, Nietzsche transcends romanticism in *both* its pessimistic and its optimistic aspects.

The content of Nietzsche's faith is conveyed by a single word: health. The healthy-minded man is the saint of his new religion.

Where health is combined with strength of character, intelligent self-interest, and a militant perfectionism, he believes it reveals the will to power that Schopenhauer had misrepresented. A will to live is primarily concerned with the propagation or continuance of existence. But nature is interested in more than that, Nietzsche insists. For nature causes each species to seek what is best and most powerful in itself. In man this means a nobility of character or hard, defiant pride that comes from healthy-mindedness rather than self-renunciation.

In describing Wagner's earlier, more naturalistic period, before he succumbed to the disease in Schopenhauer's philosophy, Nietzsche approvingly refers to the influence that Feuerbach's concept of "the great health" had had upon Wagner. Nevertheless, Nietzsche disagrees with Feuerbach about the origin of health. Throughout his life, Schopenhauer and Wagner remain as the thinkers whose genius he never ceases to confront because, like them, Nietzsche assumes that sickness is native to man and that health is achieved through the ability to overcome one's human debility. Neither Feuerbach nor Hegel nor naturalists like the utilitarians thought of mankind as sick. Nietzsche asserts this, arguing that man is by nature "the sick animal." To this extent, he reverts to an atavistic Lutheranism, but immediately rejects his Protestant beginnings by arguing that the sickness of man is not a spiritual failing. It is instead a weakness in his psychological constitution, an enervating conflict between variable ways of trying to satisfy the will to power. Health, which is the only salvation, could be found by accepting the fact of one's natural sickness and then overcoming it through the gratification of instincts, by becoming creatively self-directed rather than by cultivating attitudes that encourage one to make fruitless sacrifices.

It is in this context that Nietzsche makes his attack upon the notion of *Mitleid* (pity or compassion). He despises it in Wagner as an insincere affectation, in Schopenhauer as an empty response to the suffering caused by the cruelty of the will, and in Christianity as a glorification of weaknesses which then become institutionalized and thus give dominance to sick instead of healthy people. Through pity, compassion, and the slavish love that the Christian tradition has promoted, suffering can never be eliminated nor weakness supplanted by strength. On the contrary, those who are incapable of overcoming their sickliness are allowed to drag down the free spirits whose superior talents they cannot appreciate. Mitleid always runs the danger of causing *ressentiment*—those who are inferior resenting the fact that others can attain the kind of health which circumstances have denied to themselves.

Nietzsche's critique of pity as an unworthy emotion that weakens human beings instead of curing them, together with his more general attack on Christianity, is the part of his philosophy with which he has most often been identified. But it is only *Christian* or *Schopenhauerian* or *Wagnerian* pity that he really wishes to condemn. In various places he reveals the humanitarian basis of his thinking. He insists that Mitleid becomes vicious only when it does lead to ressentiment, only when it occurs apart from efforts to alleviate the suffering that has brought it into being, only when it encourages self-sacrificial behavior that defeats normal and life-enhancing self-interest: in short, only when it fosters moral weakness in ourselves or in others instead of helping us to overcome our sick animality. In *Beyond Good and Evil* Nietzsche remarks: "a man who is by nature a *master*—when such a man has pity, well, *this* pity has value."

The master morality that Nietzsche advocates, as opposed to what he calls slave morality, includes "caution regarding compassionate feelings." Though pity may exist in Nietzsche's nobleman, it is not what makes his goodness. That comes from pride in himself, from an aretaic awareness that he alone creates values, and from contempt for those who recommend selflessness. In such a man, pity and humanitarian compassion will occur but they will always be controlled by the necessities of action, by stoical adherence to enlightened projects that may sometimes involve the increasing of human suffering.

There is in everything Nietzsche writes a fascination with cruelty, harshness, and evil—even though he wishes to eradicate the Western idea of evil, which belongs to slave morality, in order to substitute the more secular notion of the "bad," i.e. that which is inimical to the free expression of natural impulses. His language is often militant and he frequently uses the image of the hammer to suggest the hard-headedness and even hard-heartedness that is required to drive out sentimental attitudes. In all this, one may detect the influence of the Marquis de Sade as well as the excuse for the Nazification of Nietzsche that took place after 1930. Yet Nietzsche himself condemned German nationalism as well as virulent anti-Semitism; and sadistic philosophizing he constantly transcends by the moralistic fervor that pervades all his immoralist writings. Hardness and acceptance of pain are for him mainly the steeling of one's will. They are needed as instrumentalities for the creative leap into a new humanity. They are not to be relished as a source of pleasure in themselves, or justified as the fulfillment of some idealized destiny. On the contrary, it is because human nature in the present is subject to so much pain and pointless suffering that Nietzsche, with all the thin-skinned sensitivity native to his poetic soul, yearns for a superman who will supplant the wretchedly infirm beings that now exist.

The longing for the next, superhuman stage in man's development dominates *Thus Spake Zarathustra*. But that book is too rhapsodic for it to yield much clarification about the Jesu of Nietzsche's desiring. Nor in his more discursive attempts to present his mature philosophy does Nietzsche really help us to understand the future he envisions. It is clear that his concept is not Darwinian, that he is not referring to a new species into which man will evolve through natural selection: the superman is not a biological entity. He is a moral and even religious abstraction, the messiah for which Nietzsche's predecessors among the prophets of the Old Testament were clamoring. And it is through him that Nietzsche, like the Hebrew prophets, expresses his ambivalent ideas about the love of humanity. Mankind is to be exceeded in the sense that the superman will rise above the frailty, the weakness, the moral disease that oppresses most human beings in their search for self-defeating sympathy. Yet this act of rising, Nietzsche claims, involves superior love and not a hatred of human nature. The superman does not love humanity for what it is, but he loves it for what it may become.

The great paradox in Nietzsche's philosophy issues from the fact, to which we shall presently return, that he also wants to accept existence as it is. That is for him the equivalent of cosmic love and he sometimes sounds as if it alone reveals the excellence of the superman. It is not, however, a love that includes humanity as presently constituted. An understanding of what life is like for members of the herd—their massive hopes, their petty pleasures, the awesomeness of their immense sufferings—none of this appears in Nietzsche, as it often does in Schopenhauer and in the utilitarians that Nietzsche so arrogantly disprizes. Though Nietzsche extols the goodness of friendship or fellowship, he actually has little to say about it, and one can hardly imagine a society consisting of his kind of supermen. On the contrary, Zarathustra has no place to be at home except the mountaintop where he can meditate in isolation about the new race, the heroic Siegfrieds of his imagination.

In this respect, Nietzsche's attacks on Rousseau are particularly interesting. He sneers at Rousseau for believing in the natural goodness of man and thus encouraging the assumption that only the structure of Western society needs to be changed. He also blames Rousseau for Romantic self-expressionism, which Nietzsche considers an emotional escape from the realities of life at moments when tough and relentless action or analysis is required. At the same time, there is in all of Nietzsche a proud and tormented loneliness which suggests that he is much closer to Rousseau, in character if not in thought, than he himself may have recognized. In his book on Nietzsche, Karl Jaspers argues that all his life Nietzsche had a fear of friendship and was unable to live with other people. Nietzsche often *seems*, at least, to approximate the recurrent paranoia of Rousseau; and like Rousseau he could find no way of living in the world even though he wanted to spread his messianic message throughout it. Jaspers quotes letters of Nietzsche to show how much he suffered from an isolation that he both dreaded and also welcomed, accepting it for the sake of his unique mission. To this extent Nietzsche resembles Kierkegaard as well as Rousseau. One cannot infer from the pathology of their similar conflicts that their ideas about love must be erroneous. But the comparable syndrome in all three may be taken as indicating realms of human achievement about which none of them had much personal acquaintance.

This is not to say that Nietzsche was unaware of the limitations imposed upon him by his personal problems, any more than Kierkegaard and Rousseau were in their own cases. Nietzsche's intellectual self-portrait, *Ecce Homo,* is too studied in its aggressive assertiveness to reveal what was really going on in this remarkable man, but in *The Genealogy of Morals* his discussion of asceticism tells us a great deal about himself. Ostensibly he is there investigating the psychology of philosophers who "pay homage" to the ascetic ideal, philosophers like Schopenhauer who deny the possibility of "healthy sensuality," as Feuerbach called it, and attempt to defeat the will by rejecting bodily enjoyment. But to some degree, at least, Nietzsche is talking about himself as well as Schopenhauer when he says that philosophers are driven to the ascetic ideal by a desire to gain release from the "torture" of the appetitive life. And Nietzsche may also be read as speaking about himself when he says that Schopenhauer "*needed* enemies in order to keep in good spirits; that he loved bilious, black-green words, that he scolded for the sake of scolding, out of passion; that he would have become ill, become a *pessimist* (for he was not one, however much he desired it), if deprived of his enemies, of Hegel, of woman, of sensuality and the whole will to existence, to persistence."

Nietzsche says this of Schopenhauer in order to prove that even the denier of happiness makes his denial because he thereby finds his own happiness. But Nietzsche also recognizes the greatness of Schopenhauer's mind and he characterizes him in ways that he (rightly) considered appropriate to himself as well: "a genuinely independent spirit . . . , a man and knight of a steely eye who had the courage to be himself, who knew how to stand alone without first waiting for heralds and signs from above." Moreover, Nietzsche's account of why philosophers find asceticism so attractive implicates him no less than others. For though he is speaking in this place as a psychologist, Nietzsche has the same attitudes as the philosophers he describes. He says that every philosopher must abhor mundane bonds that threaten his independence as a thinker, his freedom of thought, his emancipation from "compulsion, disturbance, noise, from tasks, duties, worries."

Nietzsche rejects the ascetic claim that the philosopher inevitably denies existence—he argues that the philosopher is rather affirming his own existence—but he admits that the need to escape the demands of ordinary life explains why philosophers have often defended asceticism. Its rigorous commandments of poverty, humility, and chastity Nietzsche accepts as governing principles for free and creative spirits. While attacking the *metaphysics* of asceticism, he also admires it as possibly the highest development toward the single-minded, intense condition requisite for human nature to overcome itself and thus attain spiritual health.

Nietzsche's view is paradoxical insofar as he asks us to affirm our being in the process of denying it, to achieve the goods of this world through a lean and unyielding rejection of them. The superman is presumably a pinnacle in human nature, a superior being enjoying superior consummations and a superior love of all things; and yet there seems to be little in reality with which he can be identified. Toward what ends will his heroic striving actually direct itself? Humanity, and life in general, seems too meager, too insignificant for him. In his long struggle to overcome the nihilism of Schopenhauer's negative philosophy, Nietzsche may only have entangled himself in it that much more securely. He must have sensed this possibility. Perhaps it explains the incredible stridency of his prose and its inclination to burst into a marching song that soars above the turmoil of his doubts. He sings about strong and vibrant beings to whom one can devote one's total allegiance, but he has virtually no idea of how they might come into existence. In his lyrical outcries, he voices a love of humanity which is nevertheless empty of affection for real men and women, either as Nietzsche knew them or as he could imagine them at some future time. What kind of love is this?

❋

In discussing Nietzsche on the love of humanity, I have tried to show that his scorn for pity and compassion, particularly as they are advocated by Christianity, issues from his attempt to recommend heroically natural and healthy-minded love, an attempt that he himself could not render coherent or persuasive. It will not do to suggest, as Santayana has, that Nietzsche was merely in love with the turbulent feelings that come from playing with love rather than committing oneself to an actuality related to it. Nietzsche's imagining of health, discipline, self-control, and self-overcoming in strong-willed persons who proudly insist upon their superiority to those who are weak, sickly, resentful, and therefore destructive of what they cannot emulate—all this introduces a content to Nietzsche's new morality that is more than just an infatuation with one's own feelings. A more serious defect, as I have been arguing, results from the fact that neither the supermen of Nietzsche's conception nor the Zarathustras crying for them in the wilderness are defined in ways that would enable us to recognize concrete possibilities. Nietzsche's noblemen cannot be human beings that now exist, since all such are to be transcended, but neither are they portrayed as surrogate humanoids whose life—as individuals, as social entities, as creatures in nature—one can describe with any degree of precision. Nietzsche knows very well what he hates, as most ascetics do, but so much of his genius goes into his repudiation of the real world that his philosophy has room for little more than a hazy and largely cerebral attestation of the contradictory desire to love everything and to say yea despite his very good reasons for saying nay.

This residual piety in Nietzsche, so foreign to his wit and wisdom in revealing the falseness of traditional morality, appears most vividly when he proclaims the love of all being, amor fati, which he offers as a metaphysical support for his longing for the superman. "My formula for greatness in a human being is *amor fati:* that one wants nothing to be different, not forward, not backward, not in all eternity. Not merely bear what is necessary, still less conceal it—all idealism is mendaciousness in the face of what is necessary—but *love* it."

The love of cosmos which Nietzsche here demands is quite different from anything Spinoza or Hegel meant. For these thinkers, as for the Christian theologians who preceded them, universal love made sense because "what is necessary," that in the face of which one must avoid all "mendaciousness," revealed an organic totality or absolute spirituality with which human beings could feel a kinship, as in a lesser way they do with the people they love. Nietzsche has no such conception of the universe. For him it is the same field of meaningless force that Schopenhauer and any number of naturalists depicted. It has no purpose, it has no spiritual goal, it has no concern for any of the intellectual or aesthetic achievements that mattered to perceptive and refined persons like Nietzsche himself. But then, we may ask: why should this horrid fatality be loved instead of hated as a monstrosity from which the imagination must systematically detach itself? And even if such total hatred lies beyond our capacity, should we not withdraw as much fidelity to the universe as is needed for the humanizing of nature whenever possible? In other words, how can amor fati be justified, assuming it is even feasible?

In ridiculing Nietzsche's concept, Santayana claims that it neglects man's ability to learn from experience, and therefore it ignores the way human beings improve their lot through dedication to abstract ideals rather than through a mystical acceptance of the world in general. I think Santayana is mistaken insofar as he believes, good Platonist that he is, that ideals must be pure essences whose being transcends an otherwise meaningless existence. To that extent, he shares the same negativism about nature as Schopenhauer (and Nietzsche). In all three alike, one fails to see how anything good, or even the desire for moral ideals, could have sprung out of so wretched a world as the one they describe.

Santayana is right to think that forcing oneself to love the cosmos—not in part but all of it and for all eternity—need never lead to amelioration. But neither can one hope for significant improvement unless our ideals reflect the structure of the very universe whose waywardness we are trying to correct. In itself, the mere act of loving an ideal does not change reality for the better any more than does Nietzsche's saying yes to everything. In both cases, love can even deprive us of motivation for altering nature as we should. To love something is to accept it as it is. Neither Santayana's love of ideals nor Nietzsche's cosmic love can account for moral behavior. Nothing we can do will ever satisfy perfectionist ideals, and indiscriminately squandering our love on mere reality will not enable us to create a new world.

Nietzsche undoubtedly thought that the difficulties I have been suggesting would be answered by his conception of the will to power and of eternal recurrence. Amor fati would not lead to quietism or resignation, he believed, if it was predicated upon an awareness that man dynamically searches not only for life but also for ever-increasing mastery over life. This is the meaning of will to power, and Nietzsche would deny that cosmic love prevents us from acting to strengthen ourselves in the world, since every moment of our existence is already directed toward greater control.

Moreover, Nietzsche held that "the highest formula of affirmation that can ever be attained" would follow from his notion of eternal recurrence. This is the idea, which Nietzsche proposes as "the most scientific of hypotheses," that all events in the universe have already happened and will forever recur exactly the same, an infinite number of times from cycle to cycle or within an unending spiral. He thought that belief in the perpetual return of the past would require us to ask at every moment in the present whether we can will that eternity be always burdened by just the event we are now contemplating. Would not this reflection encourage us to make each moment meaningful, to focus it to the brilliance of a hard, gem-like flame, to discover in ourselves the heroic intensity needed for acts that really change the universe in desirable ways? Far from being passive, human beings would effectively realize their power as men and women who create reality in the process of coping with it. Willing that what they do should indeed return everlastingly, the new breed would become godlike. They would not only accept and ratify their destiny; they would also exercise dominion over it.

In trying to evaluate this cluster of ideas, I shall largely ignore the usual ad hominem arguments that are employed against them. It is easy to say that Nietzsche was just a sick and neglected professor living in a boarding house, or that his affirmations are grandiose gestures that his imagination used to overcome personal misfortunes, or that he is (or is not) responsible for the criminality that resulted when self-appointed disciples interpreted the will to power as total mastery—willed by them for all eternity—over other people. What seems to me more relevant is the fact that the concept of amor fati cannot be salvaged by the notion of either will to power or eternal recurrence. For if everything we do is motivated by the will to power, this must apply to our weaknesses as well as our strengths, the pitiful acts of lesser individuals as well as the heroic deeds that Nietzsche admires. But if the weak and lesser man is doing what he wants, which is to say in Nietzschean terms, expressing the will to power as he experiences it, why should he be condemned? And if in his simplicity he too loves the totality of things, how is he inferior to one who happens to be stronger?

Nietzsche might reply that everyone really wants to be more rather than less powerful, and therefore inferior men are incapable of having authentic amor fati. They will resent others who succeed where they have failed, and they will hate themselves as well as the world at large. But what kind of judgment is Nietzsche making? The issue would seem to be an empirical one. Yet Nietzsche adduces no factual evidence. In his speculations he merely assumes that some attempts to satisfy the will to power, namely those of weak or self-denying people, must render amor fati impossible. But his argument is circular: for he does not recognize the existence of cosmic love *except* among the strong or powerful or self-assertive.

Similarly, the notion that everything in reality repeats itself endlessly cannot support the idea of amor fati, or even provide a basis for moral choice. For if everything returns through all eternity, each decision would belong to an infinite set of identical decisions that occur at the same moment and in the same way. That being so, however, I don't see how belief in the eternal return could possibly yield the moral impetus Nietzsche wants to promote. As opposed to Kant's reliance upon the categorical imperative, which enjoins us to consider whether our choice can be universalized for all rational beings, or Christian transcendentalism, which seeks justification by reference to the will of a supernatural deity, Nietzsche asks the moral agent whether he can will the return through all eternity of the events that his act is about to bring into existence. But why would this matter if everything is part of an infinite recurrence regardless of what and how we decide? Does not the present moment with its present choice merely duplicate an endless number of moments that have occurred in the past and will recur in the future?

If Nietzsche's metaphysical principle is correct, nothing new can ever take place, whether it be itself a decision or the consequence of making certain decisions. Only if the world does *not* recur eternally can we freely will anything, including the future recurrence of particular moments in the present that Nietzsche would have us cherish. Nietzsche wants us to live at all times with affirmation and vital self-assurance rather than behaving like Kantian calculators or Christian self-renouncers deferring their real life to some other realm of being. This much in his philosophy we may well applaud. But the doctrine of eternal recurrence as Nietzsche usually formulates it, like his concept of amor fati, can only undermine his exhortation to live creatively or with a sense of heroic responsibility.

At times, however, Nietzsche ignores his pseudo-scientific hypothesis and unashamedly speaks as a moralist. He then tells us to live our lives as if each moment would *henceforth* recur eternally. The question he asks is: "Do you desire this once more and innumerable times more?" This involves a commitment to the infinite future but not the eternal recurrence of the past. And that makes all the difference. Instead of the categorical imperative or a crass concern about rewards and punishments in another world, Nietzschean ethics of this sort bids us to treat decisions as if their outcome would never end, as if their consequences would be with us forever. If we took that attitude, would we not make the greatest effort to render each moment as full and satisfying as possible? Would we not live for the maximum creation of goodness and beauty in this world?

If this is what Nietzsche means, I am not prepared to criticize him. Though his argument would be based upon optimistic assumptions about an underlying good will in man, that too may be defensible. But even so, our revised conception of eternal recurrence would still not buttress Nietzsche's faith in amor fati. To live as if our acts had infinite, perpetual ramifications is not the same as, or in any way related to, loving the world in its entirety.

If Nietzsche's vision of cosmic love is confused, and greatly in need of clarification, as I have been suggesting, it nevertheless helps us to understand his thinking about the possibility of sexual love. His more sympathetic commentators sometimes sound as if this part of his work can be detached or exorcised from the rest. He must be forgiven, they say, because he really knew very little about women, having not had much of a sex life himself and having experienced love for another person mainly with the sister for whom his feelings were so ambivalent. Yet most of the difficulties to be found in Nietzsche's reflections about the sexes duplicate and derive from difficulties one encounters elsewhere in his philosophy. And neither can we avert our eyes simply because his views about sexual love are sometimes offensive to present-day sensibilities.

As he does throughout his writing, Nietzsche presents ideas on sexual love dialectically and therefore in a way that often seems paradoxical. In different places he emphasizes one or another facet of his thought; rarely does he show us the underlying pattern that unites his scattered insights. This unity begins to appear, however, in his final books. In *The Twilight of the Idols,* in a chapter that contrasts Christian attempts to extirpate the passions with his own desire to harmonize them with the rest of life, he says: "There is a time with all passions when they are merely fatalities, when they drag their victim down with the weight of their folly—and a later, very much later time when they are wedded with the spirit, when they are 'spiritualized.'" Nietzsche puts the word *spiritualized* in quotes because he wishes to emphasize that the development he discusses, indeed recommends, is nothing like the extermination of passions that he ascribes to Christian dogma.

In a subsequent passage Nietzsche defines love as "the spiritualization of sensuality" and praises it as a means of overcoming Christianity. He does not tell us, however, what he means by the "time" when all passions are fatalities, or the "very much later time" when they become wedded to the spirit. Time in the life of the species, or of the individual as he or she gets older, or in the course of some experience of intimacy? These questions are unanswerable, I believe, but the discussion is nevertheless important because it displays the range of polarities within which Nietzsche's comments about sexual love generally occur.

At one extreme he insists upon a naturalistic perspective that traces even the most ethereal of human loves to biological and ultimately physical necessities. He interprets this to mean that love comes from and, in a sense, reduces to mere sexuality. As Schopenhauer had maintained, sexual love is a "fatality" inasmuch as it manifests ruthless laws of nature to which human beings are subject without exception. Christianity is thus a false religion, since it tends to negate these natural forces and is itself hostile to life. On the other hand, Nietzsche claims, Schopenhauer's philosophy is pernicious because it too prevents us from accepting our being as participants in nature. The concept of love to be found in Wagner's later operas Nietzsche finds "degenerate" since it follows Schopenhauer and the Christians in demanding the elimination of sexual passion. The inferiority of the philosophy in *Parsifal* becomes evident, Nietzsche assures us, once we compare it to ideas about love expressed in *Carmen*. In Bizet's opera he finds the assertion that love emanates not only from nature itself but also from nature perceived to be merciless and destructive: "Love as *fatum*, as fatality, cynical, innocent, cruel—and precisely in this a piece of nature. That love which is war in its means, and at bottom the deadly hatred of the sexes!"

This aspect of Nietzsche's thinking is related to his attack upon the idealist tradition in general. Far from being selfless and sacrificial, sexual love is for him the best illustration of self-interest and the universal will to power. For even if the lover acts for the advantage of his beloved, sometimes to a point where his behavior is disadvantageous for himself, he still seeks to possess the other person. God too "becomes terrible when one does not love him in return." Even when sexual love is not as sadistic as in *Carmen,* Nietzsche calls attention to the relentless quest for domination that motivates the lover's need to possess: "one comes to feel genuine amazement that this wild avarice and injustice of sexual love has been glorified and deified so much in all ages—indeed, that this love has furnished the concept of love as the opposite of egoism while it actually may be the most ingenuous expression of egoism."

By taking this approach to sexual love, Nietzsche remains the prisoner of Schopenhauer's nay-saying. For he never recognizes the joy and satisfying sweetness which belongs to the natural condition of sexuality as much as the bitterness and hatred that can result from a conflict of wills. At the same time, Nietzsche enriches the Schopenhauerian perspective with a cluster of psychological insights that are distinctively his own. Before we consider what Nietzsche means, at the opposite end of his polarity, by suggesting that passion can and must be spiritualized, these additions to Schopenhauer are worthy of our attention. For instance, Nietzsche tells us that the concept of love is not the same for a woman as it is for a man. He states, as Kierkegaard's Johannes the Seducer had also said, that women want "to be taken and accepted as a possession," and consequently for them love means total submission to the man who will be capable of treating the beloved as an acquisition. A woman whose passion causes her to make an "unconditional renunciation" thereby fulfills her own ideal. If, on the other hand, a man is possessed by a woman, he becomes little more than a slave, utterly worthless. Nietzsche sees no possibility of getting around this discrepancy, men perceiving love as the taking of women while for women it is a giving of themselves. Such disharmony between the sexes arises from the fact that by its very nature love is "harsh, terrible, enigmatic, and immoral."

What distinguishes these ideas about men and women, in some respects typical platitudes of the nineteenth century, is Nietzsche's assumption that the contrasting attitudes lead to inevitable disharmony between the sexes. And yet, if it were truly the case that women thought of love as a giving of themselves while men saw in it nothing but an opportunity to appropriate these willing women, there would be no grounds for antagonism. The roles of both sexes would be wholly complementary. Nietzsche does not reach this conclusion, perhaps because he thinks that renunciation is itself a kind of egoism, a submerged form of aggression that will eventually contribute to a struggle for power. But even if this is true, it does not follow that conflict results from the differing ways in which male and female conceive of love. That would have to be proved independently, on its own. Nietzsche makes no such attempt.

In the course of these reflections, Nietzsche dismisses Kant's philosophy of sexual love without mentioning his name and without offering much of an argument. "A woman's passion in its unconditional renunciation of rights of her own presupposes precisely that on the other side there is no equal pathos, no equal will to renunciation; for if both partners felt impelled by love to renounce themselves, we should then get—I do not know what; perhaps an empty space?" It was precisely this mutual renunciation of rights to possessiveness that Kant saw as the foundation for authentic love between men and women. Since the renouncing was reciprocal and institutionalized through the marital contract, each lover would get back what he or she lost to the other. Neither would thus become subservient, and for Kant that assured the possibility of a harmonious union of wills. This benign conception Nietzsche will not allow. Between him and Kant there stretches a long period of idealist thinking about love; and in view of the inflated conclusions that some Romantics drew from Kant's theory, we need not be surprised that Nietzsche finds idealism so ludicrous. This major disagreement between the two philosophers may also result from temperamental differences, and certainly it is related to altering climates of opinion in their societies. But it cannot be explained in terms of their own love life. Neither Kant nor Nietzsche spoke of marriage firsthand, and Kant would seem to have had as little experience of sexual love as Nietzsche.

The negativistic side in Nietzsche's outlook convinces him that marriage as it generally exists in the West is little more than moral degradation. In *Thus Spake Zarathustra* he says that marriage is "for the most part" a conjunction of beasts, a mutual poverty of soul, a dual filth becoming one. In *The Will to Power* he insists that marriage in the "bourgeois" and "most respectable" sense (which Kant surely had in mind) cannot be based upon love. Like Montaigne and voices in Andreas Capellanus, Nietzsche distinguishes between love as passion and the contrary conditions needed for a successful marriage. The latter include "a certain attraction between the parties and very much good will—will to patience, compatibility, care for one another."

Contrasting the demands of marriage and passion, Nietzsche might seem to be renewing Schopenhauer's cynicism. Actually he is saying something quite distinct. He thinks of marriage as a convention designed to propagate the race in the most desirable fashion, and he praises aristocracies that treat it as a breeding device without being overly concerned about the preferences of the participants. Schopenhauer had assigned the creation of future generations to mere sexual impulse following the imperious commands of the will. He thought that marriage arranged by the parents could provide social benefits, and even the happiness of the newlyweds, but that it was a less reliable guide to optimal reproduction than passionate love alone. As Nietzsche sees it, sexual passion serves an entirely different function: it constitutes an escape from the restraints imposed upon individual interests by marriages designed to maintain one or another ruling class. "Love as a passion—in the great meaning of the word— was *invented* for the aristocratic world and in it, where constraint and privation were greatest." Though an aristocrat might have had to propagate from within an approved marriage that he accepted in order to please his family, his erotic longing and imagination would create a cathexis elsewhere as a mode of passionate compensation.

Thinking of marriage in these terms, Nietzsche speaks both as a historian of psychology and also as a moralist. What he calls "the future of marriage" is a condition that he strongly advocates. It involves communal control of each and every marital arrangement, medical certificates to make sure that eugenic principles are not neglected, fixed periods of longevity during which marriages remain legal, advantages awarded fathers who beget boys rather than girls, etc. As an antidote to the bourgeois sentimentality that he loathes, Nietzsche wishes to reinstitute authoritarian attitudes he associates with previous aristocracies. His motivation is, however, the typical Romantic yearning for some future generation of great men, geniuses of the spirit. In that section of *Thus Spake Zarathustra* where he castigates the folly and the bestiality of most marriages, he concludes with a rhapsodic description of the spiritual ideal that marriage *ought* to serve. In this heroic fantasy men and women choose sexual partners in a joint effort to propagate the superman. That kind of marriage shows forth "the will of two to create the one that is more than those who created it."

Nietzsche cannot take us beyond the sheer poetry of his dream about this superior type of marriage. He does not give us names and addresses; he provides no details about the realities and practical necessities inherent in the new way of life he proposes. Nevertheless his conception does reveal a positive possibility that balances his negative comments about ordinary marriage and helps to indicate what he means by passions being "spiritualized." At times he thinks of man's ideal state as something that takes one beyond love, but often he seems to identify it with a kind of sexual love that men and women rarely achieve though they recognize it as a supreme goal for everyone.

In one of the places where he claims that what people call love is mainly just a lust for aggressive control, Nietzsche ends his discussion in a way that suggests this alternate view: "Here and there on earth we may encounter a kind of continuation of love in which this possessive craving of two people for each other gives way to a new desire and lust for possession—a *shared* higher thirst for an ideal above them. But who knows such love? Who has experienced it? Its name is *friendship*."

With this conception of love before him, Nietzsche can modify and refine even his most caustic remarks. Having characterized love as egoism, he can now criticize thinkers who reduce it to nothing *but* egoism. Properly understood, Nietzsche insists, love is an affirmation of oneself which results from "a superabundance of personality." Love cannot be defined as self-surrender, but neither is it mere selfishness: "Only the most complete persons can love . . . one must be firmly rooted in oneself." Those who are firmly rooted in this sense are, of course, the strong and hardened men or women whose egoism provides a realistic basis for the values Nietzsche wishes to substitute for those that Christianity had promoted. Only the free and powerful individual can truly love. For only he will be able to accept himself in the process of accepting another. He will not delude himself by pretending that any of his responses are purely altruistic, and neither will he be prevented by resentment or some other pettiness from acting for the benefit of those who receive his love.

Various commentators have noted that Nietzsche's ideal human being resembles Aristotle's "magnanimous man." He radiates love as he radiates all other creative virtues. "All great love does not *want* love: it wants more." The "more" Nietzsche here refers to is life in all its fullness. A "great love" refuses to limit itself to sexual pleasures afforded by the beloved. Instead it turns the relationship into a joint endeavor to conquer the world, to express a mutual will to power. In the process, love refines sensory enjoyment, transmutes it into spiritual goods that are more than, go beyond, the individual love itself.

In saying this, Nietzsche also defines love as sublimation. That concept does not begin with him, but he provides an impetus that moves it forward in the history of ideas. Its occurrence in Freud's thinking may well be related, indirectly if not directly, to Nietzsche's influence. The belief in sublimation underlies the Nietzschean assertion that virtues are really "refined passions," and that pity and the love of mankind develop out of sexual impulse. If the latter is weakened or restrained in an unhealthy way, pity and love are simply contemptible. But if the passions have been tamed without being destroyed, dominated but not impaired, their residual freedom enables them to blossom into a higher type of humanitarian concern. In this vein, Nietzsche speaks about *his* kind of pity (putting the word in quotation marks) as a feeling he can scarcely name but which he senses when he sees someone cut down to less than he might have been, or imagines talents squandered and future generations diminished through venal politics.

Since Nietzsche cannot name this kind of sentiment, he rarely discusses it. But its presence in his philosophy prepares us for those compassionate lines in *The Gay Science* where he speaks about women, particularly upper-class women, as victims of Western morality in the areas of love and marriage. Brought up in ignorance and yet expected "to experience at the same time delight, surrender, duty, pity, terror," such women awaken in Nietzsche an expression of sympathy that appears to be completely genuine. This may be compensation for his hostile remarks about females who venture beyond the limits of motherhood and servile domesticity, but nonetheless it reveals aspects of the Nietzschean dialectic that prevent him from being a one-dimensional misogynist.

Out of these reverberations, often oscillations, subtle as they are in their diversity though sometimes paradoxical, one can derive different philosophies of life. In one of his typical statements about the sense of power that the great man feels in molding his people into a unity, Nietzsche reintroduces the distinction between a "slavish love" that submits, surrenders, idealizes, deceives itself, and the "divine love" that despises, adores, changes, elevates the loved one. He then depicts the higher type of love as the greatness needed "to shape the man of the future through breeding and, on the other hand, the annihilation of millions of failures, and not to perish of the suffering one creates, though nothing like it has ever existed!" Nietzsche seems to have had little awareness of the dangerous attitudes that his bombastic prose could possibly encourage. It is as if, in his isolated situation as a neglected writer during his lifetime, he thought that no one would really take him seriously anyhow. In this respect Santayana is right when he sees in Nietzsche "an immature, half-playful mind, like a child that tells you he will cut your head off." Thomas Mann makes a similar point when he tries to account for the effect upon recent history of Nietzsche's "romanticizing of evil" by saying that Nietzsche had a worldview which was purely "aesthetic" rather than ethical. The former need not consider consequences since it is presumably detached from action.

The trouble with this kind of interpretation is that Nietzsche writes primarily as an ethical philosopher. Even when he discusses one or another art form, which he generally does with a great deal of expertise, he does not deviate from the stance of the moralist studying manifestations of the human soul. At the same time, his most original and penetrating insights emanate from his conception of life as itself an artistic creation, an aesthetic phenomenon. Though he purports to tell us how we must change the world, trying to motivate our behavior in accordance with his vision of a new race of supermen, his deepest inspiration comes from seeing how everything in life may be construed as an incipient work of art.

Santayana, so much closer in temperament to Schopenhauer than to Nietzsche, expresses his preference for Schopenhauer by saying "he thought tragedy beautiful because it detached us from a troubled world and did not think a troubled world good [as Nietzsche did], . . . because it made such a fine tragedy." But this formulation of Nietzsche's outlook does not do it justice. Nietzsche had no intention of denying the harsh and ugly character of existence. In this he differs from Schopenhauer not at all. His new departure consists in advocating an aesthetic attitude in which we could experience the world as if it were a good tragedy without our concluding that it is in fact a good world. That approach would enable us to accept our human existence instead of withdrawing from it, to appreciate its incidental beauties, and even to love the precarious life that flowed through it. Far from being nonethical, an aesthetic orientation of this sort could even reveal ways of improving the world. We would be changing it into a great work of art, more conducive to the natural interests of its participants and closer to their needs for self-fulfillment. Whether or not the Nietzschean ideal is defensible, it is surely ethical as well as aesthetic. It is a merging of the two.

Nietzsche's attempt to fuse the ethical and the aesthetic shows itself nowhere better than in his analysis of sexual love. On the one hand, his ideas about sublimation strengthen his belief that beauty, whether in art or in life, occurs as an emanation from biological pressures that are largely libidinal; on the other hand, he recognizes that love and sexuality are themselves products of man's artistic imagination and therefore have been "spiritualized" to that extent. In deriving the aesthetic from the biological, Nietzsche cites Stendhal as an ally against Kant. The latter had defined the beautiful as that which "gives us pleasure without interest." Kant thought that an aesthetic attitude involved detachment from appetitive behavior, from purposiveness, and above all from sexuality. It was under the Kantian influence that Schopenhauer portrayed aesthetic contemplation as an act of disinterestedness which defeats the will. In Nietzsche's mature philosophy, and even at times in his first book, *The Birth of Tragedy*, he explicitly rejects this separation between the aesthetic and the biological. In *De l'Amour* Stendhal had spoken of the beautiful as "the promise of happiness" for oneself, and Nietzsche leaps upon this as pointing in the right direction: "the fact seems to be precisely that the beautiful *arouses the will* ('interestedness')." Far from being contemplative or detached, Nietzsche claims, the aesthetic is really part of the self-interested search for biological goods, such as happiness, that characterizes life in all its appearances.

This return to Stendhal, whom Nietzsche calls a "more happily constituted person" than Schopenhauer, also figures in Nietzsche's belief that love is best understood as an artifact of aesthetic imagination. In *The Gay Science* he tells us that one must *learn* to love just as one learns how to listen to music. In both cases, if we are successful, we are rewarded for "our good will, our patience, fair-mindedness, and gentleness" by an object that ceases to be strange and eventually becomes "a new and indescribable beauty." In *The Will to Power* he carries this line of reasoning even further. Not only does he maintain that art represents "an indirect demand for the ecstasies of sexuality," but also that aesthetic imagination functions as the transfiguring power in the intoxication which is love. The aesthetic, operating creatively within sexual love, is thus "the greatest stimulus of life." Love provides what Nietzsche calls an imaginative "transposition" of values: "And it is not only that it transposes the *feeling* of values: the lover *is* more valuable, is stronger. In animals this condition produces new weapons, pigments, colors, and forms; above all, new movements, new rhythms, new love calls and seductions. It is no different with man. His whole economy is richer than before, more powerful, more *complete* than in those who do not love."

Nietzsche goes on to speak of the lover as a "happy idiot" undergoing a kind of "intestinal fever." But he says this in a voice that sounds like Stendhal's: it resonates with the same adulation and with a similar irony. Growing "wings and new capabilities," the lover is described as a supreme artist of the senses. Sensuality uses him as the agency of its own embellishment, just as art—which is the power of embellishing—enables sensuality to disguise itself as the ideal perfection that lovers seek. It is the wedding of passion with spirit, the spiritualization of sexuality through aesthetic imagination, that ultimately defines the nature of love in Nietzsche's philosophy. Latter-day Romantic that he is, despite his rejection of romanticism, Nietzsche finds in *this* type of love a positive goal for which man may properly aspire. The superman turns out to be the superior lover.

✳

In *The Birth of Tragedy* Nietzsche began his philosophic exploration by speculating about the cultural conditions under which man could possibly harmonize the beautiful and the vital, the civilized and the instinctual, the Apollonian and the Dionysian. In his later philosophy he tended to think of the Dionysian as already including elements of the Apollonian. An authentic will to power required both, and as he matured Nietzsche recognized that in art man achieved the deepest and most lasting re-creation of himself.

The greatness of Nietzsche consists in his gradual and sometimes painful struggle toward this idea. But his life's project was arrested, incomplete, truncated by his personal limitations as well as by his final, premature illness. He tells us that we must learn to love; but he does not tell us how to do it. He tells us that all love, particularly sexual love, is art; but he delineates the principles of this artistic activity with little of the detail and consecutive elaboration that we find in Schlegel, Shelley, or Stendhal. Seeing love as a human value through which the aesthetic and the biological intermesh dynamically, he prepares us for the naturalists of the twentieth century—for empirical philosophers no less than psychiatric theorists—and for existentialists of all descriptions. He is the pivot that turns the Western mind into its post-Romantic stage. His positive affirmations are often too vague and insubstantial to solve the moral, the aesthetic, and above all the religious problems that he confronts. But without him, contemporary thinking would have suffered a gap, an intellectual emptiness. It would be as if the new man that now begins to clamor for his own perspective, his own philosophy of love, had never had an adolescence.

Part II
The Twentieth Century

4

Freud

THROUGHOUT THIS STUDY I have refused to draw sharp boundaries between philosophical and literary concepts of love. In order to understand Freud, as well as his friendly or critical followers, we must likewise ignore precise delimitations between science and philosophy. Freud himself was very sensitive about the differences between his empirical research, mainly based upon clinical observations, and his metapsychological speculations. The latter were intended as exploratory theory that would generate new perspectives upon the raw data and thereby lead to knowledge that provides hints about effective therapy. As the theoretical constructions became more and more complex, and as Freud probed deeper and deeper into those areas of human experience that were amenable to his type of inquiry, his writing took on a philosophical cast that he himself might have scorned in his earlier years.

In the burgeoning of his speculative thought, Freud is often said to have gone through two major phases, as indicated by his earlier and his later theory of instincts. In the period up to the First World War, he distinguishes between "ego instincts," those that impel the organism toward whatever is needed for self-preservation, and "the sexual instinct," which is ultimately directed toward reproduction of the species. By 1920, however, he had decided that ego and sexual instincts made a unity, which he called "Eros," the instinct for life. The fundamental distinction in man's innate structure,

Freud concluded, arose from a conflict between Eros and "the death drive" ("death instinct" or, occasionally, "death instincts" in the usual translation). In his biography of Freud, Ernest Jones remarks that the first intimations of Freud's new conception had a "disturbing" effect upon his followers, and that in subsequent years few of them have been able to accept his thinking about a death drive. Critics have frequently seen a contradiction between the earlier and the later Freud: they argue that only one or the other theory of instincts can be defended.

In the course of my discussion I shall return to these problems of interpretation. But throughout I will be treating Freud's philosophy as an integral whole. Despite the complexities within it, his thinking retains a discernible unity, as if it were itself a developmental organism that grows and expands throughout the various stages that lead to final maturity. In seeking to be truly scientific, Freud prided himself on his willingness to discard old conclusions as new discoveries revealed ever-increasing problems. Still he also believed that a continuity linked his earlier and his later theorizing in ways that precluded radical inconsistency. With respect to his ideas about love, at least, I think he succeeded in this respect more than his critics may have realized.

Approaching Freud in this fashion, we may begin with a statement he made in 1920, in the preface to the fourth edition of the *Three Essays on the Theory of Sexuality,* which had originally appeared in 1905:

> Some of what this book contains—its insistence on the importance of sexuality in all human achievements and the attempt that it makes at enlarging the concept of sexuality—has from the first provided the strongest motives for the resistance against psycho-analysis. People have gone so far in their search for high-sounding catchwords as to talk of the "pan-sexualism" of psycho-analysis and to raise the senseless charge against it of explaining "everything" by sex. We might be astonished at this, if we ourselves could forget the way in which emotional factors make people confused and forgetful. For it is some time since Arthur Schopenhauer, the philosopher, showed mankind the extent to which their activities are determined by sexual im-

pulses—in the ordinary sense of the word. It should surely have been impossible for a whole world of readers to banish such a startling piece of information so completely from their minds. And as for the "stretching" of the concept of sexuality which has been necessitated by the analysis of children and what are called perverts, anyone who looks down with contempt upon psycho-analysis from a superior vantage-point should remember how closely the enlarged sexuality of psycho-analysis coincides with the Eros of the divine Plato.

Twice in this passage Freud refers to "enlarging" the concept of sexuality. What this means, and how it can be justified, will require careful analysis. The reference to Schopenhauer may not surprise us, since he insisted that the will to live manifested itself most explicitly in the sexual drive. But the suggestion that the psycho-analytic concept of sexuality coincides with Platonic eros seems wholly unwarranted. For Plato, eros was indeed a vital force that showed itself in the dynamism of sex. It explained the nature of sexual instinct, however, by revealing a search for perfection, a yearning for a highest good that did not exist in space or time and yet motivated the strivings of everything that did. Love (i.e. eros) being this "desire for the perpetual possession of the Good," Plato defines sexuality in terms of a yearning that is metaphysical, even spiritual. In his frequent attempt to derive all nonsexual love from the workings of aim-inhibited sex, Freud clearly belongs to the realist tradition that opposes the idealism of Plato. How then can Freud cite him as a forerunner?

In his book on group psychology, where Freud spells out the implications of his affective theory, he repeats the claim that "in its origin, function, and relation to sexual love, the 'Eros' of the philosopher Plato coincides exactly with the love-force, the libido of psychoanalysis. . . ." This kind of remark we must simply dismiss as being erroneous and misleading. Of greater promise is Freud's suggestion, in the next paragraph, that the Greek word *eros* is "nothing more than" a translation of the German *Liebe,* the ordinary term for love of any sort. For the German word is notoriously ambiguous, like the English and the Greek (despite Plato's definition). Freud shrewdly recognizes a wider and a narrower sense of love, and he is right in thinking that they are not unrelated, that there is some principle of unification that links them to each other and to all their derivative uses. In formulating the comprehensive doctrine that preoccupies him throughout his life, Freud articulates a conception of Liebe that shows how the term is variously employed in different senses that nevertheless depend on one another. While appreciating the great diversity in the different senses of the word "love," Freud attests to the feat of language that joins them in a single concept. Tracing the intricate links that bind the different uses to each other, he seeks a unitary pattern so basic to human nature as to reveal the being of man and thus to answer the riddle of the sphinx.

Without any preliminaries, let me now enumerate four different senses of Liebe in Freud, each of which we shall examine carefully throughout this chapter: (1) Love as the fusion of sexuality and tenderness; (2) Love as libidinal energy, both aim-inhibited and aim-uninhibited; (3) Love as Eros, the drive or instinct of life which attaches individuals to each other and ultimately unifies mankind; (4) Love as the mixture and dynamic interfusion of Eros with "man's natural aggressive instinct [the death drive]," which is inseparable from it.

I begin with love as the confluence of what Freud calls "tender, affectionate feelings and the sensual [sinnlich] feelings" because Freud refers to this sense of Liebe as definitely involving *more* than mere sexuality. The fusion of the two "currents" constitutes what he calls the "fully normal attitude in love." He seems to think of this attitude as an achievement, a benign completion, of human intimacy. The biblical text about a man leaving father and mother in order to cleave unto his wife he explains by saying that "then are tenderness and sensuality united"; and in the following paragraph he discusses factors that determine the success or failure of this "advance" in individual growth. Since, as we shall see, Freud believes that human beings cannot be happy unless their libido develops successfully, he may also be taken as meaning that an appropriate fusion between the two kinds of feelings is a necessary condition for happiness to exist.

In studying the two currents that merge within this confluence, we must recognize that terms such as "sensual," in the standard translation, imply no pejorative intent. Elsewhere I have substituted the word "sensuous" as a feasible translation, but that too can be misleading. In this context Freud is drawing upon the idea that sexual love is both a phenomenon of the senses and an attitude implying affection or kindliness. He is thereby returning to the tradition of Hume and Kant, each of whom defined love in terms of a benevolent concern about the welfare of another. For the libido to attain its proper development, however, love must also involve gratification of sense modalities that are activated by the sexual instinct. Instead of a fusion between tender and sensual feelings, Freud could equally well have referred to the coexistence of tenderness and overt sexuality.

In talking of two "currents," two "systems" of feeling, Freud would seem to be distinguishing between different responses that can occur either separately or in combination. And indeed, his insight is related to the distinction between self-preservative and sexual drives. The former come first in an individual's life inasmuch as the infant seeks to eliminate hunger before it searches for sexual gratification. According to Freud, tenderness and affection originate in the prudential awareness that mother or father provides the material sustenance needed for survival. "Of these two currents," Freud says, "affection is the older ... it is directed towards the members of the family and those who have care of the child." But he immediately adds that "from the very beginning" elements within the sexual current enter into the self-preservative attitude that generates affection. If this is true, however, one wonders how Freud knows that there were originally two currents. He does not suggest that we can ever observe the existence of one without the other, affection in its pure condition showing itself prior to the admixture of sexuality. He does argue, very cogently, about the later *separation* of tender and sexual feelings, and he is very convincing when he claims that the defeating of love in this manner leads to unhappiness and a spectrum of neurotic disturbances. But this alone would not indicate that the organism was "originally" endowed with two different attitudes, that one antedates the other, or that a confluence between them occurs at an early stage. Moreover, Freud never suggests that when the currents separate in later life they can exist in total isolation from one another. What then is the nature of his distinction?

In answer to this criticism, Freud can reply that his distinction between tender and sexual attitudes formalizes observations about the initial objects of love as well as the earliest sources of sexual satisfaction. The infant directs its love toward the caretaker that furthers its basic drive for self-preservation, and it first experiences sexual gratification in pleasures related to bodily functions essential for survival. We shall presently return to my questions about the separateness of the two currents, but here at least we may detect the utility in this concept of Liebe. For in identifying the original objects and satisfactions as he does, Freud is asserting that the "fully normal attitude in love" will have to accommodate feelings related to one's previous dependency upon parental figures. These are feelings of affection as well as feelings that enable one to enjoy the impulses of one's body.

Even if we find this reformulation acceptable, however, we must note that Freud never describes the "normal" attitude of con-fluence as a *likely* outcome. He shows how easily the two currents separate at various stages of development, and he offers little hope that they will recombine in the sexual life of many adults. Happiness in sexual love he considers to be a rare occurrence. In this respect he closely resembles Schopenhauer, Tolstoy, and others who were revolted by the naiveté of idealist philosophies that treated love between men and women as a common or even feasible solution to life's problems. For Freud as for these other thinkers, successful unification in love is more than human nature can expect to attain, though occasionally it may occur as a tantalizing indication of human possibilities. Having experienced a confluence of tenderness and sexuality in earliest infancy, the organism will strive unceasingly to achieve a reinstatement of that condition. This will help to explain its behavior. But Freud does not believe that mankind as a whole will ever manage to reunite the two diverging streams.

In moving on to the second sense of Liebe, we encounter the theory of the libido that Freud worked at throughout his life and that he considered one of his major innovations. It involves a gamut of interwoven concepts that we shall have to study in themselves as well as in their relationship to one another. If we think of the first sense of Liebe as primarily concerned about objects of love and sources of satisfaction, it is entirely consistent with the idea of love as libidinal impulse. For by "libido" Freud means the "dynamic manifestation of sexuality." It is the force or energy that underlies all aspects of love: "We call by that name the energy, regarded as a quantitative magnitude (though not at present actually measurable), of those instincts which have to do with all that may be comprised under the word 'love.'" Since the libidinal force is basically sexual, Freud can then go on to say that the "nucleus" of all love is "sexual love with sexual union as its aim." In another place he remarks that "in every way analogous to *hunger*, libido is the force by means of which the instinct, in this case the sexual instinct, as, with hunger, the nutritional instinct, achieves expression." Libido resembles hunger in being a "quantitatively variable force" but it differs from it in having its own "*qualitative* character . . . a special chemistry."

In this sense of the word, Liebe is merely libidinal energy. But since libido pervades so much of human nature—and possibly, in one way or another, all of it—the definition alone scarcely indicates the dimensions of Freud's idea. To understand his conception, we must realize that Freud thinks of libido as energy which is not only quantitative but also subject to mechanistic laws of a sort that apply to an enclosed fluid. Freud generally relies upon hydraulic metaphors to describe the dynamism of libido. He speaks as if it were a current whose natural flow can be dammed up. When this happens, libido is "repressed," prevented from flowing out through an opening designed by the organism's biological structure as the correct egress. Retained or held back, like an explosive liquid under pressure, libido would destroy the equilibrium in the organism unless it found some other way of issuing through the walls of its receptacle. The needed outlet occurs through "sublimation." Sexual energy then escapes by means that are not directly biological or reproductive. All the achievements of civilization result from the discharge of sublimated sexual energy.

I shall return to Freud's hydraulic metaphors. But first, I wish to enumerate several conclusions that he reaches when he observes how love as libido manifests itself in ordinary experience. The most shocking inference, which Freud long hesitated before enunciating, was the idea that sexuality does not arise in puberty but rather appears in the earliest moments of infancy. The vilification to which he was subjected for his claims about childhood sexuality Freud ascribed to assumptions by his critics that sex was inherently dirty or impure. Anyone believing that infants had sexual instincts would seem to be denying the innocence of childhood and besmirching values accepted by all respectable people in the nineteenth century. In our age we can appreciate Freud's astonishment in the face of this irrational attack, as well as the cogency of his denial that sexuality itself was either dirty or impure. As he rightly maintained, his generalizations in no way disparaged the earlier (or any other) stages of psychological development.

Clarifying his belief that sexual libido first occurs in infancy, Freud emphasizes that he is not referring to fully awakened desires of a genital sort. The reproductive drive begins in childhood, he asserts, but childhood sexuality need not include an explicit interest in coitus. He can say this because he means by sexuality more than just an attitude involving the genitals. In claiming that "germs of sexual impulses are already present in the new-born child," Freud means only that the sexual instinct has *begun* to operate at that age. He admits that it does so in ways that hardly suggest—though they contribute to—its final expression in normal reproductive behavior. Even when he analyzes the Oedipus complex as including a desire of the three-year-old boy to "sleep with" his mother, Freud recognizes that the child has only the vaguest conception of actual intercourse. His sexuality is primarily centered upon pleasures that result from events within his own organism. Though his mother is an object of desire for him, he still perceives her as the life-preservative individual that she was when he was born.

Sexuality thus involving the body but not necessarily the genitals, Freud initially relates it to sensitivity in the oral and anal regions, which he calls erotogenic zones. Subsequently he finds that any part of the body may be sensitive in this way and he extends the concept of erotogenicity to virtually all areas that can provide physical pleasure. Since sexual but nongenital activities are called "perversions," and since children are not yet capable of genital sexuality, Freud characterizes their libido as both polymorphous and perverse. From this he readily concludes that the sexuality of normal adults is not totally different from the sexuality of perverts. Both arise from the same kind of childhood origin. Though the types of sexuality diverge as individuals grow up, they are never wholly separable from one another. People who practice perversions such as fetish-love or homosexuality revert to earlier stages of libido, or else remain fixated at them, and so-called normal persons often express their sexuality in acts that are not unrelated to those of perverts. The difference between the two orientations consists in the degree of exclusivity: perverts are limited to interests that normal men and women have largely outgrown or at least subordinated to behavior that is ultimately genital and coital. Our libidinal origins in polymorphous perversity stay with us throughout our lives. In adulthood the condition is pathological or abnormal only when it interferes with the focusing of libidinal drive upon the genital demands of heterosexual appetite.

Defining libido in this fashion, Freud is consciously extending the concept of sexuality. At one point he says: "We have extended the meaning of the concept 'sexuality' only so far as to include the sexual life of perverted persons and also of children; that is to say, we have restored to it its true breadth of meaning. What is called sexuality outside psychoanalysis applies only to the restricted sexual life that is subordinated to the reproductive function and is called normal." In other words, he claims to be subjecting the word "sexual" to an expansion of meaning that is nevertheless justified by facts about man's love life. At the same time Freud insists that libido is what we ordinarily recognize as *sexual* impulse and he prides himself on not having used "more genteel expressions." Though such linguistic maneuvers would have protected him from attack, Freud rejects them as "concessions to faintheartedness" that occur only when people are ashamed of sex. Freud makes this comment while defending his belief that all kinds of love, however spiritual, are reducible to love as libido. This tenet we have not yet examined, but it is important from the outset to realize that Freud means by libido both sexuality as it is ordinarily understood and also as reinterpreted through an extension of everyday usage.

Assuming that we do understand the ordinary meaning, how can we make sense of the Freudian extension? Though Freud claims that children experience sexuality, he does not believe that their sexuality is identical with what adults experience. He merely holds: (1) that the two are alike in important ways, differences resulting from the fact that (normal) adult sexuality eliminates some of the ingredients of childhood sexuality while organizing the rest into a structure specifically directed toward coital behavior; and (2) that the earlier and the later sexualities are linked together within a developmental process that reveals the presence of an instinct manifesting in time its preordained pattern to the extent that environmental factors permit. Both of these assertions are summed up in Freud's statement that "normal sexuality has arisen, out of something existing prior to it, by a process of discarding some components of this material as useless, and by combining the others so as to subordinate them to a new aim, that of reproduction."

Freud calls this an "obvious inference," and if we take his words in their most obvious, i.e., superficial, sense, he must surely be right. As he repeatedly says, it would be astounding if human sexuality suddenly appeared at puberty. Freud cites scientific authorities antedating psychoanalysis who attested to the not infrequent occurrence of activities in childhood that could only be considered sexual. In the years since Freud began writing, we have acquired much more evidence of this sort, including hormonal data that reveal a continuity of sexual chemistry before and after puberty. Similar hormones are present in childhood and adulthood, though greatly different in quantity. Furthermore, Freud deserves everlasting praise and gratitude for having been virtually the first person, at least the first major thinker, to have delineated the implications of there being a developmental process underlying sexuality (and therefore love) just as there are developmental processes for locomotion, muscular capacity, acquisition of language, etc. Nevertheless, I am convinced that the two propositions enumerated above are both untenable.

To see why this is so, we must take Freud's inference in a manner that is less "obvious" than he himself may have intended. For while it is probably true that children and adults are more alike in their affective natures than anyone before Freud may have realized, it does not follow that sexuality has the pervasive and even constant importance in childhood that Freudian theory suggests. Freud's contemporaries, particularly in medical circles, were under no illusions about the occurrence of sexual behavior—sometimes involving intercourse—in very young children. What seemed scandalous was Freud's insistence that sexuality belonged to the early infancy of *all* human beings and explained not only adult perversions that were modeled upon its first manifestations but also a large segment of prepubertal experience that had never been associated with sex.

In answering his critics, Freud had to show that universal activities of infancy—such as suckling at the mother's breast—revealed the sexual drive at work, or else led to its immediate activation. Since he is not a pansexualist, having insisted that the self-preservative instincts preceded the libidinal ones, he can readily accept the idea that the infant who initially turns to the mother's breast does so for the sake of nutrition. But once the infant has found organ-pleasure in suckling, Freud maintains, it responds in ways that indicate that the sexual drive has now grafted itself onto the self-preservatory activity and made the breast into an erotic object. When the infant has been weaned, and usually long before, it may derive great satisfaction from thumb-sucking. Since this behavior has no nutritive value whatsoever, Freud interprets it as a libidinal expression related to the sexuality present in suckling at the breast. It is this mode of reasoning that seems to me highly dubious, and therefore unable to justify Freud's extending the term "sexuality" into childhood as he does.

Let us accept the assumption that a self-preservatory instinct leads or causes an infant to find nourishment at the mother's breast. Let us assume further that the act of suckling is pleasurable in various respects, and that the oral satisfaction of sucking the nipple may renew itself in the sucking of one's thumb. We may also assume a causal link between these childhood activities and adult practices such as kissing and fellatio. The latter are explicitly sexual and Freud may very well be right (indeed, I think he is) in believing that they partly originate in the gratifying acts of sucking that characterize infant and childhood behavior. It does not follow, however, that the previous pleasures are *themselves* either directly or indirectly sexual. The most that Freud could infer from his scenario of human development is the idea that a great deal of adult sexuality includes traces, sequelae, sometimes duplications of affective occurrences that belong to the individual's earlier life. In a way that he himself does not specify but that is wholly coherent with his inspiration, we may even draw the causal link beyond the moment of birth, since the fetus also sucks its thumb and thrives within a slippery, fluid environment that seems to be unitive and comforting. But these traces of past pleasures need not be considered *sexual*. Freud says that from the very beginning they are taken over by the sexual instinct, which "leans upon" them and henceforth renders them into parts of its domain. But Freud's reasoning is circular. Since it is the existence of any such pervasive sexual instinct that he must demonstrate, he cannot presuppose it in advance.

I am contending that Freud assumes what he set out to prove. He did not wish to limit himself to showing the importance of non-sexual behavior in childhood as a basis for sexual behavior in later years. He wanted to make the stronger claim that in reality the former was itself sexual. But his reasoning posits that there must have been, from the start of each person's development, a sexual instinct that was operative in the requisite ways. This argument involves a logical fallacy—what logicians call *petitio principii*.

In one place Freud confronts, with his usual fearlessness and trenchancy, the kind of criticism I am suggesting. He has an imaginary interlocutor say the following:

> "Why are you so set upon declaring as already belonging to sexuality those indefinite manifestations of childhood out of which what is sexual later develops, and which you your-self admit to be indefinite? Why are you not content rather to describe them physiologically and simply to say that ac-

tivities, such as sucking for its own sake and the retaining
of excreta, may be observed already in young infants,
showing that they seek *pleasure in their organs?* In that way
you would have avoided the conception of a sexual life
even in babies which is so repugnant to all our feelings."

The reference to repugnancy is obviously irrelevant, and so too
is Freud's immediate insistence that he himself has "nothing
against" pleasures of the body. He then goes on to ask his interlocutor two ad hominem questions that are also irrelevant: "But
can you tell me when this originally indifferent bodily pleasure
acquires the sexual character that it undoubtedly possesses in later
phases of development? Do we know any more about this 'organ-
pleasure' than we know about sexuality?" The answer to both of
these questions may well be "No." But that merely means that the
linkage between earlier nonsexual occurrences and their associated
expressions in later life does not lend itself to precise characterization. This, however, does not enable us to extend the word
"sexual" as Freud suggests. Though the interlocutor cannot specify
the moment at which sucking, for instance, becomes sexual, he is
surely justified in refusing to say that it must always have been so.
Despite Freud's denial, one could very well conclude that activities
such as the infant's thumb-sucking are often merely a search for
organ- (or rather body-) pleasure.

As a final thrust at his critics, Freud introduces a biological
analogy. Imagine, he says, that we inspect two seedlings that look
identical but actually come from different plants. In view of their
indistinguishable appearance, should we assume that the seedlings
are exactly alike and that the eventual disparity between the two
plants arises at a later stage of development? Would it not be
preferable to believe that the difference between them is in the
seedlings themselves? And, similarly, is it not rational to think that
sexuality already exists in the organ-pleasure of infants, long
before it is fully developed after puberty?

But here too Freud's argument is untenable: this mode of ana-
logical reasoning is also circular in its logic. In the case of the seedlings, we know that each will eventuate in its own kind of plant. In
the case of organ-pleasures, we do *not* know whether they are non-

sexual originally but sexualized, so to speak, later on or whether they manifest an innate sexual instinct from the very start. The analogy with seedlings fails because we can properly assume that some organ-pleasures in childhood are not sexual either in themselves or as part of a further development. Freud dismisses the problem by saying: "Whether each and every organ-pleasure may be called sexual or whether there exists, besides the sexual, another kind of pleasure that does not deserve this name is a matter I cannot discuss here." Yet this, one feels, is the underlying problem. Freud seems not to have resolved it anywhere in his writings.

Even so, one might say, why is it worth fretting over the use of the term "sexual" in this context? Is it not sufficient to recognize that Freud was right in arguing about the effect of childhood experience upon adult sexual behavior? Having agreed that sexuality arises from a process of development, have we not digested the crucial part of the Freudian concept? Isn't the rest merely verbal? I think not. For underlying Freud's speculation in these areas, there resides a metaphysical and even teleological bias about the nature of sexuality. He invests libido with such great significance as an explanatory principle because he considers it a uniform and in some ways predetermined flux of energy that is basic to all human nature and that must be operative throughout man's existence. Freud is very sensitive to, and wonderfully observant about, the vicissitudes of libido as it encounters the infinitely varied circumstances of individual experience. But he treats them as variations superimposed upon a constant theme, or—to alter the musical metaphor—as chromatic excursions bound within a diatonic regularity.

Freud believed there would be something lacking—there would be a flaw or imperfection—in a science that ignored the libidinal germs from which all affective life issues forth. It is central to his conception that there be a drive or instinct of sexuality so pervasive and universal in man that no moment of human existence can be wholly free of it. But this is to say, using the term as I have defined it, that Freud's notion of libido is an "idealization," a bestowing of importance upon an aspect of life that particularly quickens and enthralls his imagination. We need not question Freud's wish to idealize, and we are always free to join the faith that he establishes by means of idealization. It is nevertheless incumbent upon us to recognize the nature of this commitment, the fact that neither logic nor knowledge of empirical data can generate it by themselves.

❋

Further problems in the theory of libido will recur throughout our discussion. The third sense of *Liebe* immediately involves us in questions about the relation between libido and Eros. Formulating his ideas about Eros in *Beyond the Pleasure Principle* (1920), Freud develops the concept of libido in directions that alter his earlier theory. In the paper on narcissism, which appeared in 1914, he had already modified his former distinction between ego instincts and sexual instincts. Previously, as we have seen, he had assigned to the former an individual's interest in self-preservation, considering it a force that operated independently of libido. Since libidinal energy infused the ego instincts, however, it could point the organism toward other objects for the sake of reproducing the species.

The hypothesis of narcissism required a major revision in this position. Freud now envisaged libido as being directed inward, toward the ego itself, as well as outward toward other objects. Since Freud always thought dualistically, he transformed the distinction between ego instincts and sexual instincts into an opposition between ego instincts and *object* instincts. Both were now considered libidinal, and this enlarged concept of libido constitutes what Freud calls Eros. He refers to Eros as "life instinct," sometimes in the singular, sometimes in the plural; he invariably treats it as sexual, in the extended sense of that word; and in several places he tries to identify it with the kind of universal dynamism that Plato had in mind. He sees it operating in the individual cells of everything that lives. Having started out with libido meaning roughly what the ordinary man means by the physical drive that unites male and female in coital behavior, Freud stretches the concept to a point where it includes all energy that "seeks to force together and hold together the portions of living substance." Libido is thus tantamount to Eros—that which "holds all living things together."

Freud recognized that his speculations about Eros provided a concept of love rather than mere sexuality in a narrow sense. At the same time, he maintained that Eros is wholly libidinal in character. His thinking about narcissism was stimulated by Jung's insistence that cathexis of energy flowed inward as well as outward. Jung concluded that the fundamental force was psychical and therefore that it need not be considered *inherently* libidinal. The libido is one of the manifestations of psychical energy, he claimed, but not its constant quality. In effect, Jung was suggesting a kind of élan vital such as Bergson had appropriated, as we shall see, from nineteenth-century idealism.

As against any solution of the Jungian or Bergsonian variety, Freud vigorously held that the psychical energy of Eros was itself libidinal. He implicitly criticizes Bergson when he asserts that there "is unquestionably no universal instinct towards higher development observable in the animal or plant world, even though it is undeniable that development does in fact occur in that direction. . . . Both higher development and involution might well be the consequences of adaptation to the pressure of external forces." This Darwinian-sounding statement keeps Freud within the realist camp. Unlike Bergson (or Plato and, we might add, Hegel), he denies that the cosmic force which binds all living substance is oriented toward perfection. The universal love that Freud calls Eros does not progress toward stages of greater spirituality.

It is because Freudian Eros is libido extended to its maximum scope that various recent commentators are mistaken when they see Freud's final theorizing as a radical departure from his earlier period. Rollo May claims that Eros, as Freud conceives of it, is "an aspect of human experience that must not only be distinguished from libido but is in important ways *opposed* to libido." In the long discussion of Freudian instinct theory that Erich Fromm appends to his book *The Anatomy of Human Destructiveness*, Freud's later view is characterized as "not only without antecedents in his former theory, but in full contradiction to it." Fromm does recognize that Freud repeatedly states that the old and the new theories were continuous with one another, but Fromm merely interprets this as proof of Freud's "unawareness of the contradiction." Fromm's reasoning is not, however, very cogent. He argues that, without being aware of it, Freud had given up his earlier mechanistic model in biology for one that was "perhaps closer to a vitalistic philosophy." But since Freud explicitly and consistently identified the energy in Eros with libido as he had interpreted it all along, it is hard to see how the suggestions of either Fromm or May can have any merit.

In his last book, *An Outline of Psychoanalysis,* Freud says that "the greater part of what we know about Eros" is the libido and that the word "libido" designates "the total available energy of Eros." Fromm remarks that while Freud thinks of Eros as "life instinct" or "love instinct" he specifies no physiological source, no "specific organ," as its determining basis. Fromm correctly states that "in the libido theory the excitation was due to the chemically determined sensitization, through the stimulation of the various erotogenic zones." Since Freud does not say this about Eros, Fromm wonders how he can treat it as instinct. But the reason for this seems evident to me: Freud did not discuss the organic origin of Eros because all that was encompassed by his belief that Eros *is* libido. His new analysis of instincts goes beyond the old one, and certainly modifies it insofar as libido is considered to be present within self-preservatory as well as sexual instincts, but the idea that this libidinal component arises from chemical determination remains constant throughout Freud's expanding conception.

Thus far in this chapter I have not mentioned Freud's theories about civilization. When I do so, I shall have to study the claim—made by Fromm and several other critics—that the notion of Eros as a unifying energy which contributes to the existence of civilization contradicts Freud's earlier belief that civilization thwarts libido. Here I need only comment that these two ideas about civilization are not mutually inconsistent. Once we have mapped out the coherent structure of Freud's approach to Liebe, we shall be able to understand how he could enunciate both ideas within a few paragraphs of each other.

❋

The fourth ingredient in Freud's conception of love is the notion that Eros and destructiveness are interfused within all erotic cathexes. In a letter dated 1910, Freud writes to a friend: "I have, as you agree, done much to show the importance of love. My experience, however, does not confirm your view that it is at the basis of everything unless you add hate to it; which is psychologically correct." In the remaining decades of his life, Freud examined very carefully this fourth sense of Liebe, predicated upon his belief that—as a matter of psychological fact—negative sentiments such as hate accompany love on virtually all occasions and even function as constituents within it. In his book on group psychology he maintains that "the evidence of psychoanalysis shows that almost every intimate emotional relation between two people which lasts for some time—marriage, friendship, the relations between parents and children—leaves a sediment of feelings of aversion and hostility, which only escapes perception as a result of repression."

In this place, as in a similar context in *Civilization and Its Discontents*, Freud allows the possible exception of a mother's relation to her son. But otherwise he sees no way in which love can exist apart from elements of hatred. Though he introduces the term "ambivalence" to refer to this combination of sentiments, he must not be interpreted as meaning that love and hate are of equal valence within all cathexes. He recognizes that their relative strength within a mixture varies from case to case and he by no means suggests that every instance of human affect can be characterized as "love-hate." He merely wishes to emphasize two truths about hatred: first, its inevitability as a pervasive component *within* a loving relationship; and second, its importance as a causal factor throughout the *development* of love.

In seeing love and hatred as integral to each other, Freud aligns himself with nineteenth-century realism, particularly as it manifested itself in pessimists such as Schopenhauer. In several places Freud ascribes his later views to Schopenhauer. Freudian Eros, as the universal principle of life, is quite similar to the Schopenhauerian will to live. When Freud articulates the distinction between Eros and the death drive, he remarks: "We have unwittingly steered our course into the harbour of Schopenhauer's philosophy." He goes on to say that for Schopenhauer death is the "true result and to that extent the purpose of life," while the sexual instinct is "the embodiment of the will to live."

What Freud principally derives from Schopenhauer is the rejection of all benignly Romantic beliefs that love can occur in a pure or even purified form, untainted by the emotional bitterness that utopian lovers think they have eliminated through love alone. Flying into each other's arms in the hope of escaping the pain and ugliness of the ordinary world, they merely create a microcosm that includes the hatred and hostility which belong to the very being of intimacy. To this Schopenhauerian insight Freud then adds an analysis that links his own previous ideas about hatred with his eventual conception of a death drive that interacts with Eros. Formulating the stages of individual development, Freud begins by noting that early attitudes are generally ambivalent. The infant's oral impulses reveal a desire to incorporate or devour. They express "a type of love which is consistent with abolishing the object's separate existence." The pregenital "sadistic-anal" phase likewise involves indifference to the injury or even destruction that may be inflicted upon the object. "Love in this form and at this preliminary stage is hardly to be distinguished from hate in its attitude towards the object. Not until the genital organization is established does love become the opposite of hate."

In describing adult love as a condition that turns into something other than the contrary element from which it was formerly indistinguishable, Freud illustrates his general belief that libido attains through maturation a state quite different from what it was originally. But just as genital sex normally exists by including within itself bits of the polymorphous perverse, so too does mature love incorporate some of the opposing destructiveness of hatred. Freud even implies that hate endures as more deeply ingrained than love, for it is older in the organism. Hate "derives from the narcissistic ego's primordial repudiation of the external world with its outpouring of stimuli. As an expression of the reaction of unpleasure evoked by objects, it always remains in an intimate relation with the self-preservative instincts; so that sexual and ego-instincts can readily develop an antithesis which repeats that of love and hate. When the ego-instincts dominate the sexual function, as is the case at the stage of the sadistic-anal organization, they impart the qualities of hate to the instinctual aim as well."

Starting with these ideas about hatred in relation to love, Freud required only a single step in order to reach his conception of a death drive that forever vies with Eros. It was a very big step, however; and though Freud took it only in his sixties, it is surprising that he took it at all. For the notion of a death drive, even more than the idea of Eros, creates what Freud recognized as "a positively mystical impression." But having taken this momentous step, or rather leap, he felt that only by positing instinctual forces of death and Eros could he explain the polarity between hate and love.

As early as the first edition of his *Three Essays on the Theory of Sexuality,* Freud had called attention to the aggressive and harmful tendencies inherent in oral and sadistic stages of childhood libido. At that time he considered them to be components *within* the sexual instinct. In normal development they would be transformed and subordinated by the genital orientation of adulthood, becoming perverse or pathological—as in sadism proper—only when they dominated an individual's sexuality. Having made his distinction between Eros and the death drive, Freud now interpreted these evidences of aggressiveness as manifestations of a destructive principle intruding upon the erotic instead of being a *part* of it. The conflict between love and hate, the vast dialectic of human ambivalence, would thus play itself out on the plain of Eros as the preserver of life struggling with *contrary* impulses oriented toward death. Sadistic elements in childhood would not arise within the libidinal development but could nevertheless be used as a device that enabled Eros to counter the self-destructiveness of the death drive by deploying it against an external object. Masochism would reveal a failure of Eros in this respect, for the hurtfulness of the death drive is then turned against oneself.

In *Beyond the Pleasure Principle* Freud enumerates several considerations that led him to his hypothesis about a death drive. Libido theory had always assumed that throughout its instinctual behavior the organism sought for pleasure, but Freud felt that compulsions of repetition, the need to return to an earlier state of affairs, could not be explained by means of the pleasure principle. He associated them with a "drive for mastery" which might not be a source of pleasure. Even within the pleasure principle itself he detected two conflicting vectors: one furthering life by increasing tension and admitting external stimuli; the other closing off excitation and enacting what Fechner called the "tendency towards stability." In the latter Freud found a conservative element that belonged to the nature of instinct itself, for he assumed that instincts always tried to reinstate an earlier condition. Since the earliest of all conditions is the inorganic and inanimate state from which life arose, he concluded that behind the pleasure principle, and contrary to our efforts to retain or further life, there lurks an irreducible motivation toward death. Having originated as inert matter, we are all programmed with an instinctual need to return to it.

The fanciful character of Freud's speculation has been ridiculed by many critics, and Freud himself made no claims for its scientific certitude. As time went on, however, he found himself wedded to these metaphysical beliefs and it would be presumptuous for anyone else to suggest that they should be detached from his thinking as a whole. Their mythological aura does not disturb me, and Freud's error in asserting that they are supported by the laws of thermodynamics need not concern us. I am more interested in the way in which Freud continues the Romantic ideology while also undermining it. Though he opposes benignly Romantic visions of innocent love, his notion that the aim of life is death reminds us of Wagnerian ideas about Liebestod. Regardless of how Freud actually developed his conception, its basis in Romantic pessimism seems unmistakable to me. At the same time, Freud transcends this source by trying to encase his theory about an instinctual search for death within a realistic, and uncompromisingly materialistic, perspective that never leaves him. There is for him no further life toward which the death drive impels us. There is only a return to matter, whose presence in our being becomes total at the end.

In the idea that man's need to master his environment is not adequately explained by the pleasure principle, and in the belief that repetition compulsions signify a primal and inescapable recurrence of something prior to this life, one might detect some of Nietzsche's own attempt to combine Romantic pessimism with a more realistic approach. But though Freud was influenced by

Nietzsche, however little he may have read him, Freud's conception is much more sophisticated in these areas, and his reasoning much more dialectical. For in declaring the struggle between Eros and death to be the very fabric of life—"This struggle is what all life essentially consists of"—Freud concentrates upon the mechanisms by which the two contrasting systems cooperate and interpenetrate with one another. Different as they are in principle, they constantly undergo what Freud calls "a fusion of the two classes of instincts with each other." Three years after his initial distinction between Eros and the death drive, he states: "This hypothesis throws no light whatever upon the manner in which the two classes of instincts are fused, blended, and mingled with each other; but that this takes place regularly and very extensively is an assumption indispensable to our conception."

As a corollary to his idea of fusion, Freud introduces the concept of "defusion," which occurs when the two basic elements separate from one another. He thought that the existence of sadistic components within sexuality exemplifies instinctual fusion, the death drive having been transmuted into a need to control some other person in ways that may actually further the reproductive ends of Eros. But when these hurtful impulses become autonomous, as in the perversion called sadism, a *defusion* of instincts will have occurred to some extent. Freud never describes a condition in which the two instinctual systems are completely separate from one another. The energy in the death drive he ascribes to the dynamism of Eros; and the pleasure principle, which seems to manifest most obviously the workings of Eros, he finally describes as functioning in the service of the death drive as well. For the attainment of pleasure is itself a discharge that relieves tensions and restores the organism to a state of quiescence. "The greatest pleasure attainable by us, that of the sexual act, is associated with a momentary extinction of a highly intensified excitation."

In general, Freud is very careful to argue that the two instinctual forces "seldom—perhaps never" occur apart from one another. They are "alloyed" in varying degrees and in subtle configurations that prevent us from realizing their separate identities. When the death drive is dominant and relatively unaffected by Eros, the organism destroys itself through one or another type of suicidal behavior. When the death drive is directed outward, it appears as hatred, aggressiveness, or a desire for mastery that benefits the organism (inasmuch as something else is being attacked) while also furthering life to the extent that Eros can harness this energy it has already invested in destructiveness.

Some critics denigrate this stage in Freud's development as merely another indication of his inability to escape dualistic thinking. In a similar context, Jones remarks: "Someone once said facetiously that [Freud] had never learned to count beyond the number two." The strength of such criticism is mitigated, I think, by the importance Freud attached to the concepts of ambivalence and fusion. For these show him going beyond the limitations of simpleminded dualism. What troubles me more is the fact that Freud's speculations about Eros and the death drive are inherently chaotic, even confused. For instance, Freud states more than once that while Eros operates in ways that can easily be observed, the contrary system of instincts shows itself only indirectly. This follows from his belief that all the energy in the death drive comes from Eros. In one place he claims that the death instincts "do their work unobtrusively"; elsewhere they are said to be "by their nature mute"; and at another juncture he remarks that one might have assumed that they "operated silently." This last account he rejects because he finds it more profitable to say that the system "comes to light" in the form of aggressive and destructive behavior.

But even with this emendation, there is no way that Freud can clarify his metaphorical references to death instincts whose being cannot be understood apart from their appearance through the agency of Eros. Moreover, there is nothing in the nature of hatred, aggressiveness, desire for mastery, or destructiveness that could not have been derived from Eros itself. When an individual hates or tries to destroy some other object, this can be explained as the organism's attempt to eliminate whatever is capable of threatening its self-interest. Masochistic or suicidal tendencies may be interpreted as a failure of Eros, an inability to control one's environment as required for the fulfillment of self-love. There would seem to be no need to hypothesize the existence of drives or instincts oriented toward death itself.

In his detailed critique of Freud's theories about life and death instincts, Fromm argues that their main deficiency consists in the assumption that a tendency to revert to the inorganic is the same as an impulse to destroy either oneself or something else. Fromm finds no evidence for this identification, and he concludes that Freud's reasoning is circular. Freud might well reply that his conception is purely speculative. He freely suggests that the question of proof baffles him. But Fromm's point is nevertheless well-taken. Even if we agree to the (dubious) idea that an instinct is basically a return to a prior condition, or that organisms have a lingering need to revert to their inorganic origins, or that destructive and aggressive tendencies are basically instinctual, the yoking together of these disparate possibilities seems insupportable. Fromm also complains that Freud confuses "the destructive instinct" with sadism or sadistic components in sexuality. The former, Fromm states, "aims at the destruction of the object, while sadism wants to keep it in order to control, humiliate or hurt it." Since the sadistic elements in sexuality are the principal data that Freud cites to show how death instincts fuse or defuse with Eros, Fromm's objection seems quite formidable.

Finally, Fromm complains that Freud's theory would force us to postulate a reservoir of aggression and destructiveness such that an individual must vent his hostile emotions either upon others or upon himself. In *Civilization and Its Discontents* Freud does sound as if he thought that innate aggressiveness left no alternative—one had to choose between destroying oneself or destroying something (or someone) else: "any restriction of this aggressiveness directed outwards would be bound to increase the self-destruction, which is in any case proceeding." But in defense of Freud, one must also recognize that the outward aggressiveness to which he refers need not include violence or *physical* destruction, and overtly at least, it might not involve another human being. To this extent, Freud may escape the charge of holding a Hobbesian approach to human nature. He need not be interpreted as meaning that the life of man is warfare, each against all, as a matter of genetic constitution.

It seems to me, however, that the vagaries of Freud's final theory do lend themselves to insurmountable criticism. As he had earlier maintained that hate precedes love in the development of the organism, so too does he speak of the inorganic state as being older and therefore somehow more fundamental than the eventual transformations of Eros. This would imply not only that death is the original goal of life, but also that the impulse to return to the inorganic exists at a more profound level of our being than the vital striving away from it. That is the aspect of Freud which Santayana elaborates in his essay "A Long Way Round to Nirvana," whose very title interprets Freud as meaning that life is just a circuitous search for the nothingness of death. Freud does say that the organism wishes to revert to nonbeing "in its own way," which is why Eros resists the death drive as it does, but this would seem to be a peripheral, secondary consideration.

Even Schopenhauer takes a more balanced view of human nature in much of his writing. In a passage where Freud cites Schopenhauer's reference to an ambivalence between love and hate, the differences between the two thinkers appear most clearly. To make a related point, Freud quotes Schopenhauer's parable about freezing porcupines. Crowding together to warm themselves, the animals quickly separate because of each other's quills: "so that they were driven backwards and forwards from one trouble to the other, until they had discovered a mean distance at which they could most tolerably exist." Schopenhauer was describing human nature in terms of the equilibrating compromises between love and hate that people must undergo in order to attain an optimal condition in life. What Freud extracts from Schopenhauer's symbolism is significantly partial and much more defeatist, namely, that "no one can tolerate a too intimate approach to his neighbor." Freud's concept of ambivalence entails much more than just this misanthropic insight, but possibly it indicates an underlying stratum within Freud's total outlook, a realistic though vastly cynical rock bottom beyond which he thinks one cannot go.

In my discussion thus far I have been analyzing Freud's theories about love in terms of the four senses of Liebe that he employs. I have tried to show that, despite the difficulties they engender within themselves, these four conceptions make a developmental unity evolving over a period of decades but coherent in its overall structure. We must now focus upon a number of related ideas, some that pertain to the general approach and some that are subsidiary to it. For instance, Freud is commonly regarded as having "reduced" love to sexuality. Properly understood, this characterization is correct. To appreciate its implications, however, we must remember that the first sense of Liebe includes affection as well as physical impulse, and also that Eros is depicted as the combining of individuals into a oneness that may eventuate as "the unity of mankind." In what sense, then, is love being reduced to sexuality?

When Freud speaks of Eros creating interpersonal unities, he says that people are thereby "libidinally bound to one another." But this does not mean that they engage in overtly sexual behavior. The paradox is resolved by the concept of "aim-inhibition" that Freud uses in various places. As vital energy conceived in terms of hydraulic metaphors, libido remains constant even when deflected from its natural direction and instinctual goal. The latter derive from reproductive necessities that are fulfilled whenever libido is uninhibited in its aim. When inhibition occurs, for whatever reason, libido does not go out of existence but rather expresses itself in ways that often mask its subterranean presence. Love reduces to sex in the sense that all types of love—even those that are aim-inhibited—dispense libidinal energy which is, by definition, the force that propels the organism toward sexuality.

Freud employs the concept of aim-inhibited sex to explain group psychology and the growth of culture. But, in his usual manner, he traces the origins of aim-inhibition to phenomena that belong to individual psychology. By the time the child is five years old, he says, its sexual instinct has found an object in one or another of the parents. When repression thwarts sexual interests of this sort, they become inhibited in their aim and the libidinal drive turns into emotions of affection. Without necessarily showing their roots in sexuality, these feelings continue into puberty, at which time they are joined by a current of overt sexual impulse normally focused on someone outside the family. When the two currents, the affectionate and the aim-uninhibited, stay separate from one another, there eventuates the pathological condition that Freud describes so brilliantly in his essay "The Most Prevalent Form of Degradation in Erotic Life" (also translated as "On the Universal Tendency to Debasement in the Sphere of Love"). This is the article in which he describes patients who are impotent with their wives, for whom they may have great affection, although these men are sexually unimpeded in their relations with mistresses they do not love. Freud remarks that where such men love they cannot lust and where they lust they cannot love.

As we shall see, Freud uses this analysis to explain the differences between heavenly and earthly love. But here I want to emphasize the fact that he thinks this tendency to separate the two currents does not preclude their frequent harmonization. He notes that most adolescents combine the aim-inhibited and the aim-uninhibited, the affectionate and the overtly sexual, to some degree. And he even says that "the depth to which anyone is in love, as contrasted with his purely sensual desire, may be measured by the size of the share taken by the aim-inhibited instincts of affection."

This being Freud's belief, one could well conclude that—far from thinking love is sex—he fully recognizes the differences between the two. But then, why have Freud's critics been so greatly dissatisfied with this area of his work? Even as devoted a follower as Theodor Reik finds Freud's ideas about the relationship between love and sex totally mistaken. Arguing that "sex and love are different in origin and nature," Reik claims that: sex is an instinct, a biological drive dependent upon organic chemistry, whereas love is not a biological need; sex is common to the species, like hunger or thirst, but "millions of people" never experience love, since there are "many centuries and cultural patterns in which it is unknown"; sex aims for a release of physical tension while love seeks for happiness, which is found in relief from "psychical" tension; sex is directed, almost indiscriminately, toward any object that will satisfy, but in love the object "is always seen as a person and a personality" whose nonphysical qualities are valued in themselves; sex is selfish inasmuch as it cares about using the object for its own satisfaction, while love cares about the welfare of the other person and discovers happiness in whatever makes the other person happy; sex, unlike love, seeks variety in its choice of objects—"there are many possible sexual objects, but only one who is loved"; sex arises from a drive that has a rhythmic recurrence occasioned by internal stimuli and bodily events such as appetite, spasm, discharge, whereas love has no such relationship to temporal processes. Reik sums up his critique of Freud by saying: "Sex and love are so different that they belong to distinct realms of research fields; sex to the domain of biochemistry and physiology, love to the domain of the psychology of emotions. Sex is an urge, love is a desire."

There are various ways in which Freud could reply to Reik's account of the differences between love and sex. For one thing, he would be shocked at the assumption that human affect can be so sharply divided between the physiological and the psychological. When Freud talked about sexuality, in even its most obvious and physical expression, he always stressed the modifications that psychological phenomena continually effect. On the other hand, he never gave up his hope of ultimately basing psychoanalysis upon physics and chemistry, in view of the fact that psychological changes must always correspond to alterations at the level of physiology. That sex is an instinct of a sort that love is not he could well admit. But he would immediately add that this results from the fact that the word "love" is now being used to refer to one of the transformations that the sexual instinct undergoes as the individual develops. When Reik refers to "sex," he talks about the instinct in its aim-uninhibited states, and Freud always understood how greatly it then differs from its mode of appearance once inhibition enters.

Together with this kind of response, Freud might also have taken exception to Reik's assurance that love is not universally experienced whereas sex is. In saying that millions of people in many cultures never find love, does Reik mean to suggest that they have grown up with parents whom they did not love and who did not love them in any sense at all? And is it likely that sexual love could be so remote from the experience of these individuals as to remain wholly "unknown"? The *idea* of love may never have been formulated in the culture of many people, for the concept is not overtly present in all societies, but it seems plausible to assume that one or another form of love has occurred throughout human history.

Reik was probably thinking of romantic love as it developed in the West during recent centuries. That phenomenon is not at all universal, but neither is sexuality in many of its varieties. Although some of the basic chemistry and physiology of sex is identical in mankind as a whole, differences in response, in frequency, in expression, and in the choice of suitable objects contribute to the diverse patterns that distinguish cultures from one another and each person from the next. Moreover, one can make a much stronger argument than Reik allows for the idea that human beings have an instinctual need to love and be loved. I shall return to this in my chapter on recent scientific explorations about the nature of love. Reik dismisses T. D. Suttie's belief that the infant is born with "an instinctual need for companionship," but he offers no arguments and one feels that his judgment has been warped by his notion that love must be only psychological.

The inadequacy of Reik's critique may also be measured by the fact that Freud himself mentions most of the characteristics that Reik uses to distinguish sex from love. With his awareness of the ambiguities in our ordinary use of words such as "Liebe," Freud remarks that "in one class of cases" being in love means an interest in sexual satisfaction—"a cathexis which expires, moreover, when this aim has been reached; this is what is called common, sensual love." But even here, in this limiting case, Freud points out that more is involved than just the having of a momentary pleasure of the senses. For the individual knows that his sexual need will soon revive, and this realization serves as "the first motive for directing a lasting cathexis upon the sexual object and for 'loving' it in the passionless intervals as well." At the opposite extreme, Freud recognizes the existence of love that is predominantly aim-inhibited and therefore to all appearances affectionate, benevolent, and "unsexual." He says that it is "very usual for directly sexual impulses, short-lived in themselves, to be transformed into a lasting and purely affectionate tie; and the consolidation of a passionate love marriage rests to a large extent upon this process." When he talks about the emotional bonds that unite a group, or civilization in general, Freud emphasizes that they all depend on love in the aim-inhibited sense.

What distinguishes Freud's approach, therefore, is his belief that the different types of love are internally related as diverse manifestations of a single class of instincts. To this extent Freud sees himself as merely following what he calls the "entirely justifiable" unification that language imposes in the ordinary use of the word "love." It is here that Freud mentions his kinship to Plato (and St. Paul); and if all he means is that they too are employing this term in a wider sense that involves its unifying functions, he is surely right. But, unlike Plato and St. Paul, Freud also wants to prove that libido underlies every type of love, which therefore emanates from the sexual instinct. He argues this case in passages such as the following:

> The nucleus of what we mean by love naturally consists (and this is what is commonly called love, and what the poets sing of) in sexual love with sexual union as its aim. But we do not separate from this—what in any case has a share in the name "love"—on the one hand, self-love, and on the other, love for parents and children, friendship and love for humanity in general, and also devotion to concrete objects and to abstract ideas. Our justification lies in the fact that . . . all these tendencies are an expression of the same instinctual impulses; in relations between the sexes these impulses force their way toward sexual union, but in other circumstances they are diverted from this aim or are prevented from reaching it, though always preserving enough of their original nature to keep their identity recognizable (as in such features as the longing for proximity, and self-sacrifice).

It is now, I think, that we can see what is dubious about Freud's theory. In what way, we may ask, is a "longing for proximity," or even self-sacrifice, an indication that nonsexual types of love are examples of aim-inhibition? In a later context, Freud claims that "even an affectionate devotee, even a friend or an admirer, desires the physical proximity and the sight of the person who is now loved only in the 'Pauline' sense." But how can one conclude that a desire to see or be in the presence of someone signifies a sexual interest? Freud obviously means that if friendship or benevolent admiration were wholly nonlibidinal, such types of love would be content with communication at a distance, with oneness in thought, with mere intellectual agreement, rather than physical presence. To say this, however, is to assume that everything physical, everything sensory and immediate in our interpersonal experience, must be libidinal. But why should we make this assumption? It seems like an article of faith. There is no objective or scientific justification for any such belief.

In more than one place Freud enunciates his fundamental tenet, though he offers hardly any evidence to support it. In the *Three Essays on the Theory of Sexuality* he says that "it may well be that nothing of considerable importance can occur in the organism without contributing some component to the excitation of the sexual instinct." But he then admits, quite honestly, that he cannot clarify this idea to any great degree because "the whole nature of sexual excitation is completely unknown to us." That being so, how can he justify maintaining that all sensory interest contributes to, or is even related to, the libidinal instinct? I think of the old dictum about metaphysical theories of the soul: "If there is anything about which you know nothing at all, explain everything else in terms of it."

This difficulty has extensive importance. When Freud tries to show how a boy's "affection and esteem" for his mother, or a comparable adult, becomes identical with sexual love, he claims that in the process of caring for her child the mother must inevitably induce sexual feelings in him. However much she may try to avoid genital stimulation, she cannot eliminate her own sexual interest: "She strokes him, kisses him, rocks him and quite clearly treats him as a substitute for a complete sexual object." But is the child's affection or esteem elicited *only* by the kind of quasi-sexual behavior that Freud mentions? If a mother is more circumspect with her son, does the child grow up incapable of loving? And are girls at a disadvantage because their mothers are heterosexual? Finally, are we prepared to infer from the fact that many childhood experiences linger on as affective influences throughout adulthood that *every* type of tenderness, kindliness, benevolence, warm and friendly feeling, group solidarity, or sense of unity is explicable as the residue of repressed and now unconscious excitations that occurred in early sexuality?

Freud is most convincing when he argues that emotional ties of a cordial and affectionate kind, as between a teacher and his pupil or an audience and a performer, may readily *turn into* a relationship that is overtly sexual. He is also persuasive when he notes that libidinal interests can become purified and apparently nonsexual in circumstances where obstacles make it impossible to attain sexual aims. But from none of this can one conclude that all love must be either aim-inhibited or aim-uninhibited sexuality, or that the former partly derives from the latter and always retains some vestige of it.

In raising doubts about these dogmas of the Freudian canon, I am not suggesting that (as Reik puts it) "sex and love are different in origin and nature." For this would encourage one to think they are separate, though possibly overlapping, categories within a single genus. But that falsifies their logical status. As a function of bestowal as well as appraisal, love is a state of valuation; it enhances the importance of the object through our active acceptance of it. In itself love is neither sexual nor nonsexual. It may exist in situations that are not sexual as well as in those that are. Love is a way of responding to something or someone, whereas by sexuality we refer to the content in one particular class of responses. Sexual love is not a mere conjunction of sex and love. It is sex being used as a manifestation of love, and love revealing itself by *how* the sexual object is treated.

Though Freud does not analyze appraisal and bestowal, he says nothing that would question the distinction I have made. What he principally wishes to defend is the idea that love always involves libido and exists as a force in human experience only because it embodies sexual energy in one form or another. In a sense, Freud agrees with Reik in assigning a nonlibidinal *origin* to love since he believes that it arises as a kind of primordial gratitude toward those who enable the helpless infant to survive. The question is whether Freud can justify his belief that this response is immediately, and necessarily, infused by the sexual instinct.

To some extent Freud's reasoning does seem to be predicated

upon his habitual dualism. In order for the loving attitude to have any importance in human life, it must discharge psychical energy; Freud would seem to have recognized only two forms of energy—nutritive and libidinal; love is not explicable as a nutritive process and so it must be a libidinal one. Throughout his writings Freud harks back to Schiller's dictum that "hunger and love are what moves the world." At first he thought of hunger as representing self-preservatory interests that are independent of libido. Later he decided that the ego-instincts were themselves libidinal. At no time does he consider the possibility that love involves benefits to the organism as well as to the object, helping them both to survive in their relationship to one another, without the bond being necessarily sexual. That way of thinking constitutes a pluralistic approach that Freud scarcely entertains.

Interwoven with these difficulties there is another that is even more fundamental. Freud's ideas about love as aim-inhibition presuppose that the theory of the libido is acceptable. Based on hydraulic metaphors, that conception assumes that the organism does not generate energy within itself: it merely vents it in accordance with innate machinery that provides a predetermined goal. Libido is considered to be sexual because Freud thinks that by its very nature it seeks to reproduce the species. When libido has no apparent relation to reproductive processes, either in themselves or in their development, Freud concludes that it is inhibited in its natural aim. Sublimation, which accounts for the waywardness of libidinal energy, occurs when its normal outlet has been thwarted by hostility from the environment, or resistance from a chosen object of the opposite sex, or possibly some malfunction within the organism itself. In finding an outlet to express blocked libido, sublimation can be very beneficial to society. Freud thinks that without the sublimating of libidinal energy there could be no civilization. But all this presupposes that sublimation can be described in the Freudian manner. That is what I now wish to question.

As always, Freud began with paradigmatic cases drawn from his own clinical experience. Activities that seemed to have no connection with a sexual aim—chopping wood, let us say, or overeating—he could analyze as occurring in a situation where someone is actually suffering from sexual frustration and attempting to eliminate it by means of redirected behavior. No one before Freud understood this phenomenon as well as he, and I see no reason to doubt its frequent occurrence in human beings. It does not follow, however, that sublimation has the role that Freud assigned it within his conception of libido. Freud is not only calling our attention to sublimation as a mechanism of displacement, but also he claims that all interests and desires, all passions and predilections, all emotions and excitations other than those explicitly related to the sexual aim are to be explained as oblique expressions of it. This makes sense only if we assume: first, that energy with any psychological import must always be libidinal; second, that the libido is a fixed quantity of force directed toward a pre-established aim; and third, that this aim is ultimately reproductive. But neither Freud nor any of his followers ever gave scientific proof for these claims, and the few efforts that have been made more recently to test them in experiments have yielded very little substantiation. The most one can possibly say on Freud's behalf is that he extended the ordinary use of the term "sublimation" as any philosopher or metaphysician might. That, however, provides no empirical support. It cannot assure the plausibility of his doctrine.

Finally, one must realize that the theory of libido, as Freud presents it, belongs to what I have elsewhere called an "essentialistic" view of man's affective nature. By essentialism I mean the belief that there is a single structure that defines the instinctual being of men and women. I have argued that there are sexual responses that may be considered innately programmed and based on biological predisposition but that they do not constitute a unity that would enable us to believe in any one goal, aim, or system of behavior as uniquely natural and preferential. On the pluralistic view that I recommended, even heterosexual coitus defines the purpose of human sexuality only in the sense that it is the most common means of attaining procreation. Terms like "perversion" must therefore refer to statistical infrequencies rather than pathological abnormalities. From the pluralistic perspective, so-called normal behavior is not *normative*. It includes activities that most people pursue, often with great intensity and enjoyment, but it cannot serve as an exclusive criterion of what man ought to do or become in order to fulfill his biological nature.

The implications of the anti-essentialistic approach are quite far-reaching, and I cannot enumerate them here. It is crucial, however, to see that Freud's theory of libido, and all the ideas about love and sexuality that issue from it, are grounded in essentialistic assumptions. The libido, as Freud conceives of it, has a single, fixed, and definite goal toward which it drives itself. Freud sees this goal as heterosexual coitus because he thinks the libido comes into being as an agency of the reproductive instinct which (together with hunger) "moves the world." Having this genetic function to perform, libido develops through determinate stages programmed within the structure of its being. Someone who becomes "arrested" at an earlier stage of development will undergo in later life a sexual perversion, since that generally involves regression to infantile behavior. An individual who manages to pass through all the pre-ordained stages but still experiences little pleasure in coitus, or in his love life as a whole, will end up as a neurotic. The character of the libido itself would thus indicate the differences between psychological health and sexual disability, between the correct way to live in accordance with one's nature and abnormalities that signify deviations from the innate program.

At the same time that Freud accepts this kind of essentialism as the basis of his theories, many of his most revolutionary ideas involve vast modifications within it. Essentialism goes back at least as far as Aristotle, whose point of view predominated in the philosophy courses that Freud took as a university student. But Freud was virtually the first person to argue that the goals of all adult sexuality were themselves the products of the polymorphous perversity of childhood. While accepting genital interest as the proper outcome of libidinal development, Freud goes beyond previous essentialisms in believing that normal sexuality is not wholly unrelated to the abnormal, which it merely subordinates and employs for its own purposes. It is instructive to study the various places in which Freud uses terms like "normal." He generally introduces phrases such as "the so-called normal" or "what is commonly considered normal," etc. In these passages he is usually undercutting the traditional belief that all sexuality which is not directly genital or coital must be pathological and even degenerate. And when he complains, as we shall see, about tyrannical restraints that society imposes upon sexual and amatory possibilities of an unconventional sort, he does so in order to show that normality may include activities that prevailing opinion often disallows.

These modifications in the essentialistic outlook undermined it much more than Freud could have foreseen. He himself thought he was clarifying essentialism; he never intended to give it up for the sake of a pluralistic alternative. As Jones remarks, in a slightly different but related context, "Any kind of pluralism was quite alien to him." Without his residual essentialism, Freud would have had no theory of a goal-oriented libido, and neither could he have sustained his ideas of repression, sublimation, or aim-inhibition. His philosophy of love and sexuality is not tenable unless one can justify the essentialistic approach to affective life which it presupposes. To me, at least, this seems like an insuperable hurdle.

❋

In discussing Freud's general theory of love, I have sought at various points to place it historically in relation to Romantic philosophies it uses while also rejecting. This rich and inventive employment of the past is particularly evident in Freud's ideas about love as a sense of oneness with the universe. The entire discussion of *Civilization and Its Discontents* begins with an analysis of "oceanic feeling," similar to what I have called "merging" in my analysis of romanticism. Freud reports that Romain Rolland had written to him about "a peculiar feeling, which he himself is never without. . . . It is a feeling which he would like to call a sensation of 'eternity', a feeling as of something limitless, unbounded—as it were, oceanic." Freud immediately informs us that he himself has had no such experience, but that he understands what is being suggested: "it is a feeling of an indissoluble bond, of being one with the external world as a whole."

Rolland interprets this sense of merging with the cosmos as the source of all religious inspiration. Freud explains it in a different

---

Freud

fashion. He remarks that the sharp separation which the ego usually maintains between itself and the external world may sometimes disappear. In various pathological conditions the lines of demarcation become blurred or inoperative. In the ecstasy of sexual love—what Freud calls "an unusual state, but not one that can be stigmatized as pathological"—they may even seem to evaporate completely. "At the height of being in love the boundary between ego and object threatens to melt away. Against all the evidence of his senses, a man who is in love declares that 'I' and 'you' are one, and is prepared to behave as if it were a fact." These diverse occasions of apparent merging Freud traces back to the period of infancy in which the ego felt no separation between itself and the external world, in which its oneness with its mother was such that it could think that everything was a part of itself. The mother's breast, which the infant desires "most of all," thus becomes the first object of love. Losing it is the first cause of sexual trauma, according to Freud, and finding it once again renews the oceanic feeling that later instances of merging partly duplicate.

Elsewhere Freud says that the image of an infant blissfully at peace on its mother's breast serves for us all as the greatest symbol of joy and fulfillment in sexual love. Referring to the mother's breast as the first object of erotic desire, Freud states: "I cannot convey to you any adequate idea of the importance of this first object in determining every later object adopted, of the profound influence it exerts, through transformation and substitution, upon the most distant fields of mental life." Thus the mystical feelings of saints and sinners in all religions, the tender sentiments of spouses who cherish one another, the fervent yearnings of lovers—whether they be the split hermaphrodites in Plato's myth or men and women longing for oneness with their alter egos in the modern world—all this Freud explains in terms of the oceanic feeling that human beings experience until that traumatic day when they are driven from the paradise which is their mother's breast.

Related to Freud's analysis of the oceanic feeling is his conception of primal narcissism. Strictly speaking, however, the two ideas are not wholly coherent. Through narcissism the individual loves himself as the sole and immeasurably valuable object of devotion.

Originally, Freud tells us, the infant has no other object since he has no awareness of a separate world. Assuming that the fetus is also totally narcissistic in this sense, Freud states in one place that being born is the first step out of "absolutely self-sufficient narcissism" and toward the eventual "discovery of objects." Since the mother's breast is the first of these external objects, the oceanic feeling that comes from attaining it would have to be different from the absolute oneness in primal narcissism. But in that event, which type of merging is fundamental? Do we secretly long for the self-sufficient narcissism of the fetus or for the oceanic feeling of the infant?

This difficulty is, however, trivial, scarcely worth considering. The mentality of fetuses and newborn infants can only be a subject for speculation, and Freud uses the concept of primal narcissism with clear recognition that it cannot be defined too precisely. As part of his criticism of Freud's conception, Reik claims that since the infant has no ability to discriminate between himself and other objects, neither can he be narcissistic. He cannot love anything else, Reik says, because his awareness is limited to himself; and since he has no way of seeing himself as a separate entity, neither can he be said to love in the narcissistic manner. Reik concludes that self-love or so-called narcissism is "only the reflex of the love and admiration of mother, father or nurse toward the self." But in answer to this, Freud need only remark that prior to the state in which the child is capable of imitating a love for himself that he has received from others, he lives through a period in which all aspects of his experience seem oriented toward his own interests and their exclusive gratification. To call this state "self-love" is to talk metaphorically but that alone should not be troublesome. Of greater importance is the way in which Freud employs his metaphor of primal narcissism to explain subsequent developments in erotic life.

Originally the term "narcissism" had been used by sexologists to refer to a pathological condition in which a patient treated his own body as if it belonged to another person with whom he was making love. Freud alters this meaning by eliminating the component of literal lovemaking and by suggesting that narcissistic self-love is part of the normal development of human sexuality. Freud uses the concept of narcissism to explain how libido can be directed toward other objects, and how ego-libido (love for oneself) need not be wholly independent of object-libido (love for other things or persons). Though the former could result from a deflection inwards of the latter, the flow of energy might go in the opposite direction as well. This bivalent conception not only helped Freud to see how ego-instincts could be considered libidinal and therefore capable of being classified with object-instincts as joint components of Eros, but also it provided new insights about the structural workings of the libido. The more it flowed out of the ego and into other objects, the less it would remain as sexual impulse directed inward. The more the ego drew libidinal energy from other objects, the more it would have for itself.

This "economic" approach to the nature of libido derives from the hydraulic character of Freud's general theory. It assumes that the amount of energy available to an organism is limited in quantity, though capable of being routed in or out through numerous types of interaction. When an ego expends too much upon an external object, it exhausts its libidinal resources. When it withdraws too greatly from object-love, its massive accumulation of libidinal interest in itself prevents it from dealing profitably with the outside world. Both extremes are economically unstable, creating difficulties in the balance of libidinal trade, so to speak, and therefore sure to end in pathology. In the former circumstance the individual undergoes a depletion of ego, an insufficiency of love for himself; in the latter case he is cut off from reality and suffers because no one else is loving him.

The simplicity of these dynamic and topographic concepts attracts Freud most of all. By means of them he can readily demonstrate how various conditions, both normal and pathological, may be represented in terms of different vectors within the panorama of possible economic transactions. His theory fails, however, in at least one respect that many economists (in the literal sense) have recognized as a basic element in the activity of a market. That is the fact that no system of exchange—particularly one that is governed by human choices—can be explained as merely a state in which objectively predetermined quantities of value are being expended. Freud assumes that outflow of libido lessens the ego's inner wealth, as if this were a fixed and even calculable amount. But life is not like that. The model cannot account for bestowal, and love in general. Love creates additional vitality. It generates libidinal energy that would not have existed otherwise. In loving another person, we increase, not diminish, our self-love, since the ability to bestow is itself a good that we attain even though it may eventually lose value and undermine our sense of worth if our love is not reciprocated.

Freud's economic theory may sometimes be useful in the analysis of unhappy or pathological love. He, however, considers it applicable to erotic experience as a whole. He thinks that by studying the behavior of human beings in love we can best understand narcissism. He rightly suggests that people who are not loved have a lower opinion of themselves, whereas being loved tends to increase self-esteem. But then, in accordance with his economic theory, he claims that the act of loving another person ("libidinal object-cathexis") detracts from self-esteem: "The effect of the dependence upon the loved object is to lower that feeling: the lover is humble. He who loves has, so to speak, forfeited a part of his narcissism, which can only be replaced by his being loved. . . . Love in itself, in the form of longing and deprivation, lowers the self-regard; whereas to be loved, to have love returned, and to possess the beloved object, exalts it again."

How is one to interpret this passage? Is Freud suggesting that *every* love for another person lowers one's self-esteem, that *all* lovers are dependent in the sense of being humbled and deprived, that loving is by its *very nature* a depletion of the ego? Or is he merely talking about unwholesome cathexes that impoverish the ego because they are inherently self-destructive? In context he would seem to be making the former set of assertions. For he does not limit his analysis to failures in love. On the contrary, he maintains that "the return of the libido from the object to the ego and its tranformation into narcissism represents, as it were, the restoration of a happy love, and, conversely, an actual happy love corresponds to the primal condition in which object-libido and ego-libido cannot be distinguished."

In saying this, Freud unwittingly echoes Ficino's belief that in mutual love each person gives his self to the other but then gets it back as part of the self that the other is yielding reciprocally. I can only say that Freud's conception is just as fanciful as Ficino's. In what way is happy sexual love similar to the infantile condition that is supposed to illustrate primal narcissism? In virtually no respect, I suggest, except that both are examples—under vastly dissimilar circumstances—of psychological security and deep gratification. Despite the appearance of having followed a line of reasoning to its conclusion, Freud has not presented an argument. He has merely indicated a minor likeness between two different kinds of experience, and in the process he has introduced dubious generalizations that presuppose his economic theory.

As a corollary to the postulate of a primary narcissism in everyone, Freud describes "fundamental differences" between object-choices made by men and women. He claims that a "complete object-love" is characteristic of men in general but not of women. He gives no reason for this assertion other than the fact that object-love originates with the child's dependence upon the mother or her surrogate. When he elsewhere describes the dynamic, active character of the libido, he says that it is inherently masculine (since women are presumably passive by nature). He seems to believe that narcissism in the male child transforms the all-supportive mother into a sexual object, whereas for the female child this cannot happen. Moreover, Freud's concept of narcissism leads him to assert that only men typically undergo what he calls "the peculiar state of being in love." For complete object-love (being in love as opposed to narcissistically loving oneself) involves "sexual overestimation" of the object. Freud thinks this originates in the little boy's love for his mother and is not experienced by little girls.

The characterization of love for another as overestimation (or what he sometimes calls "overvaluation") recurs throughout Freud's writing about love. In the first volume of this trilogy I tried to show that such reasoning is based upon a faulty theory about types of valuation. Freud believes that love is *over*estimation because he thinks it assigns a value to its object which no appraisal could possibly justify. I criticized Freud's approach by means of my distinction between appraisal and bestowal, and I shall return to that criticism later in this chapter. Of equal interest, however, is the fact that Freud gives only the flimsiest evidence for concluding that women do not typically overestimate their sexual objects. He maintains that after puberty original narcissism becomes relatively more intense in the average woman and therefore, compared to men, she more often wants to be loved rather than to love. He says that she reaches "a certain self-sufficiency (especially when there is a ripening into beauty) which compensates her for the social restrictions upon her object-choice."

Freud ends his remarks about narcissism in women as opposed to men by admitting that there are "countless women who love according to the masculine type and who develop the over-estimation of the sexual object." From this, one might infer that Freud's distinction is only a statistical one; and in fact, his discussion of the self-sufficient female who primarily loves no one but herself includes phrases like "such women," "this type of woman," "the narcissistic woman," etc. To the extent that he is merely describing one among different types of women, what he says need not alarm us. But Freud is also differentiating between men and women on the basis of types that he considers *characteristic* of each sex. Though there may be many women who love in the masculine fashion, he implies that they are not representative of women as a whole and he is convinced that there are biological grounds for this to be the case. In other words, his distinction is essentialistic, not purely statistical. Until someone is able to provide a stronger case than Freud does, I see no reason to think that his account is accurate.

Even for narcissistic women, Freud cites one kind of relationship that makes possible to them a complete object-love similar to the male's. This happens, he says, when these women give birth to a child, which they can love as a separate object that nevertheless has been a part of their own body and can therefore satisfy their own narcissistic feelings. Freud believes that parental love in general fits this pattern. Parents dote on their children, ascribe perfections to them, and even think that through them they attain immortality. They experience each new birth as an opportunity for combining object-love with narcissistic love of themselves. "Parental love, which is so touching and at bottom so childish, is nothing but parental narcissism born again and, transformed though it be into object-love, it reveals its former character infallibly." Primal narcissism would seem to be the inescapable constant.

✸

Narcissism being self-regarding by definition, Freud devotes chapters of his book on group psychology to analyzing mechanisms that would enable individuals to love persons other than themselves, to form libidinal ties within a society, and even to transform their primal selfishness into a concern for the welfare of others. These mechanisms are considered secondary because Freud assumes that the native condition of man is not socially oriented. On the contrary, he thinks that basic narcissism makes all human beings distrustful, even hostile toward other people. At the same time Freud asserts that "in the development of mankind as a whole, just as in individuals, love [for others] alone acts as the civilizing factor in the sense that it brings a change from egoism to altruism." He had previously told us that narcissistic love "knows only one barrier—love for others, love for objects." The problem, then, consists in showing how it is possible for ego-love not only to tolerate object-love but also to employ it in the gratification of interests that are fundamentally narcissistic.

The first, and earliest, of the mechanisms Freud detects is what he calls "identification." Freud defines the term mainly by giving examples from child development. In the Oedipus complex, which Freud believes to be universal, a little boy undergoes object-love for his mother while also identifying with his father. He takes his father as his "model" and begins to duplicate his father's behavior, mannerisms, general attitudes. To some extent, at least, the boy acts (to the best of his ability) as if he were trying to *become* his father. Though Freud later discusses the interrelationship between identification and object-choice, he first distinguishes between identifying with the father and choosing him as a libidinal object. "In the first case one's father is what one would like to *be*, and in the second he is what one would like to *have* . . . identification endeavors to mold a person's own ego after the fashion of the one that has been taken as a model."

Not only is Freudian identification one of the "original" means by which an emotional tie to others may occur, but also it is presumably a permanent development and may thus be distinguished from the more transitory phenomenon of imitation. Nevertheless, identification cannot explain how the love of persons supervenes upon the narcissistic limitations that constitute ego-love. The additional mechanism Freud invokes is "idealization." He uses the term to mean that an object "without any alteration in its nature, is aggrandized and exalted in the mind." We have already encountered this concept, for it is the genus of which sexual overestimation is a species. Before an object can be overvalued, however, idealization must have created in each person an ideal of what that particular individual would like to be. Freud calls this the "ego ideal" and he argues that it is aways a product of parental and social expectations combined with processes (such as repression) that prevent one from expending libidinal energy in ways that would provide immediate gratification. The ego ideal is an image of perfection that one would like to attain. It eventually becomes the basis of one's standards of value. To the extent that we satisfy the ego ideal, we magically reinstate the infantile condition of narcissism. As Freud says in his reductivistic manner, an ego ideal is *"merely"* a substitute for the time in childhood when each person "was his own ideal."

In order for idealization to succeed in taking the individual beyond his primordial narcissism, it must affect the way in which libido flows into object-loves that develop at the same time as the ego ideal is being formed. Since he thinks that cathexis on an outside object must result in an impoverishment of the ego, and since the formation of an ego ideal is for him an enrichment only to the extent that one believes the ideal has been attained, Freud concludes that an object cannot be loved unless it is elevated onto a level of perfection. In other words, the ego manages to love something other than itself by exalting that object to the position of ego ideal. Being in love with another person is thus a state of projection: the lover transfers to his beloved an ego ideal that he has difficulty achieving within himself, for one reason or another, and that he believes he will have fulfilled if he possesses her as an object of libidinal gratification.

In general, Freud's argument presupposes that the love of persons other than oneself arises from the universal attempt to recover the security of primal narcissism. Identification with someone who serves as a role model is only partly satisfactory because that individual, usually a parental figure, seems to embody a perfection which constantly eludes us. It nevertheless contributes to our ego ideal, and when that is transferred to a sexual object—someone in the world toward whom we feel a libidinal cathexis—we love this other person in a desperate hope of realizing our ideal by means of him or her. Freud sums up this aspect of his argument in the following formula: "Whoever possesses an excellence which the ego lacks for the attainment of its ideal, becomes loved."

This conception makes the Freudian doctrine sound almost like Plato's philosophy of love. And for good reason: both approach love as a type of appraisal. For Freud, however, love of persons arises from developmental processes that enable us to cope with an environment—the reality principle—that thwarts our infinitely selfish desires. Ego ideals, as Freud interprets them, originate in parental or social repression. According to Plato, they are built into the structure of a cosmic order that sustains man's being through his innate desire for them. For Plato, love is not inherently delusory, although the love of persons must be transcended if we are to gain the metaphysical goodness that comes from fulfilling our love of the ideals themselves.

For Freud, love must always be a kind of delusion, since perfection can never be attained. Moreover, one person loves another in an effort to recover infantile narcissism, and—given the nature of things—that must always be futile. If one cannot satisfy the ego ideal within oneself, Freud seems to say, why think that one could satisfy it in some other person, superior though she may be in some respects but inevitably imperfect like everything else? On the Freudian view, a lover's valuation of his beloved *must* be excessive, for he has chosen her in an irrational attempt to find the solution to an irresolvable problem. One frees oneself of Freud's approach by seeing, as I have suggested, that Freud mistakenly treats love as if it were basically nothing but appraisal. Being an agency of imagination, love is bestowal that creates values, and does not merely appraise them. As a result it is neither veridical nor delusory in itself. Hence it cannot be defined as *overvaluation*.

✳

Freud uses his ideas about identification and the development of an ego ideal to show how emotional bonds arise within a group. He has been criticized, correctly I think, for taking groups that are inherently authoritarian—the army and the church—as the exemplars of social organizations. This led him to overemphasize the identification among group members jointly submissive to a single leader who embodies their common ego ideal. At the same time Freud's analysis of group dynamics does help us to understand the power exercised by so many political leaders who have manipulated and subdued entire nations, in the sophisticated twentieth century as much as (or even more than) in previous eras.

Freud recognizes that the libidinal ties which keep a group together are generally aim-inhibited (except in the case of sexual orgies, which have limited importance within human societies). Since the state of being in love is often aim-uninhibited, directed toward sexual goals that include the genital and the reproductive, Freud discerns a fundamental antagonism between sexuality in that sense and the demands of society. All of *Civilization and Its Discontents* addresses itself to this conflict, which Freud discusses within the framework of his final theories about Eros and the death drive.

According to Freud, the problem arises from an inevitable split between two needs of mankind as a whole. On the one hand Eros, being the principle of life which forges new unities, creates sexual love between man and woman: "In no other case does Eros so clearly betray the core of his being, his purpose of making one out of more than one." On the other hand, Eros cannot be limited to the oneness of the heterosexual couple. For reasons of security and the development of cultural benefits, it must also extend itself into libidinal groupings that involve more than just another man or woman. All of civilization, Freud insists, "is a process in the service of Eros, whose purpose is to combine single human individuals, and after that families, then races, peoples and nations, into one great unity, the unity of mankind." This more inclusive aspect of Eros results from environmental necessity, communities being required for the survival of the individual as well as the species. Also, Freud perceives that material needs would not suffice to keep groups together. Their inner unity results from libidinal oneness throughout each collectivity, and that generates a type of Eros that often opposes erotic bonding between individuals.

The basis for the conflict between (genital, aim-uninhibited) sexuality and civilization as a product of Eros Freud describes in various ways. In one place he says that "sexual love is a relationship between two individuals in which a third can only be superfluous or disturbing, whereas civilization depends on relationships between a considerable number of individuals. When a love-relationship is at its height there is no room left for any interest in the environment; a pair of lovers are sufficient to themselves, and do not even need the child they have in common to make them happy." In another place he shows how communal life originates from labor as well as love: the advantage of working as part of a group supplements both the man's desire to stay with a woman for sexual reasons and the woman's reluctance to leave her child. The question that Freud finds most puzzling and therefore most fruitful for analysis is why the two types of Eros fail to cooperate, why the forces of love and social necessity do not jointly create a civilization that provides happiness for those who participate in it. Why should there be any struggle between civilization and sexuality, since that leads to so much misery?

Formulated in this fashion, Freud's problem may remind us of the theory of love in Schlegel's *Lucinde,* which greatly influenced the development of benign romanticism. Love, as there envisaged, links man and woman in a oneness that naturally issues into the coherent and wholly complementary unities of a loving society. In principle, Schlegel thought, the love of mankind (and of the universe as a whole) could not be inimical to an authentic love between the sexes. In denying that this conception is realistic, and in tracing the causes that make all such utopian dreams impossible, Freud is completing, from his own perspective, the work of Romantic pessimism.

For one thing, he says, we must note that genital sexuality provides man with the most compelling of satisfactions. But to the extent that people seek happiness in this plausible direction, they make themselves dependent "in a most dangerous way" on a love-object that can henceforth cause great suffering by rejecting them or by dying. In a statement about sexual love that may seem whimsical, in view of Freud's unmatched knowledge of human irrationality, he remarks: "The wise men of every age have warned us most emphatically against this way of life; but in spite of this it has not lost its attraction for a great number of people."

Freud knows that love can escape the unhappiness these wise men fear, but the only circumstance he mentions in which this happens involves total aim-inhibition. He names St. Francis of Assisi as one who possibly went furthest "in thus exploiting love for the benefit of an inner feeling of happiness." This kind of love protects itself from the sorrows of sexuality by no longer having a genital orientation and by directing love not to an individual, who may frustrate one's desires, but "to all men alike." Such love is "a state of evenly suspended, steadfast, affectionate feeling which has little external resemblance any more to the stormy agitations of genital love, from which it is nevertheless derived." Needless to say, these words provide no comfort to a benign Romantic of the Schlegel sort. Far from showing how sexual love can survive its relationship with society, Freud would seem to be eliminating it as a possible source of happiness—even at the level of total intimacy with one's beloved.

Furthermore, Freud insists that when sexual love enters into society through the formation of the family its warfare with civilization intensifies. Within the family, love is partly genital, partly aim-inhibited. The former, being an exclusive bond, sets husband and wife apart from everyone else. The latter, involving activities that arise out of friendship or affection, moves beyond the couple and forms bonds with other members of the group. But then a conflict of interest develops between family and society, since each wishes to attach the individual to itself.

Freud also ascribes the animosity between civilization and sexuality to differences between men and women. He sees women as preoccupied with the values of family and sexuality while men do the work that creates culture. Being excluded from this kind of pursuit, which also drains the limited energy of their husbands, women feel hostility toward civilization and that accentuates the basic rift. Why it is that women cannot follow cultural interests as well as the men, even alongside them, Freud does not say. He merely refers offhandedly to "instinctual sublimations of which women are little capable."

The strongest argument that Freud presents for believing that conflict between sexuality and civilization is unavoidable issues from his ideas about death instincts. After reminding us how deep-rooted is the human inclination towards aggression, Freud claims that civilization survives only by rearing psychological defenses against this destructive element. "Hence, therefore, the use of methods intended to incite people into identifications and aim-inhibited relationships of love, hence the restriction upon sexual life." But what is the logic in this argument? How can restrictions upon sexual life make it easier for civilization to control the aggressive instincts? One would have thought that pacification is more likely to occur when sexuality is fully and freely gratified. We know with great assurance, thanks to the work of Freud and his followers, that frustration of libidinal impulse generally leads to increased levels of aggressiveness, much of it directed toward other people. One might have thought that, in its attempt to diminish the destructiveness of man, civilization would *further* the pleasures of sexual life, not restrict them.

Freud does give one reason for considering sexuality a threat to social harmony. Rejecting Marxist belief that the abolition of private property would result in a diminution of human aggressiveness, he mentions that even under communism sexual competitiveness would lead to "the strongest dislike and the most violent hostility among men who in other respects are on an equal footing." Even if free love prevailed, Freud insists, man's "indestructible" aggressiveness would not disappear.

Despite the informal experiments that have been carried out by sexual communes in the last twenty years, we have too little evidence to know whether Freud was right in this surmise. But even if there is residual aggressiveness in utopian societies that encourage sexual expression instead of restraining it, this alone would not establish Freud's principal thesis. In the world as he knew it, and in which we still live, man's aggressive tendencies are all too obvious; society is aware that it must defend itself against aggressiveness; and in the process it also controls, even thwarts, sexuality. It is not at all clear, however, that civilization can lessen aggressiveness only by extensively limiting sexual freedom. And neither is it clear that civilization would be greatly endangered by whatever aggressiveness persisted after complete sexual liberation had occurred. The most that one can say is that so radical a change in mores would have implications for the social order that transcend the merely sexual. The status quo in any particular society—for instance the bourgeois or managerial one most common nowadays—would certainly be threatened by major alterations in sexual behavior. But this does not mean that civilization itself would be undermined or that it needs to forestall such eventualities in order to survive.

In essays such as " 'Civilized' Sexual Morality and Modern Nervous Illness," and in various books, including *Civilization and Its Discontents,* Freud himself points out that civilization is unduly harsh in its restraints upon sexual behavior. In this context he speaks as a moralist and not merely as an analyst of psychological or sociological data. While he believes that society limits the amount and controls the nature of happiness in an attempt to achieve greater security for civilization itself, he also sympathizes with the suffering that results. He pleads for greater flexibility and the elimination of unnecessary restraint. As he himself says, he wishes to "reform" civilized sexuality in the direction of greater freedom.

This is the aspect of Freud's thinking that popular opinion magnifies, and possibly Freud is more responsible than anyone else for the increased level of sexual freedom that exists today as compared with a hundred years ago. Yet Freud himself felt that all people must choose between one or another type of renunciation. They have to forgo important values of civilization—propriety, cool rationality, single-minded dedication to knowledge—if they want to achieve the greatest sexual happiness; or else they must give up sexuality, through self-control and even abstention, if they are to satisfy the professional and largely cerebral demands that civilization imposes. As a doctor ministering to those who suffer, Freud advocated instinctual gratification, considering it necessary for personal happiness. As a social and moral philosopher, however, he insisted that men and women could not attain the intellectual, artistic, and social goals which are distinctively human unless they accepted considerable deprivation of sexual love. He saw no means by which this chasm could be bridged, no way that man could ultimately be happy as well as civilized.

Apart from the flaws of reasoning that I have already mentioned, I think there are two basic difficulties in Freud's pessimism. First, he assumes that civilization and sexuality are fundamentally distinct. In his usual dualistic manner he considers them two separate and opposing facets of human nature. The truth is quite different, I believe. Though man may sometimes resemble a raging beast and at other times act like a cog within the organization of society, it is through his sexual being that he largely becomes a *social animal*. In the past as well as in the present, civilization has often and pervasively contrived to further the ends of sexual expression while also curtailing them in some respects. This is most apparent in contemporary civilization, where the eroticization of advertising serves as the means by which social values are vividly conveyed. But our society is not unique in this. Something comparable has happened throughout Western culture, and possibly in all others as well.

Furthermore, Freud undermines his own dichotomy in his concept of "organic repression." Over and above the restraints upon sexuality that society imposes, he thinks there may be something in the instinct itself which prevents its total satisfaction. He speculates that the libidinal function may have been impaired when man acquired his erect posture, thereby losing acuities of smell that quadrupeds still enjoy. He also suggests that the development of the libido may be inherently curtailed by unavoidable difficulties related to component-instincts such as the sadistic. Neither Freud nor anyone else has been able to carry the investigation into organic repression very far. To the extent that it accounts for the incompleteness of sexual pleasure, however, one may exonerate civilization as a necessary antagonist. Its "inevitable" conflict with sexual love may not even exist. What looks like the imposition of social and therefore external controls may often be the result of disabilities within the instinct itself. In an enlightened society of the future we may find that even when civilized restraint upon sexuality is minimal, organic repression remains as a cause of frustration. However much society devotes itself to the care and rectification of the basically imperfect instinct of sexuality, human beings may not be able to avoid the problems they have inherited through their biological evolution. The difference between the sexual reforms that Freud advocates and the more radical measures proposed by utopian theorists would then turn out to be a difference of degree rather than of type.

Despite his pleas for moderation, Freud himself was not sanguine about the outcome. Imagining a community of "double individuals" happily bonded to one another through sexuality but also devoted to the common interests of civilization, Freud insists that "this desirable state of things does not, and never did, exist." The attempt by thinkers such as Herbert Marcuse to interpret Freud along utopian lines has therefore little basis in what Freud actually believed. Marcuse argues that Freud's concept of Eros shows how the conflict between sexuality and civilization may be eliminated. But in view of the fact that Freud articulates this concept in the very book (*Civilization and Its Discontents*) in which he most fully depicts the inevitability of the conflict, one would have to conclude that he was rather confused about his own ideas. It seems much more likely that Marcuse's reading of Freud is inaccurate. Since Eros combines human beings into ever greater unities, Marcuse wonders how Freud can possibly maintain that sexuality is inherently asocial. In context, however, Freud clearly specifies that he is dealing with a split between civilization and *genital* sexuality. The energy that propels Eros being libidinal, Freud considers all forms

Freud

of Eros as sexual in one sense or another. Genital love is only one type
of Eros, only one of the ways in which Eros creates a larger unity. Eros
includes aim-inhibited as well as aim-uninhibited sexuality. The
conflict that concerns Freud is, in effect, a conflict between these two
aspects of Eros. Whether or not his idea is defensible, it involves no
contradiction of the sort that Marcuse describes.

To escape the alleged inconsistency, Marcuse argues that the
concept of sublimation enables us to think of libido as including not
only aim-inhibited nongenital interests and aim-uninhibited genital
interests but also nongenital interests that are themselves aim-
uninhibited. Marcuse claims that Freud's suggestion that object-
libido may change into narcissistic libido allows a reinterpretation
such as this. He speculates that a nonrepressive kind of sublimation
might bring about a libidinal transformation that would lead to
"erotization of the entire personality." Even though it is non-
repressive, sublimation could then direct libido toward the growth
of civilization. While still being sexual and aim-uninhibited, it
would nevertheless transcend or even displace the merely genital.
These circumstances do not exist under present capitalist conditions,
but in a revolutionized political order Marcuse believes that they
would be attainable. It follows that sexuality and civilization are not
inherently or necessarily in conflict with one another: "The culture-
building power of Eros *is* non-repressive sublimation: sexuality is
neither deflected from nor blocked in its objective; rather, in
attaining its objective, it transcends it to others, searching for fuller
gratification."

Leaving aside difficulties in Marcuse's use of the term "repressive," the first thing one must say is that Freud would have
denied that there can be sublimation which is not aim-inhibited.
Freud's entire theory of the libido is predicated upon the belief that
sexual energy is controlled by reproductive necessities which
require an orientation toward genital intercourse as the normative
goal for the erotic instinct. Freud always maintained that liberating
sex from the "organization of genital interests" could only be a
regression to the polymorphous perversity of childhood. That
condition has its utility, he believed, but only as a stage in libidinal
growth. As such, it is not a sublimation but rather an early develop-

ment that must later be superseded for the achievement of the uninhibited aim. Marcuse's reshuffling of Freudian concepts merely stands Freud on his head: it renders his vision compatible with benign romanticism by giving him precisely the kind of theory he wished to refute. And even though Freud did want to liberate sexuality inasmuch as he treated polymorphous perversity as an ingredient in the normal behavior of adults, he never envisaged liberation as a stage in which the supremacy of genital sexuality would be undermined.

❁

It is because Freud so thoroughly doubts the possibility of harmonization between sexuality and civilization that he opposes all idealistic thinking about the nature of love. For idealism extols the values in communal oneness which—however small or large the community may be—Freud sees as serving the needs of civilization rather than those of the individual who longs for happiness. He says that human development is a product of both "egoistic" and "altruistic" impulses. The former seek self-oriented satisfactions; the latter are directed toward social unity even at the expense of happiness for the participants. Since men and women are all programmed to be egoistic, idealist philosophies err in assuming that altruistic love can be achieved without a significant loss in personal well-being.

Freud does not develop this argument fully, but he reveals the direction of this thinking in a passage that discusses the differences between narcissism and egoism (selfishness). He feels that these must be distinguished because they might look like similar concepts, though they are actually quite distinct. Through narcissism a man turns toward himself libidinal investment that would otherwise go out to other objects. His attitude may be selfish, but not necessarily more so than if his libido were directed toward an external object. On the other hand, object-love may or may not be egoistic. It is what Freud calls "altruistic" when one's interest involves overestimation of the object. In that event, the object is not treated as merely a vehicle for sexual satisfaction. Instead it elicits submissiveness and a concern for its welfare. When this happens, as it does in love relations, libidinal energy has been withdrawn from the ego's narcissism as well as from its native egoism. That is the state that all idealistic theories of love would seem to be promoting in one form or another. According to Freud, their recommendations are misguided and pernicious. For the condition I have mentioned, in which an individual loses both his narcissism and his egoism, is one that renders the object "supreme." And this means, as Freud says, that "it has entirely swallowed up the ego."

If we now return to the passage in which Freud discusses the kind of love that St. Francis of Assisi illustrates, we can see why he finds it suspect. For though love then avoids the hazards of genital dependency, and may indeed provide a feeling of happiness resulting from successful aim-inhibition, Freud remarks that people who follow this path can be protected against disappointments only by "displacing what they mainly value from being loved onto loving."

But, we may ask, why is that undesirable? Why does Freud assume that real, lasting, and profound happiness cannot be attained in this manner? His initial answer, I think, would be that such love is unnatural, that it runs counter to the dynamics of human instinct. Like all self-sacrificial love, it reveals how the ego can be subjugated by an object through its own excess of altruism and insufficiency of narcissism. In order to prove his case, Freud would have to show that the lover's feeling of happiness is actually shallow and precarious, providing no true evidence of what is really happening to the ego. As a matter of fact, Freud never carries out a demonstration of this sort—perhaps because he thought that people like St. Francis are extremely rare and unrepresentative.

On the other hand, Freud spends considerable time arguing against the moral principles that have been enunciated by Western religions of love. Though he claims to be seeking the "deeper motivation" that underlies these ethical systems, he also speaks as a moralist advocating a different code. "A love that does not discriminate," he says, "seems to me to forfeit a part of its own value, by doing an injustice to its object; and secondly, not all men are worthy of love." In thus summarizing his opposition to ideas about universal love, Freud is arguing on the basis of normative generalizations about objects that receive this love. They undergo an "in-justice" if we do not love them in proportion to their merits; and if they are wholly lacking in objective goodness, they are not "worthy" of being loved at all.

Freud's remark occurs in a place where he has just been talking about the transformation of genital interests into aim-inhibited love. He has portrayed this as a defensive mechanism, designed to protect the ego against frustration or other harm that may issue from the object. Similarly, when he refers to the value of an object, or conditions that cause injustice to it, he approaches these moral concepts from the point of view of personal, ultimately libidinal, benefits that might accrue to an individual who seeks to love indiscriminately. Thus when he examines the biblical injunction to love one's neighbor as oneself, he asks: "Why should we do it? What good will it do us? But, above all, how shall we achieve it? How can it be possible?" By way of response, Freud tries to show that this love—like every other—must be seen as a search for psychological advantages to ourselves. It involves other persons but only because they further, directly or indirectly, our own narcissistic interests. The relevant paragraph runs as follows:

> My love is something valuable to me which I ought not to throw away without reflection. It imposes duties on me for whose fulfillment I must be ready to make sacrifices. If I love someone, he must deserve it in some way. (I leave out of account the use he may be to me, and also his possible significance for me as a sexual object, for neither of these two kinds of relationship comes into question where the precept to love my neighbor is concerned.) He deserves it if he is so like me in important ways that I can love myself in him; and he deserves it if he is so much more perfect than myself that I can love my ideal of my own self in him. Again, I have to love him if he is my friend's son, since the pain my friend would feel if any harm came to him would be my pain too—I should have to share it. But if he is a stranger to me and if he cannot attract me by any worth of his own or any significance that he may already have acquired for my emotional life, it will be hard for me to love him.

Having begun with this account of love as narcissistic even when it is concerned about another's welfare, Freud then introduces what looks like an ethical argument that goes beyond an interest in what is advantageous to oneself. For whether or not he can overcome the difficulties of loving the stranger who is worthless to him, Freud insists that it would be "wrong" to love that man: "For my love is valued by all my own people as a sign of my preferring them, and it is an injustice to them if I put a stranger on a par with them."

In saying this, Freud is assuming that his "own people" have a moral right to his love such that he does them an injustice if he gives any of it to an outsider. But though Freud does not say so explicitly, he thinks that ethics also reduces to an exchange of benefits: I want my people to prefer me, to give me their love, and so I must recognize their right to a comparable love on my part. Freud takes this for granted. Similarly, he assumes that the quantity of love must be limited in accordance with his economic theory. Whatever goes to the stranger leaves that much less for one's intimates. Belonging to a closed and finite system, like libido itself, love cannot be distributed to all mankind without being subdivided to a point where it does no one any good. In this vein, Freud says of the person one is to love even if he is a stranger: "If I am to love him (with this universal love) merely because he, too, is an inhabitant of this earth, like an insect, an earth-worm or a grass-snake, then I fear that only a small modicum of my love will fall to his share." Freud then states that this modicum would be less than what reason tells us we are entitled to retain for ourselves.

These being the grounds on which Freud argues that not all men are worthy of his love, he easily concludes that it makes more sense to feel hostility and even hatred toward the neighbor or the stranger who does not belong to one's own closed system of affective interchange:

> He seems not to have the least trace of love for me and shows me not the slightest consideration. If it will do him any good he has no hesitation in injuring me, nor does he ask himself whether the amount of advantage he gains bears any proportion to the extent of the harm he does to

me. . . . If he behaves differently, if he shows me consideration and forbearance as a stranger, I am ready to treat him in the same way, in any case and quite apart from any precept. Indeed, if this grandiose commandment had run "Love thy neighbour as thy neighbour loves thee," I should not take exception to it. And there is a second commandment, which seems to me even more incomprehensible and arouses still stronger opposition in me. It is "Love thine enemies." If I think it over, however, I see that I am wrong in treating it as a greater imposition. At bottom it is the same thing.

Freud argues not only that Judaeo-Christian precepts about a universal love of mankind are unreasonable, even irrational, but also that they violate the "original nature of man." They cannot be fulfilled and they undermine love that hews more closely to reality. He ascribes the motivation for these idealistic injunctions to civilization's overwhelming attempt to control human aggressiveness by encouraging individuals to be self-sacrificial in their attitude toward others. But since men are so aggressive, according to Freud, one runs the risk of being hurt by them if one actually lives up to the biblical precept. And, in any event, he is sure that this desperate effort of civilization will not succeed in pacifying human nature. The intolerance and even violence that have pervaded Christianity's attitude toward nonbelievers Freud considers an "inevitable consequence" of its faith in universal love. "It is always possible to bind together a considerable number of people in love," he sardonically remarks, "so long as there are other people left over to receive the manifestations of their aggressiveness."

From this kind of statement one might well conclude that Freud found no redeeming or residual value in the Judaeo-Christian commandments about love. Two years after he published *Civilization and Its Discontents*, however, he wrote an open letter to Albert Einstein (published as "Why War?") and what he says there has sometimes been adduced as evidence of a change in his thinking. After repeating his distinction between Eros and the death drive, Freud suggests that whatever satisfies Eros by uniting mankind will help to eliminate war. Emotional ties that can have this effect, he says, are of two kinds: either "relations resembling those towards a loved object, though without having a sexual aim," or else identifications that result from the sharing of interests. About the first kind of emotional tie Freud states that psychoanalysis need not be "ashamed to speak of love in this connection, for religion itself uses the same words: 'thou shalt love thy neighbor as thyself.'"

Discussing this passage, Fromm claims that Freud's thinking had undergone "nothing short of a radical change." He finds a "profound and irreconcilable contradiction between the old and the new theories." I think Fromm is quite mistaken. For immediately after Freud's quotation of the religious injunction, he adds a single sentence that reveals his basic attitude: "This, however, is more easily said than done." In other words, even though psychoanalysis can recognize the possibility of indiscriminate love, Freud is no more confident now than he was previously about its actual attainment. Nor does he really place much weight upon the ability of identifications to create a "community of feeling." Freud does mention that all human societies are founded on them, but he in no way retracts his earlier belief that the inner cohesiveness of a people may tend to augment its hostility toward outsiders. Indeed, the only real prospect for peace that Freud adduces comes from his suggestion that civilization—in its progressive restraint upon instinctual drive—may enlarge the intellect's control over affective life and thereby amplify internalization of the individual's aggressiveness.

Both of these developments have drawbacks that Freud laments. Sexual pleasures diminish and even disappear once they are subjected to cultural inhibition, and the internalizing of aggression leads to a strengthening of the superego's propensity to impose painful and often damaging guilt-feelings. Unfortunate as these by-products may be, Freud offers no hope that they can be avoided. Without the dominance of intellect, as in dispassionate reasoning and scientific analysis, he believes that civilization cannot survive. Eros may bind mankind in ever greater unities, but only reason prevents the death drive from using them for destructive ends. And while Freud recognizes, in fact emphasizes, that the motivating energy within reason must itself be erotic, he staunchly refuses to believe—as all the idealists did—that the condition of being in love supplements and improves upon the rational attitude.

We thus return to our view of Freud as a consistent and thoroughgoing realist. He examines every type of love and shows how each resembles the other in their common derivation from organic instincts and developmental patterns systematically misunderstood by idealist philosophies. Despite the many phases through which his own thinking progressed, Freud's approach to love remains coherent and unified throughout. He is often described as a throwback to the eighteenth-century enlightenment or even the rationalism of Spinoza. But true as this may be, he also reflects the proximate influence of Romantic pessimism. It remains constant in him from beginning to end. As a young man he writes to his fiancée that every woman must expect to lose her lover once she marries him, and in later years he systematically shows how love can be manipulated by political leaders, by the church, and even (for beneficial reasons) by psychoanalysts eliciting transference. Rarely does he suggest that love solves human problems as well as causing them. All love, as Freud conceives of it, suffers from the same defect: it overvalues its object and therefore must traffic in delusion. Like Lucretius, Freud says of sexual love: "If the sensual impulsions are more or less effectively repressed or set aside, the illusion is produced that the object has come to be sensually loved on account of its spiritual merits, whereas on the contrary these merits may really only have been lent to it by its sensual charm."

If we change the phrase "sensual charm" to "sexual or libidinal import," this remark about illusion applies to religious love, to love for mankind, to married love, and in general to all love as Freud interprets it. Though he perceives the meritorious dispositions included in each type of love, and though he would approve of married or humanitarian love if only they could survive in the coldly factual world, their common dependence upon illusion makes them all equally suspect. Like the "wise men" to whom he refers—the classical moralists and traditional rationalists—Freud turns against love because he distrusts its tendency to ignore the laws of reason. Few writers, if any, in the history of mankind have studied human passion more exhaustively than Freud, and none with greater insight into the sufferings to which it often leads. Nor is he lacking in sympathy, even compassion, though these qualities are not his most outstanding. But at every moment in his writing, he stands back from the affects that he analyzes and says, like Hamlet, "Give me that man/That is not passion's slave, and I will wear him/In my heart's core. . . ." Therein lies the august purity of his genius, and also the boundary that defines its limitation.

❀

In presenting Freud's theories as an attempted solution to problems in the philosophy of love, I have neglected several concepts that are only peripheral to the theme of this book: for instance, his ideas about bisexuality within all men and women, penis envy as a female trope, latent homosexuality as a constant within social activities of males, etc. In *The Goals of Human Sexuality* I discussed the effect of Freud's essentialism upon various aspects of his sexological theory. In the first volume of this trilogy, I criticized at length his ideas about religious love and tried to show how they were related to his faulty approach to the nature of idealization.* I argued that Freud, like Plato and Santayana, from both of whom he differs in many other ways, failed to understand how love exceeds appraisive modes of valuation. Through appraisal we establish what an object is worth on the basis of its direct or ultimate capacity to satisfy needs within ourselves. Without denying that Freud made great advances toward discovering the psychodynamics of human needs, I suggested that his theory of love was vitiated by his inability to see how love depends on nonappraisive bestowals of value. Through bestowal we create value in another person rather than finding it in his or her utility to ourselves. The object of bestowal is made valuable not in having acquired a new attribute but only in the importance it has received as that to which we attach ourselves by means of our bestowal.

*See *The Nature of Love: Plato to Luther,* particularly pp. 23–38, 97–99, 101–4, 173, 182–83, 198–200, 208–31, 234–36, 263–64, 302–7.

The act of bestowing is neither rational nor irrational. It is non-rational, and probably instinctual. In his devotion to sexuality as a biological instinct that is basic to all types of love, Freud seems to be unaware of the ways in which creative and imaginative bestowals may also be innately programmed in organisms such as ours. His conception of human nature is thus deficient. His view of biology is too greatly circumscribed for him to recognize that the bestowing of value may satisfy its own deeply structured need.

By invoking bestowal as a concept that Freudian doctrine neglects, I am proposing a different method of interpreting human cathexes. For Freud, all affective efforts are designed to capture objects that can satisfy the libido. If bestowal is not a device for obtaining libidinal benefits, he will conclude that the expenditure of energy must be pathological. On economic grounds, it makes no sense. It is not what he would consider purposive. Upon analysis, Freud insists, we should be able to demonstrate that an illusion has eroded the lover's experience of reality. To the extent that love is a cathexis involving bestowal, Freud would say, it is dangerous and generally harmful. Even when its effects are beneficial, as in the state he calls a confluence of tenderness and sexuality, he would deny that emotional goods can be realized unless bestowal is thoroughly subordinated to what dispassionate observers recognize as accurate appraisals.

In opposing this perspective, I have been claiming that Freud misconstrues the affective matrix out of which love arises. Because he ignores the creative capacity of bestowal, he cannot see how it may indeed be harmonized with appraisal. He is right to insist upon the importance of making correct and reliable appraisals. As I indicate in Chapter 10, that is the great lesson he taught the twentieth century. But he is wrong to minimize the desirability of imaginative bestowals. To say this, however, is to say that we must go beyond Freud's mode of realism. In no other way can we understand what is both possible and actual in the relationship between the two valuational categories.

5
Proust

Throughout This Trilogy I
have often listed Proust among the realists. He is easily categorized
as a twentieth-century critic of idealist attitudes toward love. He
seems to condemn them as completely as Flaubert and Zola did in
their novels, and sometimes with a quasi-scientific detachment
reminiscent of Claude Bernard and other positivists of the nineteenth century. With clinical coolness Marcel, the narrator of *A la
recherche du temps perdu,* sums up his relationship with Albertine in
these words: "J'appelle ici amour une torture réciproque"—"What
I here call love is a reciprocal torture." Proust recognizes no other
kind of passionate love. He and Freud may well be linked as the
two greatest opponents of Romantic theory.

But Proust differs from Freud in criticizing romanticism from
within, as if he were a kind of fifth column. In that role Proust
develops the implications of idealist concepts more thoroughly
than any other realist had. Before rejecting the Romantic ideology,
he identifies with it, employing its fundamental ideas and showing
how they arise out of concrete experience. Proust is related to the
romanticism of someone like Stendhal much as Spinoza was to Car-
tesianism or Hume to Berkeleyan subjectivism: he carries the original premises to their most extreme consequences and thereby
reveals—in a manner even more devastating than Freud's—the
hidden imperfection of the prior view. Proust is the last of the Romantics in the sense that he is romanticism destroying itself and

doing so, as I shall be arguing, for ends that are themselves idealist and even Romantic in their inspiration.

Though Proust may not have read much of Freud, various scholars have called attention to parallels between the two. During the years when Proust was writing *A la recherche,* Freud's ideas would have been available to him from many sources. In the alembic of his imagination as a novelist he uses, even duplicates, them at many junctures of the narrative: for instance, when Marcel associates the agony of awaiting his mother's goodnight kiss with the jealousy Swann must have felt in thinking that Odette was in a "place of pleasure" where he could not be admitted; when he later speaks of his interest in Albertine as the rebirth of his childhood love for mother, leaving us to infer that he imprisons the former just as he would have liked to have kept the latter in his room indefinitely; when he remarks that no mistress has ever given him the happiness in love he used to get from his mother, whose affection was constant and reliable to a degree unequalled by anyone else. At times Marcel recognizes that his responses are pathological, and like a patient in therapy he constantly struggles with the possibility that his psychological difficulties are systematically preventing him from perceiving reality.

There are other respects, to which I shall return, in which Proust's analysis of human affect seems to fit the Freudian pattern. But the fit is never perfect. Though Proust and Freud share common tangents, the figures they describe are not wholly congruent. Their conception of love is not the same. I discount the fact that one was writing what purports to be fiction while the other was a scientific theorist, since I am treating both of them as philosophers in the broadest sense. What really separates them is the fact that they approach love in terms of different philosophical problems and use different methodologies for resolving these problems.

The contrasts between Proust and Freud appear most sharply when we consider how each would interpret the relationship between Marcel and his mother. Freud would have described the child's condition as follows: It is an unhealthy manifestation of the Oedipus complex, stemming from a frustrated desire for sexual intimacy with the mother. His development out of the Oedipus complex remaining unresolved, Marcel is prevented from enjoying love in relation to anyone else. The severity of the child's maladjustment results from his extremely ambivalent attitudes toward a pampering mother who does not give him what he really wants as well as toward a father who disciplines him but does not stick to repressive commands or manifest a requisite authority.

There is nothing in Proust to rule out this interpretation of what the narrator tells us. Indeed there is much to substantiate it, and Marcel even traces his failure of will to the acute feelings of a Freudian sort described in the goodnight episode at the beginning of *Swann's Way*. But however much Proust might accept Freud's method of anaylsis, he scarcely uses it to define love or criticize the idealist conception. Where Freud reduces love to sublimation of sexual desire, as explained by states such as the Oedipus complex, Proust employs an alternate mode of thought.

For Proust, as for most of the Romantics, sexual instinct is not the fundamental category in love. Though it may contribute an essential ingredient, it is taken as neither the cause nor the defining principle. Freud analyzes love as a complex attempt—often unrecognized but distinctly human—to satisfy biological drives, bodily demands. Proust insists that it is based upon a need that cannot be located in the body, a need that may issue into physiological events but that nevertheless remains different from them. Unlike Freud, he makes no attempt to reduce love to sex. He thereby avoids the conceptual and terminological difficulties that we considered in the previous chapter in relation to Freud's ideas about "die Liebe."

Although he often refers to it, Proust never names this other "need." I shall call it the "need to feel" in order to distinguish it from both sexual impulse and love itself. While the Romantics thought that love satisfies the need to feel, all of Proust may be read as an attempt to deny this, to argue that love cannot fulfill this need except in a temporary and ultimately unsatisfying way. What Proust inherits from the Romantics, and from the idealist tradition in general, is the conviction that one must search for (*research,* as in the title of his masterpiece) a means of experiencing reality that will put one's feelings in direct communion with the being of persons, things, and the world as a whole. To respond in this fashion is to have a sense of reality which combines vibrant emotion with accurate understanding. Romantic love claimed to have effected this harmonization through metaphysical merging with another person, that being an ecstatic interpenetration of souls which reveals the ultimate structure of reality. Freud takes all such metaphoric utterances as examples of self-deceptive rationalization about sexual dynamics. Proust makes no interpretation along those lines. For him poetic language of this sort makes sense as an expression of man's need to feel at one with his human and cosmic environment. Proust believes that this need to feel is basic in our nature and not reducible to any other need. He refutes Romantic idealism by arguing that it is an erroneous approach to problems of feeling. He substitutes for it an analysis that seeks to be realistic while also providing justification for his own kind of post-Romantic idealism.

Studying Proust in terms of problems about feeling, we do well to begin with Henri Bergson. His philosophy dominated French thought at the time that Proust wrote, and it belongs to the background of Proust's conception no less than the Dreyfus case or Parisian adulation of Wagner. Proust himself denied that his novels were "romans bergsoniens." While recognizing that literature often attaches itself to the reigning philosophy of a period, Proust asserted that the distinction between voluntary and involuntary memory, which he employs in his novel, is not to be found in the philosophy of Bergson. Scholars have discussed at great length the relationship between Proustian and Bergsonian ideas about memory, and we shall return to this question later. What has generally been ignored, however, is the way in which Proust used Bergson as the contemporary manifestation of the Romantic idealism that he found so seductive, and that he had to test against his own experience, subject to realist criticism, and finally incorporate—transfigured and transcended—within his own theories about the nature of feeling. Bergson forever looms before Proust as the one philosopher whose influence he had to overcome.

Throughout his early philosophy Bergson distinguishes between intelligence and intuition, between interpretation and immediacy, between habitual responses justified on pragmatic grounds and the artist's imaginative attempt to portray the flow of lived experience. While the basic outline of these distinctions reappears in Proust, they also underlie the metaphysics in Bergson that Proust could not accept. For instance, when Bergson describes intuition—that is to say, feeling which puts us in touch with reality—he refers to a faculty that places us "inside the object itself." In this relationship we acquire knowledge that Bergson describes as "absolute" rather than relative. We can then attribute to the object what Bergson calls "an interior." For living creatures, this would mean "states of mind." He immediately adds: "I also imply that I am in sympathy with those states, and that I insert myself in them by an effort of imagination."

I begin here because it is essential to see how Bergson rehearses the Romantic concept of merging that Proust investigates throughout his writing. Bergson's kinship to the previous forms of idealism becomes evident when he says that "coincidence with the person himself would alone give me the absolute." He then defines intuition as "the kind of *intellectual sympathy* by which one places oneself within an object in order to coincide with what is unique in it and consequently inexpressible."

This much of Bergson may hardly seem novel. But it enabled him to formulate, with greater insistence than anyone else, a dualism between intuition and analysis. Contrasting it with intuitional processes, he treats analysis as the mental operation that reduces an object to its elements, relates these elements to what is already known, and then categorizes the object instead of sympathizing or empathizing directly. Analysis explains the object by reference to elements that are "common" to various objects, and therefore it can only place reality—the person or thing we wish to understand—within an endless system of symbolic representations. For that reason it never provides absolute knowledge but only an imperfect and relativistic symbolism. Intuition, on the other hand, puts us directly in touch with reality. Intuition is the basis of metaphysics, Bergson concludes, and metaphysics is "The science which claims to dispense with symbols."

Without mentioning Bergson as a philosopher whose ideas he is probing, Proust investigates the nature of intuitive feeling by studying what happens when one person seeks to coincide with the interior being of another. Examining sympathy and imagination as contributing factors, he finds that the latter introduces distortions that prevent the former from effecting identification with another person. Like Bergson, Proust documents the dangers of analysis. But he never denies that symbolization, in its proper employment, is capable of yielding a reliable sense of reality. Through his doctrine of essences, as we shall see, Proust finally asserts that it is precisely by means of "elements" common to different objects that reality may be reached.

Bergson's ideas about intuition recur throughout his philosophy—in his notion of *élan vital* as the unforeseeable energy within evolution, which he therefore calls "creative"; in his concept of duration as the seamless continuity of lived experience which he contrasts with the spatialization of time effected by analysis; and in his description of artistic efforts to embody intuition within a permanent presentation. In *The Two Sources of Morality and Religion* Bergson uses related ideas to understand the nature of love. Though this book was published ten years after Proust's death, it expresses the same idealist approach that fascinates Proust and provides a background to his entire investigation into human affect.

Like Proust, Bergson begins with the assertion that love is not *natural*, in the sense that it cannot be explained by any system of instincts with which man is endowed. In what Bergson calls the "closed society," people do manifest a programmed need for other members of their family or tribe; they are motivated by a communal pressure that nature instills for the sake of social harmony; and from this there arises a sense of moral obligation. But Bergson ascribes love to a different dimension of man's being. It is a "stirring of the soul" rather than a "surface agitation." Bergson portrays it as the kind of emotion that cannot be produced by concepts or any representation derived from the empirical world. In a way that is reminiscent of Proust's remarks about Vinteuil's septet or the musical phrase that embodies Swann's love for Odette, Bergson sees an analogy between amorous feeling and our response to music:

We feel, while we listen, as though we could not desire anything else but what the music is suggesting to us. . . . Let the
music express joy or grief, pity or love, every moment we are
what it expresses. Not only ourselves, but many others, nay,
all the others, too. When music weeps, all humanity, all
nature, weeps with it. In point of fact it does not introduce
these feelings into us; it introduces us into them, as passers-
by are forced into a street dance.

Bergson means that in their musical works people create new
kinds of feelings rather than duplicating those that occur in nature.
Music presents emotions engendered by the composer's attempt to
cope with his condition as a human being. Bergson thinks that the
emotion of love is similar, and therefore not reducible to instincts
such as the social and sexual ones that nature provides as a means of
survival. To the extent that his morality depends on such instincts,
man resembles the ants and the bees. Their mode of sociability best
illustrates life within the closed society. To the extent, however,
that man is capable of new and unforeseeable feelings, like those
expressed in music or in love, he acts creatively. In each case the
relevant emotions arise from what is unique in someone's personal
experience. In the "open society" that Bergson depicts as the basis
for spiritual growth, people bind themselves to each other's individuality through a unitive feeling that stirs the soul and is different
from a natural instinct.

Though Bergson insists that these emotions express a person's
own perspective, he emphasizes their ability to communicate to
other people new affective possibilities that they too may henceforth
experience. He describes Rousseau's love of mountains, and of
nature in general, as something that Rousseau created out of himself. Being an emotion, it was not just "elementary feelings" that
mountains have probably elicited from many others before Rousseau. It was, Bergson claims, something unique within Rousseau's
life that he nevertheless conveyed to other human beings who could
now undergo a comparable emotion. As with any work of art or
imagination, Rousseau's love of nature is thus an invention that all
humanity may enjoy even though it resulted from his own idiosyncratic response.

In an extension of this type of reasoning, Bergson maintains that what he calls "romantic love" is not a universal phenomenon of human nature but rather a creative development that arose at a particular moment in history: "it sprang up during the Middle Ages on the day when some person or persons conceived the idea of absorbing love into a kind of supernatural feeling, into religious emotion as created by Christianity and launched by the new religion into the world." Under the influence of romantic love, people could now react to one another with adoration. But since that means treating another person as if he or she were a god worthy of religious devotion, Bergson considers romantic love an illusion.

Earlier in this trilogy we have frequently encountered the notion that love between the sexes is an invention of the Middle Ages, and the belief that it is illusory we have studied in various contexts. As against this approach, I have argued that concepts of love (and the ideals to which they contribute) occurred at different times in history, but that love between the sexes is a psychological and even biological constant belonging to human nature itself. Far from being necessarily dependent on one or another illusion, love is part of the imaginative equipment that enables man to satisfy his instincts in the most gratifying manner. This way of thinking is unacceptable to Bergson because he wishes to hold that emotions of love—whether involving adoration or some other unifying attitude—originate as creative achievements beyond the predictable limits of nature. He also thinks that if the romantic lovers recognized that their attachment to one another is basically religious, they would be cured of their illusion. In other words, they would no longer love each other romantically. Bergson has no conception of passionate sexual love that is an authentic stirring of the soul apart from religious love.

Bergsonian theory is limited in this respect because it singles out the mystic's attitude as the only true expression of love. Bergson maintains that the "open soul" is inherently mystical, and he insists that its love cannot be defined in terms of any particular object. All objects are available to it since it does not aim at any one person or group. In its love of mankind, mystical love "has shot beyond and reached humanity only by passing through humanity." The open society is thus the society of mystics, not anchorites who live in isolation from others but rather men and women whose behavior reveals the ideal morality intuitively accepted by everyone. They are superior models of what we would all like to be, inspired personalities whose example we may seek to emulate through social action.

While Bergson thinks of the open society as a remote condition that mankind may yet attain, he is primarily interested in advocating the mystical attitude as a present possibility. It is a way of life that enables one to make contact with "the creative effort which life itself manifests." This current of life is the élan vital, and Bergson identifies it with love. At times he says that God is merely the creative energy, this cosmic love immanent within all life; at other times he hedges by suggesting that it *comes* from God. True mystics open themselves to a stream of love "flowing down and seeking through them to reach their fellow-men." The love that engulfs the mystic is not man's love for God, but rather God's love for men: "Through God, in the strength of God, he [the mystic] loves all mankind with a divine love."

Since Bergson tells us nothing about divine love except that it is the élan vital propelling life through evolution, his mystical doctrine would seem to be little more than a twentieth-century variation upon Western idealism of previous generations. Hegel too saw existence as an evolutionary process motivated by a dialectic of love, and as recently as 1893 Charles Sanders Peirce had argued that "evolutionary love" was a creative, non-Darwinian force operating through all reality. Like many idealists of the nineteenth century, Bergson claims that mysticism shows itself most clearly, and with greatest purity, in dispositions fostered by Christianity. He thinks that Christian mystics have a superior capacity for merging through sympathetic identification, and he ascribes it to a preferential awareness of divine love. From their experience Bergson derives his ideas about the meaning of life. He says that all mystics, but the Christians most successfully, teach us that God needs human beings as the recipients of his love. All creation is to be seen "as God undertaking to create creators, that He may have, besides Himself, beings worthy of His love. . . . Beings have been called into existence who were destined to love and be loved, since creative energy is to be defined as love. Distinct from God, Who is this energy itself, they could spring into being only in a universe, and therefore the universe sprang into being."

In Proust we shall encounter no mention of the Bergsonian doctrine of mystical intuition, even though its outlines were present in Bergson's earliest writings. What we find instead is an implied belief that concepts such as these are worthless unless they can be reconciled with the crude realities of experience. Though Proust's conclusions are not Bergsonian, he often seems to presuppose an approach not wholly incoherent with Bergson's. In portraying love as the emotion by which a mystic expresses his own personality while responding to the personality in others, Bergson subsumes the love of persons within a love for creativity as Proust also does. They mainly differ in their ideas about the ultimate source of creativity. Neither in his theory of essences nor in any of his statements about artistic imagination does Proust suggest that moral and religious experience should be elevated above the aesthetic. His thinking stems from Bergsonian intuitionism and then veers off in another direction. Nevertheless it is only in the context of Bergson's philosophy that we can understand Proust's attempt to synthesize a kind of idealism with his own supervening realism.

We thus begin by noting that Proust and Bergson are alike in rejecting sexual love as a solution to life's problems but that Proust retains little, if any, of Bergson's assurance about the ultimacy of mystical love. After Proust's death Bergson is said to have lamented the basic orientation of *A la recherche du temps perdu*. While admiring Proust's psychological insight and the opulence of his style, Bergson could only conclude that "ce cher Marcel" had never liberated himself from the worldly and snobbish interests of his youth. In the words of his interlocutor, Bergson remarks that Proust "had not at all understood that there is no truly great work of art which does not exalt and fortify the soul, and which does not leave the door open to hope."

One might reply that the final pages of Proust's masterpiece express a positive, even optimistic, attitude toward the problems that Proust had been examining. With renewed faith in his own creativity, the narrator attains the spiritual clarification needed to write the volumes we have just finished reading. By writing them, he will have succeeded in regaining the past. This is not Bergson's solution, however. Not only does Proust deny the validity of social action, whereas Bergsonian mysticism shows itself as moral dedication through which the love of mankind comes into existence, but also Proust does not believe that creative energy sustains the universe as an omnipresent force. Unlike Bergson, Proust recognizes no divinity that gushes forth as love bestowing itself throughout the cosmos.

I shall return to the relationship between Proust's philosophy and Bergson's later in this chapter. Here I only wished to emphasize that Proust's thinking about love originates from his attempt to determine whether feeling can ever have the metaphysical significance that Bergson ascribed to it. Bergsonian intuition is feeling that puts one in harmony with the world. It is sympathetic identification that provides both veridical insight unobtainable any other way and also spontaneous joy, intense happiness, as if one were satisfying what is deepest in one's being. The ability to express our intuitions, to communicate them through verbal or visual or auditory signs, is for Bergson the justification of art. Proust ends up with a similar belief. Yet most of his work consists in re-examining the nature of intuition, which turns out to have a different meaning for him as well as different implications about the nature of human affect.

In this connection consider the passage in *Swann's Way* in which the narrator describes a sexual revery he had as a child walking through the countryside. It occurred on the Méséglise way, and was indeed part of his response to the Méséglise way. We are first told that Marcel sees the beauty of the landscape and tries to express his enthusiasm with strokes of his umbrella, disjointed cries, words like "Damn, damn, damn." None of this enables him to articulate his feelings, but with the sense of frustration comes an awareness that "between our impressions and the usual modes of expressing them" there is a profound disharmony. At this point the sexual revery occurs. In the midst of his solitude, in the discomfort of his blocked exaltation, the child feels the desire for a woman, for a peasant girl of the neighborhood who would magically spring up from behind a tree and throw herself into his arms.

Who is this girl? Is she someone Marcel has known? Obviously not. As a figment of his probing spirit, she has been created from a rib of his imagination. She is an abstract possibility that functions as a means by which the child hopes to communicate with the surrounding world that bursts upon him. The petite paysanne embodies nature as a whole, the trees in the forest of Roussainville, the wild grass, even the town itself—which Marcel has long wished to visit—its church steeple, the pink reflection of its tiled roofs. Proust describes the girl as if she were a part of the landscape, a local plant but of a higher order than the rest, capable of introducing the child to the intimate life of the countryside. The simple peasant called forth by Marcel's revery grows to the dimensions of a supernatural nymph, a goddess, an Eastern divinity with many faces, many arms, many legs to signify the pervasiveness of her being: "It seemed to me that the beauty of the trees was hers also, and that the very soul of those horizons, of the village of Roussainville, of the books I read that year, would enter into me through her embrace. . . . To wander thus through the woods of Roussainville without having a peasant girl to embrace was to remain ignorant of their hidden treasure, their deep-rooted beauty."

Bergson never associates intuition with sexual desire. On the contrary, he separates the two inasmuch as he considers intuition to be independent of material instinct. By the end of his investigations, Proust reaches conclusions that are not wholly different. But here, at the outset, he is more interested in showing that Marcel's hunger for a woman who will embody the objective scene results from a fear that without her his response to external reality is incomplete. Through her the child wishes to overcome the disharmony between his impressions and his current ability to express them. To have a vague and inarticulate enthusiasm for the Méséglise way is not enough. Marcel yearns for the peasant girl because he thinks that intimacy with her will enable him to commune with nature. Just what does Marcel really want? Why does he feel that his experience remains inadequate? The boy is not incapable of enjoying the natural goodness and sustaining beauty of Roussainville. But they seem inaccessible because he senses that something is lacking in his response. On a psychiatric interpretation, one could say that Marcel feels alienated from the beauty of Méséglise just as he feels cut off from his beautiful mother; his need to express his feelings about nature are an extension of his wish to exhibit affection for the mother; since he cannot show this love as he would like, he creates the petite paysanne through whom all losses are to be regained.

This kind of interpretation is not erroneous, at least not obviously so. But it is largely irrelevant to Proust's thinking in his novels. Despite all the psychological analysis in them, they are scarcely dependent upon psychiatric generalizations. Anecdotes about Marcel's mother, father, grandmother do not yield the needed evidence. Proust continually insisted that he was not writing an autobiography. Even in *Jean Santeuil,* the earlier work that more clearly uses events in Proust's own life, the personal details that would be essential for a psychoanalytic interpretation have largely been omitted.

Instead Proust devotes himself to a study of feeling that questions man's ability to respond adequately to nature or other people. He is primarily interested in distinguishing between objective and subjective elements in experience as a whole. Proust begins with the assumption that all men need to find a direct and satisfying means of communing with their surroundings and that this cannot occur unless one develops modes of expression adequate for intuitive awareness. If we can say that Méséglise symbolizes the mother, Proust implies, we can also say that Méséglise and the mother symbolize the world in which one lives.

In the pages that immediately precede the Méséglise experience Proust prepares us for it by discussing how Marcel annoys the servant Françoise after the death of his aunt Léonie. Françoise experiences Léonie's death as an occasion of intense, even savage, grief. For some unexplained reason Marcel goes out of his way to irritate her by speaking of his dead aunt in a cavalier manner. He scorns Françoise's display of emotion, arguing that he has no obligation to mourn a woman just because she was his aunt. When Marcel embarrasses Françoise with his clever reasoning, she remarks: "I don't know how to express myself." Since she is the only one who really does feel the death of Léonie, we need not take her statement literally. I see it as one of many clues, silver nails as Henry James would have called them, which Proust has scattered throughout his work in order to alert us to moments at which the narrator suspects that his emotional response may not have been appropriate to an objective situation.

Something similar applies to the "often, but little at a time" ("souvent mais peu à la fois") anecdote about Swann's father. It deals entirely with the old man's ambiguous response to the death of his wife. While the corpse is being put into the coffin, Marcel's grandfather manages to lead the elder Swann into the open air. He is astounded to see his friend's grief suddenly change into joyful appreciation of the beauty of nature. An outburst such as this, which might have been suitable on another occasion, is inappropriate at the funeral of one's wife. Swann's father is himself shocked at his own apparent lack of feeling. As in all moments of trial, he passes his hand across his forehead and wipes his eyes—a gesture that Swann inherits and employs whenever he too detects some discrepancy between his feelings and their expression. For the two years he survived his wife, Swann's father remained inconsolable; and yet he could say to Marcel's grandfather: "It's odd. I very often think of my poor wife, but I can't think of her much at a time." This leads to the grandfather's refrain "often, but little at a time," and it makes the child suspect that Swann's father was a monster. That is obviously not what Proust himself believes, for he has the child defer to the grandfather's insistence that his friend actually had "a heart of gold." As Marcel matures he learns that all feelings are unstable, and that our ability to express them appropriately is always precarious. He accepts this as a law of nature, a regularity that structures the inconstancy within experience. As in all of his analysis, Proust uses the technique of the lanterne magique, the kaleidoscope, which causes haphazard pieces of existence to fit together in complex and unpredictable patterns.

When Swann himself enters, we are presented with a man who appears to be the photographic negative of his father. Chatting in the garden at Combray, he seems like a cultivated person who would have no problem expressing what he feels. As a matter of fact, as we soon discover, his ironic stance is merely a device for masking or thwarting feelings instead of letting them develop properly. In Swann's affair with Odette, as in his devotion to the cause of Drey-fus, he acts like one who is still beset by his father's difficulty. In his first appearance, however, the disability is hidden, and Swann serves as a dramatic contrast to Marcel's aunts Flora and Céline. Where they want to express gratitude for the gifts he has sent them but fail to communicate any sentiment whatsoever, Swann plays the role of the dilettantish gentleman who has no feelings and therefore cannot be troubled by any awkwardness in expressing them.

Swann's tortured love for Odette arises from his fear that he may be lacking in sensibility or, at least, the capacity to express it fully. And the same is true of all the lovers in Proust. He generally sees love as an attempt to resolve problems of feeling through passionate response. His critique consists in showing that, given what human beings are like, the love of persons—and erotic love in particular—cannot succeed in this attempt.

Though he analyzes love in terms of feeling, Proust also insists upon the close relationship between love and sex. He does not idealize sex, as some of the Romantics had. He merely observes that it is usually indispensable if love is to make its greatest impact. When Albertine repels Marcel's sexual overtures at Balbec, his amorous interest largely disappears. It returns when she allows, indeed encourages, his physical advances. Even after the affair has turned into mutual misery, the narrator assures us that it was "not as fruitless as those to which, through lack of will, one can descend, for it was not com-pletely Platonic; she gave me carnal pleasures."

In saying this, the narrator does not mean merely that sexual love provides a good that is lacking in so-called "Platonic love." Proust also believes that physical intimacy contributes to a love that is most fully realized, and therefore is best capable of illustrating success or failure on any occasion. Discussing the relationship between Mlle Vinteuil and her lesbian friend, he defends "l'amour physique" on the grounds that even in an unwholesome context it brings out moral qualities of considerateness and self-sacrifice. Proust recog-nizes that cruelty, as well as kindliness, often accompanies sexual interest. But he insists that without sex neither of these sentiments would develop in the manner most characteristic of love.

I do not wish to suggest that all the instances of love Proust examines are overtly sexual. He intimates that, for all we know, Charlus' relation with Morel might not have been physical; and Jean Santeuil falls in love with Madame S—— even though he realizes he can never go to bed with her. These particular cases, however, are presented as corollaries to a rule, rather than counterinstances. In behaving as lovers, Charlus and Morel act toward one another as if their relation were sexual; whether or not it is actually consummated hardly affects its erotic character. In the other case, Proust remarks that Jean's awareness that he cannot possess Madame S—— would ordinarily have destroyed the possibility of love. Though this does not happen, Jean's love is presented as a diminished variant. It is short-lived and "denuded of its purpose," which Proust calls "waiting to see in what fashion, at present unknown, our possession of the beloved will be fulfilled." Proust usually means by "possession" more than just sexual intercourse. But in this place he is referring only to that. When the theme of Jean's love for Madame S—— was later expanded into Swann's love for Odette, like a slender melody being transcribed for full orchestra, the affair becomes wholly sexual.

That love should have a sexual base is important for Proust because of his pervasive interest in seeing how feelings are affected by bodily states. In the midst of his painful relation with Gilberte, Marcel undergoes heart flutters and is forced to reduce his consumption of caffeine. The flutters immediately cease and he wonders whether the suffering he ascribed to his anxieties about Gilberte may not actually have resulted from the caffeine. He takes this possibility very seriously, finally concluding that the drug increased the amatory anguish which was originally caused by his fevered imagination. But Marcel also remarks that the avoidance of caffeine, and the subsequent improvement in his health, did not cure whatever suffering the chemical may have created. "Even if this drug had been at the source of misery that my imagination had interpreted mistakenly (which would not be extraordinary at all, the cruelest moral pains often being caused in lovers by the physical habit of living with a certain woman), this occurred in the manner of the philter which, long after having been drunk, continued to bind Tristan to Iseult."

As the causal mechanism in this version of medieval courtly love, the philter thus becomes for Proust any stimulus that activates a physical response and thereby disposes an individual to search for love. In other words, we cannot understand the onset of love without considering our immersion in the realm of matter. Because Charlus' ideal of manliness pretends to have no basis in physical attraction, Proust condemns his homosexuality as dishonest and delusory. Though Marcel admires Saint-Loup tremendously, he harbors the same doubts about his behavior. A great lord steeped in heroic traditions that have formed his personality, Saint-Loup manifests the ideal of military comradeship and eventually gives his life for his men. Yet he never sees that he is repeating Charlus' mania about virility, and he too deceives himself into thinking that his noble sentiments exist totally independent of physical desire.

Proust's conception of the relationship between love and sexuality best appears in a passage that does not seem to be talking about love at all. Having taken an interest in the sons of Mme de Surgis, Charlus cultivates the mother's company. He enjoys the way she incorporates the charms of her children, "much as a portrait which does not itself excite desires may nevertheless nourish, by means of the aesthetic admiration it causes, desires it awakens." So too, Proust thinks that love nourishes sexual interests without which it could not be understood, though love itself cannot be reduced to sex.

At the same time Proust also insists that love for a particular person can occur prior to any erotic interest in that person. This is what happens to Swann. Until he falls in love with Odette, he feels no antecedent desire for her. She is not his type, not the kind of woman he is used to pursuing for sexual purposes. Having had a great many love affairs, he can begin this one in medias res—as if it too had been caused by a physical mechanism. As a matter of fact, Swann's love originates from his desire to love "for the pleasure of it"; and with the help of memory, suggestion, and imagination he causes the chanson d'amour already engraven in him to play itself out.

Sex has this secondary role in Proust's conception because he approaches it (and love in general) as part of man's search for reality. Swann, Marcel, and the other would-be lovers are described as persons who turn their sexual instincts into antennae that reach for the inner being of whatever object awakens their interest. The question that pervades his work is: how much of the resulting experience can be accepted as intuition that actually reveals reality, and how much depends upon subjective and distorting properties of the probing device which is sexual love?

This way of formulating problems about love occurs at the very beginning of *A la recherche*. In the fourth paragraph of *Swann's Way* Marcel describes a recurrent dream of passion. The woman who looms within his sleeping consciousness has been created by an awkward position of his body, just as Eve was born from Adam's rib. "Herself caused by the pleasure I was about to enjoy, I imagined it was she who offered that pleasure to me. My body, feeling my own warmth penetrating hers, wanted to unite with her." If the woman resembles someone Marcel has known in life, he resolves to devote the future to finding her again. As we eventually learn in the course of the narrative, he never meets the girl of his dreams. But from the start, we know that the endeavor will be fruitless. Proust mentions two paramount difficulties: memory is short-lived (Marcel quickly forgets the woman), and anyhow dreams contain a fascination that can never be duplicated with a real person.

Within his dream Marcel experiences what Proust believes that all men want—a joyous intensity without which life is meaningless. As far as the dream itself is concerned, Marcel's feelings are completely realized and wholly expressed. But a dream is only a small part of one's life, and what is sufficient in the former may be inadequate for the latter. While he is dreaming, Marcel thinks his joyous feeling has been evoked by an independently existent woman and he is prepared to sacrifice everything to search for her identity. But once he is awake and outside the dream, once he is able to reflect about it with some detachment, he recognizes that the entire experience is a figment of erotic fantasy. Powerful as his feeling was, and fully consummated within his dream, it nevertheless was based on illusion. Veridical intuitions, appropriate feelings about other people, are not of this sort. They are directed toward realities, not phantoms.

❋

This questioning of the sexual object, this attempt to determine the authenticity of one's emotional involvement with it, is basic to Proust's investigation. The procedure recurs in all the love affairs he considers. But it is not always apparent to the lovers themselves and that enables Proust to distinguish between different phases of love. In several places he discusses a fundamental change in the attitude of men as they mature. While the child or adolescent (or in general the youth who has seen little of the world) continues to seek love as a means of penetrating the reality of another person, the older man—Swann, for instance—despairs of the enterprise and falls in love with someone who will satisfy his needs at that moment of his life. In the first stage "what we seek in love is the Absolute"; in the second stage "we have learned more about life and are more self-centered in our search for happiness."

I have spoken of these as different stages because Proust defines them by reference to the inexperience of a young man and the worldly-wise maneuvers of an older one. Actually, the two attitudes are phases that occur within each love affair Proust describes, though with varying strength and a shifting emphasis. Those critics who complain that all the love affairs in Proust are really a single one repeated over and over ignore the enormous differences between the phases as well as the significant diversity of their combination. If we trace the affairs of the narrator, for instance, we find a continual development beginning with the dominance of the first stage and ending with variations on the dominance of the second. What each stage contributes to the quality of love is never the same on all occasions.

Throughout his walks on the Méséglise way, Marcel was looking for a woman he could enjoy as an external reality rather than as a figment of his dreams, a woman native to this soil and therefore capable of objectifying it for him, a woman who would gratify his desires without reducing them to the merely physical. The child never encounters this petite paysanne and eventually he despairs of ever finding someone like her. Even if such a girl were to appear, he fears she would reject his overtures as those of a madman. He ceases to believe that there is in other persons anything coherent with or corresponding to his own erotic desire, anything that would enable him to appreciate the reality of the other person by means of his ardent feelings. If this is so, he can never hope to express his emotions adequately and his desires must arise within himself as deceptive emanations of his own temperament. "They no longer had any connection with nature, with reality, which thenceforth lost all charm and all significance and meant no more to my life than a purely conventional frame, just as the plot of a novel is framed by the railway carriage on a seat of which a traveller is reading it in order to kill time." Through this early experience—or rather inexperience—of hoped-for love, the narrator thus enunciates the theme of lost time. For Proust it means alienation from one's surroundings and the living of a life that affords no determinate means of intuiting reality or expressing one's feelings authentically.

As against Marcel's despair, there remains the irony of someone having offered herself without his realizing it. This is Gilberte, whom Marcel meets for the first time while admiring the hawthorns in Swann's park. The hawthorns, like the Méséglise way, symbolize reality. The hedge Marcel discovers shortly before seeing Gilberte is said to burst forth with the festive spirit of nature itself. Yet he feels a characteristic uneasiness: "the sentiment awakened in me remained obscure and vague, seeking in vain to free itself, to graft itself upon the flowers themselves." At this point Gilberte appears, a human embodiment of the place who feels toward Marcel desires reciprocal to his own. She makes a gesture of invitation to him, but he misinterprets it—as he learns in later life—and so he cannot use her to express his feelings. When, a few pages later, Marcel must return to Paris, he bursts into tears as he says farewell to his beloved hawthorns. He is weeping for both his separation from nature and his failure to have found a means of overcoming it.

Despite the fact that the narrator has informed us that his experiences on the Méséglise way immediately led to metaphysical despair, the first stage continues for quite a while longer. When Bloch introduces him to houses of prostitution, Marcel feels a resurgence of his earlier quest. Bloch convinces him that all women are amenable to sexual suggestion, that his desires are neither uncommon nor delusory, that (at least in principle) reality conforms to them and can be appropriated by means of them. But experience with prostitutes does not satisfy Marcel, and Proust is very explicit about the inferiority of this kind of relationship. As something fully determined in advance, sexual intercourse with a prostitute fails to stimulate the imagination. A woman is not even sexually exciting unless she can induce some unforeseen gesture, like Swann's in offering to arrange the cattleyas on Odette's bosom. This kind of behavior seeks much more than physical possession. It is a creative response to a situation that involves another person, another life, not just another piece of manageable flesh. When Marcel learns this, he finds that his interest in women's bodies becomes subordinate to something else—an interest in their souls.

At this time Marcel is also engaged in the unhappy relationship with Gilberte. His involvement with her still belongs to the first stage of love. It serves to carry out—or in the psychiatric sense, to "act out"—Marcel's fantasies on the Méséglise way. In his love for the Gilberte of the Champs-Elysées Marcel attempts to redeem his lost moment with the little girl among the hawthorns in Swann's park. But just as he initially misconstrued Gilberte's invitation, so too he now mistakes the nature of her friendliness toward him. To her he is just a playmate. This is the reality of their situation, but he cannot accept it. His will to love leads him to expect something different from Gilberte, and from himself. Unable to believe that her life can be separate from his own, he has chosen Gilberte as the means of objectifying his feelings. It is characteristic of this "first love," however, that Marcel is not aware of having *chosen* anything. For him at this stage, love is predestined and objectively determined.

Certain that his love for Gilberte must be a preordained necessity, Marcel thinks it is something over which he has no control. He feels he is *fated* to love her, made for that purpose. He still assumes that love enables one to make contact with the independent reality of the beloved. For if he is destined to love Gilberte, she cannot be a figment of his imagination like the woman in his dreams. She must be a person who was created to love him just as he was created to love her. Is not "true love" always reciprocal? And since "love existed in reality outside of us," it had to develop in an orderly progression which could not be altered by the participants: the lovers must exchange vows, declare their mutual devotion, and open their hearts naively rather than feigning indifference for the sake of attaching the other more securely.

Marcel's experience with Gilberte liberates him from the first stage of love. In renouncing her even as a friend, he gives up the belief that love can be pre-existent in any sense. After repeated frustrations, he realizes that the Gilberte he loved, the girl he experienced in his thoughts and feelings, was not the same as the Gilberte who frequented the Champs-Elysées and lived in the house off the Bois de Boulogne. The latter was a real girl who had a being separate from Marcel's. The girl he loved was a fiction he had fabricated in order to have someone to love. Marcel's final detachment from Gilberte occurs after he notices her walking on the Champs-Elysées with what he takes to be a young man. Some readers have wondered how this apparently innocent promenade could strike the deathblow to Marcel's affection. It is indeed baffling until we realize that for Marcel the view of Gilberte strolling at nightfall with another person proves that their interests are not congruent and that their lives do not coincide. This makes love between him and Gilberte impossible.

By the time Marcel reaches Balbec and settles into the shade of the jeunes filles en fleurs, he has moved beyond the first stage. Proust prepares us for the change in a transitional sequence on the train. Traveling to Balbec, Marcel notices a laitière, a milkmaid, who is selling coffee at a small station in the mountains. As he watches her walk along the platform, Marcel experiences the kind of sensation he felt on the Méséglise way. If anything, his incipient love is stronger since he never had the hoped-for paysanne before him whereas now he actually sees a girl who seems to embody the charm of the countryside which she inhabits. In feeling a powerful impulse to spend hour after hour with her, to enter into country life through intimate association with this young woman, Marcel responds as he had on all the occasions we have already discussed.

But there is also a difference. In the midst of his lived experience, not merely from the narrator's subsequent point of view, Marcel knows that his love may very well have been caused by conditions that have little to do with the external existence of the laitière—for instance, the fact that he was more excitable than usual, his habit of sleeping late having been interrupted by the stopping of the train. The issue is left in doubt: "Whether my exaltation had been caused by this girl, or else had it itself caused most of the pleasure I felt in being close to her, in any event she was so completely involved in my pleasure that my desire to see her again was above all the human wish not to let this state of excitement perish entirely, not to be forever separated from the being who had participated in it, even if she did so unawares."

Since the matter can remain unresolved, there must still be in Marcel the continued presence of the first stage. But his willingness to admit the alternate possibility, his capacity to accept love despite his doubts about its objective determination, already takes him into the second stage.

In this stage the lover no longer seeks the absolute. He has lived enough in the world to recognize that love is, as Proust now calls it, "a subjective sensation." Having attempted to use love as the means of communing with other persons, and having failed each time, the lover turns inward. He has learned what gives him pleasure in human relations, and he devotes himself to getting it. The lover renounces his former interest in the secret reality of his beloved. He has come to realize the hazards in searching for another's being. He readjusts his sights as a way of avoiding frustration and achieving satisfaction for himself. Love thus becomes a medium for arousing sexual and poetic sensations that are cultivated for their own sake, not for the sake of any metaphysical goal external to themselves. In the second stage the Proustian lover, expecting much less of the world, has the appearance of greater maturity but he is also subject to greater egoism. He resembles the undaunted roué in the anecdote about a woman who protests that she can never give him her heart. "Ah, Madame," the man replies, "I never aspired that high."

Being a state of lesser aspiration, the second stage leaves the lover free for limitless experimentation. If the beloved is merely a device for satisfying one's impulses, any number of women may be suitable. This is what Marcel gleans from his experience with the girls at Balbec. In a very real sense, he is in love with them all, as a group. His attention eventually focuses on Albertine, but in a purely haphazard manner. It might just as well have been directed toward Andrée, as it intermittently is. Once he realizes this, Marcel finds that he cannot feel for Albertine what he had felt for Gilberte. For if Andrée—or even someone outside the little group, like Mme de Stermaria—can equally perform Albertine's function, there is nothing necessary or predestined about his attraction to either.

In the midst of his "grand amour" for Albertine, Marcel does think they were made for each other. But it is a different kind of love from what he experienced with Gilberte. For one thing, he no longer senses the importance of declaring his ardent feelings. With Gilberte he assumed that lyrical outbursts were an essential element in the development of love. But if love is not predetermined, it has no necessary progression. If, far from being an "external reality," love is only a "subjective pleasure," one can never be sure how the beloved will respond to one's declaration. In fact the lover might be better able to snare the woman into the system of his amorous desires by pretending *not* to care about her. This is what Marcel considers most expedient as his love for Albertine increases. And so begins the history of calculated deception which pervades their excruciating affair.

I have spoken of the two stages as simultaneous phases, complementarities, within a relationship. So much is this the case that the drama in the Proustian narrative consists less in the temporal succession from stage to stage than in the conflict between them at every moment. Even after the second stage has been reached and Marcel decides that his love for Albertine is purely subjective, he feels vestiges of the earlier condition. They manifest themselves when Albertine first invites him to her room at Balbec. He suddenly thinks that love is "not only external, but also realizable." While the real Gilberte was different from the Gilberte he dreamt of loving, he now feels that Albertine as he has come to know her might really be the same as the Albertine his erotic interests have imaginatively created. In loving Albertine, Marcel would thus be satisfying a subjective need at the same time as he directly communicated with the objective, independent existence which is the being of another person. So thoroughly is Marcel enthralled by this possibility that the sight of Albertine in her room awakens a rapture that briefly destroys his usual feelings of isolation. With a sense of cosmic merging that borders on intoxication, he locates the reality of nature no longer in a separate, unattainable world but in the torrent of his own sensations. The visual apprehension of Albertine's uncovered neck "had broken the equilibrium between the immense and indestructible life which now reverberated through my being and the life of the universe, so meager in comparison. . . . Life was not outside of me, it was within."

When Albertine bursts the bubble by repelling Marcel's advances and ringing for the servants, he recognizes that his experience was delusional, just another dream like the one at the beginning of *Swann's Way*. While his ecstasy existed, however, it was not the second phase alone which determined Marcel's emotional response. He was not putting on an act for the sake of satisfying personal desires. Nor should the subjectivistic language with which he describes his excitement lead us to think that oneness with nature was less important to him than savoring his own sensations. On the contrary, his transport illustrates precisely the kind of communication with reality that he had sought on the Méséglise way. It is not by accident that Marcel sees Albertine next to a window that discloses the ocean at Balbec, together with its cliffs and surrounding valleys. In embracing Albertine, he hopes to touch more deeply than ever before the objective being which shows itself in this particular landscape. To experience love here, in the midst of Balbec and through intimacy with Albertine, is both to commune with nature as she embodies it and also to penetrate her independent selfhood by locating it in its natural environment.

When Marcel later succeeds in making love to Albertine, he does so in Paris, not Balbec, in the secluded room where he takes his comfort and acts the invalid, not by a window overlooking the sea. But the first phase, the initial stage in love, still continues. Remarking once again that his love could just as easily have been directed toward Mme de Stermaria as toward Albertine, Marcel reminds himself that "it was not therefore—as I nevertheless so greatly desired, needed to believe—absolutely necessary and predestined." Throughout the miseries which define his liaison with Albertine, the two phases interact within Marcel's personality. They cause what Proust calls "ce rythme binaire" which constitutes Marcel's alternation between tenderness and hostility. As long as Marcel can relax within the first phase, he allows himself to believe that he really loves Albertine. This being so, he feels that his sentiments must have the special relation with the being of a beloved that could only subsist if she too were in love with him. Marcel's desperate need to love and to be loved in return then issues into spontaneous demonstrations of affection as the pendulum touches one of its termini.

No sooner does it do so, however, than it swings toward the opposite extreme. The second phase replaces the first. Marcel now despairs of his ability to love or be loved. He cannot forget that the same hopes and anxieties have been aroused in him by any number of other women. His imagination having invented the same romances and concocted the same speeches for use with one woman after another, how can he believe in the authenticity of his amorous responses? Why think that his sentiments bring him into relation with a particular person as she is in herself? It now seems to him much more likely that the woman he loves has been fashioned as the artifact of his erotic craving. If so, his feelings cannot put him in direct communication with her; they bypass her, splatter and circumvent her, as the surf does when it breaks against the rocks. But if Albertine is "a mere accident" placed before the flux of Marcel's desires, how can he be anything else for her? And without the sense of reciprocity he dare not declare his tenderness. The fear and shame of neither truly loving nor really being loved force him to act with hostility and deception, to dominate and to hurt.

Only in Marcel's love affairs are the phases described as interacting stages within an individual's development. Above all, the relationship with Albertine achieves a thematic complexity that is not present in the other affairs. In each of them, even l'amour de

Swann, the two phases have been telescoped, intermixed rather than analyzed separately. The affairs of Swann and Odette, Saint-Loup and Rachel, Charlus and Morel, Jean Santeuil and Madame S—— are constructed out of the same elements as Marcel's experience with Albertine, but without a comparable unfolding in time. Describing Jean Santeuil's love, Proust clearly indicates that this youthful adventure belongs to the second stage as well as the first. The same is true of Saint-Loup's involvement with Rachel. In the affairs of Swann and Charlus, however, we are confronted with mature men whose love is mainly of the second type though also influenced by residues of the first. These differences of emphasis contribute to the variegated texture of Proust's work. They also illuminate from different angles the philosophic principles that underlie it. All of the Proustian lovers desperately *want* to accept the possibility of idealist, Romantic love. Consequently, each of them is caught in the same dilemma as the older Marcel, though only he comes to understand that it is a dilemma. They all feel the lure of the absolute—the need to effect through love a metaphysical merging with the being of another person. Yet love is always shown to be a subjective phenomenon that they themselves create but finally destroy because they can no longer believe in its objectivity.

As we have seen repeatedly, the idealist tradition considers love a solution to cognitive as well as affective problems: since it is a merging with another person, the experience of love enables lovers to acquire knowledge about one another. The burden of Proust's critique consists in his proof that such aspirations are wholly ungrounded. To the extent that love is desire, he argues, it reflects the needs of the organism that has this desire. It therefore lacks cognitive validity, much as the dreaming state does. To the extent that love can be directed toward many different persons, whom one may desire indiscriminately, it cannot give access to the individuality in any of them. Since it is not predestined but rather results from variable conditions in one's life, love can never attain the absolute. The second stage is therefore closer to the truth than the first, and Marcel's progression from one to the other reveals an increase in wisdom. In aging, he learns how to emancipate himself from what Proust considered the deceptiveness in idealist theories of love.

As I have said, Proust always makes his critique by beginning with assumptions that both he and his audience have inherited. Love having been defined by various Romantics as sympathetic identification by means of imagination, Proust argues that it is precisely the element of imagination which makes both sympathy and identification impossible in love. He never doubts that Shelley, for instance, is right in seeing the dependency of love upon imagination. But he reaches negative and subjectivistic conclusions contrary to Shelley's by insisting upon the unreliability of imaginative processes. His entire narrative is designed to prove that, far from enabling us to resonate with the independent being of another person, imagination subsumes the beloved within the lover's fantasies and personal needs. The prolonged efforts by which the lover seeks to understand what the beloved is like are constantly defeated by imagination, which distorts the particular qualities he or she may have. As opposed to observation or analysis, imagination prevents a lover from achieving the detachment needed to experience an object as it really is.

Proust's ideas about imagination may also be taken as a commentary upon those of Stendhal on crystallization. Like Stendhal, Proust is doubtful about the possibility of love at first sight. Both claim that imagination, unlike desire, takes time to develop. Desire can be excited instantly. It can be spontaneously elicited by a silhouette, an image, or even a name. This is the coup de foudre, the bolt out of the blue, but it is not yet love. Though in Stendhal crystallization may occur fairly quickly, Proust believes that it requires a long incubation before its imaginative chemistry can operate fully. Ideas, sentiments, memories must be processed over a considerable period of time in order to achieve the intensity that Proustian love demands.

Like Ovid and Andreas Capellanus, Stendhal had emphasized the importance of *difficulty* if love is to exist. He remarks that a woman who succumbs too readily may thereby prevent a man from making crystallizations needed for him to love her. Proust seizes upon this idea and uses it not only to show how love depends on imagination but also to prove that imagination introduces the falsifying element in love. The narrator's friend Saint-Loup is passionately in love with Rachel, an actress who keeps him at a distance and imposes frustrations that cause his imagination to spin at a feverish pace. She, however, has also worked as a prostitute in a brothel where Marcel had previously encountered her. Knowing that she could be had for a few francs, Marcel cannot feel love for her and neither can he understand how Saint-Loup or anyone else might be able to. The direct and easy relationship established by her selling her body is such as to deaden the imaginative response. But that is precisely what she cultivates in Saint-Loup merely by being aloof with him, difficult to attain. And as one who performs on stage, she participates in artistic activities that create new obstacles to accessibility and stimulate the imagination even further.

Emphasizing the role of difficulty, Proust even concludes that without it the imagination cannot bring love into being. It is necessary, he says, that "the imagination awakened by the incertitude of being able to attain its object, should create an end which hides its other end, which it does by substituting for the sexual pleasure the idea of penetrating into a life." As we have seen, Marcel's experience with prostitutes teaches him that enjoying the bodies of women cannot provide the sense of reality he sought in love, and therefore he directs himself toward their souls. Since love is for Proust, as it was for the Romantics, primarily a search for the innermost core of another person, it depends on this uncertain process of using the imagination to penetrate the life of the desired object. Like Stendhal, Proust employs the term "l'imprévu" to designate the unforeseen, unpredictable quality of another's being, and like Fichte he generally characterizes it as "l'inconnu," the unknown. Love is thus an imaginative effort—inevitably unsuccessful—to reach the unforeseen and unknown reality toward which our feelings direct us.

That is what Proust means when he speaks of love as a quest for "the absolute" in someone else. What he calls the absolute is itself the unknown substance of another person. As Fichte had defined love as the "desire for something altogether *unknown*, the existence of which is disclosed solely by the need of it," so too does Proust state: "All that love requires to be born is that we should believe that a being participates in an unknown life in which our love will enable us to penetrate." This explains Marcel's love for the abstract peasant of the Méséglise countryside and for the milkmaid he sees from the train. It also accounts for his interest in Gilberte, which arises from his wanting to enter the new and unknown literary life that he associates with the author Bergotte, who is a friend of hers. Love for Gilberte was thus a triangulated means of attaining two absolutes: hers and Bergotte's. Later on, Marcel is attracted to Albertine because he wishes to enter the unknown existence of the group of blossoming girls at the seashore. Though his infatuation with the Duchesse de Guermantes never achieves much intensity, it too results from the desire to penetrate a reality—the world of high society—from which Marcel had hitherto been excluded.

One might say that here Proust reveals the deficiency in his critique of love. For in describing love as an attempt to reach the being of another, is he not assuming that each person's reality is already hidden and that we live in isolated compartments which do not communicate with one another? But if that is what he presupposes, his attempt to prove that love is limited by our own subjective needs would scarcely seem to carry his argument beyond its own premises. If people cannot be merged because their beings are inevitably separate, why blame love for not effecting the impossible?

This kind of criticism misses the point in Proust's demonstration. For he is addressing himself to philosophies that consider love uniquely capable of *overcoming* the separation between human beings, thereby causing the interpenetration of their realities. Proust accepts this as an accurate account of what love wants to achieve. His critique is designed to show that the venture cannot succeed.

For one thing, Proust argues, the desire to penetrate another reality is also a desire to possess it. Seeking the unknown absolute in another person, the lover is always trying to capture it for himself. Proust uses terms suggestive of sexual behavior—"penetrate," "possess"—not only because he defines love as a product of erotic imagination, but also because he thinks the facts of sexuality reveal that true penetration and possession must always elude the lover. Even if a man has sexual intercourse with a woman, he has not penetrated *her* except in a trivial sense pertaining to male and female anatomy. "La possession physique," Proust remarks, is a condition in which no one really possesses anything. For by occupying a woman's body, even implanting seed that can possibly take root as impregnation and the furtherance of his own being, a man has not actually possessed the woman he fertilizes. If anything, Proust would say, she has taken possession of him, or at least of some part of him. But in the most important sense, neither possesses anything of the other. For no sexual act can deprive a person of his or her separateness.

The lovers in Proust all experience this "sad and senseless" need to possess other people. Swann is an art collector and he seeks to acquire Odette, in whom he sees a resemblance to Jephthro's daughter painted by Botticelli, as if she too were a work of art that one might collect. Marcel imprisons Albertine much as a man places a jewel in a vault to keep it from being stolen. Although the person one loves cannot be possessed, both Swann and Marcel (and all the others who exemplify love in Proust) invest a great deal of time and money as if they were dealing in commodities.

All such attempts fail to provide happiness or a sense of reality that would justify the emotional expenditure which is love—the Proustian beloved never really belongs to the lover. In each case the man (we rarely see women as lovers in Proust) loses on his investment. The woman's absolute forever eludes the lover, he never captures her soul whatever he may do to her body, and she generally deceives him with other men or women as a way of proving to herself that she is not for sale even though she takes money from this man. And since imagination feeds on obstacles, Proustian lovers never attain a condition of security, or even stability, in their love affairs. Rearing ever greater difficulties in the pursuit of an impossible goal, imagination deludes lovers about the object they truly want. "My love for Albertine was only a passing form of my devotion to youth," Marcel says in one place, and elsewhere he remarks that his interest in various mistresses made sense only as a reflection of his love for his mother. Sexual love results from this kind of transference effected through the insatiable imagination. In general "the most exclusive love for a person is always love for something else." Being based on so little awareness of what the lover ultimately desires, love for a particular man or woman is sure to founder.

As persons who elicit erotic imagination by being difficult and perpetually elusive, the loved ones in Proust are always what he calls "êtres de fuite" (beings of flight). They are loved, he says, *because* they are elusive. Assuming that "one only loves that which is not totally possessed," he infers that one can only love by pursuing the inaccessible. As Freud had said that a woman should expect to lose her lover on the day that she marries him, so too does Proust maintain that even if one could have possession of another, it would mean the destruction of one's love for that person. For in the state of complete possession the lover—like the gods in Plato—can no longer desire anything or imagine gratifications beyond those immediately given. But then love is no longer possible. Time and again Proust shows how even desire is caused by the play of imagination. Far from being wholly instinctual, sexual impulse results from imagination presenting to the organism objects for it to seek. There would be neither desire nor love if possession could occur.

Love depends on imagination in other ways as well. Proust remarks that Swann is eager to make sacrifices for Odette because he knows that others will take them as signs of the passionate love affair he is having. His imagination idealizes love to the point where it becomes self-justifying regardless of the pain and humiliation to which it leads. And in fact, Swann in love experiences a great development of his imagination. He not only sees Odette as a Florentine painting, but he also finds a meaning in art—as when he reflects about "la petite phrase" in Vinteuil's music—that he would not have discovered otherwise.

For the most part, however, Proust insists that love's dependence upon the imagination merely leads to increased suffering. Love cannot succeed in its search for possession; it cannot penetrate to another's unknown being; and therefore its incidental goodness must always be outweighed by its failure as feeling or emotion. Nor are these failings extraneous to it. When the Duchesse de Guermantes laments that Swann should have fallen in love with so worthless a creature as Odette, Proust comments that "it is as if one would be surprised that a patient should deign to undergo cholera given him by so petty a thing as a bacillus." While denying that love is predestined in the Romantic fashion, Proust nevertheless thinks it follows a preestablished pattern, just as susceptibility to a disease will result in one attack after another.

The metaphysical disease which is Proustian love may renew itself with different objects of affection but it always evolves in a consecutive and predictable manner. Proust suggests that for each lover the loved ones are usually the same type of person because otherwise the imagination could not fit them into the system of drives and aspirations that motivated the lover in the first place. If only for this reason the lover's search for the unknown must always miscarry. His subjective needs prevent him from seeing the truth about his beloved, even when it is obvious to everyone else. Only after Marcel no longer loves Albertine does he begin to learn things about her that had remained hidden to him before. The blindness of lovers partly results from the fact that all the world conspires to conceal the damaging evidence that lovers try to uncover. But more essentially, Proust tells us, their inflamed and infected imagination keeps them in the dark.

As we have already seen, Stendhal also depicted sexual love as delusion and even madness. He did so, however, in the context of recommending love as a noncognitive attitude that can be justified on the basis of the happiness it provides. Proust's approach is radically different. Though he recognizes the noncognitive elements in love—all of them resulting from the imagination—he thinks they inevitably undermine love's primary mission, the attempt to penetrate another's reality. And since the outcome must always be diseased, Proustian love provides very little happiness and a great deal of pain. It is what Baudelaire called "an oasis of horror in a desert of boredom," its momentary joys arising from a world of emptiness and issuing into a nightmare of mental anguish.

The genesis of love, as Proust describes it, is itself usually a state of suffering. For that is what gets the erotic imagination started. When Marcel feels slighted by Gilberte the first time he sees her, he instantly begins both to hate and to love her. When Swann is disappointed after expecting to find Odette at the Verdurins, his hurt feelings give a strong impulsion to his love. Step by step, Proust shows love beginning and developing as an expression of inter-personal agony, which perpetuates itself like a sore one rubs uncon-trollably. This is not the only way that love exists in Proust. He recognizes that it can also result from pleasure—for instance, the joy that Marcel gets from the Duchesse de Guermantes' unexpected smile. And in fact, Marcel's love for her remains devoid of much suffering. But neither does it issue into a grand passion.

In literature prior to Proust, lovers generally suffered either because the world would not tolerate their private and ecstatic merging or else because their personalities—their characters, their ideals, their individual desires—conflicted in one respect or another. Proust's analysis of love is more extreme and much more negative. It maintains that by its very nature love is basically a state of suffering. Having been caused by difficulties, love must always be painful. Since the lover tries to overcome the insurmountable and relies upon imagination that creates cognitive distortions, he and his beloved perpetually misunderstand each other. Their love can only induce reverberating anguish in them both.

At an even deeper level, the lovers in Proust suffer because of a constant fear that they are not being loved in return. Rather than encouraging them to look elsewhere in the hope of finding recipro-cated love, their fear intensifies their passionate need for the other person and prevents them from liberating themselves. Stendhal mentioned a "second crystallization" in which the lover finally believes that the woman he considers perfect also loves him. For Stendhal the happiness of love depended on this more than on any previous stage in its development. But Proustian lovers never undergo the second crystallization. We are never shown, and Proust never analyzes, a reciprocal relationship in which both persons use their feeling and imagination to merge or unite effectively with one another. The beings in flight would seem to be fleeing this most of all. The consequence can only be suffering for those who love them.

Such suffering is inescapable, Proust believes, because true reciprocity cannot exist. "When we love," he says, "the love is too great to be contained within us; it radiates toward the person loved, encounters in her a surface that arrests it, forcing it to return to its point of departure, and it is this rebound of our own tenderness that we call the other's feelings and that charms us more than its going forth, since we do not recognize that it comes from us."

Since Proust describes love as a hopeless desire to possess another person, one might say that he believes the suffering of love is ultimately based upon the lover's feeling that absolute possession is really impossible. But while Proust implies this, he also argues that passionate love involves jealousy and that jealous suffering is the fear that the beloved is being possessed by someone else. So great is the agony this causes that the lovers in Proust are generally willing to accept the fact that the beloved does not love them if only they can be sure that no other man or woman is possessing her. And yet, jealousy makes the beloved more desirable to the Proustian lover. Marcel reports that Albertine seemed less and less pretty to him until he had reason to think that others found her attractive. His possessive need to keep her away from all possible rivals makes her more interesting to him, not only because he sees her as a woman who awakens desire but also because his anxiety about other lovers intensifies his emotional involvement.

At the same time that Marcel is undergoing his miseries of jealous possessiveness, he himself engages in promiscuous lovemaking with other women. From this we may infer that it is himself, or people like himself, that he really distrusts and considers unworthy of the ultimate merging that he has presumably been seeking all along. Swann's jealousy is also based on insecurity about himself as a lover. He is afraid that Odette "would experience with Forcheville and others maddening pleasures that she had never known with him and which his jealousy created out of nothing." In a similar fashion, Marcel is tormented by the fear that with her female lovers Albertine enjoys pleasures he himself can hardly conceive.

In being a combination of possessive hopes and jealous fears, pleasure mingled with suffering generated from within, Proustian love may easily be interpreted as unconscious hatred—or at least, as a mixture of hatred and love. Even characters like Aunt Léonie and her servant Françoise are presented as both hating and loving each other, often loving when they seem to hate and hating when they seem to love. Though the same can be said about all of the lovers in Proust, one rarely finds them expressing *strong* hatred or a powerful desire to inflict pain. Even in the acts of sadomasochism to which Charlus submits, he is whipped by men who feel kindly toward him and merely wish to accommodate his whim.

In saying this, I do not wish to deny that Proust portrays love as a kind of sadism. Though not usually violent or explicitly hostile, sadistic motivation underlies the lovers' attempts to possess as well as the beloveds' tactics in eluding possession. It appears in Odette's routine handling of Swann. Her experience with men like him leads her to believe that she can ignore Swann's impassioned complaints about her conduct since those who make such complaints must be in love, and if so, one has no reason to heed their feelings—they will be even more ensnared if one does not. Though she knows Swann anxiously awaits her return to Paris, she does not inform him that she is back. His sadism in wanting to control her would seem to justify, in her eyes, a reciprocal cruelty in manipulating his affections.

This much of love-as-hatred Proust could well have derived from various Romantics or post-Romantics, such as Nietzsche in his assertion that Carmen reveals the true character of love better than Parsifal. But more than anyone who preceded him, Proust emphasizes the extent to which the lover's behavior is also masochistic. He portrays Swann as a man who is ready and willing to undergo a passionate love affair that will make him suffer. Swann does not seem to mind being jealous. We are even told that he is less interested in escaping the pain of his anxieties about Odette's deceitfulness than in avoiding the boring effort to find out whether she is really betraying him. When he notices the enlargement of a tumor in his body, he accepts it calmly. Like the character in Proust's early short story "The Death of Baldassare Silvande," he finds life easier to live if one submits to the comforting limitations of being (or acting like) an invalid. At the end of *A la recherche* Marcel asks Gilberte to introduce him to girls who will make him suffer, as if this was all that mattered in his previous love for Albertine and others. Proust comments that love has "virtually only a single utility, to make unhappiness possible." We have travelled a hundred and eighty degrees from Stendhal.

Part of the logic in Marcel's request to Gilberte is explained by the character Bergotte, the great author. The young girls who permit him to become intimate with them do so in order to get money out of him. Bergotte tells the narrator this, but then he adds that though he suffers from their behavior he uses the girls as material for his novels and thus makes much more money than they ever cost. On the assumption that one learns most from suffering, Marcel believes that it will better help him to write his masterpiece than if Gilberte provided girls who made him happy. And indeed, the novel we have just been reading expresses everything the narrator has discovered about love by means of his amatory sufferings together with his reflections about the sufferings of Swann and other characters.

For Proust the justification of passionate love thus turns out to be its ability to teach us that love of other persons must be futile. Without the experience of love we could not have known that it leads to suffering rather than happiness, and to delusion rather than merging with another's being. When Stendhal described the presence of suffering in love, he saw it as a tonic component within a joyful enterprise—much as Shakespeare's Cleopatra refers to the lover's pinch "which hurts, and is desired." But more than Stendhal, Proust is sensitive to the unbearable pain of love, based as it is upon an impossible striving for possession and eventuating in miseries of jealousy that no incidental pleasures can ever outweigh. On the other hand, Proust does not minimize the utility of love: not only does it instruct Marcel about the limitations of human nature, but also it provides Swann with vivid, albeit unhappy, experiences that make life meaningful for him. In the emptiness of his normally wasted existence, Swann's love affair is the greatest thing that has ever happened to him. If only by stimulating his imagination, the disease of loving Odette rejuvenates his interest in art and helps him to return to his unfinished book on Vermeer.

As we shall see, Marcel's erotic failures culminate, in a parallel fashion, with his discovery of essences. Put to such employment, the experience of love can be useful for resolving problems about the nature of feeling. But in itself passionate love, and in general the love of persons, is not an ideal that Proust finds even partially defensible. In words that are reminiscent of Lucretius or Schopenhauer or all the other sages who prescribed ascetic remedies for love, Proust asserts: "The more the desire advances, the further real possession recedes. So that if happiness, or at least absence of suffering, can be found, it is not satisfaction, but rather extinction of the desire, that one must seek. We try to see the one we love; but we should do our best not to see her, since forgetfulness alone brings about the extinction of the desire."

Proust's critique of passionate love has been attacked in various ways. In *Being and Nothingness* Sartre criticizes what he considers to be Proust's "intellectualistic" mode of analysis. He sees Proust as one who follows associationist psychologists and empiricists such as John Stuart Mill in their attempt "to find bonds of rational causality between psychic states in the temporal succession of these states." Since Sartre believes that consciousness is a whole that consists of interpenetrating psychic processes, he rejects Proust's approach to love on the grounds that it mechanistically seeks causal connections between feelings or mental states that in fact have no such relation to one another. Neither love, nor any other conscious phenomenon, Sartre insists, can be understood if it is analyzed as Proust does.

Sartre illustrates what he takes to be Proust's methodology by quoting a passage from *Swann's Way*. I reproduce part of it, retaining the italics that Sartre adds: "As soon as Swann could picture (Odette) to himself without revulsion . . . and as soon as *the desire to take her away from everyone else was no longer added to his love by jealousy,* that love *became* again a taste for the sensations which Odette's person gave him. . . . And this pleasure different from all other *had ended by creating in him a need of her,* which she alone could assuage by her presence or her letters. . . . Thus *by the very chemistry of his affliction,* after having *created jealousy out of his love,* he began to *manufacture tenderness,* pity for Odette."

Sartre believes that Proust is trying to understand the fluctuations in Swann's feelings by treating them as elements that succeed one another within a causal and mechanistic system. Sartre considers this procedure faulty because the components of consciousness do not lend themselves to chemical analysis as if they were bits of matter. Psychic states cannot "create" or "manufacture" or "add" anything in relation to each other, he says. They are not separate agents that can then be connected in a causal sequence. What holds for human beings in their totality does not apply to states of jealousy, pleasure, desire, or love. Consequently, Proust has explained nothing: "How does jealousy 'add' to love the 'desire to take her away from everyone else'? . . . And how does love *manufacture* that jealousy which in return will add to love the desire to take Odette away from everyone else?"

I think Sartre is correct in suggesting that Proust wishes to do more than merely illustrate the variations within Swann's experience. As Sartre suggests, Proust is trying to explain how it is that a lover's experience can undergo an oscillation between jealousy and tenderness. It is also true that Proust speaks (metaphorically) of the "chemistry" of Swann's affliction because he wants to align the analysis of psychological states with analyses in the natural sciences. But it does not follow that Proust's approach is therefore mechanistic or guilty of treating feelings and motivations as if they were "animated agents" existing in separation from one another. For that would mean that Proust thought of material phenomena in that fashion. As a matter of fact, however, he continually shows how body and mind each expresses the other without either being analyzable into self-sufficient elements.

Proust's analysis of love requires a different reading from the one that Sartre imposes upon it. Though Proust deals with jealousy, revulsion, possessiveness, pleasure, tenderness as events that constitute love through their interaction with one another, his approach is not mechanistic. In order to prove that we are misled when we think of love as if it were a single entity, a constant and uniform affection that binds one person to another, a kind of white light unsullied by impurities, Proust analyzes the whiteness to prove that it contains within it a vast spectrum of varying and even conflicting hues that idealist writers had often ignored at their peril. "For what we suppose to be our love, our jealousy are," Proust says, "neither of them, single, continuous and individual passions. They are composed of an infinity of successive loves, of different jealousies, each of which is ephemeral, although by their uninterrupted multitude they give us the impression of continuity, the illusion of unity. The life of Swann's love, the fidelity of his jealousy, were formed out of death, of infidelity, of innumerable desires, innumerable doubts, all of which had Odette for their object."

If Proust had indeed subscribed to mechanistic psychology as Sartre thinks, he would not have referred to an "infinity" of loves, or "innumerable" doubts and desires. He would instead have demarcated elemental states distinct from one another. He does not do so because he is primarily concerned to demonstrate that love has no unitary being, that the idea of its essential unity is an illusion. This is the point of his analysis. It shows itself in his thinking about "l'intermittence du coeur" (the inconsistency of the heart, in the sense of inexplicable cessation and recurrence of feeling). For a long period after his grandmother dies, the narrator feels guilty because he undergoes so little grief and even forgets her. When the memory of the grandmother as someone who mattered greatly to him returns, suddenly and unpredictably, he concludes that love exists only as an intermittent, sporadic occurrence composed of diverse responses—including forgetfulness—that interact within it. These are not separable elements, but their variable configuration indicates that love has no single or continuous uniformity.

The relationship between Swann and Odette, or Marcel and Albertine, or any of the other lovers, progresses as it does because the heart operates not only intermittently but also in accordance with psychological patterns that Proust analyzes. As long as Albertine is an elusive being, Marcel wishes to attain her inner absolute, to penetrate and possess it. Out of this attitude there arises his emotional and sexual interest in her, eventuating in jealousy and therefore in massive suffering that outweighs all moments of pleasure. Once he feels, however mistakenly, that he possesses her, he begins to take her for granted: his responses become habitual and boring, and his passion diminishes correspondingly. Far from being a uniform experience, love is the succession of these oscillating feelings which are not identical for all lovers and do not fit together as causal units. Nevertheless there is an isomorphic development in all occasions of love, just as different patients will undergo similar stages of the same disease. Throughout this analysis Proust is looking for laws of nature, what he calls "the laws of love," that govern the recurrent patterns. His generalizations may be faulty but his approach need not be considered mechanistic.

From a totally different point of view, Proust's thinking about love has also been attacked as merely a reflection of his own homosexual orientation. Writing in a medical journal, one critic says: "Under the name of love, Marcel Proust described nothing but a guilty sexual inversion. Love as he understands it and as it is practiced by his heroes always presents homosexual characteristics: a fundamental narcissism, dissociation between tenderness and physical desire, morbid jealousy, absence of woman and permanence of the mother figure."

A statement of this sort implies not only that heterosexual love is basically different from homosexual love, but also that Proust's analysis of the former is modelled upon his experience of the latter in a way that distorts both. Instead of being a realistic portrayal that remedies the false pretensions of Romantic theory by providing a more factual and accurate account, the Proustian argument would thus involve the substituting of a very partial and limited perspective. In other words, it gives us an idealization that expresses and projects Proust's own homosexuality. Those who refer to what is sometimes called the "Albertine strategy" would seem to be reasoning in a comparable vein when they insist that Proust thought he could deal with heterosexual love merely by adding a feminine ending to the name of an Albert or Alfred he himself knew intimately.

In some respects, this type of criticism is legitimate—not because all homosexuals are alike or because there is a single something that can uniquely be called homosexual love, but rather because Proust's vision is so greatly dominated by problems that (male) homosexuals in Western society tend to experience more vividly than heterosexuals. There is nothing particularly homosexual about narcissism, or the split between tenderness and desire, or morbid jealousy, and so forth. But the combination of these characteristics, together with the special importance that his mother retains both for the narrator and for Proust himself, may be taken as grounds for describing the Proustian approach as a homosexual point of view. Though he occasionally portrays women in love, it is usually lesbian love and almost always presented in a schematic fashion quite different from the detailed introspection that Proust lavishes upon male lovers. For that matter, we learn very little about the experience of women who are loved by heterosexual men. As the elusive creatures of flight, they remain hidden and unknown beings whose reality Proust scarcely penetrates any more than do the lovers whose love consists in hopelessly seeking to possess them. Proust finds marriage inimical to passionate love, and in the context of his total perspective this too may be taken as characteristic of his own experience as a homosexual. One does not need to be a homosexual in order to have doubts about married love— think of Montaigne. But neither is it surprising when a homosexual of the sort that Proust was dismisses the possibility out of hand.

Having said all this, however, we must still determine whether Proust's critique is valid. Its being a homosexual conception proves nothing about its truthfulness or lack of it. To claim that Proust presents "nothing but" homosexual love begs the question, for it is entirely possible that a homosexual who writes from his own experience but is also a man of genius, as Proust was, can perceive truths about heterosexual love that may be inaccessible to those who participate in it. Moreover, Proust would surely claim that love retains an inner resemblance throughout the differences that separate homosexual and heterosexual attachments. If this is so, the heterosexual writer has no advantage as far as getting at the truth is concerned.

An alternate type of criticism takes the following form: whether or not Proust's homosexuality diminished his comprehension of heterosexual love, he was both psychologically and physically a sick man whose ailments prevented him from appreciating how others might achieve a healthy-minded love. In other words, Proust's asthmatic neuroses made it impossible for him to understand how normal men and women could have experiences different from his own. This kind of comment has been made by many critics in the last sixty-five years. We may readily discount it insofar as it takes the form of an ad hominem argument about Proust himself. But the fact remains that the narrator in *A la recherche* admits to being neurotic and recognizes that his own disabilities may have given him distorted perceptions of other people's behavior. The love affairs that he undergoes or observes are all based on mutual selfishness and deceit. Rousseau would have considered them examples of amour-propre, and Stendhal would have insisted that far from revealing the nature of passion-love, they illustrate the inferior condition he calls vanity-love. Not only does Proust admit no possibility of a second crystallization in which the lover believes that his affection is being reciprocated, but also he generally ignores the part of Stendhalian crystallization which discovers beauty or excellence in the beloved. Though the imagination of a Proustian lover has endless versatility for creating erotic bondage, only rarely does it result in perceiving the beloved as the embodiment of an ideal. In seeing Odette as someone out of Botticelli, Swann subsumes her within aesthetic categories that matter very much to him. But he does not find perfections in Odette herself. This aspect of crystallization being absent or minimal in Proust, Stendhal could very well have dismissed his analysis as largely irrelevant to passion-love.

Ortega y Gasset makes a similar point when he says, in one of the earliest testimonials to Proust's greatness as a novelist: "Proust describes Swann's love as something that has nothing like the form of love. All kinds of things can be found in it: touches of flaming sensuality, purple pigments of distrust, browns of habitual life, grays of vital fatigue. The only thing *not* to be found is love. It comes out just as the figure in a tapestry does, by the intersection of various threads, no one of which contains the form of the figure."

Ortega implies that the figure that appears in Proust's tapestry is not an adequate presentation of love. By extrapolating from Ortega's later writings, we may interpret him as meaning that the condition Proust depicts as love is only what Ortega calls "falling in love." For love itself to exist, Ortega believes, the lover must take a permanent interest in the welfare of the beloved, an interest based upon, and conducive to, knowledge of what she is in herself. If this is "the form of the figure," Proustian theory deals with nothing but the state of falling in love, which is a violent expression of need, a self-centered desire to possess whatever goods the beloved can provide, an obsession that dissipates once the lover realizes that his intense feelings have deluded him.

All such criticisms of Proust consist in the belief that his analysis is skewed toward a type of passion which does not represent love as a whole. Other kinds of passionate love, those that are more wholesome or benign, he seems to ignore completely. Even if Proust's investigation is realistic and precise with respect to the phenomena it takes as paradigmatic, his outlook would still remain too partial, too narrow, to support the philosophical conclusions he wishes to draw from it. Rather than concluding that love is always futile, he can make that claim only in relation to the sick and self-defeating types of love that his characters—particularly the narrator—experience throughout their lives. In the process of trying to possess Odette like a work of art that he is collecting, Swann defeats the possibility of loving her as a person. Marcel feels that he possesses Albertine when she is asleep, unconscious, but to that extent he loves her merely as a thing. Not everyone loves in this manner.

There are several ways in which Proust might answer criticism of this kind. He could maintain that falling in love, or something close to what Ortega means by that phrase, is more than just one among other types of sexual love. On the contrary, he would say, it is fundamental to them all. He could argue further that passion-love reduces on analysis to little more than vanity-love, as Stendhal himself sometimes suspected although he was finally too timid or tenderhearted to accept that conclusion. As for Rousseau, Proust could have cited him as a precursor. Rousseau ultimately rejects sexual love because he finds that there is no way of eliminating the inherent selfishness in its amour-propre. Proust might well have claimed to be one who offers convincing arguments in support of this opinion.

Moreover, one misunderstands Proust unless his treatment of sexual love is placed in the context of his thinking about love as a whole. He concentrates upon the different love affairs we have mentioned because he wants to determine whether romanticism is justified in thinking that problems of feeling can be solved by means of such experience—that is, whether men or women in love might hope to attain a sexual relationship that is intensely passionate, a source of lasting happiness, nondelusory, and capable of providing reliable knowledge about the person with whom one merges. In arguing that these conditions are unsatisfiable, in maintaining that in this sense sexual love is a futility, Proust does not deny that other types of love exist. While insisting upon the selfish character of passionate love, he emphasizes that the love he received from his grandmother, and to some extent from his mother, was both constant and unselfish. Theirs was devotion based upon concern for another's welfare. It was an expression of tenderness toward a child they understood, appreciated, and above all, considered a valuable person in himself.

The grandmother's capacity for love, which she extends toward her husband as well as Marcel, assumes great importance within the narrative structure of *A la recherche*. It provides a counterpoint for the theme of neurotic suffering that later dominates Marcel's experience with other women. Though the grandmother resembles all his future mistresses in being willing to let him suffer, only hers is a loving attitude. She sees him as a child who needs discipline and even punishment. Marcel reports that his bad habits in maturity resulted from the fact that his grandmother's suggestions, based on wisdom as well as love, were overridden by his father's haphazard goodwill, which was really a lack of principle. Throughout the narrative, the grandmother's devotion serves as a touchstone. Marcel recognizes the magnificence of her love and continually feels guilty because he cannot reciprocate. His need to suffer in his relations with other people may well be taken as self-imposed retribution for his inability to emulate or return his grandmother's love.

Over and above the grandmother's attitude, Proust also studies mother-son and wife-husband relations of love. In *Jean Santeuil* he depicts the affection and gratitude that may well arise from a normal family situation, together with the bitterness and hostility that also accompany it. In *A la recherche* filial and marital emotions are generally portrayed as an unsatisfying compromise between the purity of the grandmother's selflessness on the one hand, and the ardent excitement and focusing of feeling in passionate love on the other. We learn that Swann reasoned accurately when he concluded that marrying Odette would cure him of his diseased need for her. Having complete access to Odette as her husband, he no longer craves her presence or undergoes excruciating jealousy when she is absent. He feels the comfort of their dependence upon one another as husband and wife within a bourgeois family. She becomes a habitual appurtenance to his life, and to that extent he finally does succeed in possessing her. He is not troubled by the fact that she no longer pretends to feel strong emotions toward him. Though he knows she is sexually unfaithful, he experiences a modicum of peace. But, of course, the passion has gone out of his life. While Proust accepts family ties as valid in a variety of ways, particularly for the rearing of children, he sees no reason to believe that they can provide intuitive awareness or solve the problems of feeling to which he addresses himself.

Proust finds a more promising type of love in Saint-Loup's capacity for friendship with other men. Despite intimations that friendship in Saint-Loup was often motivated by latent or explicit homosexual desire, the narrator sees it as an expression of nobility that he himself cannot approximate. Even though Saint-Loup's dedication to the soldiers who served under him during the First World War was "clouded by ideology" since he failed to realize that his sentiments arose from sexual rather than wholly spiritual sources, Proust disassociates Saint-Loup's attitude from Charlus' baser interest in male companionship. "Saint-Loup admires the courage of young men, the intoxication of cavalry charges, the intellectual and moral nobility of friendship, wholly pure, between men, in which each is prepared to sacrifice his life for the other." Proust continues to insist on the element of "falsehood" in all this, but he nevertheless evinces great admiration for Saint-Loup's ability to live in accordance with his "ideal of virility."

For the most part, however, Proust uses the experience of the narrator to illustrate how wasteful friendship can be. He depicts it as a killing of time, an accommodation to the idiosyncrasies of others, a distraction that prevents one from learning about oneself or enjoying the beauties of nature. Though it enables us to create superficial happiness in other people, friendship—like family life—is based on animal instincts of gregariousness. It belongs to the life of the clan, the closed society, and this suffices for Proust to consider it a condition scarcely preferable to snobbishness. In general, all of Proust's "sociologie amusante" tries to show that what now exists as society is mainly a perversion of the spirit. Presumably this applies not only to men or women seeking paramours, and snobs trying to be accepted by those who are glamorous and wealthy, but also to political and even humanitarian activities of virtually every sort. While Bergson saw the furthest reaches of ideality in the mystic's talent for finding God's love throughout the everyday world and deploying it in moral action, Proust emphasizes the extent to which all life in society degenerates into pettiness and aggressive self-aggrandizement.

In view of this overall pessimism about social ideals, Proust's approach to passionate love seems less negative than one might originally have thought. In effect, Proust articulates a hierarchy of values. The love of social prominence represents the lowest rung of the ordo salutis. A little higher are the loves within a family, those between husband and wife or between children and parents. Further up, friendship establishes a more elevated love between men and perhaps between women. Heroic friendship such as Saint-Loup's would attain the highest reaches on this level; and possibly the grandmother's love can be classified as a parallel achievement, taking family love beyond its usual limits. On the highest rung stands passionate love. Though it cannot claim to be ethically superior to friendship or the grandmother's type of devotion, it elicits our strongest feelings and teaches us truths about ourselves that may be attainable in no other way.

Proust places sexual love at the top of this hierarchy because, more than the other types of love, it is explicitly based upon instinctual need while also stimulating the imagination through a metaphysical search for another person. All the levels within the hierarchy turn out to be inadequate, according to Proust, but he thinks the disillusionment and necessary suffering that results from passionate love best prepares us for the creative life, and that is what his philosophy defends as the solution to problems of feeling. For Proust the highest love, that which takes us beyond the hierarchy I have been describing, involves a dedication to artistic creativity. All his ideas about love presuppose, and finally proclaim, his belief that only art is worthy of our total devotion.

❋

To see why Proust prefers art to passionate love while also finding the latter superior to other affective possibilities, we must return to some of the philosophical problems that pervade Proust's writing. On the one hand, he wants to establish and then make sense of the fact that our experience is so discontinuous and its contents so chaotic that one may easily doubt whether we exist as individual substances evolving through time. On the other hand, he wants to find the grounds for thinking there is an external world whose independent reality we encounter through our experience. Bergson had maintained that since duration (lived time) was fundamentally continuous the human self must also be. And though he did not believe in a knowable world wholly distinct from experience, Bergson claimed that we could perceive the oneness of reality in the same manner that we intuited the flow of duration in ourselves. Proust undermines this simple faith by showing that even in passionate love, where one intuits one's being with greatest intensity and makes the most concerted effort to intuit the being of another person, the Bergsonian conclusions are unwarranted. Even in the flowering of sexual passion at its best, one cannot validate idealist beliefs about the continuity of self and its unity with the external world.

Nor does Proust ascribe this failure merely to the nature of love. On the contrary, he sees love as the greatest revelation of shortcomings in mental life as a whole. He begins his investigation by discussing the young boy's dreams because he believes that the false sense of merging so common in dreams recurs not only when we love but also throughout our normal waking consciousness. Though the body informs us about the reality in which it is immersed, Proust says, our need to interpret and to idealize prevents us from understanding its messages. In this vein he mentions the idealist philosopher "whose body takes account of the external world in the reality of which his intelligence does not believe."

Proust uses his subjectivistic analysis of love to reveal truths about human consciousness that are ignored by naive realists as well as idealist philosophers. Habit fits Marcel's room to his own experience of it without telling him what the room is really like, just as his love for Albertine molds her behavior—or rather, his ability to know what it is—in conformity with his preconceptions. As a result, he never learns (until after he has lost the intimate habit of her) the burning secrets about this person whose being he desperately wished to penetrate. The self-centeredness of love, and the fact that its dependence upon imagination prevents lovers from possessing the hidden absolute they seek, leads Marcel to wonder whether he can ever be sure that he is perceiving an objective reality. "When I saw an external object," the narrator tells us, "the realization that I was seeing it remained between me and it, framed it in a thin subjective [i.e. nonphysical] border which prevented me from ever directly touching its being; it volatilized so to speak before I could come into contact with it."

Seeing Mme de Guermantes for the first time, after having constructed in his mind an illusory image of her, Marcel tries to match his idealized portrait with the person there before him. He fails completely—"as if there were two disks separated by an intervening space." Time and again Proust shows how this separation turns our encounters with reality into frustrating and disillusioning experiences. "C'est cela, ce n'est que cela, Mme de Guermantes!" the narrator exclaims. His words—"that's her, Mme de Guermantes is only that!"—duplicate the "ce n'est que ça" with which Stendhal's Fabrizio expresses astonishment at what a battle turns out to be and Lamiel vents her disappointment after having first experienced sexual intercourse. But Proust extends the Stendhalian analysis. He shows the difficulty in *all* attempts to know or perceive the world. He argues that love teaches us about this condition by augmenting our involvement with other people and thereby sharpening our sense of disillusionment.

Proust's attempt to overcome the subjectivity of love is best approached through his ideas about memory. *A la recherche* is a calling back, a recall, of past time, the narrator's as well as that of all the others whose amatory failures Proust documents. The book proves that memory can indeed regain the past. When Proust remarks that the only paradises are paradises lost, he means in part that the experience of recovering past time contains within it joys that could not have been felt apart from memory. Through its proper use we attain not only a sense of personal identity that unifies past and present experience but also assurance that something in our being surmounts subjective limitations. Memory of this preferential sort Proust calls "involuntary" and "affective." Unlike processes of remembering controlled by the intellect and therefore subservient to practical necessities, involuntary memory cannot be summoned up at will. It occurs fortuitously, through no direct effort of our own. Proust calls it affective because he believes that it is closer to feeling than to reason or intelligence.

Scholars have argued extensively about the similarity or difference between Proust's distinction between voluntary and involuntary memory and Bergson's distinction between "habitual" memory and "pure or spontaneous" memory. Though Proust denied that his distinction was the same as Bergson's, various commentators have pointed out that the two analyses of memory overlap significantly.

These critics are right insofar as Bergson asserts that pure or spontaneous memory reveals the unity of our self and its continuity with the external world. This is similar to the function that Proust thinks involuntary memory performs. But Bergson's idea occurs as part of a theory of memory that is nevertheless quite different from Proust's. Bergson maintains that within the ongoing flow of time—which is life as we live it—the past remains permanently in us, hidden but finely etched in the recesses of the brain. Total recall, he says, is inhibited by the controlling hand of reason, which nature endows with the office of helping us to adapt pragmatically to each new environment. When pure memory breaks through, in a sudden, spontaneous, and unforeseeable outburst released by intuition, our past reality shows itself in the pristine condition that has endured throughout all subsequent experience. More often, however, memory operates in the habitual mode, as when we learn how to walk or ride a bicycle, to solve mathematical problems, or to reason in all the diverse ways needed for survival.

Proust's distinction differs from Bergson's inasmuch as he assigns no underlying permanence to the past. On the contrary, Proust searches for a method of *reliving* past experiences. For Bergson this makes no sense at all. Time being a constant progression in which the past is always retained within the present, he likens one's experience to a snowball that forever enlarges itself without repeating or duplicating any of its earlier moments. The harking back to the past is, however, the culminating goal of Proust's investigation. Bergson says the past is always present; Proust insists that most of it is absent—as in the intermittences of the heart—and needs to be re-created in a manner that will reveal its original import. However much Proust agrees that habitual responses impede involuntary memory, he has very little to say about memory that is needed for the *making* of habits. That is what Bergson contrasts with spontaneous memory. Proust's distinction emphasizes the differences between remembering something through a volitional effort and the having of a more or less passive experience in which memory re-presents the past by suddenly causing us to undergo it a second time. The datum that results is not a continuous entity but one that has disappeared and now returns to life.

The concept of involuntary memory underlies all of Proust's thinking about essences. Dipping the madeleine cake into tea, Marcel finds himself flooded by memories he could not have evoked through any voluntary means. They reveal a unifying, but previously unrecognized, pattern within his earlier life. Only in the last segment of *A la recherche* does Proust fully articulate his doctrine of essences, but after the madeleine incident he often describes other occasions on which they are intuited. Most relevant to our theme is Swann's experience of the little phrase in Vinteuil's music. It tantalizes him with the suggestion that beyond the falseness and self-deception of his love affair with Odette there remains a joyful encounter with ultimate reality that artists are able to achieve. Once he has clarified his thinking about essences, the narrator understands how aesthetic experience reveals the meaning of the little phrase. Swann's love life is wasted because—due to lack of intellectual courage and creative talent—he could not regain past time or fully appreciate the nature of essences. But the narrator succeeds where Swann has failed. He learns from Swann's suffering as well as his own, and he manages to decipher the bizarre events that befall him in the courtyard of the Guermantes palace.

Proust presents these as revelatory occurrences involving different sense modalities. In the case of the madeleine, essences were elicited by the sense of taste, but now they result from other types of sensation: kinaesthetic feelings when he steps on the uneven paving-stones, the touch of the starched napkin, and then the metallic sound of the spoon against the tray. In each of these events a particular sensation causes the reliving of similar moments from the past, providing an intuition of identity and disclosing what Proust calls "the permanent and habitually hidden essence of things." The narrator finds a joy, an insight, and a feeling of direct communion with reality that he had never known in the experience of anything present or in remembrance of the past through voluntary memory.

It is crucial, I think, that the essences Proust describes are mainly nonvisual. The example of the three steeples of Martinville, which he sees from a distance, is an exception. Usually sensations other than those of sight are named as the ones that produce the experience of essences. The nonvisual modalities are the least likely to be controlled by habit; they are mostly unpredictable; and they are the hardest to evoke at will. Above all, they are especially conducive to affective response. Proust contrasts essences with the memories that he used to have. The latter were like snapshots in an album, collected as if to prove to himself that his life had included some lovely moments. Memories of that sort, presumably quasi-visual illustrations of the past, were unable to reinstate the original reality. Essences, on the other hand, reveal a single, though developing, identity within his consciousness while also providing important knowledge about the content of his experience.

At times Proust uses words like "eternal" and "extratemporal" to characterize essences. Though they enter through the senses, he occasionally speaks of their having a "spiritual meaning." From this, many critics have assumed that Proust's conception is Platonistic. Yet Proust never speaks of essences as belonging to a separate metaphysical realm apart from or even underlying the everyday world. They are universals, but they have no being prior to existence. If they are not "temporal," this can be true only in the sense that we discover them by extending our attention beyond a particular moment in time. Proust says that the task essences accomplish is to "interpret sensations as signs of so many laws and principles." The Proustian essence is not a mystical epiphany that reveals a transcendental reality. It is just a link between similar or identical sense experiences. It leads on to interpretations that culminate in laws of nature which are capable of explaining the ordinary world. When earlier Proust referred to "the general laws of love," this is what he had in mind. Through the experience and the comprehension of essences, he feels at the end of his narrative that he can now formulate those laws.

If my reading of Proust on essences is correct, he must be categorized with the empirical and scientific tradition in philosophy more than with the Platonic. This is much as one might have expected from his overt acceptance of the realist approach. Even as a fellow pessimist he differs from a metaphysician such as Schopenhauer, who thought that salvation could be attained through Platonic contemplation. Far from being contemplative, Proustian experience of essences is not even intuitional if by "intuition" one means a faculty of mind that employs no elements of interpretation and no generalization from particulars. Though Proust's essences must be experienced as identities whose quality cannot be exhausted by any of the individual occasions of their occurrence, they are only a unifying oneness among these different occasions. They have no being apart from them. To experience Proustian essences is to undergo an amalgam of interpretation and sensation, which is quite different from what either the Platonists or the Bergsonians meant by terms such as "contemplation" or "intuition."

For this reason Santayana's discussion of Proust is both inexact and misleading. In his essay "Proust on Essences," Santayana begins with a definition of essence that fits his own conception but is largely foreign to Proust's. "An essence," Santayana says, "is simply the recognizable character of any object or feeling, all of it that can actually be possessed in sensation or recovered in memory, or transcribed in art, or conveyed to another mind." We shall return to Santayana on essences when we discuss his philosophy of love. Here we need only recognize that he contrasts their realm of being with the factuality of existence, which is to say "the material occasions" on which they occur. While the latter constitute a temporal succession that lends itself to interpretation and rational analysis, Santayana's essences—the qualitative whatness and formal character in everything—are sheer possibles that cannot be located in time or even said to exist. They are experienced only through an intuition of their inherent design. Santayana claims to find in Proust "a beautiful and impassioned" account of these essences, and he quotes a long passage from the last volume of *A la recherche* in which he considers Proust to be describing not only their ability to take us beyond their momentary appearance in the present but also "entirely outside of time."

Though Proust uses similar language, his conception is not at all the same as Santayana's. For Proust, essences have no separate being of the sort that Santayana describes. Proust says that they are "real," and he insists that they disclose the reality of what has occurred in time without being temporal themselves. But he consistently depicts essences as nothing more than the recurrence of similar or identical contents within experience we have actually had. That is why memory has such great importance for him, and why involuntary memory can evoke his kind of essences while voluntary memory cannot. For the former reinstates the totality of an experience, duplicating affective as well as cognitive dimensions that appeared in the past. There is in Proust no suggestion that essences are formal qualities or abstract possibilities. On the contrary, they are for him that which is real in existence as it progresses through a temporal order. If it is taken as a haphazard, possibly random, succession of momentary events, time has no reality for Proust. That was what the narrator's experience in the earlier volumes had continually demonstrated. His frequent suffering, in love but also in the rest of his life, the disappointments he portrays as "our inability to find our real selves in physical enjoyment or material activity"—all this is caused by living from moment to moment instead of recognizing that the reality of time consists in the essential and reverberating unities that bind its successive ingredients. Proustian essences are not *outside* of time. They are the fundamental structures of human experience *in* time. They enable us to understand what is really happening in our life as it exists *throughout* the flow of time.

Santayana's doctrine of essences being so different from this, it is not entirely surprising that after welcoming Proust's testimony Santayana ends up by criticizing it. Proust is confused, Santayana thinks, insofar as he requires two experiences—one in the present, another in the past—to reveal a single essence: "A mind less volatile and less retentive, but more concentrated and loyal, might easily have discerned the eternal essence in any single momentary fact." Santayana pursues this line of criticism by wondering whether it is likely that an essence could occur exactly the same on two occasions: "The repetition of similar events is common: the recurrence of a given essence in a living mind is rare, and perhaps impossible. . . . The earlier impressions . . . may help to deepen and fix the intuition when it comes at last. But the persuasion that this new intuition is not new, and that we have had it in exactly this form before, is probably an illusion; the well-known illusion of the *déjà-vu.*"

It is, however, literally déjà-vu that Proust describes as the basis for his conception of essences. He does not consider them illusory since they signify *only* the occurrence of similar events. They are not the appearance of qualities that transcend existence. Santayana's essences belong neither here nor there, neither in the present nor in the past. For Proust they belong *both* here and there, *both* in the present and in the past. That is why they require more than one experience. They would have no being otherwise.

Since Proustian essences can be experienced only through memory, Santayana may be right in complaining that they are never intuited with certainty. Proust does not address himself to this problem. He gives us no guarantees that involuntary memory is necessarily correct or reliable. He offers no criteria for verifying affective memories, for accepting some as more accurate than others. So powerful is the feeling of assurance and of joy that the narrator undergoes in experiencing essences that he slurs over all such questions. Though he fails to recognize how greatly Proust's conception differs from his own, Santayana is justified in seeing a difficulty here. He is also right in speaking of Proust as "a tireless husbandman of memory, gathering perhaps more poppies than corn." Even if Proust can defend, as an act of realism and fidelity to natural truths, what Santayana considers the harvesting of worthless weeds, there may be merit in Santayana's further suggestion that Proust rarely felt "the scale of values imposed on things by human nature," and that if he had, he "might have been carried towards some by an innate love and away from others by a quick repulsion."

This remark of Santayana's can seem puzzling at first. For who is more discriminating in his moral observations than Proust, more attuned to the shams and self-deceptions of virtually every player in the variegated world that he portrays? As with all realists, it is the return to values imposed on things by the truths of human nature that Proust holds aloft as a guide to personal authenticity. Essences affect him deeply because he is convinced that only through them can one pursue the artistic vocation as an expression of the innate love to which Santayana refers. Having clarified his ideas about essences, the narrator states that he must now "try to think, that is to say, draw forth from the shadow what I had felt, to convert it into a spiritual equivalent. And this, which seemed to me the only method, what was it but the making of a work of art?" What Santayana calls poppies would thus become integral parts of an aesthetic object that gets its value from being a truthful representation of how things really are. What more could one demand?

Nevertheless, and despite its imperfections, Santayana's criticism does contain a suggestive insight about the limitations of the Proustian doctrine. In his attempt to show how the narrator finally attains the capacity to regain lost time, Proust seems blinded to the possibility that pursuing ideals of interpersonal love, communal action, or intellectual exploration can provide happiness and a sense of reality equivalent to what he hopes to achieve through artistic experience. Even Schopenhauer's pessimism eventuated in an enumeration of different paths that the enlightened soul could take in the search for salvation. In addition to aesthetic contemplation, Schopenhauer recommended philosophy and science as means by which one dominates the universal will in the process of comprehending, even mastering, its ultimate meaninglessness. Proust advocates something comparable insofar as the work of art he envisages, and himself has written, includes within it a detailed search for truths about human nature, as if his investigation was at least parallel to science or philosophy. But in Proust these pursuits remain subordinate, as they must be in a work of art. He never dignifies them as equally valid activities on their own.

All of Proust's thinking presupposes that *only* in art can one redeem the past and resolve the problems of feeling with which he began. Having finally experienced and understood the joy that essences bring to him, the narrator ponders: "Was this the happiness that the little phrase of the sonata promised to Swann, who deceived himself by assimilating it to the pleasures of love, not knowing how to find it in artistic creation . . . ?" But one could also have interpreted Swann's failure in love (and in a sense, Proust himself does) as the consequence of reducing human beings to works of art—productions that may be beautiful and highly significant but that nevertheless pertain to the category of things rather than persons. The truth is that Swann fails as *both* lover and creative artist. And even if he had been successful as an artist, this would have had no bearing on his or anyone else's ability to succeed in love.

Proust offers no examples of happy lovers, with the possible exception of the artist Elstir. Apart from the kind of love that the mother and grandmother feel toward Marcel, Elstir's devotion to his wife is virtually the only love that Proust depicts in a sympathetic and constructive manner. In her youth Mme Elstir had been a great beauty whom the painter used as a model. When Marcel observes the two together, after they had been married for many years, he interprets Elstir's expressions of tenderness as adoration of an "ideal type" of female beauty that he perceives as still inhering in his wife. Proust scarcely elaborates upon the nature of this relationship, and Marcel (characteristically) finds the presence of Mme Elstir "tedious." Had he wished, Proust could have seen in Elstir's love an illustration of how artistic and amatory imagination can reinforce one another. Proust makes no such attempt, nor does he try to show—as Santayana does, in his philosophy of love—how passionate feelings may be related to a yearning for ideal types.

In the final analysis, Proust's philosophy of love fails because it never fully emancipates itself from its Romantic origins. Having shown that love does not provide a fusion with another's absolute, and in general that it is a delusion to think that in love "some other life is fused with our own," Proust infers that the love of persons is futile. But this reasoning is valid only if we assume that merging of that sort defines the nature of interpersonal love. Had Proust enclosed his realistic observations within a theory that no longer retained the basic presuppositions of romanticism, his insights into human affect might have been less radical but more persuasive.

We may also treat the deficiencies of Proust on love as an inability to understand how interpersonal response, particularly when it is erotic, flourishes by being more than mere appraisiveness. In a reductivistic manner similar to Freud's and no less extreme, Proust systematically neglects the fact that people in love benefit from bestowing value on one another. From this it follows that all sexual love must appear to him as vanity, possessiveness, and jealousy. Rousseau believed that in this condition the imagination works at a high intensity, simulating creativity, but really being feverish and diseased. Proust portrays the syndrome with a thoroughness that never has been and probably never will be equalled. He then concludes that passionate love cannot be purified and that no kind of love—except for the love of art—can possibly liberate itself from the chains of selfish misery. But Proust never or rarely shows us the joy, the sweet delight, the consummatory splendor that lovers feel when they bestow value on one another. For the most part, he only sees how imagination can operate for goals that directly benefit oneself. He does not realize that imagination can also satisfy our needs by giving us the pleasure of making another person valuable through our bestowal—above all, as it occurs in sexual love. Misguided as he may have been, even Rousseau had greater understanding of that potentiality.

Though Proust presents a coherent defense of art as the exclusive source of creativity or justifiable love, we have little reason to accept it at its face value. Having proved himself lacking in virtually every kind of love for another person, the narrator may well turn to art as his only possibility of redemption. And since for him art consists, to a large degree, in writing about "the botched work of amorous illusion," he may plausibly infer that happiness is useful only as the prelude to a creative kind of unhappiness: "It is necessary for us to form in happiness sweet and strong ties of confidence and attachment in order that the breaking of them should cause us the precious tearing away which is called unhappiness."

As a perception into the problems of a writer, whose imagination can easily be lulled by the distracting joys of successful love (or any other success), there is much wisdom in Proust's disdain for happiness. His comment reminds us of Stendhal's complaint that a happy marriage yields only "a few very commonplace ideas." Stendhal and Proust make the same mistake. They assume that creativity such as theirs exhausts the gamut of human excellence. Like all lovers, they think that no other love can rival their exhilarating dedication to art. But aesthetic love—the love of art and of its ability to fructify experience through imagination—is not the only kind of love that can provide authentic satisfaction. No love gives us preferential access to reality, and aside from individual need none can claim to be inherently superior as a source of goodness.

❋

Stendhal's mistake had less effect upon his general theory of love than in the case of Proust. One feels that the Proustian approach illustrates how research into reality can undermine the thinker's capacity to appreciate what is involved in a love of persons. In a statement about another artist, Freud says the following: "Not to love before one gains full knowledge of the thing loved presupposes a delay which is harmful. When one finally reaches cognition, one neither loves nor hates properly; one remains beyond love and hatred. One has investigated instead of having loved." These words were written about Leonardo da Vinci. They apply to Proust.

6
Twentieth-Century Puritanism
D. H. Lawrence and
G. B. Shaw

Proust And Freud Attacked
romanticism from a perspective that sought to be realist or scientific. Alongside their approach, and interwoven with it, there also existed a strand that derives from seventeenth-century Puritanism. I choose Lawrence and Shaw to exemplify Puritanism in the twentieth century despite, and *because of*, their differences from one another. Like Milton or Calvin or Luther they are moralists and self-conscious creators of new religions. The same cannot be said of Freud or Proust. Though Lawrence and Shaw both accept Bergsonian vitalism as the metaphysical doctrine required by modern man, they do so in a way that scarcely detracts from the Puritan attitudes they presuppose. Neither Shaw nor Lawrence *identifies* himself with Puritanism, and many of their remarks run counter to it. But in them, as in all other theorists of love, their presuppositions are often a better clue to their mentality than what they say explicitly.

In his long essay "A Propos of *Lady Chatterley's Lover*," Lawrence speaks of Shaw as one who knows nothing about "the profound, rhythmic sex of man's inward life." I shall return to this criticism, and others that Lawrence makes against the Shavian outlook. But first we must see how the philosophy of each of these thinkers begins with two concepts that preoccupied Milton throughout his writings. As I argued in volume 2, Milton ambivalently treated love as a condition of merging between man and woman, and also as a "conversation" between equal and autonomous partners. Employing Neoplatonic ideas about oneness in love, Milton portrayed the relationship between Adam and Eve as a merging. She had originated from Adam's rib, and he was so thoroughly bound by this primordial fusion, this link of nature, as to be incapable of withdrawing from her even when she violated God's commandment. On the other hand, Milton emphasized the divisiveness, the conflict of wills, that results from their moral crisis. In his writings on sex and marriage, Milton resorts to Protestant ideas about a marital love that overcomes such intersexual hostility through benign communication between the spouses. This would create a unity between men and women who admired each other without feeling adulation, who cooperated in the joint enterprise of constructing a family unit without aspiring to anything like a merging.

Luther had tried to harmonize these different attitudes in what was later to become Puritan thought by his use of the concept of agapē. Since human beings were in themselves unable to love, no true or ultimate merging could possibly occur between man and woman. But since God could and did descend as a free bestowal of agapē, his infinite love would then unite a husband and wife in a mystical oneness with himself which destroys the separateness of their being.

Milton had no desire to undermine the Lutheran synthesis. On the contrary, he felt that he had strengthened it by showing how a Christian marriage could effectively combine the values of sexual intimacy and cooperative individuality. But he also delineates these virtues as the natural capacities of human beings who struggle in the world. In doing so, he provides the groundwork for the non- and even anti-Christian Puritanism of both Lawrence and Shaw.

We can see this most vividly in a late essay by Lawrence that illuminates the erotic structure in many of his novels. It is called ". . . . Love Was Once a Little Boy." The title is ironic. For Lawrence ridicules all love that is a sentimental attachment between people who seek "true" or "perfect" oneness with one another. He warns us against love which aspires to be "absolute and personal," and he says that "we must always beware of romance: of people who love nature, or flowers, or dogs, or babies, or pure adventure." At a time when Lawrence's descriptions of erotic behavior had been banned because they were considered obscene, these words could easily be taken out of context and interpreted as a defense of sexual freedom in opposition to romantic love. In the popular imagination, Lawrence is still thought to have revered liberated sex above everything else.

This conception of Lawrence distorts his thinking in various ways. For one thing, it ignores the fact that he was attacking only what he deemed to be inferior and unwholesome romantic love. He reviles the kind of relationship that involves submissiveness of the man to the woman or of the woman to the man—*self-sacrificial* love that destroys the individuality of either or both of the lovers. He repudiates love that seeks a total fusion between personalities. It leads to a "guttering mess" and neglects the human need to assert one's separateness, to preserve one's difference, to recognize the fundamental isolation of each person's being.

The major dichotomy in Lawrence is therefore not reducible to the difference between love and sex. In making his distinction between merging and individuality, he wishes to unify them within a type of love that will be preferable to either. Lawrence has difficulty articulating the nature of this harmonization. He gets at it obliquely, by dramatizing the inadequacy of its two contrasting ingredients when they exist apart from one another. Writing about Walt Whitman, whom he considers a great poet and a moral pioneer, he finds him limited by his exorbitant belief in merging through love. Lawrence claims that Whitman's search for "allness," for "one identity," can only manifest the actual impossibility of merging with another person. "He found, as all men find, that you can't really merge in a woman, though you may go a long way." And where Whitman extols the manly love of comrades, Lawrence concludes that here too the concept of merging has misled him. He locates the center of Whitman's thought in lines that describe death as the final merging and ultimate goal of life. These are lines that reverberate with the Romantic notion of Liebestod, as in Wagner, and the association with the sea accentuates the Wagnerian influence:

Whereto answering, the sea
Delaying not, hurrying not,

Whispered me through the night, and very plainly before
  daybreak,
Lisp'd to me the low and delicious word death,
And again death, death, death, death.

In criticizing this, Lawrence insists that death is not the universal
goal, even though the search for merging through love or comradeship—on the part of those who believe in merging—may express an adoration of death. As commentary on Whitman's lines,
he says:

> Merging! And Death! Which is the final merge.
> The great merge into the womb. Woman.
> And after that, the merge of comrades: man-for-man
> love.
> And almost immediately with this, death, the final merge
> of death.
> There you have the progression of merging. For the
> great mergers, woman at last becomes inadequate. For
> those who love to extremes. Woman is inadequate for the
> last merging. So the next step is the merging of man-for-
> man love. And this is on the brink of death. It slides over
> into death.

Lawrence ascribes the failure in Whitman's message to the lingering effects of Christian ideas about love. The belief in caritas as
a universal self-sacrifice he sarcastically calls a "highroad of Love."
He says it undermines Whitman's deeper faith in the Open Road.
In an essay entitled "Love," Lawrence condemns Christian love as
bondage to eternity, infinity, which is really "endless travelling"
and no arrival. Since the theological ideal involves a merging with
God, a becoming one which results from man's total sacrifice of
himself, Lawrence can see it only as a wish for total self-destruction.
Any such glorification of the nothing which is death is abhorrent to
him.

One might remark that Lawrence has ignored orthodox Christianity's repeated attacks on the notion of merging. One could say
that his critique applies to mystical and Romantic concepts that the
church also rejected. Nevertheless, Lawrence negates all belief in

Christian love when he explains why he considers merging to be unacceptable: "there is in me this necessity to separate and distinguish myself into gem-like singleness, distinct and apart from all the rest, proud as a lion, isolated as a star." The words are overly brave, perhaps, but they affirm a post-Romantic attitude that aspires to goals of self-realization quite different from the Christian love of God or one's neighbor.

Lawrence's Byronic stance, or rather Nietzschean assertion of individual self-sufficiency, defines the other pole in his dialectic. In *Women in Love* Birkin tells Ursula that there is a "real impersonal me, that is beyond love, beyond any emotional relationship. So it is with you. But we want to delude ourselves that love is the root. It isn't. It is only the branches. The root is beyond love, a naked kind of isolation, an isolated me, that does *not* meet and mingle, and never can." Though this speech precedes the culminating stage in Birkin's relationship with Ursula, it establishes the parameters of his intimacy with her. He offers himself as a "final me which is stark and impersonal and beyond responsibility." He recognizes that she too is an "unknown" being, an "utterly strange" creature.

To Ursula this attitude seems indistinguishable from selfishness. She associates it with the attempt of males to impose their dominance upon females. It runs counter to the kind of love she seeks throughout the novel and hopes to solidify with Birkin. That is love based upon "self-abandonment" as well as "absolute surrender" to the fact of love itself. The differences between her ideas of love and those of Birkin illustrate the Lawrentian dialectic to which I am referring:

> She believed that love far surpassed the individual. He said the individual was *more* than love, or than any relationship. For him, the bright, single soul accepted love as one of its conditions, a condition of its own equilibrium. She believed that love was *everything*. Man must render himself up to her. He must be quaffed to the dregs by her. Let him be *her man* utterly, and she in return would be his humble slave— whether she wanted it or not.

Though critics have often identified Lawrence with Birkin,

Lawrence's thinking includes Ursula's ideas as well. The dialectic served as a creative device in his fictional writing because he was convinced that *both* of its poles were correct within themselves. Each needed to be clarified and transmuted in relation to the other. The outcome of their confrontation is a synthesis that surpasses either element. But prior to this final harmonization, which Lawrence's characters rarely achieve, his basic dialectic provides him with a series of dramatic conflicts that serve as generative motives within each narrative.

In *The Rainbow* Lawrence uses the dialectic to reveal the flaw in Will and Anna Brangwen's marriage. Despite their moments of passionate love, "they fought an unknown battle, unconsciously." Will feels that Anna does not respect him in himself, in his individual aspirations, his spirituality—"She only respected him as far as he was related to herself." Even in their sexual abandon, neither Will nor Anna can adequately respond to what is deepest in the other. At its most intense, their lovemaking becomes "a sensuality violent and extreme as death. They had no conscious intimacy, no tenderness of love. It was all the lust and the infinite, maddening intoxication of the sense, a passion of death." Will, and possibly Anna too, remains incomplete as a human being. Ursula, who is their daughter, learns from their example. Though she appreciates, even loves, Skrebensky, she distrusts his affection for her and hers for him because she feels "none of the dreadful wonder, none of the rich fear, the connection with the unknown, or the reverence of love." Eventually she leaves Skrebensky and continues to search for a love that will unite her to "something impersonal" in a man who "would come out of Eternity to which she herself belonged."

The Lawrentian dialectic between separateness and passionate union appears most explicitly in the drafts he wrote for what finally appeared as *Lady Chatterley's Lover*. The first version, usually referred to as *The First Lady Chatterley*, differs from the later ones in the stridency with which the conflicting extremes oppose one another. The gamekeeper, whose name is now the harsh-sounding Parkin rather than the mellifluous and cultivated Mellors it was later to become, attracts Constance because he embodies a strange, unknown, and primitive individuality. Despite the passionate communication between him and Constance, we are left with the feeling that they are not likely to overcome the personal and social barriers that separate them. She cannot understand his proletarian hatreds, and he cannot believe that they could ever make an ideal couple. As he says despairingly, when someone suggests that they might eventually get married: "She'd niver open to me proper—niver the last bit. If I gave in to her she'd hold the last bit back. She couldn't help it."

Lawrence's final words in this version do offer a modicum of optimism—"The future was still to hand"—and in *Lady Chatterley's Lover* he works out a viable resolution. But *The First Lady Chatterley* has more dramatic power than its successor because Lawrence accentuates to a much greater degree the antagonistic elements in his dialectic. He uses them to reveal conflicts not only between Parkin and Constance but also between him and her husband Clifford. Even if the two men were not engaged in class warfare, they could never become friends. Lawrence suggests that they are as different as the black and the white horses in Plato's *Phaedrus*. The distance between their personalities symbolizes an absolute separation of body and mind.

The possibility of love between men who differ more or less in this fashion, which *The First Lady Chatterley* excludes, is central to the drama of *Women in Love*. Birkin's yearning for a manly love that he might experience with Gerald contributes to the imperfection of his relationship with Ursula. After Gerald's death she denies that Birkin could have had two kinds of love, an "eternal union" with a man as well as the love he now has with her. Birkin refuses to believe that she is right, but much earlier Gerald too had rejected Birkin's suggestion that married love had to be supplemented by "the unadmitted love of man for man." Birkin thought that men could thereby enable each other to retain their individuality while also benefiting from the intimacy of heterosexual love. Gerald never shares this faith.

Though Birkin's ideal is not realized in the earlier novels, Lawrence pursues the possibility of a love between men that would be more than merely friendship in works such as *Aaron's Rod* and *The Plumed Serpent*. His descriptions of physical contact between men have often been interpreted in terms of latent or explicit homosexuality, despite his own disclaimers; and his notions about political action arising from a passionate male bonding have been attacked as inherently fascistic. I think there is some basis for reading Lawrence in both of these ways. His thinking is nevertheless speculative, and options he proposes in one context or another must always by seen as imaginative themes with which he is merely experimenting. In the last two or three years of his life, he went beyond his earlier ideas, finding in heterosexual love a solution that seems more definitive of his genius. Without denying the other elements in his thought, we may well take this final development as his most important contribution to the philosophy of love.

Lawrence's attempt to harmonize the element of merging in self-sacrificial love with self-assertiveness that manifests authentic individuality dominates " . . . . Love Was Once A Little Boy." He there proposes a kind of merging that is not truly self-sacrificial since it does not involve the submission of one person to another or the fusing of their total personalities. What merges, in Lawrence's conception at this point, is the *desire* that streams through individuals and flows together in heterosexual love. The love that Lawrence recommends is neither "absolute" nor "perfect." For these terms imply conditions of homogenized oneness between the sexes that never can exist. Instead, he sees men and women as separate conveyors of vital energies that arise from deep and unknown springs within each individual. "In its essence, love is no more than the stream of clear and unmuddied, subtle desire which flows from person to person, creature to creature, thing to thing. The moment this stream of delicate but potent desire dries up, the love has dried up, and the joy of life has dried up."

In saying this, Lawrence emphasizes that no one controls the streaming of his desire. He portrays the ego deceiving people into thinking that they, as self-activating persons, can truly love other persons. In reality, he says, it is only the streams of desire that meet and mingle and thereby bring love into being. Since love results from the confluence between the desiring maleness in a man and the desiring femaleness in a woman, the other properties that define their individuality have nothing to do with it. For that reason love, by its nature, does not impair individuality. Lovers remain inevitably and eternally separate as particularities and as persons. For their unison occurs only at the level of desire: "But it is never *himself* that meets and mingles with *herself:* any more than two lakes, whose waters meet to make one river, in the distance, meet in themselves." This is what Birkin means when he offers Ursula not the Romantic love for which she craves but rather "an equilibrium, a pure balance of two single beings:—as the stars balance each other."

As it stands, this much of Lawrence's thought is quite incomplete. In asserting the separateness of lovers, it largely disregards what binds them together. Though Lawrence uses words like "desire" and "equilibrium," his analysis does not give adequate weight to the complexity of ties that unite a man and a woman. In ".... Love Was Once A Little Boy" he even denies that people (or animals, e.g. his cow Susan) can really be equilibrated. To say this, however, is to make individuality into a principle of insurmountable separation. The desire of this woman might mingle with the desire of that man, and yet there would be no way in which the two human beings could accept or appreciate one another.

Lawrence must have recognized the importance of this problem. *Lady Chatterley's Lover,* in its last version, is a prolonged attempt to solve it. Unlike *The First Lady Chatterley,* the narrative structure is no longer dialectical, and neither is it especially dramatic. As in Wagner's *Tristan and Isolde,* it is developmental, revealing the progressive growth in Lady Chatterley's awareness of what it means to be a woman who realizes her emotional potential as an organism that exists in nature. In her sexual awakening and eventual fulfillment, she goes through several stages that create a forward momentum in the novel. Although her ability to live with Mellors is still problematic at the end, she achieves a oneness with and through him that Lawrence now considers paradigmatic of love.

In "A Propos of *Lady Chatterley's Lover,*" which Lawrence wrote shortly before he died, he condemns Western civilization—and above all, Christian religion—for having idealized "apartness" and "the mean separateness of everything." Through the idealization of abstract spirituality, Western man had lost the ability to recognize his "togetherness with the universe, the togetherness of the body, the sex, the emotions, the passions, with the earth and sun and stars." In the novel, Lady Chatterley's experience provides her with an intuitive understanding of this togetherness. In the essay, Lawrence analyzes it as a threefold relationship:

> First, there is the relation to the living universe. Then comes the relation of man to woman. Then comes the relation of man to man. And each is a blood-relationship, not mere spirit or mind. We have abstracted the universe into Matter and Force, we have abstracted men and women into separate personalities—personalities being isolated units, incapable of togetherness—so that all three great relationships are bodiless, dead.

Seen from this point of view, *Lady Chatterley's Lover* is a novel of quest not greatly different from the medieval romans d'aventure. To reach the relationship, the togetherness, that Lawrence idealizes, Constance must explore all levels of desire in herself. When he uses the word "desire," Lawrence means more than merely sexual impulse. He also means the desire to exist, to assert one's self, to live in accordance with one's nature, to sense one's instinctual being and to gratify it. In various places he expresses all this in terms of the tactile sense, the need to be "in touch"—with oneself, with other men and women, and with the universe. At the same time he thought of desire as pervasively and inherently sexual. One could reach the level of desire only through sexuality. Civilization had alienated modern man from his own desire by dulling and diminishing sexual activities.

In *Lady Chatterley's Lover* Mellors uses forbidden words in order to remind Constance of the sexual fulfillment that she—like everyone else—desires. Lawrence's erotic writing in the novel was censored as obscenity when, in fact, it is merely pornographic: that is to say, language that may well arouse some form of sexual desire in the reader while also, and primarily, depicting its ecstatic importance to the characters. What distinguishes Lawrence from others who write pornographic literature is his conviction, his sincere and fervent belief, that living in accordance with our sexual capabilities will put us in touch with the reality of our ultimate desire. In this belief there may be much absurdity, but certainly not obscenity.

As much as he wishes to identify metaphysical desire with sexuality, however, Lawrence is careful to deny that all sex is equally revelatory of desire. He analyzes types of sexual experience in accordance with a distinction that he makes between egoism and self-assertion. The former is an interest in nothing but one's own personal welfare; the latter includes a concern about the world, indeed the cosmos, in which one participates. In *The Man Who Died* Christ's final resurrection occurs through his orgasmic oneness with the priestess of Isis in Search. In relation to one another, they each have a cosmic experience of self-assertion, the higher kind of sex. But earlier Christ and the priestess are united by the fact that they jointly—though at a distance from one another—look down at two slaves who are copulating on a terrace below them. This act of coitus, performed in anger, even violence, is merely a compliant rape in which the girl submits to the young man's quivering frenzy. It is an event within the "little body," sex of a different sort from what happens when men and women attain the "larger body" which is the realization of their true desire.

Originally *The Man Who Died* consisted only of what now appears as Part I. It ended with a paragraph in which Christ, having learned that his former mission was motivated by a hatred for life, concludes that there is "no contact without a subtle attempt to inflict a compulsion." In writing Part II, Lawrence moves beyond this statement of his usual belief in individuality. For the priestess inducts Christ into the life of the larger body through physical contact that transcends all possibility of compulsion. In the process she cures him of his death-wounds, the death imposed by his Christian belief in self-sacrifice, while she also fulfills the mysteries of her own sexuality. Their lovemaking is "a passion of tenderness and consuming desire." In it Christ becomes "one with her." But they do not merge their personalities. When Christ is driven away by her people, he survives by himself, continuing elsewhere the vital mission that her healing art has clarified for him. "'I have sowed the seed of my life and my resurrection, and put my touch forever upon the choice woman of this day, and I carry her perfume in my flesh like essence of roses. . . . To-morrow is another day.'"

We may now see how Lawrence reflects and continues the Puritan tradition he inherited. His attempt to link authentic love to sex was not a deviation from Milton or Luther; and neither was his condemnation of the self-sacrificial attitude that he identifies with Christian love. Luther's attack on the caritas-synthesis consisted in his denial that man could ever attain the selfless love to which the saints aspired. Man could not rise above his subjugation to nature, and his sexual needs were merely manifestations of that condition. Unlike many Romantics of the nineteenth century, Luther (and to some extent Milton) refused to interpret sex as an interpersonal enjoyment that could be worthwhile in itself. For them sexuality was always an agency of material powers beyond one's being as a person. This Puritan idea underlies everything Lawrence says about sexual love. In rejecting the merging of lovers and insisting upon their individuality while also extolling the merging of their desires, he treats their sexual energies as impersonal fields of force. Desire is the maleness in a man yearning for the femaleness in a woman, and vice versa. It brings together a particular man and a particular woman, but it arises from a dimension that scarcely pertains to the characteristics that distinguish them as this or that person. Lawrence's thought is much closer to Puritanism and the Reformation of the sixteenth century than it is to romanticism.

Indeed, Romantic faith in the love of persons is what Lawrence ridicules when he denies that "sentimental" love can actually be "perfect" or "ideal." Men and women cannot be perfect companions or create an ideal oneness between their personalities or establish a truly sentimental attunement with one another because human nature excludes the ability to love in this manner. "Why, human beings *can't* absolutely love one another. Each man *does* kill the thing he loves, by sheer dint of loving it." These are Lawrence's words, but he could have copied them out of Luther's *Table Talk*. Only at the level of the instinctual desire, never in their totality as persons, can men and women love each other. The destructive willfulness of human beings makes any such love impossible.

But if desire is not a yearning for the individuality in another human being, must it not be indiscriminate and promiscuous? The sixteenth- and seventeenth-century Puritans would have answered in the negative, and so does Lawrence. Writing about *Lady Chatterley's*

Lover, he denies that he was encouraging women to run after game-keepers, or anyone else. He insists that a great many people are happiest when they abstain from sexuality, provided they "understand and realize sex more fully." The crucial term here is "realize." Lawrence frequently states that the *realization* of one's sexuality has nothing to do with promiscuity or a constant preoccupation with sexual activity. He condemns "Don Juanery" as a state in which the libidinal itch causes a man to perform incessantly without real desire. He calls it "sex-in-the-head," and time and again he reviles any kind of sexuality that is cerebral or deliberative. One's desire cannot be realized in behavior that is either casual or subservient to civilized conventions—even when those conventions involve a show of sexual liberation, as they did in the 1920s. That only leads to "counterfeit emotion" and "counterfeit love" as contrasted with "the warmth of a man" which Lady Chatterley discovers in the gamekeeper.

From its very beginnings Puritanism oscillated between two extremes. At one pole it wished to purify sex in the sense of cleansing it of extraneous evils that interfered with its wholesome, natural, and God-given function in human life. Milton's *Paradise Lost* is the greatest example of this development in Puritan thinking. But Milton was attacked as a "libertine" by co-religionists who were puritanical in a different sense. They represent the opposing pole, which seeks to purify sex by lessening its importance for human beings, by restraining and repressing it, and thus precluding its idealization as a goal worth dignifying or extolling.

In Lawrence we find a twentieth-century expression of Puritanism in both of these senses. Frieda Lawrence is thus accurate when she says, in her Foreword to *The First Lady Chatterley,* that this novel is "the last word in Puritanism." Despite his eagerness to repudiate the "sick" and "grey" Puritanism that was prone to find artistic representations of sex repellent and obscene, Lawrence retains more of this attitude than one might have expected. Perhaps that is why he suffered so keenly in his own feelings when his novels and paintings were considered indecent. He himself was revolted by Joyce's *Ulysses,* much of which he condemned as merely filthy; and when he writes about the problems of pornography and obscenity, he admits that "like a real prude and Puritan" he is disgusted by the sexual content in many romantic books and movies of the day. Lawrence makes it very clear that his revulsion does not arise from the fact that these works depict or stimulate sexual feeling. He wants to banish what he calls obscene not because it is explicitly sexual but rather because it is an insult to sex and to "the human spirit." But, of course, the repressive Puritan always says that.

Lawrence tells us he would censor anything that "does dirt" on sex, anything that treats sexuality as if it were necessarily dirty. He thinks he is thereby outlawing a vulgar and diseased commodity. He does not realize that merely by imposing his own sexual preferences, he joins forces with those who cannot accept sex in its totality, as just the natural and diversely human phenomenon that it is. This parochial aspect of Lawrence's thinking leads him into his vehement assault on masturbation. Having put himself on the side of the angels by condemning *real* obscenity (as opposed to the noble depiction of vital instincts he ascribes to his own writings), Lawrence remarks that what is truly obscene serves as "an invariable stimulant to the vice of self-abuse." He sees no possibility of masturbation being harmless. His entire approach to the question reveals how narrow is his sexual ideal.

In all this discussion about the nature of sex, Lawrence is neither systematic nor analytic. As in his writing as a whole, his mind works fitfully, in response to forces impinging on him at each moment of creative exploration. Though the two poles within Puritanism define the limits of his erotic vision, he allows himself to range freely between them. Together with his prolonged tirades against the shallowness of casual sex, he writes moving and persuasive lines about the needless shame he himself experienced as an adolescent awakening each morning to the recognition that sexual desire was growing in him. He calls for a world where men and women can delight in the fact that they are sexual creatures, that the person each desires at any time is also sexual, and that sex based on true desire shows forth reality. This is what he means by the *realization* of sexuality in human beings.

Though his concept of desire is philosophically undeveloped, Lawrence makes a concerted effort to defend the basic goodness of sex. He wisely perceives that sympathy between men and women depends on their mutual affirmation of the sexuality in themselves. In this vein Lawrence distinguishes between the secrecy of sex, which is harmful, and its need for privacy, which is healthy. Like all enlightened Puritans, he recognizes that sexual behavior runs the risk of contamination when it becomes a public event. It then loses the mystery that belongs to a private encounter between the intimate being of one individual and the intimate being of another. At the same time he insists that sex must not be hidden away as something *secret*. For that entails that what one desires in one's privacy is necessarily shameful and therefore dirty. Lawrence respects the importance of modesty in both men and women. He attacks those who confuse it with the self-mutilation that results from smothering or denying one's physical yearning.

At the opposite pole of his Puritanism, Lawrence's thinking is much more confused. Like Rousseau, he claims that children must not be taught the truth about sexual reality, and that early sex education is more likely to inculcate the corruptions of civilized barbarity than to encourage natural spontaneity. He even casts doubt upon the heroic pioneering work of Dr. Marie Stopes, one of the founders of contemporary sexology. As always, Lawrence dreads the possibility of cognitive interference with vital processes within our affective being. Bertrand Russell once remarked that Lawrence was a man who had no mind. It would be more accurate to say that he feared Russell's kind of reliance upon abstract or deductive rationality, and as if in reference to Russell's mind he cogently states in one place: "Logic is far too coarse to make the subtle distinctions life demands." Lawrence's mistake consisted in assuming that one gets closer to life by wholly subordinating the intellect. Even if logic is too coarse, it does not follow that profound insights occur without considerable aid from empirical observation and the rationality of common sense.

One might defend Lawrence by saying that he was not trying to thwart intellectual processes but only to harness them in the service of vital impulse. When Lawrence uses the symbolism of Plato's black and white horses, which take on thematic importance throughout *The First Lady Chatterley*, he implies that their joint functioning is essential to the good life. At other times, however, he does give passionate feeling—what he sometimes calls "blood-consciousness" or "phallic consciousness"—an interpretation that seems to exclude much of what we would ordinarily consider civilized or intelligent modes of response. When he talks in this vein, Lawrence enunciates a sexual ideal that is highly circumscribed. He even spurns sensuous acuities to the extent that they do not immediately conduce to passion.

The most explicit description of sensuousness being sacrificed for the greater glory of passion occurs in *The Plumed Serpent*. In her sexual intercourse with Cipriano, Kate initially feels a renewal of the "old desire for frictional, irritant sensation" that she had experienced with a previous lover. But Cipriano, one of Lawrence's phallic heroes, is repelled by her appetite for "frictional voluptuousness." As if she were Shakespeare's Kate, a shrew in need of taming, Cipriano withholds himself affectively in order to awaken her capacity for emotional response. His tactic succeeds and she eventually realizes "the worthlessness of this foam-effervescence, its strange externality to her." As the outcome of her newly discovered knowledge, she concludes that her old type of orgasm was in fact "nauseous." The sexuality that Kate sloughs off, like a skin she must learn to outgrow, is the sexuality that depends on foreplay and, above all, the fondling of the external genitalia. That kind of behavior finds consummation in what used to be called "clitoral orgasm." It is part of what I have described as the "sensuous" mode of sexuality. Lawrence does not tolerate this as one among several kinds of acceptable responses. He is not a pluralist in these matters. In his "dark, hot silence" Cipriano believes that his beneficial mission consists in restoring to Kate the "heavy hot flow, when she was like a fountain gushing noiseless and with urgent softness from the volcanic deeps." This inner type of sex, involving passion rather than sensuous pleasure, puts Kate in contact with her true desire. It creates an orgasmic explosion that parallels Cipriano's burst of ecstasy.

The ability to undergo passionate emotion of this sort constitutes the sexual ideal for Lawrence. His Puritanism resides in his denial that such experience—"the simple and direct," as Kinsey called

it—can ever be harmonized, can ever find an authentic accommodation with, the playful, titillating, and sometimes excruciating
delights of the purely sensuous. As a recent critic remarks: "He was
puritanically repelled by 'cuddling and petting,' and complained
that nowadays 'there is plenty of pawing and laying hold, but no
real touch.'" Though Lawrence occasionally hints that when passion rules in male or female sexuality the sensuousness of "superficial" sex need not be totally neglected, he never shows how the
two may be integrated. In his messianic voice, virtually the only one
his poetry and prose sustain, he demands the dominance of passion. He thought that the metaphysical desire reveals itself through
nothing else.

In advocating his narrow conception of sex, Lawrence sees its
deepest expression in the marital bond. For the ideal of matrimony, as he depicts it, involves a permanent "blood" relationship.
He sometimes refers to this as a "mystic marriage" between man
and woman, based upon a mutuality of passionate sex strengthened by a commitment to fidelity. "The instinct of fidelity," he says,
"is perhaps the deepest instinct in the great complex we call sex.
Where there is real sex there is the underlying passion for fidelity."

These words were written at the end of Lawrence's life, but he
had been groping toward the idea of mystic marriage throughout
his earlier novels. In *Kangaroo* he considers three relationships that
a man might establish with his wife: "(*a*) the lord and master who is
honoured and obeyed, (*b*) the perfect lover, (*c*) the true friend and
companion." Lawrence rejects the second of these possibilities on
the grounds that men and women are incapable of attaining so
high and noble an ideal for any length of time. It is a Romantic
fantasy having little rapport with human reality, and it generally
eventuates in marital failure. But neither does he find the other
alternatives defensible. Though the man in this novel, and in others of the same period, tries to achieve dominance as lord and master, Lawrence clearly sees his arrogance and duplicity. Nor does
Lawrence find any hope for a marriage between friends, however
true and companionate they may be. In friendship, as he conceives
of it, two people admire each other's mind and personality without
reaching the oneness created by passionate sex. For that to occur

there must be "blood-marriage," mystic marriage in which "the oneness of the blood-stream of man and woman in marriage completes the universe, as far as humanity is concerned."

This notion of marriage as the embodiment of passionate sexuality Lawrence traces to the traditional doctrine in Western religion. He even calls it "Christianity's great contribution to the life of man." He commends the sacramental importance that Catholicism bestows upon marriage, not only through its rituals but also through its rejection of divorce. For the most part, however, Lawrence's approach reverts to what he perceives as the pagan origins of Catholicism. To the extent that his thinking does incorporate Christian belief, it generally relies on Protestant rather than Catholic ideas about agapē. Notice the words that Lawrence uses in his advice for those who wish to realize their metaphysical desire: "let your heart stay open, to receive the mysterious inflow of power from the unknown: know that the power comes to you from beyond, it is not generated by your own will."

By saying this, Lawrence renews and revitalizes Lutheran faith in a cosmic energy that operates independently of man's will. He also resembles Luther (and Freud) in complaining that Christianity is unrealistic when it demands spiritual achievements that defeat desire and frustrate human nature. Discussing the parable of the Grand Inquisitor in Dostoyevsky, Lawrence sides with the Grand Inquisitor and not with Jesus. For the love that Jesus taught imposes too difficult a burden for man to bear. According to Lawrence, it is a love that accepts people as they ought to be, not as they really are. Only the Grand Inquisitor loves mankind "for what it is, with all its limitations." And the greatest of these limitations is the inability to generate love from within oneself. That is what Christ finally learns in *The Man Who Died*.

Since Lawrence perceives the concept of agapē through post-Romantic spectacles, what he calls in-flowing desire does not originate with God the Father or God the Son. It belongs to the "unknowable" Holy Spirit, and far from being a bestowal of love it "surpasses either love or hate." We may see in Lawrence's doctrine something similar to Eckhart's distinction between God and the Godhead, but it would also be correct to classify him with nineteenth-century pantheists or religious naturalists. He says that "We can only know that from the unknown, profound desires enter in upon us, and that the fulfilling of these desires is the fulfilling of creation." More often, however, he refers to the unknown as a "great dark God"—the God "from whom the dark, sensual passion of love emanates." Elsewhere he separates the quick and the dead, the quick being "God-flame, in everything . . . the sum and source of all quickness, we will call God." Since he identifies God with the vital impulse in life, Lawrence may be considered Bergsonian. But unlike Bergson he seeks to put Christian faith behind him. We may therefore want to categorize him among the naturalists who explain man's search for love in terms of instinctual processes that must be revered as nature's own divinity.

I do not choose to confine Lawrence to one or another of these pigeonholes. With his glistening eye and frenetic tone, he defies precise taxonomy. By mapping out the different alternatives and recognizing the extent to which the concept of agapē underlies them all, we may, however, appreciate Lawrence's idea that love is desire which harmonizes merging and individuality. As an aspect of passionate sexuality, satisfied desire fulfills the deepest cravings of life within us; as a communion of "two in one," it creates the "whole love" between a man and a woman. This bond is more secure than Christian or brotherly love: it does not require self-sacrifice and it is therefore less likely to issue into the hatred of others. Fulfillment of desire is the principal access to reality, Lawrence believes, and at times he sounds as if it is the only one.

Yet even here, at the furthest reaches of his metaphysical probing, Lawrence presents two qualifications that destabilize the analysis. First, he introduces an idea of "sympathy" which would seem to be separate from passion. Having condemned Whitman's self-denying eagerness to melt into the being of others, he commends him for his ability to *sympathize* with them. He sees it as a talent for authentic love since Whitman can thereby accept all living creatures as just the striving bit of life that each of them is. He associates this attitude with the tenderness that Mellors feels for Lady Chatterley. It transforms Mellors' passionate use of her sexuality into love rather than lust. Presumably, natural sympathy fused with sexual tenderness puts one in touch with desire, but Lawrence does little to show us how this may be the case.

Second, Lawrence insists that even the most desirable love must be subordinated to what he calls activities that are not sexual but rather purposeful, socially and artistically creative. In *Fantasia of the Unconscious* he distinguishes between man's daytime and nighttime interests. He calls the former the "primary responsibility," the one that issues from man's "deepest soul . . . his own genuine, not spurious, divinity." The daytime attitude, which Lawrence refers to as "the pure, disinterested craving of the human male to make something wonderful, out of his own head," issues into a "passionate *purpose*." In *Fantasia of the Unconscious,* and possibly throughout his writings, Lawrence assumes that a man's purposive needs must take priority over even his strongest love for a woman: "Man, in the daytime, must follow his own soul's greatest impulse, and give himself to life-work and risk himself to death. It is not woman who claims the highest in man. It is man's own religious soul that drives him on beyond woman, to his own supreme activity. . . . He must carry forward the banner of life, though seven worlds perish, with all the wives and mothers and children in them."

At this point we may detect a kinship between Lawrence and Shaw. But Shaw, as we shall see, has generally been considered a stalwart feminist, whereas Lawrence has been singled out for attack by those who believe in women's liberation. In the passage just quoted he explicitly assigns a creative and purposive role to men that he denies to women, who are relegated to a male's nighttime interests. In *Sexual Politics* Kate Millett argues that Lawrence's writings reveal a chauvinistic bias which is both fearful of woman's independence and hostile to her very being. There is some basis to Millett's claim, and even when Lawrence encourages men and women to *"Be Thyself!"* he uses language that is significantly different for the two sexes. To every man he says: *"Be Desirous!"*, but his injunction to every woman is: *"Be Desirable!"* In this change of adjectives Lawrence manifests a differential attitude to which liberated women may well object.

On the other hand, Norman Mailer defends Lawrence against Millett in a way that seems partly justified to me. Mailer concentrates upon Lawrence's development as a novelist who explored various sexual possibilities but finally outgrew the need to dominate women, as he also overcame homosexual temptations which he thought were contrary to nature. Even Millett admits that *Lady Chatterley's Lover* is "a quasi-religious tract . . . [in which] Lawrence seems to be making his peace with the female." Mailer recognizes that some of Lawrence's earlier ideas are indefensible. But he sees them as a prelude to the theory of "sexual transcendence," the mystical unification through sex that takes both lovers beyond male domination.

One may nevertheless ask whether Lawrence ever believed in true equality between men and women. And more fundamentally, we may doubt the validity of Lawrentian transcendence even as a sexual ideal. In its rejection of nonpassionate sexuality, which constitutes so much of erotic life, this idealization may seem irresistible to a certain kind of Puritan. I myself think the conception is crude and self-defeating, restricting consummation in the very process of seeking to attain it at its deepest level. In turning to Shaw, can we hope to find a more advanced form of Puritanism, closer to the needs of the twentieth century?

❋

In the Foreword to *Women in Love*, Lawrence says: "Nothing that comes from the deep, passional soul is bad, or can be bad." Are we to take this as a tautology, the words "deep" and "passional" excluding the bad as a matter of definition? Or is Lawrence reporting, as he usually does, about the infinite goodness to be found in truly passionate sexuality? In either event, Shaw gives us reason to doubt the wisdom of the Lawrentian creed. In one of his "self sketches," written in the year that Lawrence died, Shaw sums up his own attitude toward sex and marriage: "I was never duped by sex as a basis for permanent relations, nor dreamt of marriage in connection with it. I put everything else before it, and never refused or broke an engagement to speak on Socialism to pass a gallant evening." This is the image of Shaw that is reflected back by all the critics in the last eighty years who have attacked him as a cold fish, a desiccated mind devoid of feeling, or even a man who was interested in people only as puppets for his art. Lawrence adds his bit when he claims that for Shaw "all sex is infidelity and only infidelity is sex. Marriage is sexless, null."

Lawrence says this in a passage that defends marriage as a permanent bond based on ultimate fidelity between the spouses and devoted to the achievement of mystical sexuality. Throughout his long career as a writer, which begins before Lawrence was born and ends twenty years after he died, Shaw often ridicules Lawrence's kind of thinking about sex and marriage. He frequently proclaimed the values of the daytime purposiveness that Lawrence recommended only on occasion. But to say that Shaw had no understanding of man's nighttime being, or that he had the mentality of a "eunuch," as Lawrence claims in one place, is to falsify his message.

Various commentators on Shaw have pondered the significance of the last words that Marchbanks the poet utters after he has lost out in his attempt to steal Candida from her pragmatic husband: "But I have a better secret than that in my heart. Let me go now. The night outside grows impatient." Like Dubedat, the selfish and self-oriented painter in *The Doctor's Dilemma,* or Dudgeon, whose sacrificial behavior in *The Devil's Disciple* is motivated by moral commitment rather than by feelings of love, Marchbanks may be seen as the solitary Shavian artist following the lonely path of creativity. That would align him with the Lawrentian archetype of inspired men who guard themselves against merging and remain devoted to their purposive mission. But Shaw himself suggested that the meaning of Marchbanks' final words could be discovered in Wagner's *Tristan and Isolde,* "where you will find the final and complete repudiation of the day and acceptance of the night as the true realm of the poet." Lawrence considered *Tristan and Isolde* "very near to pornography." He could not understand, as Shaw did, how Wagner's erotic music symbolizes the craving for indissoluble oneness that belongs to passionate sexuality.

One might remark that Lawrence was lacking in musical sensibility whereas Shaw was one of the greatest music critics. At a deeper level, however, we can also say that they were different kinds of Puritan theorists—both Puritans, but attuned to different facets of a similar doctrine. Shaw professes his Puritanism in various places. In his Preface to *Three Plays for Puritans* he identifies himself with Reformation thinkers who banned any glorification of sex on the stage. Like them, Shaw fears that the theater's constant preoccupation with love and the vicissitudes of romantic attachment must inevitably undermine public morals. "If the conventions of romance are only insisted on long enough and uniformly enough (a condition guaranteed by the uniformity of human folly and vanity), then, for the huge compulsorily schooled masses who read romance or nothing, these conventions will become the laws of personal honor."

In declaring himself a foe of "romantic conventions," Shaw had no intention of banishing romance from his own writings. *Arms and the Man* is subtitled "A Romantic Comedy," and many of the other plays concern themselves with the question of who among the characters will finally marry whom. In *Misalliance* Lord Summerhays finds it incomprehensible that people never tire of this question, and that it "occupies all the novel readers and all the playgoers." Yet Shaw himself feeds the unquenchable thirst for romantic adventure in the imagination. He does so, however, by placing each romance within a context that tests its adequacy to the needs of human nature and that generally finds it wanting. In *Arms and the Man* the militant Romantic Sergius proves himself a fool, a hypocrite, and an inconstant lover. Raina's adoration of him is punctured as soon as she encounters a really capable man, Bluntschli, the soldier who pursues no military ideals at all but thinks only of self-preservation. Although he is sometimes called a machine, Bluntschli is more than just an unemotional calculator. He shows wit and insight, quickly revealing to Raina that her girlish dreams are Romantic self-delusions. He combines within himself both realism and intuitive feeling, and these traits become the hallmark of true heroes in all of Shaw's plays. Romance has not been destroyed; it has merely been enlisted in a practical and purposeful cause beyond itself.

I shall return to this characteristic of the Shavian ideal, but first we need to see why he considered the conventions of romance so dangerous. Discussing his own childhood, he notes that it was filled, as far back as he can remember, with a sense of sexual need: "I cannot remember any time when I did not exercise my imagination in daydreams about women." Since he remained a virgin until he was twenty-nine, as he tells us, the young Shaw devoted himself to the chaste pursuit of "Uranian Venus"—the heavenly Aphrodite in Plato. He found her in the art of nineteenth-century romanticism, in Romantic fiction and Romantic opera. Shaw describes the hazards in this kind of upbringing. Splendid as it is for cultivating a sense of beauty and perpetuating the free expression of imagination, it may "spoil us for real women and real men" by causing us to live within our own voluptuous vision. We then treat others as "something they are not and neither desire nor hope to be."

What then is the *earthly* Aphrodite, according to Shaw? What is the nature of human affect as experienced by the real men and women whose being is misrepresented by romance? Shaw has no hesitation in reverting to the category of sex, much as Lawrence would have done. He says that he always found St. Paul's attitude "pathological," and he adds: "Sexual experience seemed a natural appetite, and its satisfaction a completion of human experience." But Shaw's interpretation of sexuality sets him apart from Lawrence, who rarely treats it as just instinctual behavior that leads to reproduction. For Lawrence, desire arises out of the unknown cauldron that creates all power in the universe. It is not the force which brings into existence a succession of human beings bound to one another. Similarly, there is in Lawrence remarkably little perception of how a gratifying sexual relationship can issue into familial oneness or an eventual love between parents and children. While Shaw's plays also contain a scarcity of family love of this sort, Shaw always interprets sex as an evolutionary process that enables life to progress from one generation to the next. For Shaw, that is the most essential—though not the only—thing one can say about it.

From this we might conclude that Shaw has appropriated the major insight of Freud. Yet that too is not entirely correct. For Shaw retains metaphysical categories that Freud spurned, or at least found counterproductive as far as scientific work was concerned. When Shaw discusses sex as a reproductive energy, he portrays it as an expression of the Life Force. He feels no difficulty in using this terminology taken from Bergson, whom he names as "the established philosopher of my sect." Though he often pays homage to Schopenhauer, Shaw's conception of the Life Force is quite different from the will in Schopenhauer, as we shall see. At the same time Shaw's thinking does resemble Schopenhauer's in positing a metaphysical agency that manipulates sexual experience for the sake of procreative goals neither passion nor romance can ever comprehend.

For Lawrence sexual passion is important to human beings because it puts them in touch with the deepest level of themselves. As Shaw conceives of it, sex never has that significance. Though he acknowledges its basic function as the reproductive mechanism, he sees no reason to glorify sexuality. In the Preface to *Getting Married* he calls sexual love "an appetite which, like all other appetites, is destroyed for the moment by its gratification." Though he here uses the word "love," he is talking about it in relation to sex. In general he insists that much of love, even passion, has nothing to do with sex. His attack on "Nineteenth Century Amorism" issues from his denial that passion is always sexual and that sexual passion provides the transempirical benefits Lawrence or the Romantics sought.

As against Lawrence's tendency to denigrate reason, and mind in general, Shaw claims that intellect is itself a passion. He says that in his youth he valued sexual experience because it could produce "a celestial flood of emotion and exaltation which, however momentary, gave me a sample of the ecstasy that may one day be the normal condition of conscious intellectual activity." The fault in romanticism would therefore consist in its outlandish idealization of those transitory emotions and exaltations that arise out of sex. Of greater value and profundity, according to Shaw, is the experience of intellectual passions in no way related to sexual instinct. "And who dares say that mathematics and reasoning are not passions?" asks Secondborn in *Buoyant Billions*. He then describes scientists like Copernicus, Newton, and Einstein as thinkers who were "carried away by the passion for measuring truth and knowledge that possessed and drove them." He sets this kind of passion far above "the vulgar concupiscences of Don Juan and Casanova, and the romance of Beatrice and Francesca, of Irish Deirdre, the greatest bores in literature."

In much of his prose writing Shaw argues for the superiority of intellectual over sexual passion. Maintaining that "thought is a passion," Shaw believes that in themselves cognitive pursuits are capable of providing the emotional gratifications usually associated with sex. In its idealistic blindness, he says, romanticism put the cart before the horse. In "The Sanity of Art" Shaw remarks: "It is not emotion in the raw but as evolved and fixed as intellectual conviction that will save the world." Shaw makes this statement in the context of arguing that altruistic feelings may be as basic to human nature as aggressive or egoistic ones, but he assumes that the former exist as passions which are basically intellectual.

Shaw makes no attempt to show how intellectual and sexual passions are comparable, if in fact they are. Presumably the Life Force motivates the yearning for knowledge and moral clarity as well as the impulse to reproduce. And possibly one can speak of both as "passions." What Shaw scarcely recognizes, however, is that a love of learning—engrossing as it may sometimes be—has only an indirect relation to the passions that make us want to engage with other people in the kinds of intimacy that sexuality involves. Shaw gives us no unified theory, and therefore no means of discerning how the two types of passion may depend on one another.

What Shaw proposes, in effect, is a redeployment of romanticism, a redirection of its energies toward the achievement of purified passions of the intellect. That became the burden of his later philosophical plays. In *Back to Methuselah* the course of creative evolution takes man to a point where babies are no longer produced in the present fashion and where sexual dalliance belongs to a brief playtime lasting only two or three years. The important business of life is shown to consist in the search for immortality. Life everlasting will be attained once the human race has learned to survive without a body. In the final state, as Shaw portrays it, men and women come very close to living in the intellect, by thought alone. But though these higher beings achieve this good, they would seem to have eliminated everything that we can recognize as emotion. While freeing man from the bonds and illusions of sexual passion, Shavian evolution destroys the human capacity for passion in general. To that extent, the superman is not even man. In striving for the ideal, he has evolved into something that diminishes our natural condition. Shaw never resolves this paradox in his thinking.

I do not mean that Shaw is oblivious to the problem. At the end of *Back to Methuselah* he has one of the characters express doubts that many of us in the audience will have shared: "What is the use of being born if we have to decay into unnatural, heartless, loveless, joyless monsters in four short years?" Shaw does imply, of course, that "the ancients," who vastly outlive this character's infantile stage of development, have greater understanding of these matters. But we may also conclude that Shaw's own genius is less evident in his utopian musings than in his reflections about the current imperfection of man. His ideas on immortality achieved through the transcendence of physical nature seem quite insubstantial. They are predicated upon the flimsy assumption that mind or intellect must be deathless in itself, and we are given no help in our attempt to understand what existence could be like without the body. We encounter the same difficulty in *Man and Superman,* where Don Juan finally reaches an elysium of pure contemplation. The Devil and the Commendatore find heaven boring, empty not only of divertissements but also of stimuli for aesthetic appreciation. We are told that the "masters of reality" congregate in heaven, exercising their superiority through the search for knowledge. But we are vouchsafed no other information about this blissful realm, and we may well choose to discard Shaw's references to it as verbal filler.

All religious thinkers face a similar problem when they talk about the culminating goal of life, whether it be Nirvana or the Christian paradise. If, as I am suggesting, Shaw should be taken as a religious, indeed Puritan and post-Protestant, writer, the relative weakness in this region of his thought will not surprise us. As in the case of many other religious theorists, however, his message may also be read as a symbolic vision of existence in the present life. When Bergson identifies the élan vital with creative spirit emanating from the Judaeo-Christian God, he too tells us little or nothing about the ends toward which it is evolving. He explicates its inner being by reminding us of how mystics in the real world have actually lived. Similarly, Shaw the atheist expresses what is deepest in his vitalistic conception when he gives St. Joan the lines that reveal the nature of her questing soul: "O God that madest this beautiful earth, when will it be ready to receive *Thy* saints? How long, O Lord, how long?" There is no answer to these questions since Shaw is primarily interested in the complexity of forces that make things to be as they are right now. Despite his speculations about utopia, it is man's prior and immediate condition that elicits his true philosophy.

In naming the Life Force as the ultimate category of explanation for how the world evolves, Shaw does not mention Hegel. It is always Schopenhauer, though sometimes Nietzsche as well, that he cites as the philosopher from whom he acquired his ideas about the will. But there is in Shaw's thinking an optimistic and melioristic disposition which aligns him with Hegel much more than with theorists such as Schopenhauer or Nietzsche. In fact his conception of the Life Force could largely have been derived from Hegel's ideas about absolute spirit moving progressively upward by means of its immersion in matter. Though Shaw chooses to direct his vitalistic creed toward the possible achievements of empirical science, as Bergson also did, the underlying Hegelianism in Shaw's thought appears when he says: "To me the sole hope for human salvation lies in teaching Man to regard himself as an experiment in the realization of God, to regard his hands as God's hands, his brain as God's brain, his purpose as God's purpose. He must regard God as a helpless Longing, which *longed* him into existence by its desperate need for an executive organ." On another occasion, Shaw claims that his life "belongs to the whole community. . . . I want to be thoroughly used up when I die; for the harder I work the more I live. I rejoice in life for its own sake." In *Major Barbara* Undershaft says the power that drives both himself and the society he has created is a "will of which I am a part." His daughter sees in this the basis of a new religion, which she depicts as "the raising of hell to heaven and of man to God, through the unveiling of an eternal light in the Valley of The Shadow." All this sounds more like Hegel than like Schopenhauer, Nietzsche, or even Bergson.

For Shaw, the ideal of life is itself the making of ideals (and the struggling to attain them). In the process the Life Force manifests its being, much as Lutheran agapē showed forth through man's moral activism within the world. All of Shaw's dedication to political reform, to social change, to practical decision-making issues from this approach. It also explains his insight into the differences between his kind of wit and that of W. S. Gilbert: "Gilbert is simply a paradoxically humorous cynic. He accepts the conventional ideals implicitly, but observes that people do not really live up to them. This he regards as a failure on their part at which he mocks bitterly." Of himself Shaw says: "I do not accept the conventional ideals. To them I oppose . . . the practical life and morals of the efficient, realistic man, unaffectedly ready to face what risks must be faced, considerate but not chivalrous."

The same contrast holds for each of Shaw's comedies. He is not a master of irony as Gilbert was; he is a masterful maker of ideals— whatever their ultimate validity may be. Unlike Gilbert, Shaw employs wit and fantasy to lure us into considering radically new values once we realize that nothing could be more ludicrous than those to which we now adhere. The plays of Gilbert, including those he wrote as librettos for Sullivan, are absurdist in the manner of the Marx Brothers. Gilbert makes us laugh at the ridiculous postures that human beings quite naturally assume in trying to live up to impossible ideals. They constantly fail to attain them because of an innate stupidity or lack of logic, as when a man falls off a ladder each time he reaches for the moon.

Shaw rightly characterizes Gilbert's moral stance as "cynicism, pessimism." He is also right in thinking that he and Gilbert belong to totally different traditions. Ibsen, the quintessence of whom Shaw sought to become and to exceed, wrote that he himself was a pessimist "inasmuch as I do not believe in the eternity of human ideals. But I am also an optimist, inasmuch as I fully and confidently believe in the ideals' power of propagation and of development." Hegel (and even Luther) could have said the same. A similar attitude permeates everything that Shaw wrote throughout his life. It helps us to understand what he meant by moral or intellectual passion.

If now we juxtapose Shaw's idealization of this activism and his refusal to romanticize sexual passion, we may be able to explain his frequent condemnation of marriages based on love. In the Preface to *Getting Married* he pokes at "incorrigible sentimentalists" who do not realize that love is a tyranny that people "would never dream of proposing to or suffering from those they dislike or regard with indifference." He asserts that "healthy marriages are partnerships of companionable and affectionate friendship," and that "cases of chronic life-long love, whether sentimental or sensual, ought to be sent to the doctor if not to the executioner." Though the reference to affectionate friendship reminds one of the Puritan origins that Shaw shares with Lawrence, this kind of statement must be taken as a flat rejection of Lawrence's belief in mystic marriage. In *Getting Married* Collins seems to speak for Shaw, and against Lawrence, when he says: "Marriage is tolerable enough in its way if youre easygoing and dont expect too much from it. But it doesnt bear thinking about. The great thing is to get the young people tied up before they know what theyre letting themselves in for."

Yet Shaw is also pluralistic about marriage. The great virtue of his discussion, in the Preface to *Getting Married* and elsewhere, is his awareness that marriages differ among themselves. His own marriage was sexless by previous agreement, but he got married after he was over forty and he points out that marriages between young people are not the same as "childless partnerships" like his. This does not, however, prevent Shaw from sneering at people who "write as if the highest attainable state is that of a family stewing in love continuously from the cradle to the grave." He is convinced that "no healthy man or animal is occupied with love in any sense for more than a very small fraction indeed of the time he devotes to business and to recreations wholly unconnected with love."

Lawrence could have accepted this as affirmation of the daytime consciousness that must supervene upon love, and he might have agreed when Shaw then goes on to say: "A wife entirely preoccupied with her affection for her husband, a mother entirely preoccupied with her affection for her children, may be all very well in a book (for people who like that kind of book); but in actual life she is a nuisance." In making such comments, Shaw does not deny the possibility of love within marriage. For the most part, he can be seen as attacking the mawkish *stewing* which parodies authentic love. He need not be interpreted as ruling out the idea that a good marriage may include love as well as companionate friendship.

Shaw's most consecutive effort to formulate his philosophy of love occurs in *Man and Superman*. Its third act, which includes the dream sequence of Don Juan in hell, he called "a careful attempt to write a new Book of Genesis for the Bible of the Evolutionists." More than anything else he wrote, *Man and Superman* reveals that human nature reaches its pinnacle in "the philosophic man." For Shaw that means one whose consciousness is directed toward spiritual growth understood in terms of post- and anti-Darwinian evolutionary theory. The God whose cosmic order will be contemplated in the heaven toward which Don Juan ventures, in his pilgrim's progress, is nothing like the blind and aimless Schopenhauerian will. Though he claims to have written a play about the "biology" of male and female sexuality, Shaw always reverts to the presuppositions of benign romanticism.

Shaw's residual adherence to this idealist strand of philosophy is evident in his conception of Don Juan himself. Superficial critics, whom Shaw rebuts in advance though to no avail, have often maintained that his protagonist is a deviation from the Don Juan myth. Far from being a libertine who seduces females on a wholesale basis, Shaw's character is embarrassed by his sexual charm and flees women in a frantic attempt to retain his freedom. But the truth is that Don Juan runs away from women in *all* the versions of the myth that preceded Shaw's. In the nineteenth century he was often perceived as a questing hero whose escapades are really a search for the perfect female, herself the erotic embodiment of elevated ideals. Though Shaw discards the former preoccupation with promiscuity or constant infatuation, he does so in order to accentuate the heroic male's craving for perfection. His Don Juan is primarily motivated by the intellectual type of passion. Since it is what Shaw elsewhere calls "the mightiest of the passions," Don Juan is driven by an instinctual power that mere sexuality cannot equal. He opts for the apparent dreariness of heaven because it is the abode of those who reach fulfillment through knowledge and discovery. In heaven, he insists, "you live and work instead of playing and pretending. You face things as they are."

In choosing heaven as his destination, Don Juan is less of a revolutionary than Shaw would have us think. Like John Tanner, his incarnation, or like Shaw himself, he does speak in language that is shocking and exhibitionist. But that is a typical male display, and neither Tanner nor Don Juan is really a freethinker. Apart from their wonderful ability to express themselves—their verbal freedom or sheer loquaciousness—they speak and act like typical fin-de-siècle English gentlemen preserving their bachelorhood as long as possible while also manifesting the conventional values of their society. Here too Shaw is faithfully continuing the Don Juan myth: Tirso's protagonist behaves as he does in order to maintain his status among the other young aristocrats; Molière's Dom Juan shows himself to be a prey to considerations of "honor"; and even Mozart's Don Giovanni appears to be the prisoner of Leporello's libertine catalogue. Shaw's Tanner and Don Juan are not really identical, and I shall presently return to the crucial differences between them, but in one respect they are equally guilty of the same confusion about sexual love. They both assume, quite conventionally, that it involves bondage to external forces rather than being an acceptance of man's natural condition. This is a stock idea of men in the Western world. It is by no means revolutionary.

Devotion to nothing but the Life Force is what Tanner, Don Juan, and Shaw offer as the path to salvation. They take this to mean that the heroic male—themselves in one guise or another—must overcome the allurements of sexual impulse or romantic attachment. If Shaw had truly believed his own vitalism, he would have recognized that the superman can evolve only if his ancestors choose to give him life. His parents must will him into being. Yet Tanner and Don Juan run away from women in order to remain faithful instruments of the Life Force. They hope to further it as thinkers and artists who use their brains to map out mankind's future developments. But since these have to be *biological* developments, they require the harmonious mating of Don Juan types with clever women like Doña Ana (Ann Whitefield). If Don Juan and Tanner were really devoted to the Life Force, they would not be running away. Inasmuch as they do, their official claim to serve and even love the creative energy in nature is actually a subtle mode of rejecting it.

Nature as it exists in human beings takes the form of a complex community of persons that one encounters from day to day. And it is the love of persons, the love of other human beings as just the individuals they happen to be, that the Shavian ideal neglects and denigrates. When Don Juan describes the amatory interest he experienced for one or another woman while still on earth, he calls it "the outcome of a perfectly simple impulse of my manhood towards her womanhood." He never mentions an individualized attraction toward some particular woman, or any desire to bestow value upon her personality. Like all the other Don Juans in the myth, he has mastered the art of getting women to fall in love with him but he himself has never learned how to love. This becomes quite evident when he describes his moments of greatest intimacy. Standing "face to face with Woman," he senses that his brain, his morals, his chivalry, his pity for her and his concern about himself all say No. He observes the lady as an artifact of matter and sensation—"the strange odors of the chemistry of the nerves." When he finally succumbs to the vital impulse that courses through him willy-nilly, he does so without any joyful affirmation but merely as a victim of convulsive powers beyond his control. Though wanting to say No definitively, like Schopenhauer, he ends up saying Yes reluctantly: "And whilst I was in the act of framing my excuse to the lady, Life seized me and threw me into her arms as a sailor throws a scrap of fish into the mouth of a seabird."

Since Shaw has no conception of love as an *acceptance* of nature and the persons who embody it, neither is his thought rich enough to yield any knowledge of love as consummation. One of the first things Don Juan tells Ana is that people in hell devote themselves to pleasure and talk about nothing but love. For hell is the domain of mere amusement, of illusory gratification and meaningless enjoyment. Don Juan moves on to heaven in order to rise above all such useless preoccupations. At no point, however, does he (or

Shaw) appreciate the goodness and vital reality of undergoing consummations that result from satisfying our deeply programmed instincts. Shaw's account of biological morality would seem to require a choice between being the scrap of fish and being the elevated but unattached philosopher, between hell as delusory pleasure and heaven as pure contemplation. A love of persons that would put us in touch with our own being as well as the being of those we love, that would be enjoyable and also a fulfillment of the Life Force as it sustains us in our momentary existence—none of this enters into the Shavian philosophy.

But one can also say that Shaw is greater than his own official doctrine. For with the cunning of artistic genius he contrives to make Tanner significantly different from the Don Juan who mythically represents him in his dream. The premarital struggle between Tanner and Ann ends with their suitable and predictable marriage. They are clearly made for one another; and though Tanner says that in the name of household and family they have renounced happiness, freedom, tranquillity, and romance, we have every reason to believe that they will experience married love which consists in more than just companionable partnership. From their early conversation about their childhood together, we perceive how greatly each figures in the other's life—not as instances of manhood or womanhood but as persons whose feelings and ideas matter pervasively to them both.

In creating these two characters, Shaw was inspired by Shakespeare's Beatrice and Benedick. In both sets of lovers apparent hostility is needed to counteract a network of infinite attachments to the other person, attachments so powerful that they threaten the sense of freedom and individuality. Without the compensatory self-assertiveness thus engendered, love becomes the guttering mess to which Lawrence referred. But when couples such as these finally mate, having reached an equilibration in their feelings, one senses that the work of nature is being accomplished successfully, correctly, even ideally.

A comparable paradox between Shaw the philosopher and Shaw the dramatist appears once we consider his ideas about feminism. In everything he writes about the New Woman we may recognize a champion of women's liberation, a worthy successor to Ibsen, Stendhal, and Shelley. Combined with his Nietzschean faith in discipline and self-mastery as the prerequisites of human salvation, this part of Shaw heralds—indeed glorifies—the strong, intelligent, courageous, and creative woman of the future. But Doña Ana, who stands for Ann Whitefield in the dream sequence, reveals a different side of Shaw's mentality. For he sees her as the eternal feminine not because she lures man on to transcendental values, as in Goethe, but only because she continues to seek a father for the superman. So exclusive is her role as childbearer, as madonna who will some day give birth to Christ, that the other possibilities of human nature remain atrophied in her. In a commentary on "Don Juan in Hell," Shaw describes as follows this personage who expresses his ideas about femininity: "She cannot, like the male devil, use love as mere sentiment and pleasure; nor can she, like the male saint, put love aside when it has once done its work as a developing and enlightening experience. Love is neither her pleasure nor her study: it is her business. So she, in the end, neither goes with Don Juan to heaven nor with the devil and her father to the palace of pleasure, but declares that her work is not yet finished. For though by her death she is done with the bearing of men to mortal fathers, she may yet, as Woman Immortal, bear the Superman to the Eternal Father."

This way of thinking, which has become outmoded nowadays, is coherent with much of Shaw's vitalistic Puritanism. It is, however, less interesting than his contrasting conception of man and woman joining forces to change the future for all human beings, cooperating to evolve the new species that nature requires if it is to achieve a higher level of spirituality. This much of Shaw will endure. Nor will anyone improve upon these words of his about the meaningfulness of life for those who have learned how to control their passions: "This is the true joy in life, the being used for a purpose recognized by yourself as a mighty one; the being thoroughly worn out before you are thrown on the scrap heap; the being a force of Nature instead of a feverish selfish little clod of ailments and grievances complaining that the world will not devote itself to making you happy."

7
Santayana

In Recent Years The Works of George Santayana have enjoyed a revival of interest and scholarly attention. Professional philosophers in America and elsewhere have returned to his writings in a way that could hardly have been predicted when he died in 1952. His thinking about the nature of love has never been adequately studied. In the first volume of this trilogy I discussed shortcomings in his concept of idealization. His ideas are richer than I could there indicate, however, and they merit renewed investigation.

Speaking of Santayana as the greatest proponent of Platonism in the twentieth century, I tried to show how he combined his Platonism with an antithetical materialism. But it would have been equally valid to have started with his materialism as the basis of his philosophy. In his speculations on love, scattered through all his books, that is how Santayana usually begins his analysis. I shall do likewise in this chapter. Over and beyond Santayana's materialism and Platonism, I also detect a humanistic voice that differs from both of them. I consider Santayana's "humanism" the most promising element in his philosophy.

The materialistic strand establishes Santayana as a direct descendent of Schopenhauer. As a graduate student, he had originally thought of writing his Ph.D. thesis on him. He was finally dissuaded by the realization that a commentary on Schopenhauer would give him little opportunity to reveal his own insight and acumen. He also feared that Josiah Royce might not welcome as favorable a treatment of naturalistic concepts as Santayana's would be. By the time he wrote *Egotism in German Philosophy*, Santayana had developed a more critical approach to Schopenhauerian pessimism. He detected irresolvable difficulties in Schopenhauer's transcendentalism and lingering romanticism. Even so, Santayana praises him in that book. He greatly prefers him to "those unspeakable optimists" who thought the troubled world must be good because it made such a fine tragedy.

What Santayana admires most in Schopenhauer is his insistence on the material grounding of all experience and of all reality. Though the will might occasionally attain spiritual goals, it is not itself spirit. It is merely the dynamic but purposeless power in natural process, which Santayana calls "the realm of matter." In Santayana's ontology that realm has the same ultimacy as the deterministic force of destiny which is the will in Schopenhauer. If anything, Santayana is more of a materialist than Schopenhauer. In his attempt to dismiss Romantic ideas about the will heroically contriving to deny itself through acts of contemplation or proud defiance, Santayana accentuates and extends Schopenhauer's reductivistic belief that brute matter is the only substance, that only it sustains being of any sort.

The implications of Santayana's materialism appear even in his earliest statements about love. In *The Sense of Beauty* (1896) he introduces into a section on "The Materials of Beauty" a discussion about "the influence of the passion of love." Though he is doing aesthetics in this place, he makes remarks that are relevant to the philosophy of love. In effect, he argues that the sexual instinct needed for purposes of reproduction underlies our perception of beauty in another person as well as our ability to love that particular individual. He tells us that there exists a "machinery" (unspecified but presumably discoverable by empirical science) which directs all animals to their proper object of sexual desire. He even analyzes "lifelong fidelity to one mate" as a differentiation related to successful reproduction of the species. But though the sexual instinct cannot be satisfied unless an appropriate object is singled out, Santayana believes this process operates only with "a great deal of groping and waste." From this there arise the effects, which Santayana considers secondary, of beauty and of love: "For it is precisely from the waste, from the radiation of a sexual passion, that beauty borrows warmth. . . . The capacity to love gives our contemplation that glow without which it might often fail to manifest beauty."

In saying this, Santayana is consciously espousing a reductivistic thesis about love as well as beauty. Like many other materialists and realists, he does so with a sense of admiration, even reverence, for the creative goodness in the sexual instinct. He sees it as a "dumb and powerful" faculty that can nevertheless "suffuse the world with the deepest meaning." Unlike traditional moralists, he emphasizes the social and spiritual tendencies that sexual attraction can induce. He reminds us of Stendhal, in one place claiming that "all these new values crystallise about the objects then offered to the mind." On the next page he even cites Stendhal's *De l'Amour* after saying that when the new values focus in a single image "the object becomes perfect, and we are said to be in love."

Santayana's reductivism is of a double nature. Not only does he explain love in terms of sexual instinct, but also he derives all love from the relationship between a man and a woman. He says that we become lovers of nature when the values normally crystallized within the image of another person are "dispersed" over the world. And though "woman is the most lovely object to man, and man, if female modesty would confess it, the most interesting to woman," he remarks that repression or frustration often redirect sexual passion towards other ends. These include religion and philanthropy as well as the love of nature. "We may say, then, that for man all nature is a secondary object of sexual passion, and that to this fact the beauty of nature is largely due." In a similar vein Santayana traces back to the needs of the reproductive function virtually all the social dispositions that constitute civilization and communal enterprise.

One can only speculate about the extent to which Santayana's thinking was influenced by Freud at this stage. By 1923, however, the points at which their ideas make contact are firmly established in the essay Santayana wrote after he had read *Beyond the Pleasure*

Principle. In "A Long Way Round to Nirvana; or Much Ado About Dying," Santayana contrasts Freud's dualistic materialism with Bergson's belief in a "general impulse toward some unknown but single ideal." He recognizes that both conceptions are mythical, but Freud's he finds true to nature while Bergson's he condemns as folly. Speaking always as a moralist and metaphysician, Santayana perceives in Freud's approach a chastening insight into our condition as material entities. "The transitoriness of things is essential to their physical being, and not at all sad in itself." What Santayana does find sad is the frustration or destruction of instinctual impulses, arrested before their latent potency has had a chance to express itself and reach fruition. Assuming the rightness of Freud's dictum that "the goal of all life is death," Santayana implies that if all their instincts could be satisfied harmoniously human beings would have no further reason to stay alive. In that event, he surmises, "we should be satisfied once and for all and completely. Then doing and dying would coincide throughout and be a perfect pleasure."

Almost twenty years earlier Santayana developed a similar notion in the chapter of *Reason in Society* entitled "Love." Depicting the sexual origins of love in general, he suggests that when passion is vehement and complete it may renounce even life itself "now that the one fated destiny and all-satisfied good has been achieved." Quoting Siegfried's paean to Liebestod at the moment when he and Brünnhilde merge with one another in Wagner's *Ring*, Santayana remarks: "When love is absolute it feels a profound impulse to welcome death, and even, by a transcendental confusion, to invoke the end of the universe."

In the context of his discussion, it is evident that Santayana is not reverting to Romantic pessimism. For he immediately invokes instincts other than the sexual, instincts related to parental interest. These supervene upon passion and prevent the "transcendental illusion" from causing a total extinction. Instead of death there is the creation of new life, renunciation being followed by a resurrection in the birth of offspring. By introducing parental instincts of this sort, Santayana remains faithful to his vision as a materialist. For the nature of passionate love is still taken as basically dependent upon the needs of reproduction. In this vein he praises Lucretius as "the most ingenuous and magnificent of poets," criticizing him only because he described sex in terms of its external behavior and thus neglected the beauty of its inner life—the joy and feverish intensity of libidinal instinct as it is actually experienced by each member of a species. Santayana calls this the "glory of animal love." As a staunch materialist and naturalistic philosopher, he laments the human tendency to consider sexual passion a shame or sin rather than an opportunity for communion through "the most delightful of nature's mysteries." Later in the chapter he refers to "the quality of love" as "its thrill, flutter, and absolute sway over happiness and misery."

To explain how it was possible for the innocent goodness of sex to have been degraded in the course of man's development, Santayana suggests that emotions such as shamefulness result from the relative complexity of human nature. Having a large gamut of instinctual needs, man is subject to the continuous interaction between sexual impulses and other desires that inhibit sex while also submitting to its pressure. His brief reference to a field of interacting forces determining the nature of erotic response Santayana doubtless inherits from William James' psychology. The idea is important here because it implicitly takes Santayana's conception beyond its reductivistic limits. For if shame (or any other attitude related to interpersonal feelings) occurs as a vector of conflicting forces, it cannot be reduced to one of them. And indeed Santayana's approach changes throughout the rest of his chapter. He has less to say about the sexual basis of love than about its function as an imaginative questing for ideals. At this point, Santayana's Neoplatonism becomes the dominating theme in his analysis.

To my knowledge Santayana never calls himself a Neoplatonist, or a Platonist of any kind. In the chapter on love he complains that Plato ignored the "natural history" of the subject. Nevertheless, Santayana repeatedly acknowledges his indebtedness to much of what is most distinctive in Plato's philosophy: the idea that passion, and love as a whole, is elicited by an object that seems good; that this object embodies or represents or symbolizes an ideal goodness and beauty; and that ultimately—in its final definition—love yearns primarily for the ideal itself and not for the imperfect object which happens to prefigure it.

Though he drew upon these elements of Platonic philosophy, Santayana rightly saw that they need not conflict with his basic naturalism. In *Platonism and the Spiritual Life* he attacks the "Platonic tradition" for having assumed that ideals have any being as substances. He insists that ideals have no existence prior to the occurrence of matter. Throughout his writings, Santayana maintains that only nature or materiality exists as substance. Ideals emerge as goals that organisms create in the process of adapting to their environment. From this it would follow that the origins of love are natural even though its aim or objective is the perfection encompassed by an ideal. Synthesizing Platonism with naturalism in this way, Santayana believes that "every ideal expresses some natural function, and that no natural function is incapable, in its free exercise, of evolving some ideal. . . . For love is a brilliant illustration of a principle everywhere discoverable: namely, that human interest lives by turning the friction of material forces into the light of ideal goods."

Both early and late, Santayana frequently describes love as a "sublimation" related to an "animal basis," and to this extent his kinship to Freud remains intact. But Plato too had thought that love originates in each person's history as a physical, indeed sexual, impulse even though it signified the more ultimate longing for possession of a transcendental good. In Plato's writings, however, we constantly encounter a systematic ambiguity about natural and ideal love. To what extent must material interests be cleansed or eliminated in order for the lover to fulfill his metaphysical mission? Is love a harmonious completion of organic needs, such as the sexual, or is it rather a oneness with the principle of goodness and beauty that requires quasi-ascetic contemplation? By insisting upon the interrelationship between ideals and natural processes, Santayana continues the effort of Neoplatonists in the Renaissance who tried to resolve Plato's ambiguities. Like Ficino, Santayana sees love as a search for ideals that appear in the midst of nature, and as an inherent part of nature. Ficino, like other Platonistic Christians and like Plato himself, thought that ideals emanate from a super-world beyond nature. Santayana parts company at this juncture, but he never deviates from the belief that love consists in the transmuting of natural desires into a striving for ideals that underlie the goodness of everything that is desired.

❋

If this were all that Santayana said about love, one might have been tempted to dismiss him as a naturalist who weaves a bit of Neoplatonism into his fabric. Despite its belletristic beauties, the chapter on love in *Reason in Society* is remarkable only in its repeated claim that ideals such as married love or the love of humanity may be explained as sublimations of sexual desire. But even in 1905, when the book was published, this suggestion was hardly novel. It is only Santayana's subsequent development of his Platonistic insights that reveals the great originality in his synthesis. The major text is *The Realm of Spirit*, the final volume of *Realms of Being*. It appeared in 1940, at a bad moment in the history of the Western world, and it has never received the attention it deserves. In it Santayana's thinking about love reaches a height beyond anything he had previously attained.

Despite the connotations that the term "spirit" often has, Santayana's conception is thoroughly naturalistic. Like everything else that exists, spirit belongs to processes in the material world; it arises from the realm of matter. Spirit has no substantial being in itself. As the sole substance, matter creates spirit when it develops into a particular form of life—the disposition of organic energy that Santayana calls "psyche." "The self-maintaining and reproducing pattern or structure of an organism, conceived as a power, is called a psyche." When psyches become active in their relations to the physical world, they achieve an animal as well as a vegetative condition. If spirit then awakens in animals, it does so as a kind of "moral illumination" or "free entertainment." In his glossary of terms, Santayana defines spirit as "an awareness natural to animals, revealing the world and themselves in it. Other names for spirit are consciousness, attention, feeling, thought, or any word that marks the total *inner* difference between being awake or asleep, alive or dead." Elsewhere he says: "spirit is only that inner light of actuality or attention which floods all life as men actually live it on earth." And later, when he discusses the sense in which there may be freedom in spirit, he remarks that spirit is "the invisible but immediate fact that matter with its tropes and powers is being observed, conceived, enjoyed, asserted, or desired: a vitality essentially moral, invisible, and private, absolutely actual and thoroughly unsubstantial, always self-existent and totally vanishing as it lives."

By formulating this concept of spirit, Santayana discards all supernatural ideas about a soul or spiritual entity that could exist apart from the material world. He also rejects idealistic notions about spirit as a metaphysical power that determines the direction of the universe, whether by creating it in advance or by animating its progressive evolution. On the contrary, Santayana maintains that spirit—as opposed to psyche, which is a biological agency of material being—always remains impotent, wholly ineffectual, capable of surveying the universe but unable to alter it. Changes in the order of things may result from the psyche working upon the world as a functionary within animal activity. Spirit is one of these changes. Its existence depends on the interrelationship between psyche and the natural environment. In spirit itself there can be "nothing persistent or potential. It is pure light and perpetual actuality."

If we now ask what it is that spirit illuminates in its actuality and purified light, Santayana replies in terms of his ideas about "essences." These are the character or whatness of everything given to consciousness, either through direct intuition or analytically through dialectical reasoning or symbolically through imagination. Santayana's doctrine of essences resembles the Platonic theory of forms inasmuch as both assume that man has the capacity to contemplate the world in its immediacy and without necessarily interpreting it as something that exists. Far from being an insight into the vital impulse which is foundational to existence—as Bergson would say—intuition is for Santayana an aspect of the mind that lights upon the pattern or apparent quality of everything that is possible, whether or not it has existed or ever will exist.

Santayana's essences are nothing but pure possibilities. In thinking of anything that is not self-contradictory, we contemplate a whatness without which nothing could even be conceived—its defining attributes, its essential form. Everything that is not logically inconsistent or incoherent will be a possible in this sense. That is why we can have reveries about unicorns and golden mountains although we know that no such entities will come into existence. There can be no essence of a round square, for that yokes together logically inconsistent terms and hence there is no viable possibility for the mind to entertain. Since everything that exists must also be possible, we have access to the realm of matter through the realm of essence. But Santayana insists upon the ontological difference between these realms, as Plato also does, because he wishes to call our attention to the implications of living in accordance with one or the other way of approaching the world.

In Plato's philosophy, as it is usually interpreted, the doctrine of forms is designed to show how mankind can obtain certain knowledge about reality through the proper use of a priori reason. Santayana offers no such prospect. He is a skeptic in epistemology, and he argues that what counts as knowledge is inevitably based on mythological feeling, what he calls "animal faith." Moreover, Plato considered the forms to be hierarchically ordered in the sense that those providing greater levels of logical generality were more reliable for understanding reality than the ones that pertained to data from our bodily senses. On the highest level stood the Good or the Beautiful since everything was purposively ordered toward the achievement of ultimate values present in the universe as infinite and eternal possibilities. Little of this idealism survives in Santayana's conception. For him all essences are alike in being the content of a clarified intuition, and therefore each is a comparable revelation of possible reality as we experience it.

Plato's doctrine is the one that judges of a dog show might use in their attempt to find the perfect collie or basset hound. But Santayana considers every competitor, whatever its attributes, a valid exemplar of one or another possibility that defines its being and serves as an appropriate essence for us to contemplate. And just as he affords no causal or teleological efficacy to the realm of forms, neither does Santayana accept the Platonic assumption that the universe is innately and objectively structured in accordance with a hierarchical ordering of essences.

At the same time, Santayana does retain Plato's belief in the value and importance of the contemplative attitude. Focusing its light on the being of any object, spirit yearns for the potential goodness in everything. Since it is only a fortuitous emanation of psyche, spirit cannot change the world. But having intuited essences, it searches for what it defines as beautiful in them. This depends on imagination, and Santayana remarks that "the only possible way for spirit to create is to imagine."

In saying this, Santayana sounds more like a nineteenth-century Romantic than like a Platonist. His basic Platonism shows itself, however, when he portrays spirit's attachment to ideal potentialities rather than to anything that exists or can be physically possessed. In the first of the epigraphs that precede *The Realm of Spirit* Santayana quotes from a passage in which Plotinus, speaking of love, says "this spirit is generated out of the psyche in the measure in which she lacks the good, yet yearns after it." Such a view of love and of spirit is wholly coherent with what Santayana stated in *Reason in Society* about the "ideality" of love. He there argued that, in its purified and sublimated condition, love "yearns for the universe of values." Despite its origins in matter, i.e. reproductive necessity, love's "true object is no natural being, but an ideal form essentially eternal and capable of endless embodiments."

In *Reason in Society* these statements about the ideality of love adumbrate much of what Santayana later developed in his ideas about spirit. By the time that *The Realm of Spirit* was written, however, he had become sensitive to the contradictions within spirit itself. It was not only a light that shone upon the actuality of what was given or the possible qualities of what could be imagined, but also it included a painful awareness of its inability to make the world better. He now saw spirit as a disposition rent by two different kinds of love. Spirit, Santayana finally maintained, "is inwardly divided and confused." Since it is a product of universal Will, which Santayana capitalizes as if in recognition of Schopenhauer's German usage, spirit must love the love in everything. It must feel sympathy for all the forms that life may take and for all the ideal fulfillments that are possible to living things in their diverse manifestations. But the will in one organism competes with that of another, and each occasion of spirit occurs within a psyche that seeks its own welfare. However much spirit may wish to identify with the universal search for goodness, it is hampered by the selfish demands of its own psyche and by the limitations that this imposes upon its capacity for dispassionate love. As Santayana says:

> Will here must sympathize with all Will and must love with all lovers; yet it must condemn each Will, not for loving that which it loves but for not loving that which it does not love; in other words, for not loving the good in all its possible forms. But all goods cannot be realized or sanely pursued in any particular life. Only the specific goals of that place and hour are proper to that particular concretion of universal Will.

Articulating this contradiction within spirit, Santayana perceives an inevitable conflict between existence and what he calls justice. Being a by-product of matter in one or another configuration, spirit arises as an aspiration toward particular goals. But in itself, in accordance with its own essence, it sympathizes with all potential exemplifications of goodness or beauty, wherever and however they may occur. Santayana considers this "the most tragic of conflicts." He claims there is no way in which it can be avoided. On the contrary, he insists that spirit fulfills its nature by accepting its inability to eliminate the conflict, by submitting to its own impotence in the world, and in that sense choosing renunciation as its destiny.

When it makes this choice, spirit does not escape suffering. But it learns how to benefit from it. In its allegiance to "intelligence, sympathy, universality," Santayana tells us, spirit acquiesces in the fact that it must suffer and thereby purifies its own spirituality. For spirit does more than just intuit ideals that reveal possible goods within the universe: it also hungers to become pure spirit in itself. Herein consists another contradiction that Santayana exploits. Talking specifically about spirit in relation to love, he describes the latter as a vital attachment without which the former could not exist. Love "experiences a physical affinity between the psyche and the object." To that extent, it precedes spirit rather than depending on it. Nevertheless, as Santayana maintains throughout, love subsumes its object under the aspect of an ideal goodness, thus clothing it "in spiritual guise." Through the inner dynamics of love, each vital attachment progresses into that elevation above particularity which defines the realm of spirit. This realm is not another world; it is not an example of "cosmic animism" or any other metaphysical dimension beyond the actuality of ordinary life. In its purity spirit aspires toward the same perfection that love seeks once it sublimates its instinctual or possessive needs into a detached appreciation which renounces the world in the very process of accepting it.

There are various criticisms of Santayana's conception that one could make. In the first volume of this trilogy I argued that the principle of idealization which Santayana employs prevents one from understanding the love of persons. For if love perceives its object under the aspect of an ideal beauty or goodness that this individual symbolizes and even represents, it is the ideal which is really loved rather than the object. In that event we are in love with a possible perfection and not with this man or woman, and the love of persons is not what we are experiencing. When Santayana says that in love "the true object is no natural being, but an ideal form essentially eternal and capable of endless embodiments," he describes love as a kind of idealization that has little rapport with loving someone as just the particular person that he or she happens to be.

This difficulty applies to Santayana's later writings as well as his earlier, to *The Realm of Spirit* as well as to *Reason in Society*. In terms of his final thinking about spirit, the problems appear within the concepts we have just discussed. As jointly the products of psyche, both love and spirit result from desire for a specific good embodied in a particular object. Spirit refines love, and possibly issues into its own kind of love, as we shall presently see, by detaching the organism from mere possessiveness and focusing the light of adoration upon a universal potentiality for goodness. This means that love has two types of essences, two modalities or levels of being. In one it operates within the realm of matter. In the other it reaches for a purely spiritual love that transcends any attachment to a single object while also accepting it as the approximation of an ideal.

The first of these is what I call a love of things, and it may possibly account for the erotic bonding that instinctually causes us to seek one or another kind of sexual pleasure. The second love that Santayana defines is closer to what I have described as a love of ideals. These issue from human aspirations and they enable us to move beyond any momentary or local condition in which we happen to exist. Both are authentic modes of love, and in his supreme awareness of the role that imagination plays in each, Santayana brilliantly portrays their complex relationship to one another. What he does not understand, or recognize fully, is the fact that a love of persons involves a type of love that these two do not explain either individually or in conjunction. It is a love that involves neither possessiveness nor renunciation, neither instinctual gratification of a wholly material sort nor the sacrificial martyrdom of one's individual interests, neither a blind craving for domination nor a willed and willing detachment that culminates in contemplation at a distance. The love of persons endures by being what it was in its origins—a vital attachment. But, in being love directed towards others in themselves, as persons, it is also a bestowing of values that may create a unique and sometimes beneficial interdependency that Santayana's perspective can scarcely accommodate.

If my criticism is justified, one must conclude that Santayana's attempted synthesis has not succeeded. Matter and spirit have been interpreted in a way that does not elucidate what is most in need of explanation. I think that is what William James meant when he called Santayana's philosophy the "perfection of rottenness." He did not wish to malign Santayana or to deny his competence as a philosopher: he was not saying that Santayana's philosophy was perfectly rotten. He was referring to Santayana's combination of Platonism and materialism, which James considered faulty. For if Santayana's vision of the world included only the superimposing of possible perfections on the rottenness which belongs to its material substance, was he not ignoring man's ability to live a good though imperfect life within a natural environment that is not entirely bad or completely hostile? Santayana formulates his analysis as he does in an attempt to remain absolutely faithful to reality as he knew it. His was a tragic view of life precisely because he saw no grounds for minimizing fundamental differences between the realms of matter and of spirit. What justification could there be in putting on a brave show of confidence, as he thought that James pervasively did, instead of admitting the frightening truths of our ontology and learning how to cope with them? Santayana's courage is undeniable. But even so, his philosophy fails to show us how human beings may overcome the split between matter and spirit. In misrepresenting the love of persons, he neglects a major segment of man's reality that cuts across these philosophical categories.

❋

The crack in Santayana's golden bowl recurs in all his statements about love. As in Platonism throughout the centuries, it repeatedly introduces a note of sadness and despair. Human beings strive for ideals that lift the heart and invigorate the spirit but eternally elude our grasp because we are creatures forever bound by an alien materiality. Several times in these volumes I have quoted Santayana's epigram about Platonic love: "All beauties attract by suggesting the ideal and then fail to satisfy by not fulfilling it." I now wish to call attention to the aura of frustration and depression that surrounds these words. Though they express a view of the world that has inspired much of the greatest poetry, and though they honestly reflect the disappointments that are always possible in love despite the grandeur of its quest, they also reek of personal failure arbitrarily projected upon the facts of life. It is an outlook that belongs to the experience of those homosexuals who are not proud of their erotic orientation and who do not live in a society that allows them to attain their own type of free development.

Plato himself vacillates in his opinions about sexuality between males: he sometimes accepts it as a means of harmonizing material and spiritual inclinations, but frequently he condemns it as unnatural, even criminal. Within Santayana's writings we often find him referring to homosexual behavior in language that is quite unfavorable though somewhat veiled. Like Ficino and other Neoplatonists, he speaks of it as depraved and possibly diseased. But in a conversation with Daniel Cory he alluded to his own homosexual proclivities, and a recent biography gives evidence about the love he felt for several men. Santayana kept his homosexual feelings secret, as if he thought they were shameful. On the other hand, there is little reason to believe that he savored the varied delights of heterosexual love. All beauties—male and female—may well have attracted him, but could any eliminate the painful inhibitions with which he was reared?

I do not wish to magnify the relevance of these biographical details. I mention them only to highlight Santayana's assertion that "A perfect love is founded on despair. . . . The *perfect* lover must renounce pursuit and the hope of possession." In another work he amplifies this by saying that "possession leaves the true lover unsatisfied: his joy is in the character of the thing loved, in the essence it reveals." The first part of this sentence is reminiscent of Proust stating that in sexual possession one possesses nothing (and therefore remains unsatisfied); the second part sounds like Proust using Platonistic language to talk about essences. Despite the differences between Proust and Santayana, they write as men who have been disqualified from appreciating the possibilities of a satisfying sexual love for any other person. Santayana could be speaking for Proust when he concludes that "contemplation is the whole object of love, and the sole gain in loving."

Santayana was aware that contemplation can be problematic. In an essay on "Plotinus and the Nature of Evil," he says: "I know that in practice a devotion that passes from individuals to the ideal is . . . commonly only a sort of abstract sensuality or aestheticism, at once selfish and visionary." Nevertheless, Santayana is convinced that the "genuine Platonist" surmounts all such difficulties by loving individuals so intensely that they become "the revelation of an essence greater than theirs, of something that, could we live always in its presence, would render us supremely happy." Yet he asserts (elsewhere) that when we recognize the imperfection of the individual object "love turns into suffering." He even wonders: "If ever we have ceased to suffer, have we not ceased to love?"

Since contemplation (as Santayana interprets it) affects the experience of love in this way, we can understand why he claims "it is not persons, in their personal limitations, that can enter into a spiritual union; for the limitations are transcended in being understood, one's own limitations as well as other people's." Santayana then likens this "union of spirits" to the relationship between souls as Dante depicts them in the *Paradiso*. "Persons become translucent," Santayana says, but he does little to explain what this can possibly mean. He probably has in mind a condition such that people perceive one another as just the essences each reveals. Though Santayana describes this union between translucent spirits as different from the oneness between persons who love each other, he does state that "contact or friendship" between persons can have an important role in the emergence of spirituality. Since spirit cannot occur without psyche, he says, it requires a healthy affiliation between persons as a preliminary to the transcending of its origins. A successful love of persons might thus provide a springboard for spiritual attainments. But Santayana does not believe that spirituality and the love of persons are similar in their defining properties. For him the love of persons achieves its ideality only as it is sublimated, and therefore submerged, in the service of spirituality.

Santayana's doubts about the love of persons appear most clearly in a chapter entitled "Distraction." He begins by asserting that "frank love," by which he means lovemaking directed toward immediate pleasures of the senses, is not an impediment to spirit. In itself the flesh does not create distractions, particularly when "love turns the flesh into loveliness." Far from being threatened by an appetite for sexual goods, which Santayana considers innocent in themselves, spirit can readily arise as a purification of one's passion. This happens when love "ceases to be a craving for the unknown. . . . The object then proves to have been an essence and not an existing person or thing; and among essences there is no jealousy or contradiction, and no decay." Distraction occurs when spirit becomes enmeshed in attachments to things or persons that may create "domestic virtue" but scarcely spiritual freedom. "In marriage," Santayana remarks, "love is socialized and moralized into a lifelong partnership which it would be dishonourable to betray; and community of interests and habits buttresses that love into mutual trust and assistance." But in the very next sentence, he adds: "A household rather smothers the love that established it."

How then can spirit escape the distractions of the world? How can it liberate itself from the duties and responsibilities that it knows to be morally defensible though inevitably imposing a confinement to its free exercise? As always, Santayana's answer presupposes the need to transform personal involvement into contemplative sublimation. To avoid distraction, spirit "will distinguish the loveliness in things or the charm in persons from the existing persons and things. These were the vehicle, *that* was the revelation." What he calls "the straightjacket imposed by society" seemed less pernicious to Santayana than "the illusions, revulsions, suspicions, and disasters suffered by love itself when given a free rein." Santayana considers these possible occurrences the "vital contradictions" of love. He scarcely intimates that the love of persons can include a system of values not at all inimical to spirit.

In Santayana's defense one might argue that the condition he wishes to explicate is a *purity* of spirit that must not be reduced even to the love between persons. When Santayana talks about "pure spirit" or "the spiritual life," he should be taken as referring to a possible achievement—an excellence in spirit, a kind of superior subdivision within the realm of spirit. While Santayana defines spirit as the actuality of mind when it attends to what is given or is possible (in other words, when it merely contemplates or imagines), he defines *spirituality* as spirit trying to exclude everything but itself. Though the spiritual life, like spirit in general, is an outgrowth of psyche and the realm of matter, it seeks to disintoxicate itself from them. The word "disintoxicate" often occurs in Santayana's writings, as if to suggest that spirit becomes sober and pellucid only when it treats its material origins as if they were foreign to its being. Santayana does insist that pure spirit will recognize the goodness of all mundane loves: having disintoxicated itself, it will perceive the beauty that is in them. But it will not love anything as the world does. For it will not concern itself with existence focused in a particular object, whether a person or a thing, and it will avoid all bonds that impair its own purified kind of love.

In *Platonism and the Spiritual Life*, where Santayana discusses spirituality as a path anyone may follow, he claims that it exceeds even Plato's philosophy of love. For that still involves a search for goodness, for values that a life of spirit transcends just as they themselves transcend materiality. The greatest literary portrayal of spirituality he finds, not in the philosophic texts of Greece, but in the religious documents of India.

Closer to his own origins, Santayana uses his ideas about spirit to make sense out of Catholicism and Christianity in general. In *The Idea of Christ in the Gospels* he analyzes the Christian notion of God in man as a mythic representation of pure spirit providing the only means to salvation. Embodying the principles of renunciation, detachment, liberation from the world, but also enjoyment of its universal goodness, Christ is seen as an idealization of the suffering human spirit which triumphantly disintoxicates itself from the lures and miseries of existence. To the end of his life Santayana remained a "Catholic atheist," as one commentator has called him. He never wavered in his materialist beliefs, but his delineation of —and obvious admiration for—the spiritual life reveals the depths of his permanent allegiance to Catholic ideology.

On more than one occasion, Santayana insisted that he himself was closer to the Greeks than to the Indians, and that he aspired to a life of rationality rather than spirituality. The former seeks a harmony among interests, whereas the latter is a single-minded pursuit that would seem to cast aside everything but itself. Do we have to choose between these alternatives? That is the question that Santayana examines dialectically in one of the chapters of his *Dialogues in Limbo*. In the dialogue entitled "The Philanthropist" Socrates and The Stranger converse about two ways in which mankind can be loved. In effect, one is love coherent with the life of reason and the other is love that issues from pure spirituality.

In depicting both possibilities, Santayana voices aspects of his own philosophy that could easily appear to be in contradiction to one another. On the one hand, we are presented with a conception of humanistic "philanthropy," which Socrates defends. As against this idea, The Stranger argues for what he calls "charity." Philanthropy is a love of mankind which Socrates describes as really being "the love of an idea, and not of actual men and women."

Philanthropy directs itself toward what is truly good for human beings; it is geared to the realities of their nature and aims for a "perfect humanity" that ideally would provide fulfillment, regardless of what some individual may happen to desire. The Stranger claims that "any adoration of mankind is mere sentimentality, killed by contact with actual men and women. Towards actual people a doting love signifies silliness in the lover and injury to the beloved, until that love is chastened into charity." Santayana employs the word "charity" in approximation of the medieval concept (caritas) and not as the word is more commonly used nowadays. He considers charity godlike even if it exists only in human beings. The Stranger calls it "a sober and profound compassion . . . succouring distress everywhere and helping all to endure their humanity and to renounce it."

In this notion of charity we may recognize the disposition that Santayana generally assigns to pure spirit. Transcending the search for perfection and aspiring toward emancipation from the world, the spiritual life is an exclusive commitment to charity. The Stranger remarks that charity "is less than philanthropy in that it expects the defeat of man's natural desires and accepts that defeat; and it is more than philanthropy in that, in the face of defeat, it brings consolation." Socrates sums up the discussion with the suggestion that "philanthropy is a sentiment proper to man in view of his desired perfection, and charity a sentiment proper to a god, or to a man inspired by a god, in view of the necessary imperfection of all living creatures."

Santayana leaves the dialogue with this minimal synthesis between the two ideals. Though charity is a Christian concept, he makes little attempt to defend Christianity itself. The Stranger classifies that religion as one among other "domesticated evils or tonic poisons, like the army, the government, the family, and the school; all of them traditional crutches, with which, though limping, we manage to walk." Even this half-hearted recommendation seems overly generous to Socrates, who gives thanks that he died before the Christian era. All the same, we must realize that the dialectical play between the voices of Socrates and The Stranger duplicates the ambivalence in Christianity between its indigenous concepts of eros and agapē. In *The Realm of Spirit,* in a passage subtitled "Charity *versus* Eros," Santayana discusses the theological controversy about love that descends regardless of what the object merits as distinct from love that seeks to attain perfection. In different places he offers varying solutions to the problem.

At times Santayana insists that, properly speaking, all love must be subsumed under the concept of eros. For love arises from the psyche and can only desire something that will ideally satisfy it: "There is therefore no love not directed upon . . . something that makes for the fulfillment of the lover's nature. This good may be the good of others, but doing good to others will to that extent be a good for oneself." It would follow from this that perfect charity is not really love, and Santayana argues that orthodox beliefs about God being love are hardly coherent within themselves. In *Platonism and the Spiritual Life* he likewise wonders whether charity can really be love since, in its spirituality, it must not seek perfection as its goal. Santayana nevertheless ends his book with the idea that charity expresses a kind of spiritual love that is not properly understood by the Platonic approach or by the eros tradition in general:

> When the renunciation of the world, and of existence itself, has been hearty and radical, the love of nature can be universal; I will not say unqualified by sadness, because the spirit, having itself suffered, recognizes in many an alien form of existence a maimed effort and a lost glory analogous to its own; but a love unqualified by prejudice, by envy, by fear of being outshone or discountenanced by the marvels which nature or society may elsewhere bring to light. It is of the essence of spirit to see and love things for their own sake, in their own nature, not for the sake of one another, nor for its own sake.

This kind of statement must give us pause, since it seems to contradict what Santayana says elsewhere. Still it would be fruitless in itself, and harmful for an appreciation of Santayana's genius, if we were to charge him with inconsistency in his use of the word "love." In its detached compassion and sympathetic concern for the suffering of everything, charity (as he defines it) involves a loving attitude whether or not it is the type of love that either Santayana or Plato considers paradigmatic in the human condition. Partly at least, the love which is charity asserts that everything is worthy of our compassion since all reality suffers in the universal bondage to the wheel of karma. While renouncing the goods it cannot hope to garner for itself, spirit extends its charity to existence as a whole. In his own way, Santayana would seem to be reverting to Nietzsche's notion of amor fati.

In *Egotism in German Philosophy,* published in 1915, Santayana condemned Nietzsche for romanticizing evil, for encouraging us to accept it in order to feel the intensity of our aggressive nature. Santayana had no desire, in his later writing, to acquiesce in any doctrine that deifies the exercise of power, even if that leads to happiness for oneself or others. He resembles Nietzsche, however, not only in basing his moral philosophy on naturalistic premises but also in depicting a condition in which the human spirit may finally reconcile itself to the evils that attend the frailty and fragility of the world. Reading from the other direction, we may even see in Nietzsche's doctrine of amor fati an anticipation of Santayana's idea that spirit can liberate itself only by accepting reality through an act of self-purification. This would be the side of Nietzsche that links him to Schopenhauer as well. The Nietzschean concept implies something more strenuous and activistic than the kind of contemplation that Santayana identifies with the spiritual life. But before he returns to the everyday world, Nietzsche's superman withdraws from it—like Zarathustra on the mountain—and to this extent he is purifying the spirit within himself.

All the same, it would be a mistake to confuse Santayana's prime inspiration with either Nietzsche's or Schopenhauer's. In his attempt to create a twentieth-century synthesis between Platonism and materialism, Santayana moves further from romanticism than does either of these German philosophers. His literary criticism abounds with scornful remarks about the "barbarism" of writers such as Whitman, Browning, even Goethe, and in general all Romantics who treat the human spirit as anything more than a lonely wanderer in a universe that has no concern for its welfare. Santayana's anti-Romantic stance is evident in his assertion that spirit attends to the known rather than the unknown. His conception appears most fully in his discussion of "union" in *The Realm of Spirit*. Since substance is always material, and in living creatures individualized in one or another organism, Santayana insists that "fusion with the universe is not union but death." The Good toward which spirit may direct itself is a knowable harmony among natural interests. When spirits attain a similar oneness of this sort, Santayana says, the moral union they achieve consists in "perfect unanimity." Far from fusing or merging with the unknown, they can only affirm the ideal possibilities that the highest moral principle involves for everyone.

In relations between spirits, Santayana recognizes no possibility of union apart from the fact that each may happen to pursue the same ideals and realize that others may cooperate in some extraneous fashion. "In seeking union with any other spirit," Santayana states, "we are therefore seeking either the Good, in that this other spirit realizes the perfection to which we are inwardly addressed; or else we are seeking such conformity with power and with truth as is necessary to the attainment of our proper good."

From this it follows that if spirit can ever attain complete and authentic union, this oneness must be a unity within an individual spirit. That is in fact what Santayana does believe. He ends the discussion with a vision of spirit free and wholly unified within a concentrated, detached, but also compassionate human being who sympathizes with the yearning for goodness in every thing and every person although he can never experience fusion with them. Nor does Santayana see any reason to expect permanence or uniformity in the purified spirit. Like Proust, he tells us that "Intermittence is intrinsic to life, to feeling, to thought; so are partiality and finitude."

In a passage that reminds us of Spinoza as well as the Christian mystics, Santayana's final words about union describe a victory for spirit embracing in an ultimate restoration the world it has renounced. Having achieved unity in its own contemplative nature, spirit enjoys the essential—though not the existential—being of everything. This happens by means of "intellectual worship, in which spirit, forgetting itself, becomes pure vision and pure love."

In reaching this conclusion, Santayana touches upon spiritual possibilities that other materialists and realists have always considered
fatuous or bogus. But neither will Santayana's conception satisfy
idealists who believe in a separate spirit-world from which human
beings originate, with which they may commune in this life, and to
which they can return after death. Of greatest import from my
point of view, Santayana's ideas about spirit neglect and misconstrue the love of persons. As long as he treats the spiritual life as
the transcending of particularities in existence, he cannot explain
how spirit may achieve a love that responds to another person *as* a
person—someone who exists in time and space, an "accidental"
conglomeration of specific properties and dispositions. As Santayana defines it, pure spirit is incapable not only of merging with
other spirits but also of interacting creatively with other persons
however they are described. How else can we interpret his assertions about detachment, renunciation, and acquiescence in the ultimate impotence of spirit? A disposition such as this may certainly
be compatible with sympathy, even compassion, but it tells us very
little about the ideal of interpersonal love.

Nonetheless, we may find Santayana's conception helpful if we
wish to emancipate ourselves from possessiveness, egoism, self-
deception, and the restless hunger for dubious goods that makes it
impossible for any other kind of love to exist. Santayana shows us
how pure spirit may attain joyful serenity by accepting what is
given and contemplating what is true or imaginable. This is a kind
of satori that need not prevent an individual from returning to the
world and living in it as an organism capable of satisfying all its
faculties. Indeed, the ideal of happiness as the total fulfillment of
natural impulses is defended in much of what Santayana wrote,
particularly in his earlier work. The importance of undertaking
mundane activities, the philosopher descending from his contemplative state and participating in the wretched world, he does
not emphasize as much as Nietzsche or even Plato. But he leaves
this open as a viable project that can sometimes fill periods of spiritual intermittence with opportunities for moral behavior. The

purified spirit would then be joining forces with the psyche from which it arose, the two combining harmoniously and seeking unification with the interests of other spirits.

In Santayana's later philosophy these intimations of beneficent harmony are left largely undeveloped. They are compatible, however, with his former writings about the life of reason. He himself denied that there was significant inconsistency between the two stages in his thought. He accounted for the differences between them in terms of new areas of interest that preoccupied him as he got older. I think Santayana was right about this: he understood the nature of his philosophical development better than the critics who thought he was rejecting reason in favor of spirituality. Although *Realms of Being* calls itself ontology, it may well be taken as a quasi-literary expression of Santayana's experience after middle age. Though that was inevitably different from his experience as a younger man, he did not create a new system of analysis which contradicts his previous philosophy.

In this connection Santayana's comments about friendship, scattered throughout his writings, are extremely pertinent. They represent the humanistic strand that always accompanies, and enriches, his conception of either the life of reason or the life of spirit. In *Soliloquies in England* he suggests that "One's friends are that part of the human race with which one can be human." The kind of friendship that mainly interests Santayana is the "union of one whole man with another whole man," which he interprets as "the felt harmony of life with life, and of life with nature." Does the word "man" here refer to both sexes? Seventeen years earlier, in a chapter on "Free Society," Santayana maintained that "friends are generally of the same sex, for when men and women agree, it is only in their conclusions; their reasons are always different." A few pages later, however, he tells us that in contemporary society "a well-assorted marriage" approximates, indeed "most nearly resembles," the ancient ideal of friendship that he wants to further.

The passage is worth quoting more fully:

> In spite of intellectual disparity and of divergence in occupation, man and wife are bound together by a common

dwelling, common friends, common affection for children, and, what is of great importance, common financial interests. These bonds often suffice for substantial and lasting unanimity, even when no ideal passion preceded; so that what is called a marriage of reason, if it is truly reasonable, may give a fair promise of happiness, since a normal married life can produce the sympathies it requires.

A declaration such as this reinforces my belief that Santayana does not give us an adequate analysis of the love of persons. The statement reveals that his approach to married love mainly concerns itself with the coordinates of a suitable partnership. The "marriage of reason" that Santayana advocates is the same as the social arrangement Schopenhauer contrasted with the bond of sexual love. Schopenhauer despaired of uniting the two within the marital relation, and Santayana makes no attempt to show how that might happen. On the other hand, one could argue that Santayana's references to sympathetic and lasting unanimity do take us part of the way toward understanding how marriage can become a manifestation of heterosexual friendship.

The humanistic (and pluralistic) reach of Santayana's philosophy of love appears most prominently in his posthumous essay entitled "Friendship." In it he sketches a spectrum of affective values, friendship and charity being the two that intrigue him most though they are not the only ones he wishes to defend. He contrasts friendship with brotherly or sisterly love, since they depend on family origin rather than free choice. Friendship is "distinctly selective, personal, and exclusive: in this respect it resembles the passion of love." But friendship differs from passionate love, Santayana states, in directing the imagination outward, toward the world as a whole, rather than focusing it on the relation between the lovers themselves. "What fills the imagination of friends is the world, as a scene for action and an object of judgement; and the person of the friend is distinguished and selected from all others because of exceptionally acceptable ways of acting, thinking, and feeling about other things or other persons." Santayana concludes that friendship is "the union of two freely ranging souls that meet by chance, recognize and prize each other, but remain free."

In citing the freedom basic to friendship, Santayana sets it apart from other kinds of love that he discusses. For it is bound neither by instincts that serve reproductive need nor by constraints and moral obligations, as in marriage. Yet he insists that friendship is just as "vital and biological" as sexual or marital love. He also contrasts friendship with companionship fashioned by business or external circumstances in which "the persons are indifferent, transparent, and exchangeable. . . . In friendship, as in love, the play must have the persons for its authors."

This way of talking about friendship, and about love, is very remote from Santayana's usual variations on either Platonism or materialism. His emphasis upon persons, and the suggestion that they may have importance in themselves, takes him beyond his notion of individuals being the vehicle to some transcendental ideal. But Santayana's philosophy is incomplete at this point. Though he sees love and friendship as similar in their concern for "a vital personal sympathy," he makes no attempt to understand, or even acknowledge, the ways in which the two may coalesce. He treats sexual and marital love as sentiments controlled by the needs of domesticity, and he seems to take it for granted that the burdens they involve—to say nothing of "jealousy, masterfulness, the desire to monopolise,"—must be inimical to friendship. Predicated upon a free choice, and remaining an expression of freedom throughout its career, friendship must belong to the spiritual life. As he has little conception of how spiritual and nonspiritual love may interpenetrate, so too does Santayana ignore the possibility of a love between persons which is both sexual or marital and also a type of friendship. The rift I mentioned earlier has not been overcome.

In describing friendship as a "union of souls," Santayana might seem to be undermining his claim that spirits cannot merge with one another. As a matter of fact, his thinking is quite consistent in this regard. Although he maintains that the union in friendship is "more than agreement," he also refers to it as "a coincidence of free souls." This does not diverge from what he says elsewhere about union. Moreover, his remarks about friendship serve as a corrective to the charge that Santayana's later philosophy seeks to orient all human relations toward the achievement of spiritual purity. For he insists upon the differences between friendship and charity. The latter "not being intrinsic either to love or to friendship, requires the intervention of imaginative reason, by which we detach ourselves from our accidental persons and circumstances and feel the equal reality of all other persons in all other plights." Santayana extols the infinite beauty in charity, but he points out that love or friendship or philanthropy can also be beautiful. Nowhere does he suggest that anyone must extirpate natural virtues or devote himself to the peculiar and exclusive interests of pure spirit. That remains a matter of individual choice.

It is this pluralistic substratum that I particularly admire in Santayana's moral philosophy. It is the aspect of his vision from which we can learn the most.

8

Sartre and the Varieties of Existentialism

SCHOLARS HAVE LONG SINCE recognized that "existentialism" is a generic term that masks a great diversity among philosophers who have been characterized in this fashion. The differences between Sartre and Heidegger or Husserl, both of whom greatly influenced him, are as great as those between Aristotle and Plato, or Nietzsche and Schopenhauer. The differences between Sartre and Buber or Sartre and Gabriel Marcel are even greater. And though Sartre benefited from a cooperative relationship with Simone de Beauvoir throughout fifty years of his productive life, their development is not identical. Particularly on questions about the nature of love, Beauvoir's *Ethics of Ambiguity* and *Pyrrhus et Cinéas* anticipated important turns in Sartre's thought that he himself reached only later.

Among these writers, Sartre is the most interesting as an analyst of love. He approaches the topic in a more systematic and detailed manner than the others, and he never hesitates to modify his earlier conceptions throughout the stages of his intellectual progress. The variegated character of Sartre's philosophy has largely been ignored by his critics and even by his sympathetic commentators. Almost everyone who has written about Sartre's ideas about love mistakenly considers the presentation in *Being and Nothingness* to be definitive. That work, which appeared in 1943, does contain an analysis of love that is both extensive and intentionally radical. I shall want to give its arguments the careful attention that they merit. But shortly after he published *Being and Nothingness* Sartre saw its inadequacies and began to modify many of its fundamental points. Greatly dissatisfied with the chapters on "Concrete Human Relations," he concluded that his treatise had overemphasized negativity in love and therefore needed rectification.

Whether Sartre succeeded in his attempt to improve his earlier philosophy of love will preoccupy us later. Here, at the beginning, we need only bear in mind what he himself said near the end of his life: "What is particularly bad in *L'Etre et le Néant* [*Being and Nothingness*] is the specifically social chapters, on the 'we,' compared to the chapters on the 'you' and 'others.' . . . That part of *L'Etre et le Néant* failed. . . . Beginning with *Saint Genet* I changed my position a bit, and I now see more positivity in love. . . . I would still maintain the idea that many acts of human love are tainted with sadism and masochism, and what must be shown is what transcends them. I wrote *Saint Genet* to try to present a love that goes beyond the sadism in which Genet is steeped and the masochism that he suffered, as it were, in spite of himself."

This development in Sartre's thought involved a deepening of awareness and a sharpening of insight. Its stages parallel the periods in his own experience which he elsewhere characterizes as follows: "my life certainly consists of three parts. An anarchistic individualistic part, a transition period, wherein one may speak of a development, of a coming into contact with the societal in many ways, . . . and from that moment there is a new attitude, that of the individual in the society, of the person in society." Sartre's modified ideas about love appear not only in *Saint Genet* but also in *Cahiers pour une morale, The Devil and the Good Lord,* and the first volume of the *Critique of Dialectical Reason.* In some respects Sartre's final conception of love approximates the thinking in Marcel and Buber. He did not work out the details of his "positive" philosophy, however, and he always places it within the framework of his earlier negativism. Even at the end of his career, he leaves us with an approach that retains the skeptical realism he never wished to relinquish. This alone would set him apart from idealistic existentialists such as Buber or Marcel. Between them and Sartre there are philosophic chasms that may well turn out to be unbridgeable.

❋

Since Sartre presents us with a concentrated analysis of love only in his first stage, the major text for our discussion must remain *Being and Nothingness*. About a third of that book deals with human ontology from the point of view of "being-for-others." Sartre had previously distinguished between "being-in-itself" and "being-for-itself." Through the for-itself man as a conscious entity freely creates values out of nothing: in the external world there is nothing that can objectively tell him how to live. As a for-itself, man is a complex of possibles which he projects in accordance with whatever system of values he has chosen. We are aware of this part of our being, Sartre says, inasmuch as we individually possess a consciousness that provides an irreducible subjectivity to each of us. In being separate from everything that may cause or condition it, consciousness arises out of nothingness and is free in that respect. Regardless of what a human being has become, he can always transcend his present state through freely chosen endeavors that propel his being into new possibilities. The for-itself is thus consciousness under the aspect of freedom. It is a fundamental category in man's ontology, but it does not comprise all of human nature.

The for-itself is ourselves as we experience the world. It is nothing (or nothingness) in the sense that it is not a specifiable thing or object of any sort. At the same time we are also things, objects that have come into existence and developed in time. We have a particular body as well as a consciousness. And even our conscious being exists within a temporal dimension. It occurs as a specific, actual event in the world. At each moment consciousness is free to recreate itself, but the fact remains that it has now become what it previously chose to be. This aspect of being Sartre calls facticity or the in-itself. Since people experience their consciousness directly, they identify with the for-itself—their purposive and creative projection of possibilities that transcend each present configuration in time. To this extent, however, we undergo a separation from our own facticity. The in-itself is nature or reality impinging upon human freedom, causing it to be as it is, dependent on material forces that enable us to exist although we feel that we ourselves belong to a different order of being.

Sartre's ontology is humanistic inasmuch as he recognizes no reality other than that which enters into human experience. He is not offering us a cosmology, a philosophy of science, or anything like a traditional metaphysics. His analysis, particularly in this early stage, is always phenomenological, that is to say, concerned with the dimensions of conscious experience as it directly apprehends the ordinary world together with the reflective intuition of itself that consciousness also has.

The categories of the for-itself and the in-itself are primary in Sartre's vision. They reveal what he considers distinctive in man: the incessant need for meaning, which people create out of the nothingness of their disembodied consciousness, and the dependency upon external forces that make a human being what he is and therefore partly constitute his reality, even though he has no inclination to accept these forces as himself. In Sartre's philosophy the for-itself and the in-itself stand in dialectical opposition to one another. Man is torn between them. As a detached for-itself, he suffers anguish because he desperately seeks meaning in life which he must create entirely on his own and with no assurance of justification. As an in-itself, he is subject to objective constraints but they can only serve as hurdles that he must transcend in order to assert his essential freedom, to make his life meaningful by choosing new possibilities beyond his present state.

The split between the for-itself and the in-itself is the principal problem of human existence according to Sartre. Most of *Being and Nothingness* deals with man's attempt to harmonize the two. In the chapters on being-for-others Sartre addresses the fact that while consciousness exists only in a world in which there are other people, these others can never belong to our subjectivity. From our own point of view, they must be objects we experience. From their point of view, however, they are subjectivities and we are the objects. Sartre rejects any solipsistic philosophy that would deny the existence of consciousness in anyone else. All human beings are in the same condition. Each experiences himself as a subject and all other people as objects in relation to his consciousness. Each of us is a for-itself who encounters the Other as an in-itself, which is to say, as a factuality whose ontological being cannot be explained in terms of our own subjectivity.

The Other must therefore be a something that my consciousness inherently transcends. Nevertheless his experience of me reveals facts about my being. For though I identify myself with my own consciousness, I am also the physical expression of that consciousness as it appears in the objective world and is experienced by the Other in his own way. This is my facticity. It is my body, which I am as an in-itself, and the Other may well understand it better than I can. The Other sees me in presentations of my body that are not always available to my own awareness. He is just an object in my consciousness; yet this object is a subject that can have greater knowledge about my behavior and personality than I myself may be able to attain.

The fact of being a subject to myself but only an object in the consciousness of the Other is crucial for Sartre because it symbolizes man's pervasive alienation from his own being, and his constant search to surmount this condition. According to Sartre, man —by his very nature—tries to find a meaning in life by making himself into an in-itself-for-itself. For all human beings this is a "fundamental value" that Sartre describes as "the ideal of a consciousness which would be the foundation of its own being-in-itself by the pure consciousness which it would have of itself." Becoming an in-itself-for-itself would provide the ontological security that everyone desires. This ideal, Sartre maintains, corresponds to the concept of God. For it is through God as an ideal that man "represents the permanent limit in terms of which [he] makes known to himself what he is." From this, Sartre argues: "To be man means to reach toward being God. Or if you prefer, man fundamentally is the desire to be God."

We have encountered in the writings of Neoplatonists such as Plotinus and Ficino the idea of man wishing to be God. I tried to show that much of Christian thinking in the Middle Ages gravitated toward this as its ultimate ideal. Romanticism of the nineteenth century frequently defined itself by a similar conception. In a line that Sartre refers to more than once, Nietzsche states that "if there were gods, how could I bear not to be one?" He means that it is in man's nature to want the absolute assurance that comes with being perfect. This is the feeling of what Sartre calls "justification." Nietzsche expresses a related idea in his remark about all desire yearning for "deep, deep eternity." The eternal is divinity, and Sartre defines it as the ideal goal of man's perennial craving to become an in-itself-for-itself.

If man could succeed in amalgamating the two aspects of his being, his freedom as a for-itself and his facticity as an existing in-itself, he would achieve the ontological oneness for which his diverse projects strive. But harmonization between the two principles is impossible. Sartre conceives of them as mutually contradictory: the for-itself has its being in transcending the in-itself, and the in-itself has its being in solidifying the for-itself into something that exists as a matter of fact, as an object that is no longer free to be anything but what it is. In *Nausea,* his first novel, Sartre had introduced the idea of "contingency" to characterize man's existence as a brute occurrence that could find no necessary meaning in itself despite its inherent freedom. After his revelatory experience of the chestnut tree, the narrator tells us that contingency means "one cannot define existence as necessity. To exist is simply *to be there;* those who exist let themselves be encountered, but you can never deduce anything from them. I believe there are people who have understood this. Only they tried to overcome this contingency by inventing a necessary, causal being. But no necessary being can explain existence: contingency is not a delusion. . . it is the absolute."

In *Being and Nothingness,* and indeed throughout the rest of his philosophical work, Sartre retains his belief in man's contingency. His lengthy treatise may be read as an exhaustive portrayal of humanity struggling to render its existence as a for-itself into a self-sustaining, fundamentally necessary, irreducibly justified in-itself-for-itself. Towards the end of the book he states: "Every human reality is a passion in that it projects losing itself so as to found being and by the same stroke to constitute the In-itself which escapes contingency by being its own foundation." Man loses himself in the sense that he seeks to give up his freedom as a transcending for-itself in order to attain the ontological security of being something that exists as an absolute in-itself. But if that happened, he would no longer have consciousness, which is ineluctably free and self-transcendent. Consequently, "we lose ourselves in vain. Man is a useless passion." In his Conclusion to *Being and Nothingness*, Sartre presents the following as a synoptic view of his philosophy:

> Everything happens as if the world, man, and man-in-the-world succeeded in realizing only a missing God. Everything happens therefore as if the in-itself and the for-itself were presented in a state of disintegration in relation to an ideal synthesis. Not that the integration has ever *taken place* but on the contrary precisely because it is always indicated and always impossible.

In developing this philosophy, Sartre is formulating more than just a modern version of atheism. He is also analyzing a religious dimension that belongs to human nature and is distinctively human. Unlike positivists who consider the idea of God inconsistent or nonsensical and therefore unhelpful in our attempt to understand reality, Sartre uses it to explain man's permanent malaise in a universe that cannot accommodate his religious yearnings. As opposed to Freud, who thought that mankind might some day outgrow the neurosis of its theistic illusion, Sartre maintains that the structure of human ontology must always include the hopeless desire to become God. I do not mean that Sartre sees no way out of man's futile passion. In sketching the ethical implications of his ontological analysis, he intimates that "another fundamental attitude" may take us beyond the failure to which we are all doomed. In a famous footnote he remarks: "These considerations do not exclude the possibility of an ethics of deliverance and salvation. But this can be achieved only after a radical conversion which we cannot discuss here."

❇

Critics have often puzzled over this statement, particularly since Sartre never published during his lifetime the ethics that he seemed to be promising. We shall have to return to this problem. In the meantime we must keep it in mind as a difficulty relevant to his critique of love. That occurs in the context of Sartre's belief that the attempt to become an in-itself-for-itself always involves other people. The irreconcilable tensions between the for-itself and the in-itself structure all concrete human relations. Seeking the ideal which is God, man fails because of an inherent contradiction between the in-itself and the for-itself. And therefore, Sartre claims, a similar futility must characterize subsidiary ideals such as love.

The most basic of human relations that Sartre considers he calls "the look." By this he refers to the situation of "being-seen-by-another." Since we live in a world that includes other people—not as a fact of sociology or politics but rather as part of what it is to have human reality—our appearance to others is a fundamental aspect of our being. Since I cannot see or in general experience myself as another does when he looks at me, that relationship reveals my objectivity: what the Other sees belongs to my facticity, my in-itself. Sartre interprets this to mean that the look must always cause the "objectification" of a subject. As a free, transcending for-itself, each consciousness is a subjectivity to itself. But in his appearance to someone else, as a person whose body is looked at, an individual exists as an objectified phenomenon within another's subjectivity.

In developing his concept of objectification, Sartre combines two different meanings of that word. Not only does it signify our being as the objects of someone else's subjective consciousness, but also it entails our becoming objects in the sense of *things* or *artifacts*. Since we are freely transcendent only as consciousness, Sartre thinks, he considers our being-seen-by-another as comparable to the being of material entities. Being looked at, we are a "transcendence-transcended." For the other person sees us as an object in his visual field and not as a subjectivity. He cannot perceive our consciousness—only we can do that. He sees us as tantamount to other things, which indeed we are to the extent that we are an in-itself, although he knows that we have a consciousness like his own.

It is essential for Sartre's argument that the look involves both types of objectification. He believes that all concrete human relations must manifest the attempt to justify one's contingent existence, to ground one's fragile and insecure for-itself in the solidity of some necessary in-itself. But in our relations with one another, each person is "seen" by others and his in-itself becomes part of their experience. Since they can only perceive him as a thing, his making himself an object of their consciousness defeats his desire to bring about his own justification.

This is one of the seminal concepts in all of Sartre's thinking. To formulate it in this fashion, however, is to assume that one cannot be an object in the first sense of that word without also being an object in the second. And this, I believe, is a basic and pervasive error. Though we enter into another's experience as an objectivity available to his subjective consciousness, it does not follow that we are thereby rendered into an object in any other sense. As we know that the Other is a subject in himself even though we experience him as an object in our perception, so too are we more than just material things in his awareness of us as objects of *his* perception. Sartre insists that neither we nor the Other can actually have experience of one another's consciousness. This is true insofar as each has his own consciousness and no consciousness can occur identically in different people. But why think that our inability to duplicate another's consciousness, to experience it exactly as he does, prevents us from having access to it? Sartre attacks the behaviorists precisely on the grounds that they ignore the ways in which perceiving someone's body means seeing that it manifests a for-itself transcending its facticity. Nevertheless he resembles the behaviorists in claiming that a manifestation of this sort must be experienced by another as an objectification which negates the transcending consciousness being expressed.

I shall return to this difficulty throughout my discussion. It pertains to everything Sartre says in *Being and Nothingness* about human relationships. It underlies his belief that the look explains the nature of shame. For we are ashamed, Sartre says, to be reduced to the status of a thing. Since our reality includes the in-itself that the Other is perceiving and that we cannot assimilate to our for-itself, we feel diminished. Being just an object to the Other, it is as if we were nothing *but* an object; and that is the basis of our shame.

Sartre illustrates this in the example of a man who is peeping through a keyhole. In performing this act, he is a fully absorbed subject, a consciousness freely engaged. But then the man suddenly hears footsteps and notices that someone is looking at him as he peers into the next room. This occasions shame, Sartre suggests, and it does so because the spying individual becomes aware of himself as the object of another's observation. He who was a purely focused subject now feels himself transcended by a consciousness that perceives him from the outside, as if he were nothing but his behavior and had no conscious being of his own.

Sartre's example is a peculiar one and rather unfortunate for the sake of his argument. Though he gives us few details, he allows us to assume that this act of peeping is conduct that most people would consider shameful on moral grounds having nothing to do with the state of being a transcendence-transcended. But what if we recognize no immorality in what we are doing? One could easily imagine that the two persons involved are government agents carrying out a professional and even patriotic mission. The man at the keyhole might then experience no shame at all. On the contrary, he might be pleased to think that his colleague may give him credit for his performance of duty. Though his behavior is no longer what Sartre calls "prereflective," his awareness of himself as the object of another's perception will not make him feel that he is being treated like a thing. And on an occasion that clearly involves moral condemnation, where the peeper might be ashamed, we could explain his emotion as fear that someone else has acquired information not only about his in-itself but also about contents of his for-itself that he desperately wishes to keep secret. In the state of shame we have an exposed and threatened consciousness. We are looked at scornfully, which is not to say that we are perceived as if we were nothing but a thing.

In general, Sartre's analysis of the look suffers from a failure to recognize that even on the ontological level people have different ways of looking at one another. Sometimes we look in a manner that does diminish the being of another, regarding him as if he were indeed a thing. When a group of men stare at a solitary woman walking in front of them, they may look at her as a commodity, a sex object, a female body whose physical dimensions interest them to the virtual exclusion of everything else in its being as a person. If the woman then feels ashamed, this may happen because she believes that something she has done elicits the men's response or possibly because she senses her own inclinations—assuming the woman has them—to cooperate with their attitude even though she thinks she ought not to. But even in that stereotyped situation, there may be different kinds of looks. The men may be appreciative of the visual spectacle being afforded them, and they may even see in this beautiful woman a possibility for various kinds of consummated love. Rather than reducing the woman to a thing, their stare can signify a fascination with her as a person whose consciousness they have begun to admire as the unique subjectivity that it is. Similarly, the woman can react in any number of ways without feeling that her transcendence has been transcended or that she has been turned into an object of the sort that Sartre describes. She need not undergo ontological shame, though she may experience modesty or diffidence.

In his analysis Sartre ignores what happens in a look of love. When a mother gazes at her infant as she cuddles it, her loving attitude prevents us from thinking that the object of her attention is being treated as a thing. On the contrary, the mother may feel a sense of wonder and delight that this product of her own body—this mass of fleshy tissue—has in it all the potentialities of a separate consciousness. For her the infant is already a person of infinite value. She herself has bestowed that value. Far from reducing the object to a thing, her imaginative love has raised it to the level of a conscious person that one cherishes. She sees her baby as a being that already transcends its own materiality. That is the basis of her wonderment. It is something all lovers experience at one time or another.

Sartre's philosophy takes a different line of thought. He wishes to explain love in terms of "the" look, but he insists that the look—like all human relationships in their underlying structure—is always an expression of conflict. While the Other is looking at me, I seek to free myself of this "enslavement," as Sartre calls it, and reciprocally try to enslave him. In *Being and Nothingness* Sartre states the following as a general principle, fundamental to his approach but scarcely argued: "Conflict is the original meaning of being-for-others." In a conversation with Simone de Beauvoir many years later he remarks: "I've never had tender relations with my friends since then [his childhood experience]. There were always ideas of violence between them or from them to me or from me to them. It was not a lack of friendship but rather the proof that violence was imperative in the relations between men."

With conflict as his governing insight into the nature of human relations, Sartre proceeds to show that our being-for-others is a form of possession. Insofar as the Other's look is capable of objectifying me, "he makes me be and thereby he possesses me, and this possession is nothing other than the consciousness of possessing me." I, of course, am also possessing him, since I counter his look with one of my own. Because each person wishes to be the foundation for his own being he tries to free himself from ontological possession by the Other. And yet, each of us must also recognize that the Other "founds" our being to the extent that he is aware of its facticity. That makes us dependent on one another and, according to Sartre, therein consists the inevitability of conflict. And from conflict there arises, as a compensatory effort, the ideal of love as well as various attitudes related to it.

In approaching love as an outgrowth of conflict and the mutual desire to possess other subjectivities, Sartre continues the tradition exemplified by Proustian realism. Unlike Proust, however, he is seeking an ontological explanation for the attempt to possess another person. Though he admired Proust's work throughout his life, mentioning in several interviews that it served as a formative influence upon his early development, he clearly wished to go beyond Proust's psychological analysis by means of an investigation that probes more deeply into the nature of being and the basic structure of human relations. Where Proust contents himself with demonstrating that sexual love means possessiveness, Sartre wonders about the meaning of possessiveness. He concludes that it involves enslavement that prevents a person from overcoming his contingency or founding his being through an act of freedom. In order to recover himself as a free transcendence, Sartre says, each lover must "assimilate the Other's freedom." The ideal of love is thus explicable as possessiveness seeking to preclude one's own possession and doing so by "absorbing the Other."

In using words like "assimilate" and "absorb" in this context, Sartre aligns himself with Freud as well as Proust. For these are terms of interpersonal domination; and they intimate that one animal is somehow devouring another. Like Proust and Freud, Sartre aims his critique at the ideal of love that romanticism formulated through the concept of merging. In claiming that man wants to found his being by becoming God, Sartre represents the desired outcome as a fusion with the cosmic entity who is by definition an in-itself-for-itself. The religious aspiration to love God spiritually and to be loved by him he interprets as a concerted attempt to effect the final merging. Sartre does not consider, and scarcely seems to recognize, the prolonged efforts by orthodox Christianity, Judaism, and Islam to banish belief in any merging with divinity. Neither does he discuss alternate concepts of religious union. But for Sartre's purposes, these differences of ecclesiastic doctrine are largely irrelevant. He wishes to establish that man's sense of ultimate insecurity causes him to imagine a consciousness that by its very essence enjoys a perfect foundation for its being, thereby serving as a model of what man desires for himself. Only by merging with this superior being could man eliminate his insecurity. Though some religious authorities have conceived of oneness with God as less than actual merging, Sartre would say that their conception may be dismissed: it does not pertain to the ontological quest that he is describing.

In fact, one can even argue that Sartre's atheism duplicates the moral intention of orthodox religion in the West. Sartre believes that "man is a useless passion" because the human effort to escape contingency by being God is utterly futile. But since the ultimate identification could occur only through an intermingling of substances, Sartre's conclusion parallels the orthodox rejection of merging. When Sartre depicts the vanity of man's basic yearning, he sounds like Pascal or any number of other Christian moralists who deride human nature for its pride in wanting to become divinity. Of course, Sartre differs from the Christians insofar as he maintains that the idea of God is "contradictory." But, as we shall see, he resembles twentieth-century theists like Buber and Marcel inasmuch as they too claim that a solution to man's anxieties about his being cannot be found in the concept of merging that was proffered by religious as well as nonreligious Romantics of previous centuries.

In analyzing love between human beings rather than between man and God, Sartre treats it as a comparable search for assimilation or absorption. He nevertheless recognizes that the phenomenological context is not the same. He points out that we are always aware that the man or woman who objectifies us through the look is not an in-itself-for-itself. And though the Other is a subject to himself, as we are to ourselves, our look is always turning him into an object. To love another human being is therefore wholly unlike loving God. We love the Other in an effort to overcome our objectivity by merging with the subjectivity which is that other person confronting us and thereby rendering us into objects. In being a subject, the Other is an essential freedom. In merging with him or her, we would absorb this freedom. If only we could *assimilate* the Other's consciousness, Sartre says, it would no longer be able to objectify us. For us to be objectified there must be a subject other than ourselves, but through love we will have merged with that subject. That is the ideal goal in love, as Sartre conceives of it. His critique consists in showing that this ideal is as futile as the original ideal of merging with God.

Sartre's advance upon the Proustian argument may now be seen in a slightly different light. Proust describes love as a desire for physical possession where there is paradoxically nothing to be possessed. He then suggests that the lover really wishes to possess the hidden being of the beloved, her secret and mysterious absolute. In *Being and Nothingness* Sartre states that if love were merely a desire for physical possession it might well be satisfied. He cites Proust's narrator as an example of someone who possesses his beloved in that sense: Marcel makes Albertine a domestic prisoner. Sartre then goes on to remark that Albertine escapes, even while still imprisoned, by virtue of her consciousness. He concludes that Marcel's love was really a desire to capture her subjectivity. All lovers, Sartre thinks, want to appropriate the consciousness of their beloved. For that is where her absolute being resides. It is the freedom that every consciousness enjoys inherently: "the lover does not desire to possess the beloved as one possesses a thing; he demands a special type of appropriation. He wants to possess a freedom as freedom."

For this reason Sartre denies that the lover truly wishes to enslave the beloved. If that happened, he would no longer be merging with a free subjectivity. He would merely be controlling the Other-as-object. But then the beloved's response would be elicited mechanically, as if she were an automaton. The lover would not be assimilating another's freedom.

On the other hand, Sartre also denies that the lover wants to merge with a purely unbounded freedom in the beloved. For if his love is motivated by the attempt to recover his being from the objectivity it undergoes in its confrontation with the Other's look, he must contrive to get the beloved's freedom to sustain his own subjectivity. In Sartre's words: "He wishes that the Other's freedom should determine itself to become love. . . and at the same time he wants this freedom to be captured *by itself*, to turn back upon itself, as in madness, as in a dream, so as to will its own captivity." The beloved must remain free, but also focused in her being upon the lover as the limit of her freedom, as something that she cannot transcend or objectify. The beloved must thus define her being in terms of the lover's facticity. It will be, so to speak, a second facticity for her since it becomes the self-imposed limitation to her own free transcendence. The ideal of love is a desire to merge with someone who will "re-create you perpetually as the condition of a freedom which submits itself and which is engaged; it is to wish both that freedom found fact and that fact have preeminence over freedom. If this end could be attained, it would result in the first place in my being *secure* within the Other's consciousness."

In this kind of relationship with the beloved, the lover would no longer be one among other objects in her world. He would be protected against the danger of being used as an instrumentality. He would be the condition for anything to be valued, and also that than which nothing has greater value. In being loved by the Other, the lover would assume the dimensions of "the unsurpassable." To this extent, his being becomes the object of a look whose ontological structure has been transformed. For now he is no longer an object the beloved objectifies but rather someone the beloved has freely chosen as her "unique and absolute end." The beloved is thereby "assimilated by our freedom." The ideal of love, its culminating goal, Sartre portrays in the following passage:

> By means of this love I then have a different apprehension of my alienation and of my own facticity. My facticity—as for-others—is no longer a fact but a right. . . . These beloved veins on my hands exist—beneficently. How good I am to have eyes, hair, eyebrows and to lavish them away tirelessly in an overflow of generosity to this tireless desire which the Other freely makes himself be. Whereas before being loved we were uneasy about that unjustified, unjustifiable protuberance which was our existence, whereas we felt ourselves *"de trop,"* we now feel that our existence is taken up and willed even in its tiniest details by an absolute freedom which at the same time our existence conditions and which we ourselves will with our freedom. This is the basis for the joy of love when there is joy; we feel that our existence is justified.

Sartre's parenthetical remark ("when there is joy") may be taken as an expression of his doubts about the frequency of happy love. In his novels and short stories one rarely finds descriptions of love's joyfulness. In this respect too his conception of human nature resembles Proust's. Within the confines of his analysis, however, generalizations about the joyfulness or suffering of love must always remain merely psychological and secondary. In trying to show the futility of love on purely ontological grounds, Sartre must demonstrate an incoherence within its structure as a projection of man's being. He finds this fundamental split in the fact that love involves self-defeating mutuality. For if, in loving the beloved, the lover wants to merge with the absolute of one who accepts him absolutely, he has projected love as a desire to be loved. But the love he demands of the beloved must also include *her* desire to be loved, which she pursues just as he does. And yet, neither person intends that the other should love merely in the sense of wanting to be loved. Their sheer mutuality as participants in love must therefore involve an insurmountable contradiction within its very structure.

"Each one wants the other to love him but does not take into account the fact that to love is to want to be loved and that thus by wanting the other to love him, he only wants the other to want to be loved in turn."

Sartre calls this state of affairs a "system of indefinite reference," from which it follows that love is self-defeating. If the lover's love is merely a desire to be loved (for the sake of recovering his being from the Other's look), and if this love as it exists in the Other is likewise a desire to be loved, the mutuality of love reduces to a reciprocal but impossible demand that each provide a love that neither can actually attain.

To see Sartre's critique in historical perspective, we need only remember that Kant—and the great Romantic tradition that evolved from him—defined love as a mutuality which enabled human beings to enjoy and to appreciate one another as ultimate ends. Though each relegated to the other a gamut of rights to their private person, neither lost anything because their mutuality assured them of an equalizing exchange. As a result, their joint efforts to be loved in no way diminished their capacity to elicit love from one another. For Kant, love occurs through the act that admits another person into this preferential "union of wills." It is this interpretation of mutuality that Sartre rejects. In effect, he is denying that the desire to be loved can ever generate an ability to love, on the part of either the lover or the one by whom he wants to be loved. In works such as *Saint Genet* Sartre shows how the fundamental need to be loved may take different forms that he himself considers to be inferior for a variety of reasons. But in *Being and Nothingness*, where he limits himself to the definition of love, he argues that even at its best this ideal must always be futile.

In the course of expounding his position, Sartre makes comments such as the following: "Thus it seems that to love is in essence the project of making oneself be loved"; "The lover. . . is the captive of his very demand since love is the demand to be loved"; "The beloved cannot will to love"; "Here in fact we encounter the true ideal of love's enterprise: alienated freedom." Some of these statements, such as the suggestion that one sacrifices or alienates one's freedom in the process of trying to found it through mutual love, may well follow from the rest of Sartre's argument. But his belief that love consists merely in a desire to be loved must be taken as an a priori assumption, a presupposition. It is a guiding principle that Sartre employs as the basis of his analysis. Far from being a truth revealed by his investigation, it is an axiom that preselects the segment of human nature he is willing to identify as love. From the outset, he sees the lover as one who wishes to appropriate the consciousness of the Other. This means that the lover is primarily seeking a mechanism for using the Other selfishly. The ontological use that Sartre specifies, the very extensive one of providing an absolute foundation for the lover's for-itself, he identifies with being loved. At no point does he consider instances in which the lover bestows value upon the beloved. Though Sartre finds the essence of human consciousness in its freedom, which is to say, its power to surmount the nothingness that separates it from the world, he never recognizes that this freedom—creative as he knows it to be—is capable of making others valuable over and above their appraisive utility as persons by whom we may wish to be loved.

As Sartre portrays love in *Being and Nothingness,* it both originates and results in conflict: "This project is going to provoke a conflict." He means that the beloved will want to be loved as the lover does and therefore that neither party will be satisfied with what the other provides. But, as I suggested earlier, Sartre assumes that conflict is basic to all human relations, and possibly that explains why he ignores man's ability to fulfill his own instincts and to satisfy his own needs by freely bestowing upon others a love that does not reduce to the equally fundamental craving to be loved. Except for its ontological underpinning, Sartre's reductivism resembles Freud's belief in primal narcissism, which also entails that loving is really a version of wanting to be loved. If this were just a generalization about a frequent type of love, the view might be worthwhile. Through introspection as well as empirical observation, we know how easy it is to deceive ourselves into thinking that we love someone when we merely wish to be loved by him. As an insight into this particular danger, the analyses of Freud and Sartre could be defensible.

But even in the most extreme cases, there often emanates a new affective response which reveals affirmative possibilities of a different sort. In one place William James notes that if you want to be liked by somebody, do everything you can to make him think you like *him*. This tactic could not succeed unless the other person's liking were an authentic bestowal that we had managed to elicit from him. Our enterprise would be fruitless if he were deceiving us in the way that we are possibly deceiving him. And to some extent, we may not be acting deceptively either. For our eagerness to be liked may itself express admiration and respect which motivates our concern about this person's feelings toward us. If he does end up liking us, it may well result from his intuiting that deep down we really do care about him (or, at least, about his response).

Having argued that love fails as a project to recover one's being through the merging of subjectivities, Sartre also claims that neither can it succeed when the lover tries to attract the beloved by arousing her interest in himself as a desirable object. Sartre refers to this device as "seduction." Through it the lover hides his subjectivity while encouraging the Other to experience him as a "fascinating" and ever more meaningful object. The effort is self-defeating because the lover's objecthood can have no meaning, or truly fascinate, except as an expression of his subjective being, his free consciousness which is now seeking to seduce the beloved. Moreover, the lover always risks the possibility of the Other's awakening from her seduction and suddenly treating the lover as if he really were nothing but an object.

And even if love could succeed in assimilating two subjectivities, Sartre insists, it would fall short of its ideal aspiration unless they were each an absolute end for the other. But for this to occur, they would have to live only for one another. They would have to be separate from everyone else, alone in the world, complete within their perfect isolation. But that cannot be, or at least it cannot last. When, as must always happen, a third party looks at them, he reduces them both to the status of objectification, their oneness having become an object relative to his transcending gaze.

The importance of the third party (*le tiers*, the Third) recurs in Sartre's subsequent analysis of the we-object and the us-object, and in much of his later social philosophy. Before turning to these concepts, however, we should briefly consider his belief that love's failure cannot be overcome by masochism or sadism, by indifference or hatred, or by sexual desire. In masochism, as he perceives it, the inability to seduce the Other through one's objectivity creates an attempt to fascinate *oneself* with one's objecthood. The masochist delights in imagining himself as nothing but an object for the Other. His effort must always come to naught since he cannot escape his responsibility as the one who originates this projection: "It is in and through his transcendence that he disposes of himself as a being to be transcended." Similarly, the sadist seeks to render the Other obscene by forcing him to identify with his own body, as if the victim were merely flesh from which all freedom has been eradicated through torture. But sadism fails ontologically, and for the same reasons that love does. If the Other is unwilling to be reduced to his body or treated as a thing, the procedure cannot provide either dominance over a person or possession of the desired sort. And if the Other does accept the obscene condition into which he has been coerced, he transcends it by having freely acquiesced—which also defeats the sadist's project.

As Sartre interprets them, indifference and hatred fail no less than masochism and sadism. In being indifferent, I revert to my own free consciousness and disregard the fact that the Other is a subject looking at me. My attitude is self-contradictory, however, because my act must always occur in the context of my being aware that all other people in my world experience in *their* consciousness a freedom comparable to mine. To that extent, I am not indifferent even when I try to ignore them. Similarly, there is no resolution to be found in hatred. It merely manifests confused ideas about one's inability to cope with problems of existence. Through hatred we may intend harm and even death to the Other, but that will not enable us to recover our own being. The hated one objectifies us merely by looking at our enactment of hatred. Even if we kill him, he survives in our memory as someone whose subjectivity we could not assimilate.

❋

In the phenomenon of sexual desire, Sartre detects a more promising possibility. He discusses it as a fundamental attitude parallel to love. Where love seeks to absorb another's freedom, sexual desire directs itself to the need of each consciousness to be immersed in its own facticity as a body. In desiring the Other's body sexually, an individual allows himself to be "swallowed up in" his own body. Consciousness that would otherwise be clear or purified in its being as transcendence becomes "troubled" or "muddied" once it expresses itself bodily. Sexual desire is "a clogging of consciousness." As in love, we are striving to recover our being. But now our effort consists in trying to reach the Other's subjectivity by means of embodiment. We engage in our own clogging of consciousness through desire in the hope that our being flesh will produce a similar effect in another person. In desire "I make myself flesh *in the presence of the Other in order to appropriate* the Other's flesh."

Consciousness making itself body Sartre calls "incarnation." Through the caress, one's incarnated consciousness evokes the incarnation of the Other's consciousness. Since that too seeks another's incarnated consciousness, it causes the further incarnation of one's own. As Sartre puts it: "I make myself flesh in order to impel the Other to realize *for-herself* and *for me* her own flesh, and my caresses cause my flesh to be born for me in so far as it is for the Other *flesh causing her to be born as flesh.* I make her enjoy my flesh through her flesh in order to compel her to feel herself flesh. And so possession truly appears as a *double reciprocal incarnation.*" This, then, is the ideal of sexual desire. Like love, it involves mutuality and a search for merging. And also like love, it is a relationship between persons trying to overcome their fundamental conflict with each other.

In saying this, Sartre is quite emphatic about the differences between his interpretation of sexual desire and that of physiologists or psychologists such as Freud. He insists that through our sexuality we always desire a person, not merely an organ or a body. For he sees sexual desire as a primary structure in our social being, different from and ontologically prior to any of the instinctual mechanisms of reproductive physiology. At the same time, Sartre claims that we seek a double mutual incarnation not only with the Other, but also with *every* Other. Sexual desire is therefore present in all relations between human beings. This belief does not, however, implicate Sartre in the kind of pansexism sometimes ascribed to Freud. Since Sartre defines sex as a craving for a union of personalities, he maintains that it uses bodies to express an extra-biological intention. Whatever else it may be, he thinks of sexual desire as a search for oneness that involves more than just facticity.

Developing his argument further, Sartre distinguishes between sexual desire and sexual activity in a way that convinces him that the ideal of sex must be "doomed to failure." Sexual activity is concentrated either on deriving pleasures from one's own body or taking and appropriating the body of the Other. In the first case, we attend to the gratifying incarnation of our for-itself. But then we are ignoring the incarnation of the Other. We enjoy the caresses we receive and in the process reduce ourselves to objecthood. The result is "a rupture of contact and desire misses its goal." In the second case, the desire to appropriate another's incarnated consciousness requires one to use the Other as a thing. The caress having brought about the incarnation of the Other's consciousness, sexual activity makes her flesh into an object that one penetrates for the sake of consummations wholly unrelated to her subjectivity. The Other becomes "*all* object." In that event, she escapes with "*all* her transcendence." Yet this was precisely the condition that sexual desire sought to overcome.

It is at this point that Sartre introduces his analyses of sadism and masochism. They are hopeless even as sexual maneuvers. Masochism amounts to intoxication with my flesh as object, which the Other helps me to realize by using me as nothing else. Sadism appropriates the Other's flesh but treats it as nothing but an object of appropriation. In either event, the ideal of sexual desire is defeated. Nevertheless, Sartre claims, sadism and masochism provide the coordinates for sexuality in general: "It is because of this inconstancy on the part of desire and its perpetual oscillation between these two perils that 'normal' sexuality is commonly designated as 'sadistic-masochistic.'"

Sartre's novels and plays generally depict sex as a compendium of sadism and masochism. And among his later theoretical discussions, one could argue that none really mitigates his critique of sexuality in *Being and Nothingness*. In that book he sometimes seems to say that since sexual activity undermines the goals of sexual desire they might possibly be attainable if only we limited our behavior to caressing one another and thus instituting double mutual incarnations. But this cannot be what Sartre intends. For "the caress," as he uses that term, is an ontological projection that already includes sexual activity whether or not it leads to genital intercourse. In saying that sexual activity defeats the aspirations of sexual desire, Sartre means that sexuality as a whole, sex as it exists in concrete human behavior of any sort, cannot enable us to merge with another person as we would like.

Recent commentators have differed in their interpretations of Sartre's views about sexual perversion. If sexual activity systematically thwarts the goals of sexual desire, should the former be considered a "perversion" of the latter? If so, is it the *fulfilling* of desire that undermines it; or rather the physical behavior itself? Or are these questions dismissable as largely irrelevant to Sartre's analysis of sexual desire? If he maintains that *no* sexual relationship can succeed in its underlying purpose, is he not rejecting the entire distinction between perverted and unperverted sex? I myself find this controversy irresolvable in view of the program Sartre has set himself. He calls sadism and masochism "vices" but he does not discuss the nature of perversion. Of greater importance is his suggestion that these attitudes create inescapable guilt in all intimate relations. Sartre describes sadism as "a seed in desire itself." That is why he thinks that desire must always fail. He believes that sexual desire cannot be separated from sadism and masochism, as if it could precede them or later exist in some purified form. The "perpetual oscillation" between sadism and masochism to which Sartre refers reveals what he considers to be the very nature of sexual desire. Its guiltiness results from its inherent need to treat as an object either oneself or the Other, and usually both.

It is here that the inadequacy of Sartre's analysis appears most graphically. He maintains that double mutual incarnation—the ideal of sexual desire—is universally sought but always unattainable. His philosophy resembles that part of Plato's which holds that all beings seek their alter ego and yet can never find it in the empirical world. For Sartre the futility of the sexual ideal results from incoherence within the act of incarnation as well as in the attempt to double it. When consciousness descends into the body, making itself flesh, it becomes an object to be seen by the Other, just as the Other's body is seen by oneself. Since this contradicts what consciousness really wants, Sartre concludes that the incarnated state must be inherently unsatisfactory. But in saying this, he assumes that consciousness has a dual being: sometimes as unadulterated freedom, like water that is clear of particles alien to itself; sometimes as clogged or muddied by the materiality with which it has been mixed. One can hardly imagine how this dualistic notion comports with Sartre's belief that man exists only in a world which includes other people and that sexual desire is an omni-present craving toward community with them. For if that is true, must not consciousness always be clogged? What are the circumstances under which consciousness could possibly occur in its pure, non-incarnated condition? Without an answer to these questions, we cannot really understand how there could be consciousness which then makes itself *into* body. And similarly, we will have no way of asserting that one consciousness can manage through its incarnation to bring about the reciprocal incarnation of another consciousness. Sartre's analysis has not revealed an incoherence: it has merely generated one.

To make this criticism I do not need to question Sartre's assumption that sex is a fundamental reality in all human relations. For, like Plato and the Romantics, he means by sex the dynamic force or vital impulse that causes people to gravitate within each other's orbit. It is the integument which binds them, which creates the conflict Sartre considers basic, and which projects its own ideal for achieving a beneficial resolution. Though it requires clarification and greater precision, we may treat this much of what he says as an interesting possibility. What is bizarre and clearly unacceptable is his description of the incarnated state. Leaving aside the fact that the terms he uses for sexual incarnation—"muddied," "impure," "clogged," etc.—are distinctly pejorative, I see no reason to believe that consciousness is related to the body as Sartre thinks. If sexuality is a pervasive power within the human world to which we all belong, consciousness is *always* incarnated. In moments of sexual arousal, our feelings are suffused with what may be called the consciousness of incarnation-through-flesh. This is a particular mode of incarnation, quite different from other modes, but only one among many ways in which consciousness is necessarily incarnated.

As we have seen, Sartre insists that sexual desire is always directed toward persons rather than organs or parts of the body. He constructs his antinomies out of the fact that in sex we crave the Other in his subjectivity while being forced to experience him as a body, and therefore in his presentation as an object. But this condition is problematic only if we assume that the categories of personhood and bodily objectivity are contraries of the sort that Sartre suggests. And that seems very dubious to me. Though we use sex to make contact with other persons, and though it is uniquely attuned to various aspects of their being, it has access to their personhood only through its sensitivity to their body. This sensitivity functions within our own body, by means of our own organs, sense modalities, and appetites. Human sexuality ranges within a spectrum defined by the need for unity with other persons as one of its termini and the need for appetitive gratification as the other. Most occasions of sexual desire are explicable as a combination of these two contrasting but wholly compatible demands. There are no grounds for asserting, as Sartre does, that sex must always involve an incarnation of consciousness which hopelessly turns both itself and the Other into depersonalized objects.

Sartre may be justified in seeing the ideal of sexual desire as a mutuality which is doubled when each person's interest becomes augmented by a comparable attitude of the Other. In happy or successful sex, the participants respond to each other's feelings, which are intensified through recognition of their mutual responsiveness. Their behavior is dynamically integrated. We can say the same about quarrels or even warfare, and this may often alert us to an erotic element in these different situations. What distinguishes sexual intimacy is its capacity to eliminate hostility through the experience of organic pleasure that creates interpersonal harmony by means of the mutual bodily response. Sartre considers this consummation futile because he thinks it cannot be achieved. And yet, we may well insist, it sometimes happens—frequently or infrequently, but surely on some occasions. Does Sartre really want to deny that?

❋

In view of the many changes Sartre made as his philosophy developed, we may leave this kind of question in abeyance for the time being. Some of the difficulties in Sartre's analyses of love and of sexual desire are related to his ideas about the interdependence of individuals within a group. He devoted much of his later philosophy to the revising of his earlier theories about groups. In *Being and Nothingness* he had stated that man's ontology precluded any ultimate oneness between subjectivities. He thus rejected the possibility of an authentic "we-subject." In his relationship with the Other, man could only be an "us-object." Sartre does not wholly discard this distinction in his final thinking, but in various details he modifies it greatly.

Sartre's denial of ontological intersubjectivity first arises in his criticism of attempts by Husserl, Hegel, and Heidegger to refute solipsism. Husserl tried to prove the existence of other persons by arguing that the Other is a necessary condition for there to be a world that each individual must experience in order to be himself. Sartre attacks Husserl's position on the grounds that it is relevant only to knowledge and not to being. Hegel maintained that each person's being depended on the being of the Other inasmuch as we could not be conscious of ourselves unless we were aware of self-consciousness (*Bewusstsein*) in general, as an identical something that occurs in others as well as in ourselves. Sartre claims that Hegel's argument applies to knowledge no less than Husserl's, even though it is oneness with the being of the Other that Hegel wishes to establish. As against Hegelian optimism, Sartre insists that consciousness can only be an awareness internal to each subject as it exists for-itself. No one else has direct access to one's consciousness, and therefore one's being cannot include the being of another: "The Other is not a *for-itself* as he appears to me; I do not appear to myself as I am *for-the-Other*."

Heidegger's view Sartre finds more intriguing, but equally un-acceptable. In his attempt to get beyond idealism as well as realism, Heidegger suggested that man exists as a solitary being who is also part of a world made up of other people—and therefore every individual is a "co-existing" of consciousnesses. Sartre remarks that Heidegger's idea is best illustrated by the relationships within a crew. The oarsmen are separate entities but they share a single goal, which itself makes sense only in terms of a world that includes competitors, spectators, and others not themselves. This "common solitude" or attunement (*Stimmung*) Heidegger refers to as being-with, *Mitsein* that defines the being of each person. Sartre does not doubt that cooperation and being-with occur in human experience, but he denies that they are "the unique foundation of our being." He sees no way of moving from empirical instances of Stimmung to the ontological primacy of Mitsein, and he spurns as merely ab-stract or vacuous all a priori assumptions about Mitsein.

We do not need to go through Sartre's arguments against Heidegger. We need only attend to the rhetorical questions that he poses about the nature of Mitsein: "And what type of being does this coexistence have? To what extent is the negation which makes the Other *an other* and which constitutes him as non-essential main-tained? If we suppress it entirely, are we not going to fall into a monism?" Sartre poses these questions in this fashion because he believes, as we have seen, that each consciousness exists only as a separate entity that defines itself through opposition to the being of others. Since the Other sees us as an objective in-itself, we must defend our being as a conscious for-itself either by negating his being or somehow using it to found our own. In rejecting Heideg-ger's concept of Mitsein because it implies some kind of monism, Sartre reveals once more his usual skepticism about man's search for absolute merging or total assimilation with other beings. In his early writings, he scarcely considers the possibility of any other type of ontological oneness.

Sartre's conclusions in *Being and Nothingness* about the we-subject and the us-object are therefore almost predictable. He does not deny that human beings may occasionally have an experience of the "we." People often talk about themselves as if they had a we-ness as opposed to other individuals, and Sartre has no desire to question this use of language. Instead he argues that the basis for such experiences or verbal expressions is not to be found in an ontologically ultimate intersubjectivity or fusion of consciousnesses. The experience of the we-subject cannot be fundamental, he thinks, because it always presupposes an Other to which we are jointly related. Walking through a doorway marked "Exit" or "Entrance," I may see myself as undergoing the same experience as you do when you walk through it. But this event is derivative from the fact that the sign represents a world of human beings controlling us, a world which lies beyond our use of the doorway and which serves as the Other that conditions our similar experience. In relation to that reality, the we-subject is not only secondary but also reducible to the us-object.

In being an us-object, as Sartre conceives of it, two or more beings are unified by the Third who looks at them both. He thereby treats them as a single object. This may create a sense of one-ness, but "we experience it in shame as a community alienation." Sartre portrays the condition by describing convicts visited by a beautiful and elegant woman. Beneath her recognition of their state of misery, they undergo "a common shame and a common alienation." In *Saint Genet* Sartre depicts various relationships that operate as modifications of this kind of experience. In *Being and Nothingness* he lays the groundwork for analyzing class consciousness as us-objectification. He later develops this analysis in works such as the *Critique of Dialectical Reason*. It is the Third as the oppressive ruling class that causes the workers to realize themselves as an us-object. Similarly, Sartre describes the traditional ideal of the oneness of man as a search for a humanistic us-object in relation to a Third beyond which there can be no Third. This being "is the same as that of the being-who-looks-at and who can never be looked-at; that is, it is one with the idea of God." Since God is "unrealizable," man's effort to use him as the Third which establishes a sense of totalized humanity must always end in failure.

Sartre's analysis of the us-object reinforces his belief that the experience of the we-subject is never ontologically basic. It must always depend on the existence of an Other from whose consciousness we are alienated. "It is therefore useless for human-reality to seek to get out of this dilemma: one must either transcend the Other or allow oneself to be transcended by him. The essence of the relations between consciousnesses is not the *Mitsein;* it is conflict." In saying this, Sartre means not only that a "unified" or merged subjectivity between individuals is unattainable but also that a community of human beings must always be predicated upon conflict among them—what he calls the underlying "conflict of transcendences." Once again we return to this presupposition on Sartre's part.

Critics of Sartre have dealt with his assertions about conflict in a number of ways. Some have argued that he uses the word in a loose and even ambiguous manner. At times it seems to refer merely to the ultimate fact of separation between consciousnesses; at other times it implies that they are alienated from each other; occasionally it contains the suggestion of lingering aggression or possibly violence. Even if we eliminate the last interpretation as irrelevant to Sartre's conviction that subjects are always ontologically distinct from one another, we may still question his assurance that separability can never be overcome in any fundamental sense. We need only note that interpersonal oneness can exist even if there is no merging of subjectivities. Sartre might well reply that we would then be entertaining an ideal other than the one he was analyzing. But nothing required him to limit his analysis to that ideal alone. He does so because he assumes that the desire for merging uniquely reveals man's quest for intersubjectivity. If, however, we refuse to believe that only a merging of subjectivities could enable them to eliminate their separation, we may reject Sartre's claim that a we-subject can have no status as an ontological ultimate.

We might also argue that intersubjectivity involves a kind of merging that is different from what Sartre means: for example, the oneness that consists in having a common language or cultural viewpoint. These are undifferentiated unities ontologically prior to the being of individual consciousnesses. They are merged or quasi-merged conditions to which we are born, although we go on to exist as separate entities.

These and related problems about the nature of community and the interdependence among human beings recur throughout

Sartre's development. He was constantly aware of them and they served to propel him through each of his three stages. As he clearly perceived, *Being and Nothingness* was written during a period in his life of personal alienation. In one place he ascribes his attitude at that time to his living as an "anarchistic individualist" just before the Second World War. During the war his thinking about society and the structure of interpersonal relations began to change. Though he later regretted some of what he says in "Existentialism Is a Humanism," that lecture (delivered shortly after the end of the war) typified his new approach. The essay states that freedom which is essential to the being of each individual entails moral responsibility for the freedom of everyone else: "I am obliged to want the freedom of others at the same time as my own; I cannot take my freedom as an aim unless I equally take that of others as my aim."

Critics immediately pointed out that statements like this one, which is characteristic of Sartre's second phase, would seem to contradict his ontological assertions in *Being and Nothingness*. He there emphasized man's helplessness in the face of that "original sin" which is existence in a world that includes others. As a character in his play *No Exit* claims that hell is other people, so too had Sartre said: "Whatever I may do *for* the Other's freedom, as we have seen, my efforts are reduced to treating the Other as an instrument and to positing his freedom as a transcendence-transcended. . . . I shall never touch the Other save in his being-as-object." In context Sartre does admit that we may provide the Other with opportunities to reveal his freedom, but he denies that we can ever help him to increase it. In view of this ontological guilt, as Sartre calls it, this shameful inability to overcome our misuse of other people, this separation and alienation basic to human nature, how can Sartre consistently formulate a social ethic in which the essential freedom of each individual entails a concern for the freedom of anyone else, to say nothing of the freedom of *everyone?*

In *Being and Nothingness,* as I have remarked, Sartre mentioned the possibility of a "radical conversion." If he can be defended against the charge of inconsistency between his ontology and his later moral philosophy, the content and plausibility of this radical conversion must become evident. In the second and third stages of Sartre's development we should expect to find some solution to the problems about oneness and interdependence that beset him throughout his life.

❀

Studying Sartre's efforts to move beyond the limitations of *Being and Nothingness,* we do well to begin with two early works by Simone de Beauvoir. In *The Ethics of Ambiguity* and *Pyrrhus et Cinéas,* she attests her allegiance to Sartre's ontology and tries to show how their world outlook is relevant to moral philosophy. Written in the middle 1940s, these books belong to the years when Sartre wrote drafts for the treatise on morals that was published only after his death. Like Sartre, Beauvoir constructs a morality of freedom, i.e., an ethical doctrine in which the fundamental and principal value consists in freedom itself. Unlike Sartre, however, she sees the need to demonstrate that there is no inconsistency between the ontological premises and ethical conclusions that each of them espoused.

The difficulties in Sartre's philosophy arose because he seemed to be saying that man was doomed to conflict engendered by the need to free oneself from objectification existing in every relationship—however happy or well-intentioned it might be. If ideals such as love were futile since they failed to resolve this problem, how could one hope to construct an ethics in which people could be considered autonomous and yet all would devote themselves to freedom as an absolute and universal goal? If each man had to protect himself from the mere look of everyone else, how could he be expected—even in principle—to take responsibility for maximizing their freedom? Beauvoir's solution consists in giving importance to an aspect of individual subjectivity that Sartre had hitherto ignored or underemphasized. In seeking to found his being, she says, a person must realize that no one can successfully justify his existence unless others sustain him in this effort. Our self-esteem depends not only on our awareness of ourselves as freely transcending subjects, but also on the fact that others (who are also freely transcending subjects in their own right) acknowledge and accept us as such. In order to justify my existence as one whose being is freedom itself, I must live in the company of persons who validate my self-justification. This can happen only if they are preserved in their being as free agents. "Man can find a justification of his own existence only in the existence of other men." Beauvoir means by this that the very concept of justification or the founding of one's being already involves coexistence with others. And since it also requires their freely given recognition of our independent subjectivity, our search for self-justification must include a desire to further *their* freedom.

Beauvoir realizes that her solution is, in some respects, quite tame and even conventional. She remarks that her position is "at one with the point of view of Christian charity. . . and Kantian moralism which treats each man as an end." But Christian ideas about charity always imply that man's justification, in the ontological sense Sartre and Beauvoir have in mind, can only occur through a relationship with God. And for Kant, each man is morally an end whether or not his freedom conduces to the justification of anyone else. Having discarded these supernatural and a prioristic dogmas, Beauvoir can claim to have effected a link between ontology and ethics that enables us to bypass the usual modes of idealistic thinking. The crucial concept was the idea of freedom, as Sartre had often said. Man's reality is his freedom since the nothingness of his being and the self-transcendence of his consciousness entail it; his values arise from freedom, since he creates them himself in the absence of any objective preferability beyond his own choices; and his legitimate dependence on others, as Beauvoir now concluded, results from his need to have them freely sustain him in his freedom. This in turn requires him to respect and even foster their freedom.

Beauvoir's analysis of love is an extension of this approach. Apart from some comments about the failure of "the passionate man" in *The Ethics of Ambiguity,* she mainly writes about love as it exists in women. Her feminist philosophy is, however, comprehensive, and her negative description of *l'amoureuse*—the woman in love—makes sense only in the context of her affirmative suggestions about "genuine" or "authentic" love as a whole. In *The Second Sex* she argues that women can have no access to authentic love as long as they are subjugated by the institutions of male dominance. L'amoureuse grows up within a world that allots freedom of action to the male and defines its principal values in accordance with masculine aspirations. Young girls in general learn to think of the male as a kind of god, however diminished his divinity may show itself to be. As Sartre had stated that all human beings wish to merge with God, so too does Beauvoir explain female submissiveness in love as the debased consequence of a similar desire: "The supreme goal of human love, as of mystical love, is identification with the loved one. The measure of values, the truth of the world, are in his consciousness; hence it is not enough to serve him. The woman in love tries to see with his eyes; . . . The center of the world is no longer the place where she is, but that occupied by her lover." To illustrate this search for identification, Beauvoir quotes Catherine in *Wuthering Heights* when she says, "I am Heathcliff."

Beauvoir insists that l'amoureuse, as she describes her, is not experiencing genuine love. Even if this is true, however, Beauvoir scarcely seems to recognize that the condition she depicts has often existed among men as well as women, that it manifests an aspect of Romantic ideology which reached fruition in the nineteenth century, and therefore that it cannot explain a uniquely female subjection through love that Beauvoir considers virtually universal among women. Moreover, though she introduces Proustian and Sartrean ideas about love as the search for an absolute, she applies them to l'amoureuse as if they were primarily relevant to her situation. "The supreme happiness of the woman in love is to be recognized by the loved man as a part of himself; . . . As one necessary to a being who is absolute necessity, who stands forth in the world seeking necessary goals and who gives her back the world in necessary form, the woman in love acquires in her submission that magnificent possession, the absolute. . . . So long as she is in love and is loved by and necessary to her loved one, she feels herself wholly justified."

Beauvoir talks in this one-sided fashion because she is convinced that our society rears females to believe that males are inherently superior, even embodying an absolute or necessary value. Women accept this belief, she says, in a way that has no parallel for men, including those who fall in love. Though Beauvoir argues that masochism is one of the possible forms that love may take, she seems to ascribe it principally to the condition of women. She traces the submissiveness of l'amoureuse to the desire in all unemancipated women to assimilate themselves with the image of the god-like male. Women have been taught to revere him, she says, but they must finally learn how to liberate themselves.

The polemical burden of Beauvoir's analysis is obvious and, by now, quite commonplace. Since she thinks that female submissiveness results from social rather than biological or obscurely pathological forces, she argues that only legislation and a change in moral attitudes are needed to make genuine love feasible for women. Total equality between the sexes, particularly in their economic opportunities, will allow women to reject the futility of giving themselves in love to one or another male whose reality as a mere human being they must eventually discover through suffering and frustration.

I have no reason to question the value and validity of Beauvoir's demands for sexual equality. *The Second Sex* will endure as an early formulation of feminist enlightenment in the twentieth century. Beauvoir's claim that authentic love between men and women can occur *only* in the context of social and economic equalization has been repeated by later theorists who benefited from her suggestions. This much of what they jointly say I reserve for my comments in Chapter 10. Here I shall only remark that Beauvoir's general argument creates unnecessary difficulties for the feminist cause. For in failing to recognize that men in love often treat the female as a goddess, seeking their justification in her much as she hopes to find it in them, Beauvoir ignores the kind of oneness that even undesirable love may foster. Her analysis of male and female roles being simplistic in this respect, it is not surprising that the benign relationship which she portrays as genuine love usually sounds empty or utopian.

"An authentic love," Beauvoir tells us, "should assume the contingence of the other; that is to say, his lacks, his limitations, and his basic gratuitousness. It would not pretend to be a mode of salvation, but a human inter-relation." This seems fine as far as it goes. Men are not gods; and if one believes that the ideal of God is inconsistent or untenable, there can be no acceptable reason to act as if any human being transcends the limits of our frail mortality. In Beauvoir's reference to the "basic gratuitousness" of the male, one may also detect an intimation about bestowal as a fundamental ingredient in all love. But beyond this, we wish to know what *kind* of "human inter-relation" Beauvoir recommends as authentic love. In her preoccupation with the fallen state of l'amoureuse, which is to say, almost all women who love men in our male-dominated society, she makes little attempt to specify the details of her glowing alternative.

Even so, what Beauvoir does proffer is important and worth considering. She emphasizes the mutuality of authentic love and its ability to supersede the impossible dream of union through merging. When it is genuine, love between man and woman causes them to accept one another not only as equals but also as beings equally free by their very nature: "Genuine love ought to be founded on the mutual recognition of two liberties; the lovers would then experience themselves both as self and as other: neither would give up transcendence, neither would be mutilated; together they would manifest values and aims in the world." The last clause in this quotation derives its significance from Beauvoir's belief that society has thus far denied women the ability to be active rather than passive. They were to accept and admire values that men created, but they were not to participate through any aims of their own. If there were genuine love, however, women would cooperate as co-workers, as positive contributors to human endeavors that are meaningful because they benefit everyone.

Many writers have attacked Beauvoir's feminism on the grounds that it is anti-feminine and anti-marriage. Insisting upon equality between the sexes as a prerequisite for genuine love, she has been interpreted as encouraging women to emulate masculine aggressiveness and aversion to marital fidelity. It is true that she sees the usual demands for constancy in love or marriage as a cynical device that binds women to organizational restraints men are permitted to escape. She rightly condemns Balzac for asserting that "woman's life is love" when he means (as he then goes on to say) that "woman is man's equal only when she makes her life a perpetual offering." But Beauvoir's rejection of love or marriage which institutionalizes female submissiveness in no way implies scorn for lasting types of intimacy between men and women. She concludes *The Second Sex* by quoting with approval Marx's statement that "the relation of man to woman is the most natural relation of human being to human being." As if she were answering Sartre's analysis of love in *Being and Nothingness,* she proclaims the following about the liberated woman of the future: "Let her have her independent existence and she will continue none the less to exist for [man] *also:* mutually recognizing each other as subject, each will yet remain for the other an *other.*"

Far from denying the potential goodness of married love, Beauvoir describes it as the goal of viable marriages. She states that they would enable "entirely self-sufficient human beings to form unions one with another only in accordance with the untrammeled dictates of their mutual love." Though she and Sartre decided early in their relationship not to get married, their friendship of fifty years seems to have been similar to what nowadays would be called an open marriage. In her autobiographical writings, Beauvoir refers to the bond with Sartre as a "necessary love" in contrast to the "contingent loves" each of them had for other people. Elsewhere, she speaks of "a 'certain fidelity' " that she and Sartre maintained toward each other throughout their varying experiences. In novels such as her semiautobiographical *The Mandarins,* she reveals how hard it is to combine self-sufficiency and independence as a professional woman with the ideal of genuine love toward a man who is equally independent and self-sufficient. Genuine love nevertheless remained as a permanent goal for her as well as for representative characters in her fiction.

The utopian aura of Beauvoir's recommendations may still deter us. Though she may be right in ruling out both submissiveness and the ideal of merging, one can hardly imagine what she means by authentic love if the participants are to be self-sufficient as she says. Like the gods in Plato, they would seem to have no need of anything like the intimacy of love. In discussing Plato's philosophy, I criticized it for failing to recognize that love involves a bestowing of value which even perfect gods may enjoy as part of their nature. Throughout Beauvoir's philosophy, one finds little awareness of the role that bestowal plays in love. Her ideal includes more than mere friendliness or companionship in a noble cause, but it does not account for the ardor and intensity of ties that go beyond these associations without turning into submissiveness or idolatry. She does not quite perceive that the value lovers create in one another through acts of mutual bestowal serves to structure and to fortify their continuing interdependence. Inspiring as it may be, her conception does not extend this far.

❋

For further clarification about the nature of genuine or authentic love, we must return to the writings of Sartre. Though he offers little description of what he means by authenticity, a passage in his book on the Jewish problem (translated as *Anti-Semite and Jew*) is very helpful. He says that if man is defined "as a being having freedom within the limits of a situation, then it is easy to see that the exercise of this freedom may be considered as *authentic* or *inauthentic* according to the choices made in the situation." He then states that authenticity "consists in having a true and lucid consciousness of the situation, in assuming the responsibilities and risks that it involves, in accepting it in pride or humiliation, sometimes in horror and hate."

Sartre recognizes that authenticity occurs only rarely among human beings. If this is so, one need not be surprised that *Being and Nothingness* approaches man's ontology from the point of view of "bad faith." For that concept reveals the state of self-deception and inauthenticity that usually characterizes the human condition. By bad faith Sartre means a refusal or inability to accept the fact that one is both a self-transcending consciousness responsible for its own inherent freedom and at the same time a facticity limited by what one has made oneself into. In acting from bad faith, we confound the categories of the for-itself and the in-itself. Sartre's ontology may therefore be taken as an attempt to facilitate authenticity by analyzing bad faith for the sake of avoiding it.

Various critics have interpreted *Being and Nothingness* in a different manner. They argue that since the book reveals that bad faith is fundamental in man's being, authenticity must be considered wholly impossible. If this were true, Sartre's ontology would undercut his subsequent attempts to formulate an ethics. In the Conclusion to *Being and Nothingness* Sartre does mention that no ontology can yield ethical precepts. But his critics go beyond this in saying that *his* ontology makes it logically impossible for him to advocate the kind of ethics that he eventually proposes. If man is "a useless passion" and if he always hopelessly seeks to be a god who founds his own being, how can he ever escape bad faith? And if he cannot do so, neither can he approximate an ideal of love other than the one that Sartre has already shown to be futile.

I do not see any comfortable solution to this debate. There are passages in *Being and Nothingness* that would lead even the most sympathetic of readers to agree with Sartre's critics. Moreover, the writing is often loosely constructed and sometimes obscure, as if Sartre were not himself aware of contrary implications that could be drawn. Perhaps that is why he later felt that his treatment of concrete human relations had failed. All the same, one can make sense of his primary intention by treating *Being and Nothingness* as an investigation into the fundamental problems mankind faces because of its ontological being. By analyzing human nature under the aspect of bad faith, Sartre would then be illuminating the most prevalent propensity in man's condition. It is a structure of our reality that we all grow up with, like original sin in Christianity, but one that may be altered through determination and courage. This occurs in the radical conversion. Sartre's moral philosophy can thus appear as a consistent—at least not necessarily inconsistent— attempt to articulate the details of the sole regenerate possibility that he finds defensible.

Until recently, "Existentialism Is a Humanism" was generally cited as the only place in which Sartre had outlined the ethical system designed to supplement the rest of his philosophy. But in 1983 there appeared his *Cahiers pour une morale*, the notebooks on ethics that he wrote in 1947 and 1948. In them he discusses "moral conversion" and describes authenticity as "the new departure" that enables a man "to exist his existence." He insists that the idea of the authentic was already present within the dialectic of bad faith as analyzed in *Being and Nothingness*. With respect to the nature of love, however, Sartre introduces what he calls a "dimension" that was lacking in his earlier treatise.

Sartre begins this new departure by reasserting that love arises from the "sadomasochistic dialectic involving subjugation of liberties" as he had previously described it. Now, however, he adds the further belief that love (he means *authentic* love) exists only when there is "deeper recognition and reciprocal comprehension of liberties." Even at its best, this dimension cannot eliminate the sadomasochistic element, he says, for then love would disappear. Since it pertains to sexuality as a constant in human development, love involves *both* sadomasochism and the mutual recognition of freedom. For love to be authentic, it requires what Sartre calls the "tension" between the two—in order "to maintain both poles of the ambiguity, in order to retain them in the unity of a single endeavor [*projet*]." Without the ambiguity there is no love, and neither is there an a priori or predetermined synthesis to be attained. According to Sartre, one must "invent" any harmonization between the two components. He means that only by coping with the vicissitudes of lived experience can the duality within love be overcome.

In defining love as a tension that may be resolved in practice, through trial and error, Sartre moves beyond the pessimism of *Being and Nothingness*. Still he remains faithful to the vision of that work insofar as he continues to consider love problematic (like human affect in general). Love is not the ontological substratum that the idealist tradition extolled, and yet it is more than just an empirical fact about man. The tensions that constitute its being occur at different levels. If one loves, Sartre maintains, one also wants to love. But wanting to love implies choice, the making of a decision to love, and this would seem to go against the phenomenon of love it-self. If love involved no choice, if it were just something that happened against one's will, as the Romantics thought, that too would not be love. At least, he says, it would not be authentic love, which must therefore involve the further tension between wanting to love as an expression of our choice of being and submitting to it as a system of feelings we cannot control. This is the dilemma of love, and authenticity consists in accepting the fact that love is based upon tensions of this sort. Since it partly involves feelings that occur in spite of oneself, authentic love will also include a "fundamental anguish" about whether or not it ought to continue. And since love is willed as well as being felt, authenticity requires that we willingly acquiesce in this anguish as a part of what it is to love.

Through this conception of an authentic love resulting from tension that is recognized and accepted, Sartre modifies his earlier views about contingency. Previously he had focused upon man's search for ontological security, futile in view of the nature of subject-object relations as he interpreted them. Now, in this later writing, he calls our attention to a relationship with the Other that is different from either turning him into an objectified thing or trying to protect oneself from objectification. He speaks of a need "to accept unconditionally this finitude [of the Other], this contingency and this fragility." Acceptance of this sort is based on more than just recognizing the Other's contingency. It also entails that I acknowledge my having created his contingency insofar as my own subjective being structures it. "Here," Sartre says, "we can understand what it means *to love* in the sense of authenticity: I love if I *create* the contingent finitude of the Other as being-in-the-midst-of-the-world while accepting my own subjective finitude and while also *willing* this subjective finitude." As a further proviso, Sartre adds that "through the same gesture which makes me assume my subject-finitude, I assume his object-finitude as being a necessary condition of the free goal that it projects and that presents itself to me as an unconditional end."

Throughout this discussion Sartre continues to see the Other's finitude as a vulnerability to which one contributes, but he now treats it as a condition that one counters through the act of *accepting* the contingency of this other person. And since the Other's finitude and vulnerability are evident in his body as it exists for others, Sartre concludes: "to reveal the Other in his being-in-the-midst-of-the-world is to love him in his body."

The being that Sartre refers to in this love of another person is the being of that individual as a particularity. It is the Other as a bit of reality that depends on the universe as a whole and yet remains free to transcend it. Elsewhere in the *Cahiers* Sartre contrasts the "love of Being [which is to say, Being in general]" with the kind of love that he considers authentic. He asserts that the former belongs to an idealization of force, violence, conquest. It directs itself toward pure Being on the assumption that only that is perfect, and therefore that all love for particularities must be sacrificed as relatively worthless. It resorts to violence because nothing can be allowed to stand in the way of perfection. As Sartre states: "the scorn of man accompanies abnegation." He develops his conception of others as beings-in-the-midst-of-the-world in order to supplant the bad faith that is built into this pernicious love of pure Being. In authentic love for another person one accepts the finitude of the Other without denying its dependence upon Being in general. The goal is "to unveil the Other's being-in-the-midst-of-the-world, to recognize this unveiling and therefore its Being in the absolute; to *rejoice* in it without seeking to appropriate it to oneself; to place it in the shelter of one's freedom and to transcend it only in the direction of the Other's ends."

The word I have here translated as "rejoice" is *réjouir* in the original. This infinitive is related to *jouissance,* signifying enjoyment or consummation, as in the eighteenth-century concept I discussed in the second volume. Elsewhere in the *Cahiers,* Sartre attacks Hegel's monism by arguing that it emphasizes the destructiveness of desire rather than its ability to function as jouissance. Through merging of the Hegelian sort, one assimilates and therefore destroys the object. Sartre sees this as a desire for possession, but now he insists that desire (particularly in its "dialectical moments of tenderness and love") also seeks for recognition by the Other, whom it wants to sustain in her facticity. Though he continues to mention the desire to appropriate and possess another's consciousness through the body, Sartre modifies his earlier conception by reinterpreting what that means. Saying that "desire desires the Other *in his being-there*," he suggests that the acceptance of another's particularity may explain the nature of desire better than inclinations toward merging or possession. In the next paragraph he extends this insight to man as he exists in society as a whole: "man exists in society. And his original rapport with society is such that he can neither completely merge with it nor completely transcend it."

I shall presently return to Sartre's later ideas about oneness in society, but first it will be useful to see how far he takes his new conception of sexual and interpersonal love. In his theoretical writings, he makes little attempt to elucidate his reasons for renouncing the analysis in *Being and Nothingness*. But occasional statements indicate how greatly his thinking had changed. For instance, in the second volume of *The Family Idiot*, his work on Flaubert, he speaks of "the essence of love" as follows:

> [It] is that a man *enters totally* into a woman who receives him *totally*, which supposes that, in welcoming him, she tightens herself onto him, contains and penetrates him in turn with what Doña Prouhèze calls "the taste that I have." Love is not mute, above all when it remains silent: through the flesh, its "taste," its odors, its elasticity, its colors and its forms, across the grainy texture of a skin, the patterning of hair, the total but unsayable sense of the person transmits itself to the other person; from each of the two sides, this sense becomes a material and silent condensation of all language, of all the sentences spoken and as yet unsaid, of all the actions carried through and still to be done. The two naked bodies in the momentary present are equivalent to an infinite discourse that they promise, transcend and, suddenly, render useless.

In the context of Sartre's discussion, this passage has specific reference to sexual intimacy. At the same time, however, it deals with all love between man and woman, treating it as an affirmative achievement, not at all as futile. In several places Sartre distinguishes between sympathy and empathy in a way that is pertinent to his study of Flaubert but that also has more general relevance. Although he devoted many years to the task of understanding and appreciating Flaubert's particularity as a person, he could never overcome his antipathy toward the man. He freely admitted that—for a variety of reasons resulting from their differing principles and attitudes—he felt no sympathy for Flaubert. He nevertheless believed that he empathized with him as a fellow human being and that this was sufficient for studying Flaubert as a person. When an interviewer asked Sartre whether his concept of empathy was helpful in trying to explicate the nature of love, Sartre implied that it was—provided that the other person was lovable: "That means a lot: to be lovable. The old nineteenth-century theory claims that you love a person for psychological and personal reasons, [someone] who is neither lovable nor non-lovable, who is the loved person. But according to me that is not correct. Persons are lovable or they are not lovable, and it is to that extent that one can love them or not love them."

In this place Sartre must be interpreted as referring to the appraisive element of love. Nineteenth-century romanticism generally thought that love is an unconditioned bestowal, oneness that creates lovability in the object rather than being motivated by any prior goodness in it. Sartre is here pointing out the absurdity of this belief. He rightly asserts that love between human beings is constrained by the requirement that each find something lovable in the other. This in turn belongs to the concrete circumstances that issue from a person's conditioning in the world, what Sartre calls one's "situation." In the second and third stages of his philosophy, Sartre largely devotes himself to analyzing the social situation of men and women, who are joined to one another not only as the subjects and objects analyzed in *Being and Nothingness* but also as conditioned individualities within a particular group of human beings.

Most of Sartre's *Critique of Dialectical Reason* concerns itself with man's being as a social animal that lives in groups. Sartre thereby adds a further dimension to what he had previously written about the we-subject. In *Being and Nothingness* he concluded that it was only a psychological phenomenon, the presence of the Third preventing feelings of oneness from attaining ontological finality. He now reorients that analysis in a way that makes it possible for community and authentic reciprocity to exist as valid ultimates. He still retains the idea of inherent instabilty between two persons who act as subject and object to one another, and he still insists that their intimacy is always threatened by the look of a third party. Even in the *Cahiers,* where he defines love as the having of "the Other in oneself," he immediately adds: "But do not forget that the rapport with the Other always occurs in the presence of the Third and under the sign of oppression. Poisoned." In the *Critique* he shows how this relationship, poisoned as it may be, can nevertheless use the Third to achieve the desired goal of keeping the Other separate from oneself but also as the free source of one's own actions. Under those circumstances, the being of the Third would contribute to, rather than destroy, the reality of the we-subject: it would help to make possible the reciprocity which is love.

The *Critique* develops this line of reasoning by reinterpreting the concept of alienation. In *Being and Nothingness* Sartre used that term to refer to the isolating of persons through their objectification of one another. In the *Critique* it signifies man's inability to dominate external forces on which he depends for his survival. Like Marx, Sartre believes that scarcity of material goods is the basic cause of conflict between human beings. Men create a common group and pursue joint enterprises in the hope of eliminating scarcity and overcoming alienation. In order for there to be cohesiveness within the group, each member must serve not only as a subject united with some other member of the group but also as a Third seeing fellow group-members as subjects engaged in the same activity.

This quasi-Trinitarian concept of dialectical inner structure enables Sartre to avoid monistic beliefs about merging. As in *Being and Nothingness* he had condemned Hegel for trying to cover up "the scandal of the plurality of consciousnesses," so too does he now assert that no group can include the total merging of its members. They always remain responsible for their individual freedom. Within the unified group, their oneness can only consist in the interlocking or overlapping sameness of their feelings and their actions. Sartre consistently maintains that this sameness is not an identity among the members, and he uses the concept of the Third to indicate how each person structures the group as a single entity while also engaging in the diversified behavior that unites him with the other members.

There is no need for us to follow Sartre through the details of his distinction between "the fused group" and "the statutory group." The former arises spontaneously in reaction to an external threat; the latter springs from an act of commitment, the members having deliberately pledged themselves to the existence of this particular grouping. Though Sartre interprets both types of group as an expression of human freedom achieving goals beyond the capacity of mere individuals, he sees the statutory group as the fulfillment of the "mediated reciprocity" essential for there to be a freely chosen society. Through their mutual pledges, each member discovers in the Other (and in the Third) the basis for his own freedom. Each is the same as one another insofar as they have all chosen the mediated reciprocity which makes them into we-subjects. Reciprocity alone is always "incomplete," but through the mediation of the Third it constitutes authentic and effective interdependence.

In the statutory group Sartre finds the solution to man's search for oneness with other people. He speaks of the pledge as "the origin of humanity," and as that which creates fraternity involving a reciprocal affirmation of sameness. Authentic oneness in society results from commitments that enable the participants to experience brotherly feelings toward people whose existence is conditioned by a mutual dependence upon one another's freedom. *"Our common being* is not *an identical nature* in everyone. On the contrary, it is a mediated reciprocity of conditionings." According to Sartre, friendship and love are each derivative from this basic structure. They are a "practical enrichment," a "free specification," of the reciprocity established by the fraternal pledge as it occurs in one or another circumstance. Even in *Being and Nothingness* Sartre had said that love is more than just a momentary feeling, more than just a passionate excitement that might invade one's consciousness without altering one's conduct. In placing it within his analysis of the statutory group, he portrays love as part of man's effort to attain social harmony through interdependence which does not negate individual freedom. The Other is no longer seen as necessarily an antagonist to be seduced or transcended. Since his existence is the same as mine, I can accept him as another *myself*, and as one of many *myselves* that belong to the same society.

Sartre barely develops the idea of love as interdependence. Perhaps he would have done so if he had written a second volume to the *Critique,* as he originally planned. In statements subsequent to the first volume, mainly in the course of interviews, he often mentions the direction that his thinking would have taken. In one place he says that "love is the true relation of the self to others." In another place he laments having said that man is a "useless passion" and shortly thereafter remarks that "true social harmony" will some day be realized. For this to occur there must be a worldwide elimination of scarcity as well as fundamental changes in "the economic, cultural, and affective relations among men."

This language is utopian, and it prepares us for Sartre's further claim that in the future there will be "a form of sociality in which each person will give himself completely to someone else, who will likewise give himself completely." Sartre calls this a relationship of "transparency" and he insists that it "should always be substituted for secrecy." By making his existence wholly visible to others in his society, each person will overcome the antagonism that threatens love. Though denying all possibility of merging, Sartre's belief in ultimate transparency establishes a final—but possibly residual — concession to romanticism. Throughout its dialectical contortions, his philosophy would seem to have taken a long way round to Rousseau.

❋

In presenting Sartre's ideas about love, I have concentrated on the development from his earlier to his later work. In his printed conversations he often encouraged this way of reading him. But those who say that he simply changed philosophy in mid-life are not entirely mistaken. In some respects his final affirmations do contradict crucial statements in his earlier work. That is why critics who limit themselves to his first stage present a distorted picture of his thinking. In other respects, however, the continuity between the earlier and the later Sartre is quite evident. Even the contradictions between isolated passages may often be eliminated through a sympathetic reinterpretation of Sartre's intentions.

For instance, consider the passage in *Being and Nothingness* where Sartre analyzes love as a search for a commitment by the Other which will be freely given and yet totally bound by its devotion to oneself. He says that no lover would be satisfied "with that superior form of freedom which is a free and voluntary engagement. Who would be content with a love given as pure loyalty to a sworn oath? . . . Thus the lover demands a pledge, yet is irritated by a pledge. He wants to be loved by a freedom but demands that this freedom as freedom should no longer be free." At least one commentator has pointed out that it is precisely a pledge or oath of this sort that the *Critique of Dialectical Reason* offers as the basis not only for authenticity in love but also for communal action as a whole. We seem to be confronted by either an inconsistency or a fundamental shift in Sartre's position.

These alternatives can be avoided, however, if we see the passages as complementary rather than contradictory. In the earlier book Sartre addresses himself to man in his characteristic quest for ideal love. The later book tries to show how one gets beyond that condition through the radical conversion. One then learns how to forge relations that are not based upon a futile passion. In a sense, Sartre may continue to say, all lovers would *like* to snare the freedom of the beloved, but they can renounce this inclination in order to attain the authenticity of reciprocal love involving a sworn commitment. As he got older, Sartre saw no reason to repudiate all his earlier insights into human failure. Instead, he directed his efforts toward understanding the mechanisms by which alienation and hostility could be transmuted into friendship, love, and harmony.

Since Sartre never published a synoptic presentation of his developing ideas about love, and since most of what he wrote on the subject addresses itself to the circumstances of bad faith, the resemblances between him and Rousseau are worth underlining. Both hold before us the carrot of an eventual society predicated upon authentic love as well as transparency, and both are convinced that everything in man's interpersonal being arises from a kind of original sinfulness. Both believe in freedom as the

ontological basis of human nature, and both treat social conditioning as that which reveals how and why individuals use their freedom as they do. There is in Sartre none of Rousseau's pantheism,
but one is continually surprised to find how many of the pre-
Romantic concepts in Rousseau recur in the post- and even anti-
Romantic writings of Sartre.

To illustrate this, I turn to themes in two of his plays—*The Chips
Are Down (Les jeux sont faits)* and *The Devil and the Good Lord.* These
are not representative of his fiction inasmuch as the former was
written as a screenplay and the latter is mythic on a grandiose scale
rather than being realistic. Nevertheless, they reveal better than
Sartre's other plays or novels how his thinking about love progressed beyond its original negativism. In *The Chips Are Down* a man
and a woman from different social classes are allowed to return to
life after their deaths. They were "authentically destined for one
another"; but because of an error in the bureaucracy of heaven,
they had failed to find each other on earth. They are now given a
second chance. If they can succeed within twenty-four hours to
love each other totally, they will have "the right to a complete
human existence." Once they return to life on earth, however, the
lovers become separated by social necessities. Though the man believes that they are "alone in the world" (seuls au monde) and need
to love no one but themselves, he also recognizes his solidarity with
fellow proletariats engaged in revolutionary action. He cannot
withhold himself from their cause, for which he dies a second time.
His love for the woman is thus destroyed by his commitment to the
others, and she too dies with the knowledge that they have not
realized their one great opportunity for love.

This play was written in 1949. In its counterpoint of individual
happiness versus social responsibility, it may be interpreted as a
statement of Sartre's doubts about the authenticity of love and the
possibility of attaining we-subjectivity by either two people or a
group. But though the man and woman do not achieve the oneness
predestined for them, the play ends with their encountering another couple in heaven who also have been given a second chance
to love on earth. Though they smile with disillusionment and gentle sadness, the couple who have failed encourage the younger

lovers to make the effort. We are left with the suggestion that in the next generation, or some later one, the complete condition of human love may somehow be obtainable. Though the play was written just a few years after *Being and Nothingness*, it by no means suggests that love must always be futile.

In *The Devil and the Good Lord* the protagonist Goetz is motivated first by hatred and then by pure love. Neither is effective, neither works politically or in his personal life. For, as Goetz finally concludes: "On this earth at present Good and Evil are inseparable." He learns the meaning of love from Hilda, the woman who accepts him as he is, in his facticity and in the increasing ugliness of his mind as well as body. "If you die," she says, "you will rot away in my embrace, and I will love your carrion flesh; for you do not love at all, if you do not love everything." In *Saint Genet* Sartre makes a similar statement. Replying to the rhetorical question of a medieval author who asks how any lover could desire to hold in his arms the "bag of excrement" which is another's body, Sartre says: "Now, there is only one answer: that one loves nothing if one does not love everything, for true love is a salvation and safeguarding of all man in the person of *one* man by a human creature." He claims that no one gave this answer before Genet except for D. H. Lawrence, whom Sartre discounts because "his answer is smeared with a philosophical jam that makes one gag [soulève le coeur]."

The Devil and the Good Lord shows Goetz reaching a kind of love he had not foreseen. He resolves his moral problem by devoting himself to a social good which is inseparable from evil, and to acts of love which are compounded out of the hatred that he continues to feel. Instead of searching for a pure love, a love that exists without evil or hatred, he dedicates himself to action, violent action, that employs them both. In taking command of the army, he willingly makes his men hate him on the grounds that he knows "no other way of loving them." Like the lovers in *The Chips Are Down*, he and Hilda are alone, but now they are "alone together." She stands by him throughout his final commitment to social responsibility. And in relation to Hilda, Goetz approximates the oneness with another that he has wanted all along. "You are myself," he says, as if in an attestation of ultimate merging. These are the same words that Galatea says to Pygmalion in the playlet by Rousseau that I discussed in volume 2. Previously Goetz had told Hilda that he envies her capacity for loving others: "There you are, you look at them, you touch them, you are warmth, you are light, and YOU ARE NOT MYSELF. It's unbearable. I do not understand why we are two entities, and I should like, while remaining myself, to become you."

When Goetz says at the end of the play that Hilda is himself, we need not take that as an affirmation of merging, even on Goetz's part. His ideas about love remain chaotic throughout the play, and critics are possibly justified when they claim that Hilda is the only character in Sartre's works who really shows herself capable of authentic love. Beauvoir mentions that the fourth volume of Sartre's tetralogy *Roads to Freedom* was to include a description of harmonious and successful passionate love between two of the main characters. But Sartre never wrote that volume. Possibly he thought that the real world, the present-day reality that his fiction depicts, is not yet ready for such benign eventualities. Goetz and Hilda, both separately and together, point the way. In his honest probing and Socratic modesty, Sartre may well have felt that he at least—and possibly everyone else in our tormented period of history—could not hope for anything more than this.

❋

Stepping back from Sartre's career as a whole, we may see it as an attempt to overcome problems within his particular world outlook. He assumes that man has a need to establish his being—to find a reason or justification for it—and he eventually shows how this need can be satisfied through the oneness of an authentic community. But this achievement is inherently precarious. Not only does it lack the absolute security that Sartre thinks human beings crave, but also it involves interpersonal conflicts he considers basic to man's being and possibly inescapable. It would not be unreasonable to conclude that the harmonious relationships of love or friendship or social commitment that Sartre's morality describes cannot really show the fly a way out of the fly bottle. However much man transcends the solitary, isolated, alienated aspects of his being, Sartre may always have to see him as a failure in his core reality. Though human beings enjoy moments—or even a lifetime—of authentic oneness, will they ever satisfy what Sartre believes to be their ultimate yearning for a merged identification?

These problems would not exist if Sartre completely rejected the concept of merging, treating it as a confused idea that cannot truly characterize man's ontology. Nor would the problems remain if Sartre held that the oneness which can occur succeeds in fulfilling human nature. Sartre accepts neither of these alternatives. To that extent, his vision seems unstable. In its major sweep it may not be inconsistent, but it is less than wholly satisfying. Despite Sartre's analyses of scarcity, freedom, conditioning, and the different kinds of groups that human beings create, his philosophy never manages to explain how interpersonal unity can be the powerful experience that it is for many people.

These difficulties resulting from Sartre's premises have been recognized by many of his critics, including several philosophers lumped with him under the general rubric of "existentialism." Heidegger is sometimes mentioned in this connection, and it is true that his idea of Mitsein or we-subject, which Sartre attacks in *Being and Nothingness*, might have served as the basis for a theory about moral intersubjectivity. But even when Heidegger discusses "care" or "caring about," he scarcely touches on attitudes such as love or friendship. For him authenticity resides primarily in the honest acknowledgment of one's isolated state rather than in attempts to change it. Existentialists such as Jaspers and Merleau-Ponty take a totally different point of view. Writing in the early 1930s, Jaspers defines "existential communication" as the circumstance in which "one self in its authentic being enters into relation with another." He contrasts communication of this sort with the isolation of human beings who treat each other as objects and have no inner relations with one another.

Through authentic love in particular, Jaspers says, what is individual or "absolutely concrete" in one person communicates itself to another person as a unique infinity: "In love the individual is grasped as an infinity, which can never become the object of thought or knowledge. Between human beings love is also what is ambiguously called perfect understanding." Merleau-Ponty develops similar ideas in terms of what he calls "the experience of dialogue." When that occurs, he remarks, two persons share "a dual being." No longer functioning as units of behavior, they become "collaborators for each other in consummate reciprocity. Our perspectives merge into each other, and we co-exist through a common world."

In the writings of Martin Buber, ideas about "the experience of dialogue" and "existential communication" are developed fully and applied to the analysis of love. Buber criticizes Jaspers for having limited communication to a relationship between persons who are men or women. For this would mean that one cannot relate directly to God conceived to be a person, or if one does, that it must be a wholly different kind of relation from anything available to human beings among themselves. Indeed, Jaspers maintains that communication with the godhead hinders one's ability to communicate with people. It is central to all of Buber's thinking, however, that authentic relationship is always the same. Regardless of whether one communicates with God, human beings, animals, or even non-conscious entities, what matters most is the immediacy, directness, and mutuality in the encounter.

Buber calls this "the dialogical principle" by means of which one establishes an "I-Thou" relationship as opposed to an "I-It" relationship. When two people reciprocally communicate with one another as an I and a Thou, they respond as persons to the personhood in each. On the other hand, they enter into an I-It situation when they treat each other as objects or instrumentalities, things to be manipulated in the material world. Buber would seem to believe that virtually everything, whether or not it is a person, can be experienced as either an It or a Thou. But only when we undergo an I-Thou relationship, Buber says, do we penetrate to the foundation of being.

In his dialogical philosophy Buber articulates for the twentieth century the major tenets of religious romanticism. To some extent William James had done the same, and Buber quotes from the passage in *The Will to Believe* where James says: "The universe is no longer a mere *It* to us but a *Thou*, if we are religious; and any relation that may be possible from person to person might be possible here." In making I-Thou the prime relationship—that by reference to which all being can be explained—Buber renews the idealist attempt to see the world as ultimately striving for the realization of human values such as love between persons. In his book *I and Thou* he describes an "instinct to make contact" which includes the need to establish mutual relations of tenderness. He links childhood development to a "longing for the *Thou*," and he interprets this as a "yearning. . . for the cosmic connexion, with its true Thou."

According to Buber, only the I-Thou relationship is ontologically ultimate. In it one attains reality in the sense that this and only this relation manifests the fundamental character of being. In the I-It relationship one reduces others to objects, things that can be enjoyed, used, or fitted into a system of knowledge. The I-Thou, however, is purely immediate: in itself it encompasses and reveals another's being in its totality. It is a relationship in which a person experiences the Other as a *presence*, as something or someone to whom we are fully attending. As a moralist, Buber is principally concerned with the I-Thou bonds that people fashion among themselves, each responding to the presence of some other human being. But whenever this relational capacity exists, he thinks it can easily be extended to animals and inanimate objects—in principle to all of nature.

Making the dialogical attitude basic in ontology, Buber's philosophy is antithetical to Sartre's. Their views overlap on some major points to which I shall later return, but to see the differences between them we need only consider Buber's comments about having the I-Thou relationship with a tree. After enumerating the many ways in which the tree may be considered merely a thing— classified as a species, contemplated as a visual entity, perceived as a growing organism, etc.—he then remarks that we can become "bound up in relation to it." When this happens, we attend to the tree as a totality, as "a single whole" that is present to us. Buber insists that this new relationship involves no sacrifice of any of the other ways of experiencing the tree. Nor does he wish to suggest that he is responding to the tree as if it had a consciousness or soul of its own. He argues that the I-Thou relation simply involves an encounter with "the tree itself." Without being a living creature like myself, "it is bodied over against me and has to do with me, as I with it." It is a Thou to me because it enters into the direct relation of presence even though it is a tree and not a person.

Buber's *I and Thou* appeared some fifteen years before Sartre's *Nausea.* Roquentin's vision of the chestnut tree in that novel may have been conceived as an implied critique of Buber's suggestion that even trees can be experienced as a Thou. For this idea assumes that such a relation, which Buber calls a "mutual" relation, discloses an interconnected oneness in being which is the meaning of life. In using the chestnut tree to illustrate the brute contingency in everything, Sartre could have had in mind the contrary idealism of Bergson rather than of Buber. But in their speculations about the underlying unity of all being, Buber and Bergson are very much alike. Buber on the I-Thou relationship can be interpreted as developing what Bergson meant by intuitions that put us "inside" an object and enable us to reach its "absolute." Both philosophers are depicting a nexus of immediacy and direct response to the totality of that which is present to us. In seeing alienation as the primitive condition of man, Sartre rejects Buber's approach as well as Bergson's.

Though there is no evidence for this, one can also imagine that Sartre's early analysis of the look might have been designed as a criticism of Buber. Twenty years before Sartre wrote *Being and Nothingness,* Buber described how an expressive use of eyes, or even a casual glance, creates a communicative bond between human beings and—as Buber delights in showing—between man and other animals. Through the primal look, as he portrays it, the world of Thou comes into being. It may include creatures of any description. Among people, it creates precisely the kind of ontological we-subjectivity that Sartre originally denied.

Writing when he did, Buber does not address himself to Sartre's skepticism. But he argues that Heidegger's conception of man fails to recognize the I-Thou relationship. He interprets Heideggerian care or solicitude as an attempted corrective for human isolation, but he sees it as always remaining on the level of coexistence rather than interpersonal community. Contrasting Heidegger's approach with his own, Buber insists that we must think of the We as an extension of the Thou. Both of these concepts involve belief in the autonomy or independent being that belongs essentially to persons, and each indicates how these separate individuals may unite in a direct relationship: "By *We* I mean a community of several independent persons. . . . The special character of the *We* is shown in the essential relation existing, within the *We*, of an ontic directness which is the decisive presupposition of the *I-Thou* relation."

One might say that this conception of the We, and even the Thou, is what Sartre eventually reaches as the outcome of his later philosophy. For if Sartre comes to believe that authentic community among human beings is indeed possible, must he not presuppose an ontological basis for this achievement? And what else is Buber referring to when he says: "The *We* includes the *Thou* potentially. Only men who are capable of truly saying *Thou* to one another can truly say *We* with one another." Moreover, Buber employs the concept of transparency in ways that are similar to what Sartre would later repeat. Buber describes the I-Thou relationship as one in which a man "who gives himself to it may withhold nothing of himself." Even with respect to merging, Sartre says little that would contradict Buber. For Buber frequently denies that beings can be related to one another as I and Thou if either is absorbed in the other or deprived of ultimate independence. One sees another as a Thou by accepting him in his essential separateness, not by fusing or merging with his inner being.

Despite these similarities between Sartre and Buber, their perspectives on the world inevitably diverge since they originate in contrary presuppositions about being in general. Everything Buber writes arises from his assumption that our world reveals the presence of a personal deity with whom one may establish an I-Thou relationship. He does not argue for this article of faith any more than Sartre argues for his atheism. It leads Buber to a conception of love which Sartre may have partly duplicated in his final philosophy but which he would never have found defensible in itself.

Buber is very careful not to identify love with the I-Thou relation. He is sensitive to the fact that love can sometimes entail a misuse of the other person. It then exists in an I-It relation that refuses to accept the Other as a Thou. But though Buber gives no formal definition of love, he clearly thinks that it becomes authentic or genuine only when it binds an I with a Thou in accordance with the dialogical principle. In several places he insists that love is not a feeling or even a complex of feelings. It is a relationship *"between I* and *Thou."* He also characterizes love as "responsibility of an *I* for a *Thou."* And finally, he claims that love predicates a likeness or equality among persons who have mutually accepted the free and autonomous individuality of each other. None of this would make sense if love were merely a feeling.

Only through love, or at least the dialogical element within it, Buber maintains, can people respond to the totality of another's being. In the relations of hatred or indifference, this is not possible. Hatred must always be limited to part of a person; indifference removes one from a direct relation. Love is not identical with the I and Thou because that relationship fulfills itself in the present and in the immediacy which constitutes its nature. Love, as Buber sees it, must exist through time, through circumstances in which individuals change from what they are to what they may possibly become. This is what Buber means when he says that love "endures."

Defining genuine love as a continuing commitment that is based upon the I-Thou principle and includes social or erotic feelings without being reducible to them, Buber believes that all love must ultimately be explained as the love of God. Everything Buber writes fits within the framework of Judaeo-Christian teachings. At the same time his thought, ecumenical as it is, usually focuses on one aspect of this tradition: it reflects Hasidic ideas about the uniformity of love. As against Christians or Jews who stressed the differences between a love of God and a love of mankind in order to subordinate merely human love to a spiritual or ascetic type of religious love, Buber enunciates the Hasidic belief that no such distinction can be defended. He insists that all love is love for God inasmuch as God is present when we truly love our fellow man. And however far our carnal loves may fall, they too must be understood as an attempt to love God as he reveals himself in his creation. To say this, in the manner of Buber's Hasidic faith, is to say that the two Great Commandments about love in the Bible are really only one. In loving our neighbor as ourself, we are loving God. We cannot love God unless we also love the neighbor. If we truly love God, we do love the neighbor.

In the first volume of this trilogy, I analyzed similar beliefs as formulated by medieval thinkers within Christianity and Judaism. We may now notice how this approach issues into Buber's criticism of Kierkegaard. In several books Buber returns to Kierkegaard's dilemma about "the Single One." In his later writing, Kierkegaard concluded that man could properly love God only as a solitary individual who dedicates himself exclusively to him. Buber applauds this call to individuality, which he interprets as the manifestation of commendable self-love that is different from selfishness. In a similar vein he elsewhere supports Heidegger and Simone Weil when they caution against allowing oneself to be submerged in the faceless mass of mere humanity. But as against Kierkegaard as well as Heidegger and Weil, Buber maintains that neither self-love nor the love of God excludes the authentic love of other people. "Exclusive love to God ('with *all* your heart')," Buber says, "is, *because he is God*, inclusive love, ready to accept and include all love. It is not himself that God creates. . . his revelation does not have himself as object. He limits himself in all his limitlessness, he makes room for the creatures, and so, in love to him, he makes room for love to the creatures."

In one place Buber recognizes that a character in Kierkegaard's *Stages on Life's Way* expresses ideas comparable to those that Buber is here using against Kierkegaard himself. Buber rightly notes that this pseudonymous voice in the *Stages* is meant to present a "lower point of view" that will finally be superseded. It articulates the perspective of "the married man," and in his dialectical way Kierkegaard is arguing that earthly love belonging to marriage must eventually be renounced for the sake of loving God exclusively. "That is sublimely to misunderstand God," Buber remarks. "Creation is not a hurdle on the road to God, it is the road itself."

Coherent with this point of view, Buber defends marriage as an "exemplary bond" through which we can achieve the freedom that belongs to being genuine children of God. Though he cites the dangers in married love, as in all other ties related to our finitude, Buber tells us that "our hope of salvation is forged on this very danger, for our human way to the infinite leads only through fulfilled finitude." Buber advocates marriage as that which involves us in society—what he calls "the body politic"—but his doctrine applies equally well to all love between the sexes: "He who loves a woman, and brings her life to present realisation in his, is able to look in the *Thou* of her eyes into a beam of the eternal *Thou*."

In everything Buber writes there resides a wholesome acceptance of the goodness in reciprocal love. In relating it to our awareness and sustenance of another person who is present to us as an indefeasible Thou, he illuminates much that is fundamental in the nature of love. By rejecting any idea of merging that would blind us to the individuality of different persons, he avoids aspects of earlier romanticism that may well trouble us in the twentieth century. At the same time, however, we may also be repelled by Buber's simpleminded, and possibly delusory, vision. He depicts the cosmos as an expression of God's love; he says little about the existence of suffering, hatred, or brutality. Though he differs from the prevailing theology of the Middle Ages in refusing to separate the love of man or nature from the love of God, he duplicates the earlier conception to the extent that he interprets all reality as the creation of a kind and ever-loving personal deity.

Not only is Buber's God a person, but also he is a person who feels the need to be loved by other persons. Buber says that God created the world and placed man in it because this enabled God to "actualize" his divine being. From this, Buber concludes that God must need man just as man needs God. Involving reciprocity as it does, perfect love such as God's includes a longing that man should love him in return. How this can be reconciled with belief in an infinitely powerful deity, Buber does not explain. He says at one point that "God needs you, for the very meaning of your life." But he scarcely clarifies this highly poetic statement. He remarks that "divine meaning" fills all of life, and he asserts that the world is "divine destiny." Leaving aside the question of whether he is right, can we even claim to understand such language?

❋

In my attempt to delineate the differences between realist and idealist attitudes toward the ontology of love, I could have contrasted Sartre's philosophy with Gabriel Marcel's rather than Buber's. Marcel resembles Buber in many ways and he belongs to the tradition of French idealism that Sartre was reacting against. Like Buber, and in writings that precede his, Marcel identifies the I-Thou relation as the "structural aspect of the fundamental human situation." Marcel means by this that authentic intersubjectivity is basic to man's being. He therefore argues that it is indicative of Being itself, which he refers to as God or the Absolute. Marcel suggests that Buber elaborated the I-Thou approach further than he himself had done, but he also notes a significant difference between their philosophies. Though he agrees with Buber that intersubjectivity unites persons who are and remain autonomous individuals, Marcel claims that relationships do not come first in the order of being: "In the beginning, rather, is a certain felt unity which becomes progressively articulated so as to make room for an ensemble involving interrelated terms."

Holding this view, Marcel expresses a preference for F. H. Bradley's idealism as opposed to Buber's. One might also detect the lingering effect of Hegel's philosophy. Throughout his writing, Marcel emphasizes how human reality must be understood as a communion among separate persons who create their individual selves in relations defined by fidelity and love. It was from Josiah Royce that Marcel derived the idea that fidelity as a moral commitment to other persons revealed the essence of one's own selfhood. But much more extensively than Royce, Marcel develops the linkage between fidelity and love. He ends up with a philosophy in which all being manifests a communion ultimately based upon fidelity toward other persons which he considers indistinguishable from love. Marcel believes that such love descends from God, and even is God.

We may take this turn in Marcel's thought as merely a re-turn to Christian theism couched in existentialist terminology. To some degree the same is also true of the ideas about love and Being to be found in the works of Tillich, Brunner, and others. I will examine Tillich's ideas in Chapter 10, but since I am not writing a history of modern theology I need only mention here some of the salient concepts that give Marcel's philosophy its distinctiveness. Most prominent among these is his analysis of love in relation to death. The association between the two concepts, indeed their amalgamation, originates in the earliest sources of romanticism. Marcel's innovation consists in his claim that part of the definition of love *entails* the defeat of death. In his philosophical writing Marcel frequently repeats what a character in one of his plays asserts: "To love a person is to say: you shall not die." Marcel explains this as meaning that love is a response to the Other as an immediate presence whose being is directly experienced and permanently cherished in this relationship. Since the being of anything participates in Being as a whole, and since Being must be perennial or eternal, Marcel concludes that love inherently affirms the immortality of the beloved. In his own voice he states: "Because I love you, because I affirm you as being, there is something in you which can bridge the abyss that I vaguely call 'Death.'"

To this sonorous declaration one might readily reply that it ascribes to love more power than it can rightly claim. Even though he affirms the being of his beloved in the sense that he accepts her as she is and sustains her mere existence, no lover can truly believe that this alone will make her immortal. But Marcel is not deluded about that. He means that through love we achieve communion with what is eternal in another person, and even create it. That is why he identifies love with the concept of God as the foundation of all existence, its origin and its continuance forevermore. To love another person, Marcel insists, is to love him in God. For once we give ourselves to the mystery of love, our act of commitment, fidelity, and faith—each of which Marcel defines in relation to the other two—acquaints us with a deity that dwells within the world and shows itself throughout reality. "My deepest and most unshakable conviction," Marcel reports, "is, that. . . it is not God's will at all to be loved by us *against* the Creation, but rather glorified *through* the Creation and with the Creation as our starting point."

At times Marcel implies that faith in God is a condition for authentic love to exist. On the other hand he also says that faith results from the occurrence of authentic love, since the concepts of love and faith are defined in terms of each other. Marcel detects in both the phenomenon of unconditionality, which he elicits from the element of fidelity. In what he calls "the fullest and most concrete sense of the word, namely, the love of one being for another," he finds an affirmation that says: "I shall continue to love you no matter what happens." Marcel uses this idea as an explanation of the marital vow. Married love, and indeed all genuine love, he sees as an unconditional acceptance of the Other. Since in themselves human beings cannot hope to fulfill a pledge of unconditionality, he argues that only faith in God's presence makes it possible for people to love authentically.

Having gone this far, Marcel has only one more step to take. As he affirms the presence of God in everything, so too does he suggest that love—when it is genuine—has the ability to provide knowledge about its object. As opposed to any subjective attitude or feeling, love is to be construed as the sole means by which human beings can penetrate to one another's reality, and indeed, to the reality of the world as a whole: "In the measure in which it is now no longer permissible to dissociate being from appearance we can say that it [love] *is* perfect knowledge."

Once again we seem to have touched an extreme within contemporary existentialism that is diametrically opposite to the Sartrean philosophy. But I do not wish to end this chapter with the ontological speculations of either Buber or Marcel. Undeveloped as it was, and as it remained at his death, Sartre's defiant realism incorporates a devotion to the facts of life that one ignores at one's peril. His earlier analysis of love was often criticized by commentators, such as Iris Murdoch and Marjorie Grene, who lamented its blindness to the possibilities of communion and intersubjectivity in human experience. For the most part, however, these critics failed to tell us how one can retain Sartre's premises about man's conflict-ridden being while also believing that the ontological war of each against all may be truly overcome. In a recent book by Robert Solomon, I find a reading of Sartre that may show us the way out of this dilemma. Though he criticizes Sartre's ideas as being "overdramatized," Solomon commends them for their emphasis upon love as conflict, "a conflict which can be as constructive as destructive." In a definition that goes beyond Sartre but nevertheless remains faithful to his point of view, Solomon interprets love as a "sometimes violent alteration of self that is always torn between our ideologically all-pervasive need for independence and autonomy, and our equally all-pervasive obsession with romantic love and shared identity."

This seems like a promising approach toward understanding Sartre and possibly carrying out the positive elements in his mature conception. Solomon adheres to Sartre's inspiration when he describes love as a "balanced tension," a unity that maintains itself only through the balancing of forces that are constantly struggling with one another. This is a truth about love as it occurs in the everyday world that idealists such as Buber and Marcel do not understand, or else gloss over in their eagerness to affirm the sustaining goodness of ultimate Being. Though Sartre is only half-hearted in his naturalism, his philosophy provides insights closer to empirical observation than the abstract generalities of Marcel or Buber. Both alternatives can nevertheless be useful. Disparate as they are, both wings of existentialist theory may yet find a middle ground that will survive as the permanent value in each.

Part III
The Future without Illusion

9

Scientific Intimations

THROUGHOUT THESE VOLUMES I have suggested that the most promising opportunity for us in the twentieth century is to be found in a synthesis of scientific and humanistic approaches to human affect. Until recently science lagged behind philosophy and literature. It lacked empirical and experimental data needed for detailed investigation. Moreover, it suffered from methodological qualms—as if this particular part of human nature was too delicate or elusive to warrant a truly scientific analysis. Since Freud's grand achievement, however, and since the growth of ethology, sociobiology, sexology, and relevant aspects of developmental psychology much new work has begun. Though each investigator laments the scarcity of reliable studies about the nature of love, there nevertheless exists a sizeable body of suggestive information and piecemeal theorizing. We are nowhere near the point where scientists can expect to formulate a unified or comprehensive theory. But we are making progress, and there is no need to despair about future possibilities.

I shall not attempt to summarize the sweep of contemporary research about affect in man and other animals. Instead I focus on several problems that have motivated conceptualization and theory construction. These problems occur within a technical context that may seem to have little rapport with the ideas we have thus far considered. As a matter of fact, however, scientific investigation in these areas has grown out of the same historical matrix. The history of scientific thinking is interwoven with the history of ideas in general. There is every reason to believe that current work on scientific questions about love and sexuality will eventually alter the humanistic perspectives from which science first arose and later sought to emancipate itself.

I shall be discussing five questions, or clusters of questioning, about the nature of love that scientists have studied in recent years. I list them here before turning to each individually: (1) Is love innate in man or an acquired disposition learned in some particular environment? (2) Are there stages of development through which human beings must pass in order for them to attain the ability to love? (3) How is love related to, and can it be independent of, attitudes such as hatred and aggression? (4) In what sense is altruism a possibility for organisms, such as ours, that conform to the genetic and evolutionary principles most biologists believe in nowadays? (5) Is love, particularly romantic love, a universal phenomenon among human beings? Or does it arise only in cultures that choose to encourage it? And in either event, what does it reveal about patterns of social structure?

❀

Throughout the history of concepts that we have been examining we have often encountered the idea that love is innate in human nature. To say this is to claim that love is not merely learned or inculcated by society, but rather built into the prior structure of man's being. Some such belief characterizes the philosophies of Platonists as well as Aristotelians, Christians as well as naturalists, advocates of both courtly and Romantic love, realists no less than idealists. It is a view that existentialists bring into doubt when they deny that man has a "nature." It belongs to an approach that some feminists have considered sexist in its application. Females are thought to incorporate the instinct to love more than males, these theorists say, and this becomes an excuse for relegating women to nurturant roles as opposed to activities that are most highly valued in society. But whatever we conclude about differential ability to love—a question to which I shall return in the next chapter—we may have grounds to reject the notion that it originates in human instinct. Robert Solomon, who defends love against the charge that it is injurious to women, agrees with those feminists who maintain that "love is a culturally created emotion, not a natural need."

Among twentieth-century scientists the belief that love is an acquired disposition and not innate has, until recently, been the majority opinion. Psychologists in particular have often stated that love is "a learned response," fundamentally "a product of experience," and therefore "not given by nature." On this view, as it is usually presented, we love people who provide pleasurable and satisfying rewards to us. These people then become "secondary positive reinforcers." Reinforcement of this sort is considered secondary because the psychologists claim that love always consists in the hope that some person (or thing) will yield organic benefits and fulfill primary needs. These are generally limited to a need for nourishment, elimination, pain avoidance, and sex. It follows that love can occur only when experience teaches the agent that someone may reliably serve as a source of primary rewards. Far from being innate or fundamental as a need, love must be categorized as a "generalized" reinforcer dependent on our capacity to learn which objects are likely to be satisfying in different and diversified situations.

This kind of approach was popular among experimental psychologists because it required no commitment to instinct or a metaphysical agency of love. By avoiding such assumptions, scientists felt that they were discarding the vagaries of previous centuries. They could avail themselves of learning theory in order to understand human affect, and they could even look for support from Freud and many of his followers. In various places Freud had spoken of love arising in the infant as an "attachment to the satisfied need for nourishment." It was for this reason, Freud asserted, that "a child's first erotic object is the mother's breast." As the child learns that the mother or surrogate mother can be used to gratify other organic needs, his love becomes more extensive. This idea is entirely coherent with Freud's doctrine of primary narcissism but it is complicated by his belief that love must not only be derivative from sex but also reducible to it. For if sexual need is a primary drive, and if love is always a manifestation of the sexual as Freud maintained, then it would seem that in one sense or other love must be a primary rather than a secondary motive.

In his major work on attachment, John Bowlby claims that at the end of his life Freud was dissatisfied with his earlier reliance upon primary narcissism as the basis of love. Be this as it may, post-Freudians such as Michael Balint, Alice Balint, and Bowlby himself redirected psychiatric theory toward the possibility that love was more than just a derivative response. Where Freud's account of narcissism assumes that the infant has no conception of objects separate from itself, and therefore no capability for object-love, the Balints interpreted the infantile "instinct to cling" as an example of a primary object relation. They deemed it an active, though primitive, type of love, innately given to the organism and in no way secondary to other needs.

As early as 1937, Michael Balint argued that "this [clinging] form of object relation is not linked to any of the erotogenic zones; it is not oral, oral-sucking, anal, genital, etc., love, but is something on its own." Alice Balint emphasized that the infant's primary object-love is an "egotistic way of loving": though directed toward the mother, it includes no concern for what interests her. In his writings about attachment, Bowlby treated infant behavior as the expression of an unlearned program that manifests itself through "instinctual response systems" belonging to the first year of life. These include suckling, clinging, following, or otherwise retaining contact with the mother—all of which constitutes the initial stage in developing one's ability to love.

❋

Bowlby's conception of love as based upon an innate structure is related to the work of two other scientists. In the 1920s Konrad Lorenz began publishing his findings about "imprinting" in geese and other animals. At a very early age goslings showed a wholly unlearned propensity to follow objects that seemed to fit predetermined patterns of behavior and appearance, whether or not these objects were mother geese. In the fidelity with which the goslings then pursued a mother surrogate who was imprinted upon their sensibility, one could find a model for primary object-love even in organisms as complex as human beings.

Harry F. Harlow brought the investigation closer to our own species. He demonstrated that the capacity for love in primates, particularly rhesus monkeys, could be explained in terms of affectional systems organized as an unlearned developmental pattern latent in every individual. What underlies the infant's attachment to the mother or her surrogate is not a need to find someone who satisfies hunger or thirst, Harlow said, but rather a primary and instinctive craving for "contact comfort." Given the choice between a soft, cuddlesome terrycloth surrogate that yielded no nourishment and, on the other hand, a surrogate that provided milk but was made of welded wire, infant monkeys almost invariably clung to the former. Harlow concluded that infant love was not derivative from organic impulses related to nourishment, elimination, or sex. Instead it revealed a biological necessity different from these motives and more important for understanding the beginnings of primate love: "It is clearly the incentive of contact comfort that binds the infant affectionately to the mother."

In the nineteenth century Alexander Bain also suggested that "soft warm touch" was the fundamental pleasure in all experiences of love and indeed in sociability as a whole. "Touch is both the alpha and omega of affection," Bain concluded. William James ridiculed the idea, but Harlow's experiments support it. At the same time one might argue that in establishing the role of contact comfort Harlow merely found an additional biological motive from which love is derived. In a sense this is true, but it ignores the fact that in the infant monkey a craving for contact comfort is hardly distinguishable from a need for attachment or love. If the former is primary in the experience of the infant, the latter must also be.

Nor will it do to criticize Harlow on the assumption that he neglects the element of learning which surely belongs to the child's growing ability to love. As Harlow repeatedly points out, affective development depends on the cooperation and interpenetration of learned as well as unlearned responses. He makes his greatest contribution by delineating stages of development that provide an innate structure for behavior. But he also documents the role that learning plays at each stage, and it is significant that the title of the book in which he assembled his research is *Learning to Love*. Much of what he says is based on contemporary learning theory. For that matter, those who deny that love is innate often mean that it is "largely" or "principally" learned. At this point, I believe, the task for future scientists consists in harmonizing the two opposite approaches through a synthesis of the more moderate formulations in each.

Throughout his theory of developmental stages, Harlow tries to prove two theses: first, that the stages occur in a virtually invariable sequence; and second, that individual primates who have been deprived of success at an earlier stage will generally fail to achieve the potentialities of a later one. Subsequent research has cast doubt upon some of Harlow's generalizations about the relative importance of one stage or another. Nevertheless, his articulation of five "affectional systems" that constitute a sequential order through which human and other primates must pass if they are to reach adult interpersonal love has survived scientific scrutiny. The five stages of love, or "love systems" as Harlow calls them, are: (1) "maternal love," the love that a mother has for her own child; (2) "infant love," the love that the neonate or young child has for the mother and the mother surrogate; (3) "peer love," the love that children have for their playmates—"child for child, preadolescent for preadolescent, and adolescent for adolescent"; (4) "heterosexual love," love between adult male and female, which includes elements of romantic attraction, sexual response, and reproductive possibility; (5) "paternal love," the love that a mature male has for members of his family and, by extension, for others in his society toward whom he feels protective. In their structural design the five stages make a circle, or rather a spiral: after the last one, we return to the first and so forth from generation to generation.

Harlow recognizes that the five systems always overlap, that they function differently in the lives of different individuals, and that they merely indicate a biological blueprint for statistically normal behavior. Like most biologists, Harlow treats reproduction as the goal of sexual love. He therefore feels no need to account for homosexual love or nonsexual friendship apart from their development out of peer love or romantic elements in heterosexual love. This concentration upon reproduction as the ultimate stage in love limits the utility of Harlow's analysis. As a stage theory, however, its value is quite considerable.

Harlow summarizes the principles of affective growth in the following words: "As with other aspects of development, each love system prepares the individual for the one that follows, and the failure of any system to develop normally deprives him of the proper foundations for subsequent increasingly complex affectional adjustments." To the extent that this approach can be verified in observation, it offers an extremely promising conception of innate, programmed requirements that must be fulfilled for human beings to learn how to love. The organic character of this primate achievement is revealed by Harlow's elucidation of his findings:

> Thus the maternal and infant affectional systems prepare
> the child for the perplexing problems of peer adjustment
> by providing him with basic feelings of security and trust.
> Playmates determine social and sexual destiny, but without
> the certain knowledge of a safe haven, a potential playmate
> can at first sight be a frightening thing. By the same token,
> age-mate experience is fundamental to the development of
> normal and natural heterosexual love, whether this passion
> is deep and enduring as in most men or trivial and tran-
> sient as in most monkeys. In all primates the heterosexual
> affectional system is hopelessly inept and inadequate un-
> less it has been preceded by effective peer partnerships
> and age-mate activities.

These conclusions are based upon experimental work over a period of many years. For our purposes it is not essential to study the extensive data that Harlow and his associates collected. Neither do we need to examine all the subsidiary stages within each affective system. But some are worth mentioning. For instance, Harlow analyzes infant love into five major phases: organic affection related to nursing and dependent upon reflexes of clinging and suckling; contact comfort and the resulting attachment to the mother; solace and security which afford the infant an assurance of safety once it tentatively begins to explore its environment; increasing detachment from the mother as the infant matures; and finally, relative independence as "an almost totally infant-guided process" correlated with a phase of separation occurring within maternal love.

Other investigators may choose to analyze the affective systems differently. The empirical evidence can be sorted in diverse ways. What matters most is the demonstration that developmental processes occur within a regular and predetermined framework, that the ability to love begins with the reciprocating effect of maternal and infant affectional ties, that the interaction between these two systems has a definite though variable influence upon later systems, that failures within each subsequent stage make it harder to compensate for previous failures or to succeed at a higher stage.

Workers in the field may eventually decide that Harlow underestimated the importance of adequate peer-love, and its ability to overcome deprivation at the levels of maternal and infant love. It may also turn out that the analysis into just five systems of love is too impoverished for understanding the intricacies of human nature. But even so, Harlow has laid the groundwork for a proof, founded on experimental procedures, that love as it exists among adult human beings results from a process of maturational growth within a network of innate determinants as well as learned responses. Discussing the components of heterosexual love, Harlow emphasizes the extent to which it involves mechanical and secretory subsystems as well as the one he calls "romantic." The former make possible various types of sexual behavior, while the latter issues into emotional bonding. All three subsystems are essential for heterosexual love to exist. And though they involve substantial amounts of learning, they are preprogrammed as biological possibilities given to the organism.

In reaching his conclusions, Harlow often refers to Freud's ideas about love. He differs from Freud not only in substituting the concept of contact comfort for that of primary narcissism, but also in explaining childhood patterns of separation without invoking the Oedipus complex. At the same time, Harlow obviously derives sustenance from the fact that Freud too was groping toward a stage theory of libidinal development.

Within the psychoanalytic tradition, this quest has been furthered by theorists such as Karen Horney, Melanie Klein, and many others who followed their lead in recent years. In her lectures on "Love, Guilt and Reparation," Klein provides the basic outlines of the post-Freudian effort in this direction. Though she continues to employ many of the stock concepts of psychoanalysis, Klein uses them to describe a dialectical process through which love develops continuously in human beings. This process begins in the early experience of the baby, whose "mind" already manifests a struggle between love and hate that persists throughout each person's life. Neither Klein, nor Freud himself, ever *identifies* love with hate. That suggestion, which is to be found even in the writings of James Joyce, derives from Romantic pessimism or Sadean realism and not from psychoanalytic theory.

Klein concentrates upon the element of hate within loving relations but she treats it as a motive that propels an individual from one level of love to another. She believes that the infant's love for the mother exists independently of, and prior to, feelings of hatred. The latter result from destructive impulses arising out of frustrations the baby either experiences or imagines. Since the destructiveness of hatred undermines the child's love and puts the child in a precarious relationship with the parents (or other adults whose goodwill it needs for survival), there soon develops a sense of guilt. From the offspring's point of view, guilt feelings are merely distressful. But actually they serve to further the growth of love. Though love occurs spontaneously in the baby's response toward the mother or father who has already given love to it, the inevitable sequence of frustration, destructiveness, hate, and guilt leads the child to make equilibrating reparations. It undergoes sacrifices to benefit the person toward whom it feels guilty. Feelings of sympathy and concern begin to appear. In the process of repairing the real or imagined harm caused by its destructive hatred, the child acquires an enriched ability to love. Klein is convinced that this is an emotional accretion, and therefore wholly "genuine," rather than a mere contrivance on the part of a dependent being.

The dialectical tensions between hate and love, guilt and reparation, continue throughout an individual's development. But their operation alters as new situations occur and new faculties become available. Klein sees the capacity for identification with another person as crucial in the formation of love that is both "real and strong." Using words that are reminiscent of Ficino and Kant when they talk about reciprocal love, Klein remarks: "Since in being identified with other people we share, as it were, the help or satisfaction afforded to them by ourselves, we regain in one way what we have sacrificed in another." In order to act lovingly toward others, Klein states, we must put ourselves in their place. This happens through identification, and that makes sense psychologically because it gives us a means of restoring to ourselves the benefits we have accorded those with whom we identify. We then play the part of the good parent that we always desired when we were children, as well as the part of the good child that we originally hoped to be ourselves. In mature, adult love the combination of identification and reparation makes it possible for us to carry out the simultaneous roles—which are largely symbolic—of good parent and good child. In a harmonious marriage the spouses perform these dual functions in their varied activities with each other and to their mutual benefit.

Klein's analysis is strengthened by her recognition that the demands of an early stage in development can often be realized only under the altered conditions that belong to a later one. The infantile desire for total intimacy with the parent cannot be fulfilled in childhood. It may finally be satisfied, however, when the individual becomes fully sexual and enjoys a love relationship with someone who has reciprocal interests. By this time new needs and attitudes will have supervened upon the interests that motivated the infant's development. Though the initial stages of normal growth will influence subsequent attachments, the latter do not revert to the former except in the sense that people are given renewed opportunities to repair in the present the guilt and hatred that originated in the past. Klein is very sensitive to the fact that the woman a man falls in love with may duplicate the characteristics of his mother. This is the phenomenon that so greatly intrigued Freud. But with her superior understanding of dialectical forces that condition love in adulthood, Klein realizes that a man may also choose someone whose vast differences from his mother enable him to escape the frustrations that always accompanied his earlier attachment.

Like most psychiatric theorists, Klein associates the capacity for mature love with the ability to emancipate oneself from infantile dependence. Unlike psychoanalysts who try to explain failure in love as just "arrested" development, however, she shows how the search for emancipation through love may be thwarted systematically when the dialectic of guilt and reparation works out badly. Discussing the Don Juan personality, for instance, she wisely perceives that the faithless male succeeds in giving pleasure to one woman after another. He is not just fixated on his mother and therefore punishing womankind because no other female can give him what he wants. On the contrary, Klein interprets the promiscuous philandering of Don Juan as benign in two important respects. On the one hand, he "is re-creating or healing his mother by means of sexual gratifications (which he actually gives to other women)"; on the other hand, he frees himself from dependence upon his mother inasmuch as he renounces each woman he pursues. In both events his behavior is motivated partly by a sense of guilt for destructive impulses in himself, initially directed toward the mother, and partly by a desire to make loving reparation that will eliminate his guilt while also overcoming his feeling of dependence.

The Don Juan type of man fails in his search for love because he cannot control the forces within this dialectical mechanism. Klein does not explain why this happens. But presumably early frustrations or fantasies of destruction or the resulting guilt feelings can sometimes be so powerful in an individual as to impair his capacity to make what he himself will ever consider an adequate reparation.

If Klein's theory is right—and in its broadest dimension I think it is—it elucidates success as well as failure in love while also avoiding many of the reductionist difficulties in Freud's psychology. At the same time it has the great merit, as Freudian thinking generally does, of rejecting the possibility that any love can exist in isolation from the negative impulses of hatred and destructiveness. Even the purest, even the most elevated and self-sacrificial love occurs as an escape from the hurtfulness of aggressive attitudes in oneself, and as a compensation for them. In citing the empirical evidence afforded by normal as well as abnormal psychology, the followers of Freud who argue along these lines are providing scientific justification for Nietzsche's belief that without hostility there is no love. Whether we like it or not, we are always immersed in the destructive element. Salvation does not reside therein, but the only heaven of love that human beings have access to must be reconstituted out of the hell of some prior conflict and interpersonal suffering. This does not mean that only negative inclinations should be considered primary in the being of man. Love and strife exist together, as widely variable but interrelated ingredients in all affective situations.

This kind of approach pervades the work of many psychiatric theorists as well as behavioral biologists like Konrad Lorenz. Where Freud thought that human aggression manifests vicissitudes in the death drive, Lorenz claims that (intraspecific) aggression serves evolutionary needs. Rejecting the notion of a death instinct, Lorenz considers the self-destructive aspects of aggression as unfortunate by-products in an organism monistically programmed for survival.

Like Freud, Lorenz has often been criticized for believing that aggression is innately programmed in human nature. Though he stresses the importance of creating social machinery that will transmute aggression into cooperative behavior, his assertion that aggressive tendencies are genetically given and not wholly learned has been taken as both deterministic and defeatist. I have little to add to this controversy. What interests me more immediately is Lorenz's attempt to analyze love as a ritualistic offshoot of aggression. Contrasting human beings with social animals that have no aggression, Lorenz notes that although the latter may live in flocks or herds they do not form permanent and individualized bonds with one another. "A personal bond, an individual friendship, is found only in animals with highly developed intra-specific aggression; in fact, this bond is the firmer, the more aggressive the particular animal and species is." In the behavior of various types of fish, birds, and mammals, Lorenz finds a coherent development in which aggression against a co-specific arrests itself for some reason and then becomes ritualized in a gesture that redirects the original attack. These acts of ritualization are oriented toward specific individuals within the group, who eventually elicit the nonaggressive behavior by their mere presence in an appropriate situation. Out of this pattern grow the personal bonds of friendship and love that Lorenz shows to exist within many different species.

In arguing for love's dependence upon aggression, Lorenz in no way suggests that love is merely a veiled or deceptive form of aggression. On the contrary, he believes that human beings can achieve authentic and highly commendable love—benevolent, altruistic, and attuned to the uniqueness in other people. By undergoing the ritualizations that enlightened society is able to create, innate aggression may be harnessed by moral attitudes that use it for the goals of interpersonal love and friendship. Lorenz distinguishes between hate and aggression. While love derives from aggression, he says, hate presupposes love. Both hate and love would thus involve a basic condition of aggressiveness. When ritualized and redirected, aggression becomes love; when love is frustrated or defeated in its aspiration, it turns into hate.

Lorenz's views about love have generally been ignored by other scientists. They have been criticized, however, by one of his principal followers among those who do ethological research. Irenäus Eibl-Eibesfeldt denies that aggression is fundamental in species that have strong personal bonds, and consequently he rejects the idea that love is only secondary or derivative. Though Eibl-Eibesfeldt agrees that in the history of living creatures on earth aggression preceded love, he points out that wherever redirected aggression leads to love it does so within a species that already displays parental care. Eibl-Eibesfeldt thinks that individualized relationships result from the kind of brood or society in which parents rear and protect the young. He concludes that the development of love and friendship depends on parental care primarily and redirected aggression only secondarily: "only animals that care for their young form closed groups. Only they have succeeded in forming a bond in spite of the 'aggression barrier.' They all do it by means of behavior

357

patterns of cherishing which originate from parental care, and by
making use of infantile signals, which activate this behavior."

❋

The theories articulated by Lorenz and Eibl-Eibesfeldt, as well as
those of Harlow and Bowlby, occur within the framework of
Darwinian approaches to social bonding. The same applies to recent
sociobiologists such as Edward O. Wilson and Robert Trivers. In
their thinking about altruism, these two confront what seems to be a
paradox in evolutionary doctrine. Most scientists assume that
natural selection occurs through the development of behavior that
enables an organism to survive long enough to reproduce. But in the
process of performing self-sacrificial acts, which exist in many social
species, individuals put themselves at a reproductive disadvantage
and sometimes lose their lives. How then can altruistic behavior be
explained by Darwinians?

When sociobiologists use the term "altruism," they define it in a
way that does not necessarily imply sentiments of benevolence or
love. By an altruistic act they mean merely one that, in Trivers'
words, "benefits another organism at a cost to the actor, where cost
and benefit are defined in terms of reproductive success." But also,
the sociobiologists are trying to explain how it can happen that
various organisms, including human beings, acquire attitudes such
as love which sometimes undermine an animal's ability to survive or
reproduce. The solution to the problem begins with a distinction
between two kinds of altruism, one involving individuals who are
more or less strangers while the other relates members of a single
family or immediate clan. In both cases what looks like altruistic
behavior turns out to be founded upon considerations that are
basically selfish.

The underlying selfishness in altruism between strangers appears once we realize that members of a group who provide benefits to each other thereby increase their reproductive success. This
will happen if, and to the extent that, their behavior guarantees
mutual assistance at some other time. In what Trivers calls "reciprocal altruism" individuals are part of a biological system that

benefits each participant by compensating his self-sacrificial acts with corresponding payments which tend to increase his chances of survival. The structure of this system must inevitably remain fluid and precarious since cheating is always possible. Nevertheless, many kinds of love—and in general the ability to love someone who is genetically unrelated—will be explicable to the sociobiologist as a manifestation of the selfish advantages that reciprocal altruism can ultimately provide.

The other kind of altruism requires a totally different type of explanation. For now we are dealing with acts that unite individuals who are biologically related to each other. Since reproductive success means gene survival, and since family members have some of the same genes, an individual who sacrifices himself for a brother or a sister or their children may be perpetuating his own genes in the best way available to him. The most obvious example of family altruism is the mother who sacrifices her life so that her child may live. In doing so, the mother enables her own genes to survive. But this would also be true, to a lesser degree, if she sacrificed herself for the sake of other kin. In circumstances such as these the altruistic individual may lose his ability to reproduce, but his genes will live on to an extent that is determined by the closeness of the blood-tie. Since the sociobiologist defines selfishness and altruism in terms of reproductive success, he concludes that what seems like altruistic behavior may thus reduce to selfishness.

The sociobiological argument is very challenging. But does it prove that altruism is *always* reducible to selfishness? I do not think so. However cogent their reasoning may be, the sociobiologists can only establish that self-sacrificial behavior *frequently* serves to protect one's genes. This demonstration does not and cannot mean that on all occasions altruism or the love of others functions as a device by which individuals gain reproductive benefits that outweigh their sacrifices. To convince us of that generalization the sociobiologists would have to show that even when it does not give one's own gene pool a better chance for survival every occurrence of altruism can be traced back to an attempt to achieve genetic advantages of that sort. No such proof has ever been made, and it is difficult to imagine what the conclusive observations would be for a species that is as motivationally complex as ours. Self-sacrifice, for instance by soldiers in battle or by saints, is more easily explained in terms of ideals such as courage and a love of mankind. Though these ideals issue from one or another biological matrix, there is no reason to think that they invariably illustrate, either directly or indirectly, a search for benefits to the gene pool of those who act in accordance with them.

Being an enjoyable and gratuitous expression of feeling, love arises even when there are no reproductive incentives attached to it. Love could not have evolved if it ran counter to what is needed to survive. But it does not exist as merely an instrument in the struggle for survival. It is an end in terms of which human beings are able to define themselves.

As sociobiology matures, it will make new discoveries. I am convinced that they will be entirely compatible with distinctions between appraisals based upon need gratification and bestowals that create values in the process of valuation itself. Both operate in a world governed by natural selection. The integrity of love is not jeopardized by the fact that it results from evolutionary processes. For its part, sociobiology will not have told us much about the nature of love if it merely asserts that all successful analyses must include some reference to reproductive success.

Sociobiology is still a young science, and we should not prejudge its future capacity to yield fruitful insights about love. Its importance for theorization is already evident in one respect: it provides the outlines of a valid answer to idealist thinkers such as Bergson. The distinction between the two types of altruism runs parallel to Bergson's distinction between the closed society and the open society. Where Bergson thought that only the former evolves in accordance with adaptive principles, the sociobiologists insist that the open society must do so as well. Their approach shows that it is not necessary to invoke mystical or nonbiological concepts in order to explain even a purified love of mankind, and it alerts us to the futility of any facile solution to the conflict between the open and the closed society. Wilson points out that the distinction between the two types of altruism has particular significance because "altruism based on kin selection is the enemy of civilization." He means that "global harmony" is possible only to the extent that human beings are programmed to have social feelings that go beyond a concern for their immediate family or tribe. The scientific task consists in determining the character of the different altruistic structures and their malleability through experience. We need to know how attitudes acquired for reasons of genetic benefit can be transmuted into responses—such as those belonging to sexual and nonsexual love—that involve more than just the individual's desire to favor his own genes. Thus far, very little has been done to carry out the requisite research.

In the work of several anthropologists and sociologists, related investigations have led to fruitful debates about love as an innate potentiality for human beings. If there are instinctual patterns that structure man's capacity for love, these should be observable in a large number of cultures. The question would seem to be resolvable through the acquisition of empirical data. Sociologists and anthropologists regularly accumulate cross-cultural information about the experience of love, but as yet the evidence is sparse and rather inconclusive. While everyone agrees that romantic love which exists nowadays in the Western world has been foreign to many other cultures, scientists disagree about the significance of this fact. On the one hand, there are those who conclude that all ardent love between man and woman is a creation of ideological developments, mainly in Europe and America, of the last few hundred years. On the other hand, there are those who take its common appearance in a great variety of cultures as proof that something like romantic love is an inborn tendency for men and women everywhere. Since modern methods of investigation are hampered by the scarcity of remaining primitive societies, there may never be sufficient evidence to adjudicate this dispute. The arguments of the two camps are nevertheless worth studying.

At one extreme, some investigators insist that instances of romantic love are so infrequent in heterosexual relations that they should be classified as, in the words of Ralph Linton, "psychologi-

cal abnormalities to which our own culture has attached an extraordinary value just as other cultures have attached extreme values to
other abnormalities." Linton explains his suggestion as follows:

> The hero of the modern American movie is always a lover
> just as the hero of the old Arab epic is always an epileptic.
> A cynic might suspect that in any ordinary population the
> percentage of individuals with a capacity for romantic love
> of the Hollywood type was about as large as that of persons
> able to throw genuine epileptic fits. However, given a little
> social encouragement, either one can be adequately imi-
> tated without the performer admitting even to himself that
> the performance is not genuine.

It should be noted that in this passage Linton begins by talking
about romantic love but then allows his "cynic" to argue against its
being universal by citing the difficulty of genuinely enacting love of
the "Hollywood type." By the latter, one assumes that he means a
highly contrived and wildly fanciful conception of heterosexual intimacy belonging to an aspect of American culture in the early to
middle decades of this century. But it seems strange to think that
romantic love can be limited to that type. And it is surely ludicrous
to suggest that most ardent or passionate attachments between men
and women are merely "imitations" of a social norm and thus a
performance which is never genuine.

Linton's comment was written fifty years ago but it is often
quoted approvingly by later sociologists. In recent years they sometimes supplement their argument by references to de Rougemont's
claim that romantic or passionate love is a creation of the twelfth
century's fondness for Manichean heresies. If we reject that theory,
as I have been suggesting that we should, we are left with very little
reason to think that romantic love is primarily a cultural artifact
either in our society or in any other.

As a variation on Linton's thesis, Philip Slater superimposes
Freudian and Marxist coordinates. Defining love as aim-inhibited
sexuality, he asserts that it is a marketing device for augmenting
the value of sex. He says that love is a "scarcity mechanism [whose]
main effect. . . is to transform something plentiful into something

in short supply." He means that inhibitions which define the nature of love are created by some societies, such as ours in the West, in an ethnocentric and by no means biological attempt to give the innate propensity for sex an increased value it would not otherwise have.

Part of Slater's argument seems to me quite correct. Different societies deal with human affect in different ways that bestow a specific value and importance upon it beyond its purely biological function. Love and sexuality as they exist in any particular culture will always reflect, indeed promote, the ideals of that culture. That is why contemporary advocates of sexual liberation misconstrue nineteenth-century norms of privacy or decorum. Such evidences of restraint reveal human nature fabricating imaginative devices for increasing the value of sex. They are more than just morality curtailing nature: they are also idealizations giving significance to sex by redirecting it toward goals that were cherished in Western society. Unwanted modes of sexual expression may have suffered, but others were nurtured and rewarded.

But from this element of truth in what Slater says one cannot generate his belief that romantic love is mainly a social construct. For one thing, the empirical data do not support the idea that romantic love is always correlated with the imposition of sexual constraint. In some societies this does seem to be the case, but it is far from being universal. Even in modern America the relative freedom of sexual opportunity is often accompanied by romantic longing which is more than just a vestige of the previous generation's ideology. Anthropologists have noted that romantic love of the Western type exists in various primitive societies, some of which limit sex severely while others evince total permissiveness. Though the characteristics of romantic love are not always exactly the same as what we are used to in the West, it would seem to be an affective state that flourishes under different and largely disparate sexual circumstances.

In this connection, some of Margaret Mead's early work is particularly relevant. In one place she argues that "romantic love as it occurs in our civilisation, inextricably bound up with ideas of monogamy, exclusiveness, jealousy and undeviating fidelity does not occur in Samoa." Yet in the same paragraph Mead also remarks that young Samoans are given to the "composition of ardent love songs, the fashioning of long and flowery love letters, the invocation of the moon, the stars and the sea in verbal courtship." Mead deems all this only a "superficial resemblance" to our own patterns of lovemaking, and she may be right in view of the profound differences between Samoan and Western civilizations. But we can also conclude that romantic love takes different forms as social norms vary. In the West it may often have accompanied an idealization of monogamy, exclusiveness, jealousy, and fidelity without being bound to these phenomena in other societies. And even if it is absent in one or another culture, that would not rule out the possibility of its functioning as a universal propensity for people generally. Under more favorable conditions, its frequency might have been greatly augmented.

It is reasoning of this sort that supports the alternative approach to the problem. Theorists at this pole argue that romantic love is an innate tendency in human beings that realizes itself only in a social setting that is amenable to its occurrence. In a classic article the sociologist William J. Goode maintained that "love is a universal psychological potential, which is controlled by a range of five structural patterns, all of which are attempts to see to it that youngsters do not make entirely free choices of their future spouses." The five structures that modulate romantic love belong to a continuum. At one end there is child marriage arranged by the parents and, at the other, the development of an adolescent peer group that subtly limits its members' freedom to love and to mate. Several recent psychologists have made detailed studies about social influences on one's choice of a love-object. Important as it is, their work lies beyond the scope of the present book. It is worth mentioning, however, because the extensiveness of cultural control in this area indicates that every society feels the need to protect itself against dangers posed by romantic love.

In stressing this need, and in proposing his range of controlling structures, Goode distinguishes between a "love pattern" and a "romantic love complex." Both represent an institutionalization of love, but where the former treats love as merely a possible accompaniment to courtship and to marriage, the latter involves an "ideological prescription" about its desirability in any eventual marriage. Though Goode admits that American culture may be unique in the degree to which it has traditionally been committed to the romantic love complex, he also thinks that passionate attachments can exist in all societies and that the "love pattern" may be a relatively common occurrence cross-culturally.

More recent theorists have provided further elaborations of the thesis that romantic love may be a universal propensity. In *The Evolution of Love,* Sydney Mellen speculates about conditions of life in the Plio-Pleistocene era two million years ago. He speculates that the survival of human (or protohuman) children would have required emotional bonding between male and female. Sexual drive might have accounted for associations that could lead to reproduction of the species, but in order for adequate numbers of children to survive, the parents would have had to establish additional ties of love for one another. Since hominid offspring have a relatively long period of dependency and even helplessness in childhood, the forming of lasting bonds between adults could help to explain the reproductive success of human beings. Strong and prolonged intimacy between the parents give their children a superior ability to survive.

Seen from this perspective, love between the sexes would have to be considered part of the biological program innate to all men and women. This argument is not new. It goes back at least as far as Darwin. But Mellen presents it in the context of the recent controversy about romantic love. Asserting that attitudes basically similar to Western types of romantic love occur "in all the past civilizations of which we have good historical knowledge and in many extremely varied cultures existing today," Mellen suggests that a genetic tendency toward the formation of such emotional relations must have evolved as early as the Pliocene period.

Mellen recognizes that the programmed capacity for romantic love between man and woman has often been defeated or submerged in various human societies. But if this is so, one wonders how members of those societies could have survived as well as they seem to have done. Moreover, Mellen's speculations about love as a phylogenetic occurrence throw little light on its actual development in individuals. A recent book by Daniel Rancour-Laferriere tries to bridge the gap. Rancour-Laferriere synthesizes research from the fields of sociobiology, psychoanalysis, and semiotics in an attempt to show how they may jointly explain romantic love as a universal tendency in human beings. His approach emphasizes the maternal origins of love and of altruism as a whole. Emotional bonding between the sexes, including permanent mating, he analyzes into elements of regression, neoteny, and iconicity. Through regression adults relive with one another the emotions they originally experienced with their parents. Through neoteny they retain juvenile traits although they have long since outgrown their childhood in other respects. Through iconicity each of the lovers sees the other as a sign or representation of parental figures belonging to their own past history.

In making his synthesis, Rancour-Laferriere draws upon the work of several theorists we have been discussing. Not only does he agree with Mellen that romantic love cannot be wholly ethnocentric, but also he capitalizes upon the work of Bowlby, Eibl-Eibesfeldt, and psychoanalysts such as Klein who traced the ontogenetic development of affect to the infant's craving for maternal love. His synthesis is very useful but far too daring in some respects. Starting with the plausible idea that maternal love is the origin for love in general, Rancour-Laferriere accords this relationship an importance in all the rest of life that seems quite disproportionate. In married love, he says, "the wife tends to be a mother-icon for the husband, and the husband tends to be both a father-icon and a mother-icon for the wife." Since maternal iconicity would thus be common to both male and female adults, he concludes that the mother's role is much more basic in heterosexual love than anything related to the father.

To say this, however, one would have to know the roles that individual fathers have played in the lives of both men and women during their childhood. Rancour-Laferriere wants to say something more than the fact that everyone was born to a mother whose love, or lack of it, can influence subsequent affective development. He also wants to claim that an eventual partner in sex or in love will *represent* the mother, that the need for her love will remain as a fundamental element in female as well as male romantic love, and that it will tend to exclude a man's experience with his father as far as iconicity is concerned. But this minimizes the goods ranging from tenderness to authority that a man may have found in his father and now hopes to find in the woman that he loves. Similarly, Rancour-Laferriere's generalization assumes that the husband will be more of a mother-icon for his wife than a father-icon. In many wives this is surely not the case. For them it would not be true that maternal iconicity is more revelatory of their heterosexual love than paternal iconicity.

Furthermore, Rancour-Laferriere's notion of regression carries Klein's psychoanalytic insights to a point where they begin to lack common sense. In her ontogenetic analysis Klein showed how love develops through stages that originate with the infant's cathexis upon its mother or mother surrogate. She concluded that all the affective bonds that followed would somehow be related to these early emotional vicissitudes. This is a reasonable expectation since we know that the experiences of childhood can have a great effect upon later events in one's love life. The strength in Klein's approach comes from her conception of the progressive and developmental dialectic between hate and love, guilt and reparation, desire to separate and fear of losing security. These determinants explain the process that takes an individual out of childhood and into the relative inde-pendence of adulthood. If, however, we ignore the temporal aspects of this dialectical development, we deprive Klein's theory of its persuasiveness. In effect, that is what Rancour-Laferriere does. By insisting that sexual love can be understood as regression, he reduces it to a quasi-infantile relationship in which two adults return to the stage at which (as infants) they were wholly dependent on their mothers. Something of the sort may sometimes happen. But it is generally a meager part of love between the sexes. It cannot define romantic love as such.

As a more constructive way of making these points, one can say that Rancour-Laferriere's concepts need further refinement. If love is a universal tendency among human beings, as I believe, and if it is related to the child's need for mother's love and (wherever possible) father's love, as I also believe, we may surmise that ele-ments of regression, neoteny, and a relevant iconicity will play a role in an adult's affective life. We can also infer that these traits occur as vectors within the innate program that social conditioning always modifies. But the lingering of childhood attitudes and the regressive return of earlier feelings must not be interpreted as signifying a throwback to developmental stages long-since outgrown. Heterosexual love emanates from these previous stages, and since we are mammals they must all start with some relationship with the mother. But an individual's responses cannot be deduced from his childhood alone. His ability to love is a function of the maturational process as a whole. In love there is a continual liberation from the past. With another person we experience the future as the new occurence that each moment of life affords. The patterns of iconicity in love, and the roles that mothers and fathers play in them, differ tremendously from couple to couple. For each participant experiences the world from the other's point of view as well as from his own. Nor does the world that each experiences remain stable. It keeps changing in an endless and infinitely augmenting reverberation. That is our nature as human beings.

As one of the reasons for writing this survey of scientific research, I hoped that it would put us in a better position to reexamine the relationship between sex and love. Nowadays no one seems to doubt that sexuality is instinctual in men and women generally, though social and cultural forces can cause it to atrophy in many individuals. Even if we believe that love is a comparable instinct or innate tendency, we still need to determine how the two are interrelated and whether either is dependent on the other. And is there a significant difference between male and female types of sexual love? Is one type preferable to the other? Are radical feminists justified when they maintain that only women are truly capable of loving?

Though these questions have been studied by scientists in several disciplines, I leave them for the following chapter. Like much of the material I have covered in this cursory discussion, they need to be placed within the spectrum of philosophical issues that have guided us throughout these volumes.

10
Toward a Modern Theory of Love

As A Volume In A Work Of philosophical history, the present book need not attempt a detailed analysis of love. Some preliminary sketches will suffice. The concept of love is difficult for all of us because it touches on so much of human nature and implicates so many lines of investigation. In these concluding remarks I shall begin by discussing questions about the nature of sexual love. If we can attain some clarification in this area, we may be able to see how other kinds of love—parental love, love of mankind, and religious love—can fit into a unified conception appropriate for men and women existing as human beings in nature.

I emphasize our human nature because the tradition that treats love as somehow originating in a transcendental realm beyond our own seems to me defunct and unacceptable when taken literally. The meaning of love is to be found in our propensity to create ideals that liberate us from reality while manifesting our adherence to it. Among the philosophers we have studied, many consider sexuality in man to be a drive that is basically the same as in other animals. But love they see as something totally different from any biological category of that sort. If we take this approach, the very notion of sexual love becomes dubious and possibly self-contradictory. That is where Kant's thinking on the subject begins. As I have suggested, the problem he formulates arises only if we posit an underlying incompatibility between sex and love, between biology and morals, between nature and idealization. Kant does not deny that sexual love exists, and he recognizes its importance in human behavior. But since he relegates sex to the material phenomena of appetite and self-gratification, he is puzzled by its possible amalgamation with love. The latter, he assumes, must pertain to a trans-empirical order of values and ideality, what he calls "the kingdom of ends." This is his fundamental mistake. Eliminate such prior assumptions and the concept of sexual love, as well as its place among other types of love, becomes easier to understand.

In analyzing sexual love anew, I am returning to some of the questions about romantic love mentioned in the first chapter of this book. Discussing the dangers and the merits of romance, I shall offer a distinction between different kinds of passion. This will provide a basis for analyzing what is usually referred to as "falling in love" as opposed to two other conditions that I call "being in love" and "staying in love." We may then try to make sense of the notion of merging, both in itself and in its possible harmonization with the more prosaic joining of human interests for which I have used the word "wedding." After reconsidering my earlier ideas about idealization and bestowal, and their relation to appraisal, I shall try to map out the dimensions of a unified theory about the nature of love.

❊

In the course of this chapter I will be drawing several distinctions that cut across one another. At the outset we must recognize how loosely the term "romantic love" has been used in many recent books. When contemporary critics vilify "romantic love," treating it as a fraud or emotional disease, the object of their attack is generally a condition that many Romantics would have found quite remote from anything they wished to recommend. In recent decades psychiatrists and various types of counsellors have repeatedly claimed that those who were originally joined by romantic love could be expected to fare very badly in their subsequent marriage to one another. Although the definition of romantic love varies from book to book, the term usually refers to a situation in which socioeconomic realities and daily needs are ignored, the other person is idolized, psychological barriers are constructed in order to augment one's longing for the magnificent beloved, and yet he or she is revered as the one and only soulmate destined to share the lover's life on earth. After the appearance of de Rougemont's *Love in the Western World,* books on marriage and the family could appropriate his conception of romantic love as a self-destructive state in which men and women deluded themselves into thinking they desired consummatory goodness whereas they were really seeking death.

As I have suggested, a similar approach frequently appears in anthropological and sociological studies of love. In a chapter in which Brain argues that primitive peoples rarely experience "anything like the romantic love syndrome," he defines it in accordance with de Rougemont's theory and then rejects it as a "fraud" our society has foisted upon men and women alike. He speaks of romantic love as "illicit," "hopeless; tragic," tending to "martyrdom, despair, incest, fornication, death." Though an offshoot of Christian asceticism, it is expected to issue into "monogamous Christian marriage" and therefore, Brain asserts, it can only eventuate in misery. Pessimism of a similar sort accounts for Slater's remark, which I discussed in Chapter 9, that romantic love is a "scarcity mechanism" whose value depends on the repression of sexual gratification. According to Slater, love deludes us in two respects: "first, by having us believe that only one person can satisfy our erotic and affectional desires; and second, by fostering a preference for unrequited, interrupted, or otherwise tragic relationships." Slater identifies romantic love with "love at first sight," which he explains in terms of the Oedipus complex. Since that involves sexual desire forbidden by the incest taboo, Slater concludes that romantic love is inherently pathological just as Freud and many of his followers had often said.

We need not pursue these arguments of Brain and Slater. The term "romantic love" is ambiguous enough to cover some of the uses to which they put it. Though the conditions they cite are not the same as those recommended by any major theorist of Romantic love, and though they provide little factual basis for their generalizations, Brain and Slater are doubtless right in moralizing as they do about the love life some people lead. To a large extent they duplicate the attitude of marriage counsellors who subsume romantic love under the rubric of "immature love." In one textbook about marriage the latter is described as follows: "[It] arises through the ideas of the one and only, love at first sight. . . . The love relationship is characterized by considerable ambivalence. . . is rooted primarily in sexual attraction. . . is characterized by considerable jealousy, insecurity, and fears regarding the continuance of the relationship. . . tends to be exploitative. . . is characterized by considerable idealization based on fantasy, with marked tendency to distort the reality of the other person and to fall in love with the distorted image. . . is characterized by marked tendency to change the partner and to impose one's values on the partner without regard to the other's wishes. . . is characterized by sensing that one may be in love with more than one member of the opposite sex at one time. . . is characterized by overt competitiveness toward the other partner."

From this litany of negative possibilities, one can easily imagine the grand alternatives listed under the category of "mature love." I will spare the reader the enumeration of them. The catalogue of ills that belong to immature love, as here defined, is noteworthy because it alerts us to the many ways in which sexual love can fail in ordinary life. The failures are considered aspects of immaturity on the assumption that human beings who develop properly ("maturely") will be able to achieve a satisfying and desirable completion to love. I think this belief is correct, but I doubt that the distinction between mature and immature love throws much light on the nature of romantic love. For that need not be limited to the baleful traits associated with immaturity. There is no reason to think that romantic love—or sexual love as a whole—is necessarily destructive, delusory, or competitive in an undesirable way.

As a more plausible approach to this problem, I turn to Vernon W. Grant's theory of "amorous emotion." Grant introduces that idea in an attempt to define sexual love, which he calls: "an emotional relationship between man and woman that is distinctively *sexual,* in that it typically develops between persons of opposite sexes, yet is distinguishable from 'sexual desire' or 'sexual impulse.'

The latter terms usually refer to a motive whose goal is genital intercourse." Using the concept of amorous emotion to characterize sexual love, Grant claims that it differs from sexual impulse in being oriented toward a particular person. Amorous emotion directs attention to nongenital parts of the body like the face, and it creates an interest in attributes such as charm or strength, gracefulness or courage. It expresses itself as a fascination with the other person's beauty. It is an aesthetic attitude; it is not a hungering for direct libidinal gratification. It usually requires "a growth process of some duration" as opposed to immediate or rapid arousal of genital demand. When it declines, it does so gradually instead of subsiding all at once or becoming extinguished after physical satisfaction.

Having identified sexual love with amorous emotion and distinguished it from purely sexual impulse, Grant also distinguishes it from asexual or nonsexual love. This is a "love between the sexes" that does not involve libidinal interests. Such love, which Grant sometimes calls "friendship love," is mainly a benevolent concern for the welfare of another person. Unlike amorous emotion, it is altruistic, compassionate, and nonpossessive. It may even be self-sacrificial, and to that extent it differs greatly from what Grant considers sexual love to be. For amorous emotion, as he describes it, is not only sexual but also possessively selfish and capable of jealousy, even violence, when access to the person one loves seems threatened in any way. "We regard sexual *love*—the amorous emotion—not as tender, protective or unselfish, but as a possessive, essentially egotistic emotion."

Grant distinguishes among these three aspects of human nature as he does because he wishes to define sexual love as amorous emotion *alone*. Though amorous emotion is inherently sexual, it belongs to a category different from sexual desire as such or benevolent feelings toward a person of the opposite sex. In providing this kind of analysis, however, Grant limits sexual love to a single disposition—the amatory attitude that he considers qualitatively distinct from either libidinal craving or friendship. But to this extent his approach is radically deficient. For surely the nature of sexual love involves all three components, if not simultaneously, at least at various times within the erotic relationship.

As Grant recognizes, sexual love includes more than just benevolence, since that can occur between any two individuals however casual or sexless their acquaintance may be. And neither can sexual love be reduced to genital instinct, which often exists without love. Sexual love must therefore reveal at least an inclination to benefit the person one sexually desires, to care about that person's welfare. A benevolent attitude of this sort serves as a necessary condition for there to be love supervening upon sexual impulse. We cannot believe that love exists between two persons unless each shows concern about the interests of the other. At the same time our definition must accommodate the fact that in sexual love two people feel libidinal desire for one another. Although amorous emotion may cause lovers to dote upon each other's beauty or grace—none of which is wholly reducible to genital considerations, as Grant rightly perceives—there is no justification for treating sexual love as if it were only amorous emotion. On the contrary, sexual love combines all three of the criteria within Grant's analysis.

In itself, the sexual drive belongs to our appetitive being. It arises from organic and physiological tensions that may have no reference to the welfare of anyone else. In this respect, sex is similar to hunger or thirst. Like them, it eventuates in a system of responses that can satisfy the individual and enable the species to survive regardless of the consequences for some object toward which it is directed. Sexual love transcends this condition of nature: it bestows value and thus creates an attitude of idealization. That is why it cannot be reduced to mere libidinal instinct. Nevertheless it includes sexual desires of the usual sort. It could not exist without them.

As another way of putting this, we can say that amorous emotion is different from desire which is purely sexual but through sexual love the two reinforce each other. Being more than just the expression of an organic need, sexual love combines libidinal and nonlibidinal feelings for another human being. It generally directs itself toward persons rather than attributes. Though the lover's fancy is snared by some wondrous trait—the way a woman walks or smiles or pushes back a wayward lock of hair—his love addresses itself to her as a person, and not as a class of isolated features. Even if persons could be analyzed into the sum of their parts, it is the particular totality that we normally love, not a balance-sheet of positive and negative stimuli.

As the manifestation of an interpersonal bond, amorous emotion does not have to be accompanied by an overt sexual impulse at every moment. And while genital drive can be more or less indiscriminate, capable of being satisfied by any man or woman within a very large class of possibilities, amorous emotion tends to be highly selective. It usually limits itself to one person at a time, concentrating on what seems uniquely attractive in that person rather than qualities found in many other people. To say this, however, is only to say that sexual love, including amorous emotion as it does, is not appetitive in exactly the same manner as hunger and thirst. It is nevertheless appetitive. It is sexuality in a state of harmonization with tenderness and aesthetic delight.

In themselves, libidinal desire and amorous emotion may both be possessive mechanisms, each liable to jealousy and domination. Neither has to be benevolent, compassionate, disinterested, or selfless. But, for that reason, neither indicates how the word "love" may be appropriate rather than terms such as "obsession" or "infatuation." Love occurs when amorous emotion and sexual desire create so great an attachment to the object of one's choice that self-sacrifices otherwise repellent somehow become acceptable. For the erotic relationship to be worthy of being called love it must include elements of caring and cherishing whether or not it is also possessive and jealous at times.

Analysis of these three components, and the study of their intricate ties to one another, requires further investigation. At present I merely wish to suggest that the concept of sexual or romantic love cannot be understood if any one of them is neglected or minimized. In an adequate definition all three must be seen as indispensable—to some degree and in some dynamic interaction with each other.

In defining sexual love by reference to amorous emotion alone, Grant assumes that love must always be ardent, vehement, excited, and intense. But he is surely mistaken. Sexual love is a highly variable attitude that does not always manifest itself this way. In different contexts it may erupt in one or another emotion, but it is not *exclusively* emotional. As it develops, it will include moments of quietude and serenity. Much of it will appear as an interest in physical pleasure. Far from being definable as emotionality, it may often exist as a delectable enjoyment of sensory possibilities.

A contrast of this sort was incorporated into my distinction between "the sensuous" and "the passionate," which I formulated in *The Goals of Human Sexuality*. I argued that each of these dispositions may contribute to its own kind of sexual love. By "the passionate" I referred to the variable complex of demanding emotions that cause people to yearn for one another, to crave each other's presence, and to express their powerful and even violent need through explicit or symbolic behavior that reveals the ardor of their cathexis. By "the sensuous" I meant the capacity of human beings to enjoy other persons through immediate sensory excitation— to cultivate responses that lead to visual, auditory, tactile, olfactory, and even gustatory gratification. When thinkers such as Grant define erotic love as merely amorous emotion, they are really talking about passion and neglecting sensuous love.

My analysis of the sensuous and the passionate sought to be pluralistic, recognizing both as viable human attitudes and favoring neither at the expense of the other. It also hypothesized that each was related to a characteristic type of sexual expression. I associated the passionate with a strong interest in coital behavior, ultimately geared to reproductive instincts and generally consisting of sexual acts such as those that Kinsey called the "simple and direct." Passionate sex would thus include relatively little foreplay, vigorous thrusting by the male, and achievement of orgasm within a fairly short period of time. On the other hand, sensuous sex magnifies the opportunities for enjoyable playfulness, encouraging both male and female to use any technique that prolongs or increases pleasures of the senses, sometimes freeing itself from the need to perform coitus at all.

Leaving aside questions about the accuracy of my psychological and physiological speculations, which must be subject to the findings of empirical investigators, there is a major difficulty that my earlier writing failed to confront. Assuming that I was right in suggesting that sexual love could be either sensuous or passionate, or both in some combination, was I justified in thinking that passionate lovers tend to rely on simple and direct behavior that sensuous lovers spurn or consider less important? I had defined the passionate as an attitude of yearning and ardent need. While this might show itself in sexual behavior, I recognized that passionate lovers could also repress their sexual demands. But then why should one suggest that men and women who favored simple and direct intercourse—the male driving aggressively for orgasmic goals, the female welcoming his active response—would illuminate or even illustrate the nature of passionate love? As one astute philosopher put it: "On your view, a brutish and insensitive macho male, aggressively interested in nothing but his own orgasm, would have to be considered a passionate man." Not only was this absurd, my critic thought, but also it led one to doubt that there existed any correlation between being a passionate lover and preferring a particular type of sexuality.

I have several reasons for believing that this kind of criticism is misguided. First, I was distinguishing between the sensuous and the passionate without assuming that either would have to be accompanied by love. There was no claim that passionate response would necessarily be an example of love. To be a passionate lover one must express one's passion with love, but in my critic's example the macho male is described as one who does not act in a loving way. His forceful conduct might nevertheless be motivated by passion as opposed to any interest in the more delicate delights of sensuous sexuality. Though he may be inarticulate and rough in his bodily gestures, his crude behavior can very possibly evince the emotional need which defines the passionate.

In our post-Romantic world we sometimes think of passion as something honorific, as if it already implied a commendable, somewhat rhapsodic attitude. But that is not necessarily the case. The aggressiveness in passion can be a splendid expression of a wholesome desire for intimacy, or else it can be a gluttonous appropriation of another human being. The person who engages in the simple and direct can exemplify one or the other, or each on different occasions. Of course, it is also possible that such behavior may be mechanical or counterfeit, a mere imitation of passion. In that event the individual is not being passionate. He is disqualified not because he is unloving or his conduct is worthy of condemnation, but only because he is playacting and insufficiently motivated by relevant feelings. On the other hand, a passionate person may have the requisite emotions even if his sexuality is repressed or constantly restrained.

Though my concept of the passionate may be proof against the criticism I have been considering, it nevertheless needs further development. I have long pondered Freud's remark that a woman loses her lover when she takes him as a husband. It is impossible to know exactly what Freud had in mind, but probably he was referring to the fact that married people become habituated to each other's presence and often lose the glow of romantic excitement they may have experienced during the period of first acquaintance. To the extent that passion is augmented by obstacles and physical inaccessibility, it cannot exist in marriage as it did before the barriers to extensive intimacy were removed. Even nowadays when many young couples live together before getting married, there is still a difference between matrimony based on legal as well as personal commitment and an uncertain period of experimentation in sexual bonding. In the latter circumstance, the implicit freedom to stray may itself create a kind of obstacle that militates against the routine familiarity Freud found so destructive of passionate love.

Freud's insight is valid as far as it goes. We all recognize that the burning love that people may have in their days of courtship will not continue unabated after they live together for a long time and face the day-by-day necessities of earning a living, coping with each other's problems, raising a family, and passing through various stages of personal maturation. Our responses to one another change as the unknown becomes the known. The exotic becomes commonplace and the forbidden becomes routine, even casual. It is wrong, however, to suggest that the earlier love disappears completely once these transitions have occurred. That would mean that marriage or extended affiliation prevents men and women from loving one another passionately. Freud's intuition is better served, I think, if we distinguish between what may be called "romantic passion" and "marital passion." The latter we need not limit to marriage itself, the legal contract often being unnecessary, but since the married state symbolizes a lasting and continuous bonding between adults, this terminology is probably adequate.

Romantic passion is an emotional turbulence that most people undergo in adolescence and that many experience several times thereafter. In its origins it is surely related to a development of sexual awareness and to that welling up of libidinal energy which first occurs in puberty. In societies that encourage free and easy gratification of erotic impulse whenever it exists, romantic passion may occur less frequently or with less intensity than in civilizations that demand considerable repression. But in most societies the obstacles to sexual intimacy are very great, and therefore romantic passion generally arises in a context of doubt, uncertainty, and fear of total rejection. In all societies, a certain degree of insecurity must result from the fact that no one can ever be certain that the object of sexual preference will reciprocate. Even in the most liberated society imaginable, our hopes can always be dashed by someone whose interests tend in a different direction at that moment.

To a young person experiencing for the first time the vital power of newly awakened sexuality, the world into which his physiology has now thrown him may seem frightening and chaotic. The person who intrigues him will be a hidden reality, a mysterious entity with a secret life that must be penetrated before one dares to reveal the forces mounting within oneself. Romantic passion provides the impetus: it fires the need to discover this other person whose independence it can possibly overcome. Passion of this sort may thus be defined as a dynamic search for interpersonal unity. Developmental psychologists are probably right when they associate it with the period of life in which the child has attained considerable separation from its parents and now yearns for a compensating union with someone else. Romantic passion continues the process of separation and sometimes completes it.

A great deal of nineteenth-century romanticism focuses upon this phenomenon, making it central to the understanding of human nature. For instance, when Stendhal talks about l'amour-passion as the greatest bliss although it is a feverish state and possibly a cause of self-delusion, he is idealizing the pervasive sense of importance that results from this cathexis with another person. As we have seen, Stendhal analyzes romantic passion in terms of imagination, crystallization, and at times what I have called the bestowing of value. All these concepts contribute to a view of passion that subsumes it within a questing, burning fixation upon a sexual object which we are constantly afraid of losing because union with it provides our only hope for happiness.

Stendhal's idealization of romantic passion leads him to the conclusion that nothing in marriage can ever equal it. Like Montaigne he argues that, even at its best, marriage is a state in which husband and wife may enjoy a mutual comfort without inducing in one another anything like the fervor they experienced during their early days of intimacy. A similar conception can be found in the work of recent psychologists such as Elaine and G. William Walster. Distinguishing between "passionate love" and "companionate love," they raise doubts about the ability of marriage to incorporate the romantic elements in the former. The Walsters define passionate love as "a state of intense absorption in another. . . a state of intense physiological arousal." They speak of passionate love as "a wildly emotional state, a confusion of feelings: tenderness and sexuality, . . . anxiety and relief, altruism and jealousy." On the other hand, they describe companionate love as the kind of affection that may occur in lives that are "deeply intertwined." Compared to passionate love, companionate love "is a lower-key emotion. It's friendly affection and deep attachment to someone. . . . The only real difference between liking and [companionate] loving is the depth of our feelings and the degree of our involvement with the other person."

Though the Walsters' account is marred by the fact that they scarcely clarify what is meant by "deep" feeling, their approach enables them to explain the disappointments of married people who find that their companionate love lacks most of the passionate excitement they had once experienced and had hoped to retain in marriage. The Walsters rightly pride themselves on being more honest than marriage counsellors who glibly tell their clients to combine the passionate and the companionate. By emphasizing the differences between the two kinds of love, and by using scientific data to document the fact that a good marriage largely requires the companionate rather than the passionate, the Walsters show how unhelpful such advice may be. At the same time they fail to recognize that the friendliness, affection, and interdependence which constitutes companionate love can often (though not necessarily) result from a kind of passion not at all foreign to the nature of married life.

To see what this emotional attachment—what I am calling "marital passion"—is like, we need only return to the Walsters' definition of passionate love. Just a few of its ingredients would seem to be inapplicable to the feelings that married people are capable of having. The love that they enjoy may not be a "wildly" emotional state or a "confusion" of feelings, and it may be inaccurate to speak of their life together as a constant "absorption" in one another. But their marital experience can nevertheless include many moments of intense physiological arousal, tenderness and sexuality, anxiety and relief, altruism and jealousy.

These conditions, which make up the bulk of the Walsters' definition of passionate love, are not necessarily destroyed by marriage. To think that married love could exist without them is to reduce it to the affection and good will that might be experienced by partners in a business, or colleagues within the same profession, or neighbors who have civic interests in common. Such relationships may be deeply intertwined and predicated upon a great degree of involvement. Yet they do not create the passions that are characteristic of married love. One can certainly argue that the virtues of friendship and companionability are foundational to successful matrimony. Any viable marriage must involve joint activities and these often endure throughout a period of years. A husband and a wife who are not on friendly relations with one another, who do not respect and admire each other in the way that friends do, will not be able to cope with such long-range endeavors. But though an initial surge of romantic passion cannot suffice for the needs of marital love, there is nothing in marriage itself to prevent husbands and wives from feeling a type of passionate love that belongs to the married state.

Friends and companions who depend on one another will often

undergo strong emotions when their intimacy is threatened. They will each fear the loss or alienation of the other's affections. They will experience jealousy toward rivals who may deprive them of the company of their friend. They will worry about the welfare of this person who has come to mean so much to them. The same applies to the companionate love of married persons, except that their emotional bonds have been complicated and possibly strengthened by the fact that more inclusive activities are at stake. There may be children, there may be a continuing life with relatives, and very likely there will be a household within a community that treats the couple as a single social unit. Moreover, marriage being an accepted basis for sexual enjoyment, the spouses will have become each other's vehicles for libidinal expression. Far from precluding passionate love, their companionate love will make them more thoroughly dependent on one another. That alone can *increase* their mutual passion. If their interdependence eventuates in reciprocal trust, they will have an even greater incentive for continuing this marital condition.

What then is the difference between romantic passion and marital passion? I am convinced that the two are in many respects quite distinct and that counsellors do well to insist that marriages often fail because the spouses thought they could retain forevermore the romantic passion that brought them together in the first place. Being a sudden burst of sexual energy that grips an individual and (under the best of circumstances) the loved one as well, romantic passion can easily lead to delusory judgments. Having discovered a new and overwhelming domain of emotional possibilities, even mature men and women may easily miscalculate its durability. The condition they are in makes it difficult for them to receive untainted data about the object of their cathexis. It is awesome to undergo so blinding an explosion in one's feelings: it is as if one really were transcending or escaping from reality, or at least from all other realities. Though eventual disintoxication may be extremely painful, nothing short of a mystical experience can probably equal this sense of joy and ecstatic abandon, this feeling of total, eternal, and liberating oneness. This is not a state of mind that conduces to reliable recognition of truth.

So great is the emotional allure of romantic passion that human beings welcome its occurrence even under conditions that do not permit sexual fulfillment. Frustration can make the cathexis more powerful; and among people who doubt the goodness of the body, sublimated passions may seem to be nobler or more spiritual. On the other hand, when romantic yearning is combined with an acceptance of libidinal impulse, when it expresses itself in an eagerness to attain sexual completeness, it provides a kind of consummation that is not likely to be found within the orderly routine of even the happiest marriage. Marital passion can be very intense, but its intensity is of a different sort. This does not mean that marriage is incompatible with sexual love. It only means that marital passion is different from romantic passion in ways that require us to make further explorations.

In doing so, I must first enlarge our analytical equipment by introducing another distinction. Much of what we mean by romantic passion is exemplified by the experience known as "falling in love." But we must contrast that with two other states, both compatible with marriage, which I shall call "being in love" and "staying in love." These three differ greatly from one another.

❊

I have put these three terms in quotation marks because I use the colloquial language in a somewhat technical fashion. Traditionally, falling in love has attracted most attention. It is a dramatic event, frequently traumatic and troublesome to habitual modes of behavior. The person who has fallen in love may feel that a new reality has been revealed to him, and mystics often describe their religious conversion as a falling in love with divinity. In contrast to this, being in love requires a more continuous relationship. It is not a violent occurrence like falling in love since it depends on emotional adjustments that gradually establish themselves. Being in love is not the bolt from the blue or the love that strikes at first sight. Falling in love may sometimes fit such descriptions, but being in love involves a progressive reorientation of one's life, a focusing of one's energies that cannot occur all at once. In both conditions former interests must be newly directed, scattered commitments must be withdrawn, love that was felt for parents, school friends, or previous lovers must be transmuted into a concentrated devotion to the beloved. Falling in love does all this by uprooting the lovers and setting them apart from other people. Being in love begins the process of re-creation, the actual making of the new world.

Falling in love often manifests a craving for this regenerate society; and when two people fall reciprocally, they may assert that it now exists. But it is only being in love that effectively undertakes the constructive steps that are necessary. And if the couple are to stay in love, still more requirements must be met. Staying in love resembles being in love inasmuch as both signify an ongoing life together. But where being in love consists in the creation of a bond that still partly separates the lovers from their environment, staying in love enables the loving relationship to endure within the world at large.

Falling in love is volcanic. It is a phenomenon of great emotional stress. It may easily approach a state of obsessional fixation upon another person, often causing disruption in one's prior system of values. It is a common occurrence in adolescence because that is a time not only of erotic awakening but also of valuational questioning. But falling in love can happen at any period of life, particularly in societies where values are unstable or rapidly changing. While moralists in the ancient world considered falling in love to be a madness, and the medieval church condemned it as a soul-sickness that deflected people from a proper love of God, psychiatrists of the last hundred years have done the most to document its frequent pathology. When Freud remarks with horror that many of his patients suffer from "romantic love," he generally means falling in love. Not only is falling in love an emotional outburst, but also it is a cathexis based upon the quasi-magical—and therefore perilous—assurance of having finally encountered someone who can make life worth living.

As we have already seen, Theodor Reik's account of falling in love emphasizes its dependence on the frantic search for an ego ideal, an embodiment of perfection. Reik thought the condition would occur only in a threatened and impoverished ego. Something similar is argued by Francesco Alberoni in a recent book which approaches falling in love from a sociological rather than a psychiatric point of view. "The experience of falling in love," Alberoni claims, "originates in an extreme depression, an inability to find something that has value in everyday life." Alberoni interprets falling in love as a "nascent state" in the creation of a new society consisting of the lovers but capable of extending further. As against philosophers such as Ortega y Gasset (whom he does not mention), Alberoni insists that falling in love is "the revelation of an affirmative state of being." In the nascent state, as Alberoni describes it, we rise above the boring pattern of ordinary life and enter into a personal perspective on the world that is both imaginative and rewarding.

This conception resembles what Ortega rejected in Stendhal. Ortega attacked him for confusing "real" or "true" love with the beguiling but illusory trance which is falling in love. Alberoni recognizes the difference between falling in love and what he calls "love itself." He sees the nascent state as the beginning of a process that eventuates in an institutional relationship based upon the serenity and tranquillity of "loving devotion." But far from thinking that falling in love is a false or misleading substitute for love, Alberoni idealizes it as the exhilarating phase in the growth of an institution that remains vital only if it recreates its nascent state.

What Alberoni perceives is the life-enhancing capability of falling in love. Like Stendhal, he sees that it can be dangerous because it attempts, sometimes successfully, to find a new and uncharted world of its own. But also like Stendhal, Alberoni tells us very little about the "institution" to which the nascent state may lead. He seems to waver between considering it a satisfying culmination of the nascent state or else pervasive boredom that must be transcended by other nascent states leading to further institutional relationships, and so on indefinitely as one falls in love with one person after another. For the most part, Alberoni sounds as if the institution of love ("love itself") is inevitably limited to the banality of everyday life, so that only falling in love captures the goodness of imagination, creativity, and enthusiasm. This was the part of Stendhal that I found most dubious or deficient. We get beyond it by acknowledging the values of being in love and staying in love.

To make the contrast more vivid, I will start with staying in love.

Consider the bond between a man and woman who have spent many years in each other's company, each attending to the other's needs with recurrent and reciprocating concern. Whether or not they pursue separate careers and lead independent lives to that extent, they define themselves in terms of their special attachment to one another. They may have children whom they raise together, and they probably identify themselves with a segment of society to which they jointly belong. Assume further that each individual comes to feel that life would be greatly diminished without this other human being who has been so integral a part of one's daily existence. Eventually the relationship will lose some of its sexual urgency. It will include periods of anger, boredom, disgust, and hatred. At times it may resemble a condition of voluntary imprisonment that deprives one's affective nature of exotic opportunities one also desires.

A union of this sort may easily become habitual or prosaic, and it may reveal a fear of adventure, an impoverishment of the erotic spirit. Nevertheless, it may also illustrate the kind of love that develops throughout a lifetime. What I call staying in love involves a cherishing of the joint experience which is one's life with another person as well as a cherishing of the particular person who has lived through it with us. It manifests a basic loyalty to that person as he or she happens to be, warts and all. The realization that this loyalty exists enables each to experience spontaneous trust on many occasions. Though exuberant displays of enthusiasm may be rare, staying in love can include a large variety of passions. At moments of failure or success, there will be emotions of consternation, anxiety, triumph, or delight. If the relationship deteriorates—the participants having become too lazy in their tranquil union, too isolated from challenging possibilities beyond themselves—staying in love can be an unenviable condition. As in all love, there is no way of guaranteeing that the bond will always be desirable. Nevertheless, staying in love is probably the most meaningful form of love available to men and women. For most people it may be their one opportunity to find harmony with another person.

Between the extremes of falling in love and staying in love there is the state of being in love. When we speak of two people being in love, we mean that their relationship includes an intimate bond that has begun to establish them as a social unit. As yet their intimacy may not be based on much joint experience or coalescence of interest. Though there may not be the earthshaking excitement of falling in love, being in love resembles it to the extent that the lovers are motivated by the binding force of sexual and interpersonal exploration. On the other hand, being in love implies that a continuing union has already started, the urgency of the libidinal tie having been integrated (to some degree) with the purposiveness of a life together.

One can imagine human beings whose love for one another begins with the stage of falling in love, progresses into being in love, and ultimately matures as a staying in love that develops through the years. In the popular conception the ideal of romantic love generally assumes this configuration. But, as I have suggested, even those Romantic theorists who were optimistic about love often doubted that human beings are capable of following the desired trajectory to its culmination. There is good reason to think that the progression I have mentioned does not occur with any great frequency. The course of love does not run smooth for most of us. People who fall in love can fall out again very quickly. Though some continue their search for the perfect mate, the quest may never take them beyond one falling in love after another. This is not to say that each occasion will necessarily duplicate the errors of the previous one. People often learn from the embittering experience of falling in love with the wrong person. But however much we learn, we delude ourselves if we think that next time being in love or staying in love will follow automatically. Similarly, there is nothing in either of these types of love that requires them to have been preceded by anything like a falling in love. Some theorists, Freud and Ortega for instance, find a kinship between falling in love and hypnosis. It is surely not the case that everyone who is in love or stays in love must have gone through a prior stage that resembles hypnosis.

Between being in love and staying in love there may exist a more regular continuity. The devotion one occasionally sees in elderly couples may well have resulted from their having *once* been in love with each other. This may not be evident to us who know them now because the intensity of their sexual bonding might have long since been transformed into a calmer type of intimacy. On the other hand, it is also possible that there never was an earlier intensity. Staying in love requires an ability to cherish another person, and that does not presuppose any previous passion in the relationship.

For its part, being in love may not endure. It can be a temporary union, like falling in love, that disappears when the difficulties of living together become insurmountable. The mere passage of time cannot change being in love into staying in love. Though sexual demands moderate as people get older, emotional maturity does not assure the ability to stay in love. On the contrary, the aging process often leads to separation—a search for love elsewhere or even a feeling that interpersonal love is futile.

The three types of love are therefore logically independent of one another. Staying in love may come into existence without a preliminary stage of either falling in love or being in love. This sometimes happens (when all goes well, which is not the usual situation) among people whose marriages are created and arranged by the families. Until recently, that was the most common means of joining men and women in permanent bonds, some of which eventually became a staying in love. In the modern world, where staying in love has fewer institutions to bring it about, its occurrence is more haphazard though possibly more frequent. I leave it to the sociologists to provide the statistical data.

Distinguishing between these different kinds of love, I see no advantage in calling one of them "true love" and relegating the others to an inferior status. The pluralistic approach to human affect that I defended in *The Goals of Human Sexuality* should apply here as well. It is not an approach that has been widely accepted in previous theories of love. Though Stendhal's analysis of amour-passion includes ideas about being in love as well as falling in love, he seems to have virtually no comprehension of staying in love. Attacking Stendhal, Ortega is equally one-sided. Ortega identifies "real love" with a being in love that provides knowledge about the beloved available through no other means. In his belief that falling in love is only an erroneous substitute, Ortega neglects its redeeming values, its vivid immediacy and strenuous bestowal of importance. These are goods that may be absent, or less apparent, in the other kinds of love. In the writings of Madame de Lafayette in the seventeenth century, we find a classic representation of the conflict between falling in love and staying in love. Her protagonist, the Princesse de Clèves, experiences the latter with a loved (and loving) husband who does not excite her sexually. The Princesse must choose between him and another man with whom she has fallen in love. Though Madame de Lafayette implies that falling in love is an emotional disease, she does not limit the concept of love to one or the other relationship. For Tolstoy, however, it is very clear that falling in love is not really love, as Natasha in *War and Peace* finally decides when she marries Pierre and attains the placid staying in love that she would never have dignified with that word when she was younger.

I myself see no reason to define love in essentialistic terms, which would mean reducing it to a single possibility. Either as an ideal or as a human condition that occurs in ordinary experience, love cannot be identified with one of the types rather than the other two. Moreover, each has advantages as well as hazards. In a loving relationship vestiges or adumbrations of all three may well appear together, in varying degrees and in complicated patterns. Memories of the joyful but tempestuous time when they fell in love with each other can help a couple to stay in love. They may even forget the painful aspects of that period in their lives. Their ecstatic falling— like the fall of Adam and Eve—will linger on as the original motive in the long and difficult experience they have endured together. As they get older the couple may discover that the passionate emotions which pervaded their moments of being in love arise less frequently, but they will probably find ways of bringing them back on some occasions and to some extent. And where the attachment never moves beyond the level of falling in love, it may nevertheless include at least the dream of a permanent or prolonged union. That dream is universal and it can be realized, but only under the altered conditions of staying in love.

In formulating these three types of love, I do not preclude the likelihood that further analyses will disclose other types or subdivisions as well. In different instances of love there is apt to be as much diversity as there are different men and women differently motivated by the many springs of human nature. Whatever our system of classification may be, we should always expect to find great variety in the ways that people care for one another, express concern for each other's welfare, sympathize and feel identity of purpose, experience affection or erotic attraction, and in general attend to the being of a person reciprocally attending to one's own.

It is pluralism of a similar sort that enables me to amplify the analysis of bestowal and appraisal that I presented in the first chapter of this trilogy. Just as there are different types of love, so too are there differences in the appraisals and bestowals that constitute love between human beings. For love to exist, bestowal of value upon the other person is a necessary condition. But love can scarcely continue or prosper as a mutual interaction unless the participants also bestow value upon the relationship itself. They must want to have love for one another. They must be willing to accept as a framework for their lives the complex network of bestowals and appraisals (negative as well as positive) that binds them to each other. To see what this implies, we now need a more sophisticated explanation of how particular appraisals and bestowals combine to make the system of values which is love.

When I originally distinguished between bestowal and appraisal, I was analyzing love merely in terms of valuational categories. To love another person is to create a relationship in which that person takes on a new and sometimes irreplaceable value. The nature of this value is not immediately clear, however, and my distinction was designed to show how it should be interpreted. I argued that in appraising another person, we assess his or her utility for the satisfaction of needs, desires, appetites, impulses, instinctual drives that affect us in every moment of our lives. A woman's intelligence or a man's vigor and virility have obvious value of this sort. In the experience of love, men and women find value in each other through appraisals of an endless variety. As estimations of worth, appraisals are in principle no different from what a scientist provides when he makes judgments about matters of fact. In each case there are probabilistic predictions about the future as well as generalizations based upon empirical evidence to which one has access. In both cases, however, factual errors and inferential mistakes are always possible. Our appraisals of other people are especially liable to distortion by our hopes, our fears, our imperious sex drive, and above all, by our desperate need to find someone we can love.

In giving my analysis of appraisal, I distinguished further between appraisals that are "objective" and those that are "individual." Objective appraisals estimate a person's value in relation to the interests of some prior community. The judges in a beauty contest keep in mind features and even measurements that are accepted in their society as the most satisfying. In ranking candidates, the judges express an implied allegiance to criteria of pulchritude that reflect what people in that community consider desirable. This kind of appraisal inevitably enters into the love between two persons, sometimes with beneficial consequences but often leading to the miseries that result from wanting someone just because he or she is valued by other people. In any event, objective appraisals are always supplemented by individual appraisals in which we decide what another person is worth in relation to our *own* interests or needs. These are not necessarily identical with the needs and interests of any society, even the one to which we were born. And since "society" is itself a concatenation of statistical frequencies, there is no reason to expect that everyone in it will have exactly the same attitudes. Through individual appraisal we judge another's value in terms of preferences that are uniquely our own and often idiosyncratic.

Both objective and individual appraisal are habitual to human beings. They often occur without deliberation and in that sense may not be fully conscious. We "naturally" respond to other people in a way that indicates their appraised value for us. Only those in whom we find a positive worth of this type will be able to elicit our love. On some religious views, which I have discussed under the concept of agapē, God loves all creatures regardless of how worthless they may be in an appraisive sense and people acquire a similar capacity when godliness is in them. I myself have never held this belief. I am convinced that wholly nonappraisive love is foreign to human nature. Even saints who sacrifice their lives are motivated by evaluations that account for their behavior and that constitute an appraisive substratum for their ability to love. At the very least, they are appraising those for whom they die as suitable beneficiaries of their self-sacrifice and as more deserving of life than they themselves.

This is not to say that love is reducible to appraisal. That mistake was made by psychologists who tried to defend a "need-based" definition of love, such as the following:

> Love is the positive emotion experienced by one person (the person loving, or the lover) in an interpersonal relationship in which the second person (the person loved, or love-object) either (1) meets certain important needs of the first, or (2) manifests or appears (to the first) to manifest personal attributes (beauty, skills, status) highly prized by the first, or both.

Definitions such as this artificially limit love to its appraisive elements. The same happens when theories of "exchange" or "psychological economics" or "homogamy" are taken as *defining* love instead of merely revealing tendencies for interpersonal attraction. Thus it may be true that people mate on the basis of their similarity in various traits and in accordance with their ability to serve as need-gratifying assets within a system of psychological exchange. But that alone is not sufficient to explain the meaning of love. One might say that, in the definition quoted above, "positive emotion" specifies the additional element I am here demanding. But since the emotion (whatever it may be) is left unexamined, the entire weight of the definition falls upon the needs that people satisfy in the appraisive mode.

In denying that love can be reduced to appraisal, I have been arguing that another kind of valuation, bestowal, is necessary for the occurrence of love. When we love, we *create* value—much as the religious tradition maintained that God does in loving everything through agapē. An act of love need not change the other person (though this often happens), for it is primarily a creation in our own response to what that person is. The lover *accepts* the beloved, responds affirmatively to her attributes even though he knows that from an appraisive point of view they could be evaluated in a less positive way. Correspondingly, one who is highly ranked in relation to appraisive standards may be admired without being loved. Men rarely find themselves in love with beauty queens, and most women have difficulty loving aggressive tycoons.

One might argue that these facts merely illustrate the difference between objective and individual appraisal. For a man or woman who succeeds in the eyes of the world may not have just those traits that we ourselves require. Even so, love cannot be wholly understood in terms of individual appraisal. For that too pertains to needs and desires that may underlie our interest in some person without engendering an attitude of love rather than selfishness. Valuation through appraisal belongs to our appetitive being, which causes us to appropriate objects, including people, for the sake of our own gratification. But love implies that we want, and *care* about, the welfare of the beloved. To this extent, love goes beyond all appraisive categories. In relation to ourselves it gives another being a special goodness, a personal worth, that emanates from our own capacity to love and includes more than just the individual or objective value this person may also have. Love is a bestowal of value which supplements, and sometimes overrides, our attitudes of appraisal. As bestowal, love accords a person preferential status that is unearned in any appraisive sense. A person acquires this gratuitous value by being whatever he is. Therein lies the rich absurdity of love: for everyone, however worthless from an appraisive point of view, is what he is. In loving someone, we bestow value upon the mere being of this person.

In my previous writing, I tried to map the relationship between appraisal and bestowal by suggesting that while positive valuations in the appraisive mode serve as causal conditions for bestowal to occur, positive bestowals explain the nature of love itself. I now believe that this account needs revision or expansion in some respects. For one thing, all appraisals must ultimately depend on bestowal since they presuppose that human beings give importance to the satisfying of their needs and desires. Without such bestowal nothing could take on value of any sort. As a result, the two categories are not wholly separable. But this is a technical question that we can bypass at present. Of greater urgency is the fact that my former analysis could be taken as magnifying the role of bestowal to the detriment of appraisal. Though I maintained that all love involves elements of positive appraisal as well as bestowal, my emphasis upon the latter has been interpreted to mean that appraisal must play a minimal role in love. This does occur when love is a flight of fancy, or an emotional explosion that destroys the humdrum facts of ordinary life, or a blind allegiance, or an affirmation (however sublime) that ascribes objective perfection despite what everyone knows about the limits in mere humanity. But these are not the only kinds of love. They are not even the most representative.

Love is not necessarily oblivious to the faults of the beloved. The lover often grieves for them and refuses to tolerate the sacrifices they impose. He generally knows that his own interests must be respected if he is to live in harmony with this other person. To think of love as bestowal is to perceive that people give one another a value that goes beyond their ability to satisfy any individual or objective need (apart from the need to love, which may be basic to the rest). This does not mean, however, that the lover's other interests must be defeated or submerged for the sake of his beloved's greater glory. While love surmounts the shortcomings of another person in the sense that it creates its positive bond despite his inadequacies, it does not diminish the importance of criticizing flaws and acting for the welfare of both participants. Excessive bestowal —what D. H. Lawrence called "the greed of giving"—is not a better indication of love than a healthy-minded attempt to bestow value upon someone who truly satisfies our appraisive demands as well as her own.

To the extent that we define love as bestowal, we perceive the way in which lovers sustain the being of one another, undeterred by failures in themselves, refusing to withdraw concern or affection because of them. By recognizing appraisal as a major ingredient within love, and not merely as a *causal* condition, we focus upon the fact that love is a continuous give and take. It would be unfortunate if a preoccupation with bestowal resulted in our neglecting the appraisive element as an ever-present constituent of love.

In the first flush and excitement of amorous emotion, one may be astonished by an irresistible sense of wonderment, which is why words like "wonderful" come easily to the lips of lovers when they talk about the object of their devotion. Though outsiders who observe this spectacle feel certain that no considerations of appraisive value can justify the lovers' response, the lovers themselves may have no such awareness. They may even delude themselves into thinking that the other is appraisively better than he or she really is. But when they begin to share a life together (which does not happen for all of them), when their initial moments of ebullience turn into months and years of constant adjustment to each other and to their environment, when they mature within the new totality which is their existence as a couple, their love survives only to the extent that they make realistic appraisals of one another. If these appraisals existed without the bestowing of value, the relationship would assume the parameters of a business association, at best a well-administered partnership, at worst a power struggle between servant and master. So-called "happy" marriages often degenerate into one or another of these alternatives, debilitating comfort and habituation having destroyed the capacity for mutual bestowal. All the same, bestowal alone cannot fully explain the persistence of love, especially when the character or beauty of the participants changes for the worse and yet, as Shakespeare says, their love "bears it out even to the edge of doom."

In writing this, Shakespeare was referring to constancy as that which defines the marriage of true minds. One might assume that such love, which does not alter even "when it alteration finds," reveals bestowal in its finest flower. And that is true, for without continuing bestowal this kind of love could not exist. But I also see in Shakespeare's sonnet the portrayal of love as a willingness to recognize and acknowledge—without falsifying their import—the many negative appraisals, both individual and objective, that must belong to a life people share with one another. By telling us that love is not "Time's fool," Shakespeare insists upon its possible endurance despite the loss of moral and aesthetic virtues in the beloved. In order to be constant throughout the deterioration of mind or body, love must be a recurrent bestowal. But the splendor of that heroic attitude is augmented if the lover also appreciates, through realistic appraisal, how much the loved one has changed as he or she approaches the doom that faces all of us throughout our existence. Within itself, love includes appraisiveness as well as the bestowing of value. To neglect either is to misconstrue both.

To some readers the modification I am proposing may seem to be a trivial one. I previously argued that it is only *because* we appraise one another affirmatively that human beings are capable of love, and yet that love consists primarily in the act of bestowal. In other words, appraisal explained the causation of love—if people found nothing good in one another, they could not love each other —while the nature of love itself was to be defined in terms of bestowal as a necessary condition. But since I never denied that bestowal and appraisal are both present in the experience of love, my current formulation may now be taken as revising the earlier analysis only slightly. Even so, minor changes can sometimes have significant consequences and it is important to emphasize the part of love which is appraisal interacting with bestowal, over and above appraisal's function in the originating causal mechanism.

In the first volume of this trilogy, the idea that love is appraisal was shown to be the basis of the great eros tradition in Western philosophy. I criticized several of its proponents—Plato, Aristotle, St. Augustine, Freud, Santayana—for having ignored the element of bestowal, thereby misunderstanding the role of appraisal as well. I continue to think my critique was valid. What I now see more clearly, however, is the degree to which these thinkers were right in their insistence upon appraisal as a crucial ingredient of love. The search for need gratification which motivates so much of human behavior belongs to the core of all intimate relationships. In love one not only accepts the other despite inadequacies, but also one feels free to reject her *because* of them.

For me to say this may seem contradictory since all along I have been defining love as an acceptance of the beloved in herself and as she is—whatever our appraisal of her may be. But the concept of rejection is not necessarily incompatible with this. In a sense a husband rejects his wife if he comes to think that she will never satisfy his deepest needs, or even if he concludes that she is not the person he should have married in the first place. Rejection of this type can make love unhappy or troubled in its emotional vicissitudes, but that need not destroy love. Love ceases to exist only when our attitude turns into a more total hostility, disdain, or indifference, when we cannot live with the other person in any fruitful manner. Love that includes aspects of rejection may be considered less pure than love that involves no rejection at all. But the purest love is not necessarily the strongest or most profound. And, in any event, purity is too rare a phenomenon—here as elsewhere in human existence—for us to explain much by means of it. The innocent joy experienced by souls in Dante's *Paradiso* who have never rejected one another in any sense may be very blissful. It has little relevance, however, to love on earth.

In the works of J. M. E. McTaggart I find an analysis of love that enables me to present my ideas with greater precision. Writing some sixty years ago, McTaggart argued that love is not essentially dependent on the attributes of the object toward which it is directed. He acknowledges that one person's loving another can often be traced to the fact that the beloved has desirable qualities. But he maintains that "while the love may be *because* of those qualities, it is not in *respect* of them." He means that when we explain a person's love in terms of the beloved's attributes we are only providing information about the causes that may have brought the love into being. On McTaggart's view, such an explanation would not reveal anything about the content or inner character of the love experience itself.

McTaggart illustrates his point by contrasting love with approval. If I approve of Cromwell, he says, my admiration is directed toward one or another of his attributes. The quality in respect of which—or as we might say, the reason for which—I approve of Cromwell might be his courage (or some other trait). McTaggart believes that love is not a comparable response. We do not love others for their qualities, he insists, even though these qualities may cause our love to exist. "This, then, is the difference between an emotion being because of a quality and in respect of a quality. And my contention is that while love may be because of qualities, it is never in respect of qualities."

To support his argument, McTaggart adduces several "characteristics of love," as he calls them. In citing them, he is really listing corollaries of his major distinction. But they are nevertheless worth considering in themselves. The first one is that "love is not necessarily proportional to the dignity or adequacy of the qualities which determine it." The next he finds in those cases where we do not condemn someone's love although "we are unable to find any quality in the object of love which determines the love to arise." McTaggart thinks this indicates the nature of love since "no cause can be inadequate, if it produces such a result." In other words, love is so magnificent that we cannot doubt the suitability of anything that engenders it. Finally, he argues that there is no *reason* for love to cease when an object loses the qualities because of which the love originally arose. According to McTaggart, this characteristic shows conclusively the difference between love and other emotions. If the beloved has lost her virtue or endearing charms, our "admiration, hope, trust, ought to yield. But love, if it were strong enough, could have resisted, and ought to have resisted."

It seems to me that there are three basic claims that McTaggart is making. He wishes to establish: (1) that regardless of which qualities in the object may be the cause of love, none can serve as a necessary or a sufficient condition for either love's existence or nonexistence; (2) that the strength and quantity of love are independent of qualities that might otherwise be considered adequate or inadequate to account for our emotional response; (3) that love is its own justification and can never be condemned whatever qualities the object may have. The relationship among these propositions does not greatly concern me. The question we must ask ourselves is whether each of them is true. I believe that McTaggart's first proposition is true in part but also misleading, and that the second and third are false.

The truth in what McTaggart states results from love's dependence on bestowal. Desirable qualities in another person may explain why we love him, if we do, but no quality can guarantee the occurrence of love and none can be a prerequisite for it. In principle everyone could be loved by someone, even if we cannot indicate who that someone might be. If we are told that a hideous or evil person is loved, we do not deny the possibility. We merely alter our generalizations about what may or may not occasion love within some causal chain. At the same time love cannot be deduced from any quality in the object. Without the lover's bestowal, no quality will elicit love. And in any event, loving another as a person is not the same as loving his qualities taken separately. This much of what McTaggart claims is therefore correct.

But McTaggart also asserts that our love is not even addressed to the object's qualities. And that, I think, is false. In loving a woman as a person, a man does not love her for her admirable traits alone. He nevertheless loves them as *her* achievements and he loves her as the one who possesses them. Her attributes are more than just the cause of his love. They are a part of the woman he loves, and in loving her he is also loving *them*. "I love her grace," the lover says, "I love her kindliness [or cleverness or whatever]"—not as they might belong to someone else but as they belong to her.

What about the beloved's defects? They also belong to her. Does the lover love them too? Not in the same sense. We may love another *despite* her defects, and our love may subsume them within the imaginative act which is the bestowal of value. But only rarely do we love the defects as such. The lover is more likely to find them repugnant. It is the woman's goodness and beauty, to the extent that she has them, that he generally loves. In loving these qualities, he employs the usual processes of objective or individual appraisal as well as bestowal. His love for this woman is partly constituted by his love for her positive attributes as they exist in her. Once we perceive that qualities cannot yield necessary and sufficient conditions for love, there is no harm in saying that the desirable ones give us a reason for loving a person and that we normally love that individual in respect of them. Above all, we love her for the many ways that she is good to *us*.

If my argument is acceptable, we can readily see why the second and third propositions of McTaggart are untenable. Though he is right in thinking that the intensity or amount of love *need* not be proportional to anything in the object, the fact remains that proportionality of this sort usually corresponds to our appraisal of what the object is worth. Persons we admire and esteem, persons whose kindness or affection we can count on—which is to say, persons we appraise highly—are easier to love. That is why we speak of them as being "lovable." If they have qualities that satisfy someone's needs, all people may be lovable. By specifying which needs are relevant, we analyze the appraisive mechanism that both causes our particular love and is present in the direct experience of it.

Similarly, we would be guilty of an unwarranted aggrandizement of love, a kind of idealization of idealization, if we thought that all love is equally justified and none of it liable to condemnation. In maintaining that love is its own justification—that it can neither be justified nor condemned on the basis of the object's qualities—McTaggart fails to admit that love for a desirable object is normally preferable to love for one that is harmful or unworthy. It is lamentable (and possibly immoral) to love someone if that will lead to disaster for both of you, or for either, or for others who are affected by your love. I am not suggesting that we ought never to love persons whose attributes are considered inadequate in some respect. The saint who loves a sinner may defend his love despite, and even because of, the deficiencies in the qualities of this person. But the same would not apply to most other kinds of love. The saint who loves another saint, or ordinary people who love someone who is neither saint nor sinner, will argue for their love by pointing out the excellence of the man or woman they love. There is no reason to believe that love is invariably justifiable. At every moment we are always subject to possible condemnation for the consequences of our love, and thus for its mere occurrence under concrete circumstances.

Correspondingly, we should not be condemned, as McTaggart holds, merely because we cease to love a person who no longer has the qualities that originally caused and contributed to our love. Properly administered, a continuing love might have benefited him, and our ability to love is inherently praiseworthy. But the cessation of love under greatly altered conditions is not necessarily a failure on our part. It may even be commendable if endless constancy would have prevented us from giving our love to others and developing it further in a more promising relationship.

McTaggart slips into his indefensible conclusions because he assumes that love must be a union between two individuals who recognize each other as a separate person and are jointly conscious of the unity that binds them but each of whom ignores or disregards the other's attributes: "The fact that the union is there, or that the sense of it is there, may depend on the qualities and relations of the two persons. But if there is the union and the sense of it, then there is love, whether the qualities and relations which determine it are known or unknown, vital or trivial. . . . Love is for the person, and not for his qualities, nor is it for him in respect of his qualities. It is for him."

But what is a person apart from his qualities? We cannot love another as a person without loving the totality of his attributes. He has no being without them. It is true that we do not love him as a person if we love *only* attributes. For then it would be the particular qualities that we love, and to that degree ours would be a love of things. To love another as a person is to love him as the unique combination of his properties. We love him in respect of all his qualities as they exist in him—the good ones for themselves and the bad ones for being his despite their badness. Even if we thought that loving a totality of qualities is tantamount to loving a large class of things, this would only signify that under these limiting conditions the love of things and the love of persons coalesce. Whatever we decide about the relation between parts and wholes, however, a love of persons cannot be defined as a bare union of selves who are conscious only of each other's abstract personhood. McTaggart's mentalistic idealism led him to say this. There is no reason why we should. And having understood that love for another person includes love for his qualities, we see how appraisal interacts and cooperates with bestowal in the experience of love rather than being relegated to an extraneous category.

❉

In developing my new conception, I have profited from criticisms that appear in Russell Vannoy's book *Sex without Love: A Philosophical Exploration.* Vannoy suggests a possible inconsistency within my earlier thinking about appraisal and bestowal. He juxtaposes my stating that "love is a way of compensating for and even overcoming negative appraisals. . . . Love confers importance no matter *what* the object is worth" with my claim that "unless the beloved satisfied in some respect, no man might be able to love her." Vannoy wonders whether my saying love confers importance regardless of the object's value implies a conception of bestowal as "a blind quality that may be forced into self-sacrifice." This would contradict my assertion that love depends on positive appraisals without which it could not exist.

I do not believe that there is a contradiction in what I wrote. In its mere definition love is not bound by any degree of worth in the object. In a limiting case, one can *imagine* a love for something that is wholly worthless. This is what Christians have regularly done when they conceived of God's agapē. When, however, I insisted that a man could not love a woman unless she satisfied in some respect, I was not referring to any deity. We are not God, and we cannot hope to love one another in the manner that is said to define his being. Though it is logically possible for love to bestow itself on an object that has no other worth, human beings do not have this capacity. And if we are unwilling to accept the Christian dogma, there is no reason for us to think that anything else has it either. Appraisal occurs in love that we observe not only as its cause but also as an element that constantly accompanies bestowal. In human experience love includes both simultaneously.

Vannoy has other criticisms of my theory that also merit serious attention. He interprets my notion of bestowal as meaning that apart from it no one has value in himself. Vannoy finds this unacceptable. He believes "that the individual human soul has infinite worth, regardless of what anyone, including God, thinks of it." But how does he know this to be the case? His belief is not open to empirical verification. It is only an article of faith that he chooses to affirm. I do not share Vannoy's faith in any such absolute and unlimited worth, and I find it hard to know how he can then go on to say that "the only true value [that lovers] have is to be found in themselves alone." Does this entail that there is no other value in their relationship? Or is Vannoy saying that other types of value derive from the infinite worth that each human being possesses necessarily, regardless of the circumstances?

I cannot resolve these questions of interpretation. They pertain to a view of the world that is alien and unclear to me. People are part of nature; they live in societies; they form intimate associations with other people and become attached to various objects, institutions, and activities. Through valuation they organize their response to reality. Their mode of valuation provides a structure for their decisions. It governs their behavior. It pervades both cognitive and affective dispositions. Valuation arises from the human search for satisfaction rather than deprivation, survival rather than destruction, consummation rather than frustration. What is considered good or bad, ideal or depraved, must ultimately refer to this pattern of need and aspiration. In themselves, in their individual human souls (whatever that may be), people have neither "infinite worth" nor infinite worthlessness. They acquire value and the lack of it only as they are valued or value themselves in their relations with one another. Apart from poetic hyperbole, the concept of *infinite* worth makes no sense at all. Worth is always qualified by valuation within one or another context. And apart from all valuational contexts, worth itself means nothing.

Vannoy doubts that my theory can account for love as a caring about another person for his own sake alone. Since I maintain that the beloved acquires a new value through the lover's bestowal, Vannoy wonders whether this implies that the beloved is "utterly dependent on the lover for his or her value insofar as the value transcends his or her instrumental virtues." He then asks: "And if the beloved has such value only in relation to the lover's bestowal, is the lover as unegoistic as Singer insists he or she is? Is he in love with his beloved, or is he in love with his own power and imaginative ability to bestow value on the beloved?"

Vannoy's critique at this point involves two related problems in my theory. The first deals with the premise that love accepts the other as she is while also being concerned about her welfare. The second results from my claim that the bestowal of value is an imaginative act performed by the lover. If I really thought that the lover accepts the beloved in herself, Vannoy asks, would I suggest that the lover bestows a *new* value on her? Is this not an alteration rather than an acceptance? Returning to my belief that love is "a way of compensating for and even overcoming negative appraisals," Vannoy takes this as possibly meaning that through bestowal a lover projects upon the beloved a value "he would like to see" in her.

Vannoy misinterprets me. In arguing that the lover's bestowal compensates for and even overcomes negative appraisals, I was not suggesting that the appraisive value of the beloved would necessarily be changed in any way. This *can* happen, since bestowal provides emotional support that the beloved may use to her advantage. But in itself bestowal adds nothing to the appraisive value of the beloved. It does not project virtues or values the lover might like to see in her. Even when lovers delude themselves about each other's qualities, they are not thereby revealing the nature of bestowal, since that devotes itself to creating value *beyond* appraisiveness. Negative appraisals are compensated for and overcome only in the sense that they are counteracted by an acceptance of the beloved despite their negativity. The scales are not tilted by the addition of new appraisals unless the beloved improves in some respect or the lover's newfound intimacy gives him access to virtues in her that were hidden previously. Love is indeed an acceptance of another as she is in herself. In that respect it is "unegoistic."

Vannoy's second argument, which centers about the role of imagination, also questions the ability of bestowal—as I define it — to accept another as she is. For though bestowal does not project upon the beloved appraisive values she would not have had otherwise, it places her within an imaginative perspective that emanates from the lover. In my attempt to celebrate the goodness of the amorous imagination, I spoke of the creative power it instills in the lover. I described his transformation into one who enjoys bestowing value. Possibly my language was too florid, or my admiration for the lover's feat too emphatic. In any event, Vannoy claims that on my view "the one who bestows value seems to primarily be in love with his own imaginative powers." He correctly points up a danger lovers must always face. And without realizing it, he discloses a fundamental truth about the Don Juan character as he has often been portrayed in world literature. That kind of lover—and also the Sadean nonlover—is more in love with his own imaginative charisma than with any of the persons he beguiles by means of it. Don Juan bestows upon the woman he wishes to seduce a simulated love that deceives her into mistaking it for the real thing. His performance shows creative talent and great erotic versatility. That is why we in the audience are dazzled by it and are more likely to envy Don Juan than to hate him for all the harm he does.

But surely I never intimated that Don Juan was the exemplar of what it is to be a lover. Though I frequently suggested that bestowing value means so much to human beings because it is a profoundly satisfying type of enjoyment, I never identified enjoying bestowal with being in love with it. This would have meant that to be in love is the same as to be in love with love. There are people who have that experience, sometimes repeatedly. They often seem to be tormented by the fear of emotional emptiness or inability to love. Wallace Stevens depicts what they are trying to escape when he says: "That's what misery is./Nothing to have at heart." Moralists like La Rochefoucauld and innumerable psychiatric writers have warned us about their plight. But bestowal is not limited to a condition such as theirs. The bestowing of value does not have to be a bestowal on *itself*. Nor is this particularly representative of love in general.

In my original formulation I went to great lengths to depict bestowal's dependence upon imagination. In my eagerness to attack those who reduced love to appraisive attitudes alone, I neglected the many ways in which appraisal introduces its own imaginative quality into the experience of love. Since loving involves appraisal as well as bestowal, its totality as a creative event reflects the level of imagination in the former no less than the latter. In one place I spoke of love as "the art of enjoying another person." A commentator remarked: "This is a bit like calling gravity the art of standing up straight." She meant that I seemed to be treating love as an achievement rather than as a force in nature that may also drag us down. But this critic fails to recognize how greatly love is pervaded by a search for values and a longing for what we consider good. The art of enjoying persons is needed to harmonize and express the varied impulses in our affective being. Love is both an achievement and a force of nature. It is a prime example of imagination enabling us to enjoy the life we share with other people, and to do so by means of appraisal as well as bestowal.

❀

Having somewhat refined the distinctions between the different kinds of valuation and between falling, being, and staying in love, we may now turn to the concept of merging which has recurred throughout our investigation. I have thus far withheld much comment, partly because I find the notion so obscure. When Aristophanes in the *Symposium* has Hephaestus offer to weld the alter egos into one, can we really know what he intends? How can we make sense of Shakespeare's phoenix and turtledove being twain yet having essence but in one, or Rousseau's Pygmalion giving his entire being to Galatea, or Lawrence's tortured lovers seeking to fuse like molecules in coalescent liquids? If we can understand this use of language, we may find the courage to reconsider Lucretius' belief that one can merge with matter as a whole, or the mystics' faith that all men crave total fusion with God, or even Shelley's longing that the West Wind (and nature as a whole) be he.

My difficulty with the concept of merging has resulted from my inability to interpret it in any literal sense. Shelley and the West Wind are not the same. Lovers, however intimate, are separate individuals. This must be the case even if one of them is a divinity. We are constrained to think this way by the logic of the concepts themselves. In Lawrence Sterne's *Tristram Shandy* the following exchange occurs: "If I was you, quoth Yorick, I would drink more water, Eugenius — And, if I was you, Yorick, replied Eugenius, so would I." We laugh because we cannot imagine two people becoming one another. Though the phrase "if I was you" invokes that possibility, Sterne is ridiculing the idea of personal identities being merged. Human beings may think and feel alike, and they can share the same interests. That is what I referred to in the first volume as a "wedding" of personalities. But people cannot attain the kind of oneness that would enable them to fuse or be each other.

If, however, we consider what happens when people fall in love, we can possibly understand the feelings that motivate the language of merging. For even if there is no literal meaning in such usage, it nevertheless arises from emotions that are too profound and too pervasive to be dismissed out of hand.

Falling in love is so powerful a state for human beings because it involves an attempt to alter one's previous identity in the hope of attaining a new and radically different union with the beloved. It is often an escape from reality, but it may also be adaptive in a transitional period such as adolescence. For then we are in a precarious passage between the comforting security of childhood and the unknown demands of maturity. We are divided between the desire to liberate ourselves from dominance by our parents and the fear of venturing forth on our own. By falling in love an individual symbolically avoids both perils in this reality. He enacts something like the "displacement activity" of an animal that neither fights nor flees from an opponent but suddenly tears up the grass.

Throwing himself into the crisis conditions that falling in love creates, the adolescent withdraws from the need to choose between living as a child and becoming an adult. His fixation upon another is a movement sideways, which explains why it generally does not last very long, but it also enables him to combine elements of both alternatives. The goodness he finds in his beloved may duplicate the sustenance his mother once provided, while the possibility of sexual intercourse promises gratifications beyond anything he could have imagined previously.

For the adolescent, or anyone else who undergoes the revolution which is falling in love, there is ample reason to think or speak of merging with another person. The language is validated by the ardor of the emotion and may rightly be taken as a metaphoric expression of it. The hopeful lover who sees another as the embodiment of everything he wants in life may very well believe that he has merged with her by subjugating all interests that might have separated them. Considering himself worthless by comparison, he may sense a loss of his own identity. If his love is reciprocated, he may feel certain that nothing will ever alienate him from the object of his desire. It will be as if they had absorbed one another and thus become not only flesh of each other's flesh but also a supersoul concocted of what had once been two.

To call this aspect of falling in love merely a delusion will not advance us very far. The lovers know that they must still live their lives as separate individuals. They know that if one dies the other may still go on living. Even if they believe that molten feelings will never change and therefore that their union will continue for all eternity, this foolishness or cognitive naiveté does not diminish the *sense* of oneness that they feel so strongly in the present. In that there is no delusion. It is what it is, an affective state that people often fall into even if they soon fall out again and possibly regret the experience. Moreover, the concept of bestowal shows us why falling in love can be creative and imaginative regardless of its consequences. All bestowing tends to break down barriers between individual identities. It emanates from the lover and augments the value of the beloved, but in the process it transmutes the lover in accordance with this created value. Where bestowal is reciprocal, the being of lover and beloved must each be defined in relation to the other's identity as well as to their own taken separately. The interpersonal effect of reciprocal bestowing belongs to the two lovers in their new totality though also in themselves.

If we interpret merging along these lines, we can perceive its relevance to all three types of love. Falling in love may include the most vivid feelings of merging, but a comparable (albeit calmer) oneness occurs in being in love and staying in love. For that reason we should avoid the inclination to treat the idea of fusion as merely a "fantasy." Psychiatric writers often dismiss it in that fashion. Consider the following passage: "The concept of fusion is a fantasy shared by many people and idealized by some poets and artists who perhaps reactivated the old fantasy that, according to some writers, the baby entertains. . . . One could think of the baby as being fused with the mother when he was a fetus, but not after he was born. Any tendency to affectionate approach leads not to fusion but to the formation of a *bond of love*." Such skepticism about the search for merging is warranted, and the same applies to doubts about babies fusing with their mothers. Indeed, we can question the idea that even fetuses are "fused" in a relevant sense. But something has been lost, and the truth diminished, if we then conclude that the lover's sense of merging has no experiential base at all. His feeling is part of a development that transforms him into a self that shares its being—in part at least—with some other person. This is more than just a fantasy. As Hippolyta says in *A Midsummer Night's Dream:* "their minds transfigur'd so together,/More witnesseth than fancy's images."

To see this with greater clarity, let us move on to being in love. Some of the explosiveness of falling in love will now have subsided. The process of breaking down barriers may be largely completed. Extensive intimacy, once feared though obsessively desired, will have become a daily possibility. In giving each other access to their separate identities, the lovers change themselves by means of one another. They thereby form a *sharing of self*, which is their love relationship as it molds their individual personalities. To the extent that their love registers as feelings, they may each experience this sharing in a sense of solidarity. Far from being delusory, such feelings are the only ones that can represent their particular reality. The lovers will not have merged or fused with one another if that means annihilation of their identities, and there is no need for anything to have been sacrificed other than some of the benefits of their previous independence. Their sharing of selves is something they have jointly created. In love that endures, it is a structured state that they alone have made. Their achievement is by no means quixotic.

Discussing these matters, Robert Solomon argues that romantic lovers are engaged in a paradoxical search for what he calls "shared identity." Solomon insists that "this goal is impossible, unachievable, even incomprehensible. Two selves cannot become one, not when they start out so differently—with different origins, even from different cultures, with different tastes and expectations. And yet this does not mean that the goal is impossible to work for and to want even desperately, to *yearn* after. For this indeed is the famous *langour* of love, the play of contradictions reinforcing each other." Solomon characterizes this systematic contradiction as the "paradox of love"—"it presupposes a strong sense of individual autonomy and independence, and then seeks to cancel this by creating a shared identity." According to Solomon, the two elements are inherently incompatible: to the extent that we approach the goal of sharing, we undermine the attainment of autonomy. Since two people must always be different from one another, Solomon concludes, their individuality makes it impossible for them ever to reach the shared condition they desire as lovers.

I find this analysis unacceptable because it seems to confuse the sharing of self with an actual merging, which is what Solomon means by "shared identity." To fuse in Solomon's sense, both persons would have to lose their own identity: each becomes an indissoluble part of a larger compound. And possibly that is what some lovers do desire. The idea that a yearning of this sort is universal in love was the great mistake romanticism made. I cannot believe that it defines romantic love as a whole. Regardless of what people who fall in love may feel or say they feel, they continue to live as individuals who know they will not be literally fused in any comprehensive sense. And when their love develops further, when they experience being in love as a new life constructed out of their mutual and interacting interests, they merely share their disparate identities. In responding to one another, their personalities undergo reciprocal changes but the lovers need not lose their differences, or even care to do so. The sharing of self does not mean that lovers are no longer separate selves or that they have given up *all* their independence. There is no reason why either lover should want to lose his or her individual autonomy. For that enables each to make a unique contribution to the sharing that they crave and that their being in love makes possible for them.

Though Solomon rightly points out that two selves cannot become one, he explains this by saying they start out with different origins, cultures, tastes, and expectations. But all that is irrelevant. Even when two selves are the same in these respects, they cannot become "one" if by that we mean any total merging of identity. If their oneness involves only a sharing of their selves, however, the differences Solomon enumerates might make it difficult for them to love each other but not at all impossible.

Solomon's belief that love is necessarily paradoxical issues from his attempt to define it as what Sartre would call a dialectical "metastability." Love must therefore be "not a state of union but a never-ending conflict of pushing away and pulling together." There is much truth in this insofar as love cannot be described as a single, continuous, unchanging uniformity. It is, as Solomon and Sartre both recognize, a succession of variable attitudes that often conflict with one another, and even simultaneously. But this cannot be taken to signify that love is an impossible goal or that it is necessarily constructed out of contradictions which somehow reinforce each other. Instead it means that for any two people love differs greatly in its quality or intensity from moment to moment and as it develops through time. Love cannot, and need not, eliminate all interests that belong to us as separate selves. When divergency of interest militates against it, love may be unable to survive the onslaught. On occasion we may not be sure that we even want to be in love, with this person at least. Ambivalence in our feelings about love is probably characteristic of all human beings. Nevertheless, none of this provides any justification for believing that love itself can be defined as a state of endless alternation between wanting to be separate and wanting to be merged.

On the other hand, Roger Scruton goes too far when he describes the community that is love as one in which "all distinction between my interests and your interests is overcome. Your desires are then reasons for me, in exactly the same way, and to the same extent, that my desires are reasons for me. If I oppose your desires, it is in the way that I oppose my own, out of a sense of what is good or right in the long run." This could serve as a description of perfect fairness in human relations, and that might well be related to love. But the sharing in love is not a matter of fairness. For reasons of love, I may give your desires greater importance than my own. And if I do so, it is because my love has created in *me* feelings of concern or bestowal that count as additional reasons for *your* desire. In this sense, love is both more selfish and more altruistic than fairness. It is a sharing of selves that transcends our usual ideas of justice.

I can put these reflections in sharper focus by considering the unity that belongs to staying in love. The feeling of fusion may now have become routine, since the excitement of falling in love is likely to have been outgrown. On the other hand, the concept of a sharing of selves seems inadequate to explain the permanence and possible depth in this relationship. To understand these further dimensions of love, we must return to our earlier discussions about dependence and interdependence. Studying Rousseau, for instance, I suggested that his fear of dependence seemed to blind him to the constructive possibilities of a love between two people that would render them *inter*dependent. One feels that Rousseau, like the early Sartre, confused interdependence with the type of joint dependence that is basically hostile or demeaning. The latter is a condition of mutual enslavement. In it each person attempts to use the other selfishly and without a sense of pride or achievement in the relationship. Each is just an instrumentality for the other. Though their efforts may be orchestrated in a regular, even constant exchange of services, both persons feel entrapped. That is why Rousseau and Sartre could emphasize the loss of freedom in any such association. The participants must always be on guard against one another since neither wishes to submit to someone whose residual ill will can be inferred from the fact that he or she also feels the slavery of this dependence.

The situation is quite different, however, for people who are happily and beneficially interdependent. For now the freedoms that they lose in accommodating to one another will seem peripheral to what they care about most. They will feel free because they will have defined themselves in terms of the mutual sharing which is their interdependence. As an expression of interpersonal needs, their love will cause them to rely on one another and to that extent they will be dependent. But their dependence will no longer feel the same, and indeed it will not be the same: it now belongs to a relationship in which each wants the welfare of the other rather than merely wanting selfish benefits. It is therefore a mutuality they can freely accept. Their interdependence is an affirmation of the value each bestows upon the other as the custodian of their oneness. From within their love both attain legitimacy in seeking individual satisfactions through the other and neither feels that sacrifices are externally imposed. Nor are they. For they have become incidental adjustments within a sharing that each chooses for its own sake. What is lost in being dependent on another and in being the object of that person's correlative dependence is regained by the fact that the other likewise bestows value upon the interdependence they have jointly created.

When Ficino spoke of lovers dying through their self-sacrifice but being restored to life through their reciprocal rebirth in one another, he was alluding in his poetical metaphysics to this kind of interdependence and sharing of selves. The same is true of Kant's belief that marital union is a yielding of rights and privileges in which neither party loses anything since both win everything back through the possession of the other. As we saw in the previous chapter, some theorists interpret interdependence as the renewal with another adult of the relationship between parent and child. This makes sense inasmuch as the child who has a loving mother or father can count on them to gratify his desires for reasons of their own and without making him suffer unduly. In the happy love between mother and infant there is a natural reciprocation which does resemble interdependence. But though that relationship may be gladly accepted by both participants, only one of them could actually have chosen it and both will soon outgrow it in obvious ways. To this extent it is somewhat misleading to think that the interdependence of staying in love is a reinstitution of the union between parent and child. The interdependence of love must result from the lovers' choice, their oneness being accepted when it might have been rejected. It is not imposed upon them by infantile necessity.

In being interdependent, people who stay in love may not regret that they no longer have their earlier sense of fusion. For they will have built a system of interpersonal adjustments that resolves emotional problems without requiring an actual merging. Living with another person in reality rather than in fantasy, each comes to recognize that no oneness can be total. Instead they learn how to respect the separateness in the other person. Far from being "transparent" to one another as demanded by Rousseau's outlandish concept, they will have mastered the art of appreciating each other's privacy and indefeasible autonomy. They must be transparent in the sense of being honest and truthful, but they will have given up any pretension of revealing their absolute "inner being." Love does not define itself in accordance with that exhibitionist ideal. People in love vibrate sympathetically to each other's feelings, which are not hidden but rather shared in this respect. At the same time, they attain the ability to find satisfaction for themselves as individuals, each treating the other as an instrument while also accepting him or her as an end whose own satisfactions are distinctive to that person and equally valuable. For this to happen, one does not need Rousseau's kind of transparency.

It was Kant who most fully understood that morality means treating another as an end and that immorality consists in using others as a means *merely*. The last word must be italicized because Kant knew that people inevitably serve as means for one another. He did not realize, however, that these principles of his moral theory could also serve as the basis for a philosophy of love. Married love, the only kind Kant considers moral in sexual situations, he calls a "union of wills." Except to say that this includes an exchange of rights to each other's person, he does little to explain what married love entails. His analysis becomes plausible only if we interpret the idealized union as one in which each uses the other as a means while also treating him or her as an end on whom one bestows the privilege of using oneself in similar fashion. In this kind of circumstance there is no question of actually merging, and feelings such as the yearning for fusion must always be secondary or incidental. Interdependence will have been achieved, but that involves unity of a different sort.

As I have said, the interdependent state is more than just the sharing of selves. Though it may only be a matter of degree, I think this reveals an important difference between being in love and staying in love. The former unites individuals who define themselves in terms of their relationship. Unless their sharing persists as a governing reality to them, they can neither be in love nor stay in love. But staying in love additionally requires that the sharing of selves renders the lovers fruitfully and pervasively interdependent. Gratifications they might well have derived from outsiders they progressively choose to get from each other. For many affective needs, they stay completely within themselves. Though this may diminish the waywardness of erotic appetites, society has often felt threatened by the internal self-sufficiency of staying in love. As a character in Jane Austen cynically remarks: "Is not general incivility the very essence of love?" In a similar vein, Proust says that "when we are in love, we no longer love anyone else." Though this social hazard also pertains to falling and being in love, it can be most acute in a condition such as staying in love which has made its peace with the outside world and yet turns inward for its deepest gratifications. The couple and whatever family they engender can become an affective state within the state, an isolated clan semidetached from the community at large.

The great problem for political philosophy consists in finding means by which the interdependence of those who stay in love can be duplicated throughout society, and in a manner that integrates all units of association with each other. Despite Rousseau's ambivalence about freedom and dependency, his thought culminates with his vision of an ideal community in which all persons would be interdependent. He did not mean that everyone stayed permanently in love with everyone else. But once it has liberated itself from the dream of transparent merging, staying in love might well provide a touchstone for Rousseau's utopian state, or at least for a practical equivalent that might be approximated in varying degrees at different levels of society.

Assuming that my approach is defensible, it may enable us to harmonize concepts of merging (reinterpreted) with realistic ideas about a wedding between distinct but overlapping personalities. It may also help us to avoid two kinds of theories: those that interpret love as ecstasy and those that consider it mere dependence on another person. To the extent that he identifies love with primary narcissism—the desire to be loved—Freud reduces it to a condition of dependence. In asserting that only passion-love can yield the happiness that all men want, Stendhal sees it as the gateway to ecstatic pleasure. Some writers have described love as a confluence of these two alternatives. In one recent book love is defined as the simultaneous experience of both. The authors describe ecstasy as a fusion with something other than oneself. They think of dependence as a psychological "analogue" of physical need. Most interpersonal relations consist of the dependencies that people undergo in their desire to be loved. For love actually to occur, we are told, the striving for ecstasy must be combined with the acceptance of relationships that render us dependent: "We all have the ecstatic capacity for merger with another, but we also have a need for the Other to be available to us. . . . Melding the two in a continuous love experience is a supreme creative act."

This conception would lead us to think that love—at least when it is the real thing—is always both an ecstasy and a useful form of dependence. The formulation is inadequate for a number of reasons. For one thing, it conceives of ecstasy as an actual fusion with another person, much more than just a feeling of oneness. At the opposite pole, it depicts human relationships as dependencies without considering the differences between love and slavery, between an authentic interdependence where each bestows value on the other and sadomasochistic jockeying for domination. Finally, a view such as this implies that all "true love" is the same and therefore that an attachment without ecstatic feelings cannot really satisfy the definition of that term. In their own modern way the authors revert to the errors of nineteenth-century Romantics who assumed that falling in love is the only kind of love that matters.

I detect a similar confusion in our ordinary language about love. In common parlance, people often speak of love as something that *happens* to them. We are all familiar with metaphors—the bolt from the blue, the arrows of Cupid, the fateful meeting of glances —that represent love as an unwilled and generally unforeseeable event. Sudden bonding of this sort may sometimes occur, and I have no reason to doubt that people do occasionally love at first sight. But all of this pertains to falling in love. It is hardly compatible with being in love or staying in love. These require a different kind of analysis.

Imagine a typical situation in which a man says to a woman "I love you." If falling in love were paradigmatic of love in general, we might assume that the man is reporting upon the remarkable condition he is in. We could infer that his attention is fixated on this woman almost to the exclusion of everything else and regardless of what he wills: he thinks of her obsessively, he finds it difficult to cope with the usual necessities of daily life, he may even feel that their essences are inseparably united in some metaphysical realm. Or else he is telling the other person about the great tenderness he has toward her, or the sense of delight that her presence creates in him. In all these possible meanings, "I love you" is a declarative assertion about the man's current state of being. To that extent, it makes no reference to the future.

Yet a prediction is often built into statements such as "I love you." Using these words, the speaker then claims that he will care about the other person for some time to come, and in many circumstances that can arise throughout succeeding months or years. He may even be expressing a desire to share the rest of his life with her, to form a permanent bond to which he will continue to dedicate himself. There need not be any implications of bolts from the blue or a yearning for mystical fusion. Telling someone that you love her need not be taken to mean that you have *fallen* in love with her.

This type of utterance can also serve what logicians call a "performatory" function. In that capacity, it is related to (and possibly anticipates) performances like the saying of "I do" in the wedding ceremony. The words themselves enact something in the world instead of merely expressing feelings and asserting propositions about a present or future state of affairs. We bind ourselves by what we say. With this formula we make the beginnings of a vow and become part of an affective unity that we hope the other will ratify by using language in a similar way. When that takes place, "I love you" plays a role in the sharing of selves which is integral to being in love and ultimately to staying in love. Much more must also happen, of course, and words can always be used deceptively. I introduce these meager linguistic details in order to illustrate the need for a pluralistic analysis. Even the timeworn phraseology of lovemaking does not mean the same on all occasions. What makes good sense in one erotic context may be ludicrous or inappropriate in another.

The philosophy of love I am here outlining offers itself as an alternative to reductivism. In contemporary theorizing reductivistic approaches take different forms. It will be instructive to consider samples from psychiatric, feminist, and theological literature.

Erich Fromm's popular and influential book *The Art of Loving* exemplifies a kind of reductivism that many psychiatric writers find attractive. Fromm argues that love is primarily an "orientation of character" which manifests itself in a person's attitude toward the world as a whole. From this he concludes that it cannot be directed to any individual exclusively: "If I truly love one person I love all persons, I love the world, I love life. If I can say to somebody else, 'I love you,' I must be able to say 'I love in you everybody, I love through you the world, I love in you also myself.'" Fromm reaches this counterintuitive conclusion only after depicting love as an overcoming of separateness through a "universal, existential" craving for union. Though he wishes to discount any "symbiotic" union that diminishes an individual's selfhood, he interprets the oneness which is love as a relation that either originates in fusion or else terminates in it. In motherly love he finds original fusion; in erotic love the terminative kind. Fromm believes that all sexual desire aims at a fusion with another person. This cannot be attained, he thinks, unless each of the lovers "loves in the other person all of mankind, all that is alive." When Fromm discusses religious love, he argues for the "paradoxical logic" which claims that the love of God is the mystical feeling that one has fused completely with God. The love for another person must involve a love of everyone and everything because all love, as Fromm conceives of it, craves a totalistic fusion that no individual object can yield independently of the cosmos as a whole.

In saying this, not only does Fromm glorify merging, which he considers attainable though possibly unwholesome under some conditions, but also he perpetuates the reductivistic shortcomings of the idealist tradition. Whether they are Platonists claiming that true love yearns for the highest good, or Christian theorists maintaining that only the love of God is really love, or Hegelians asserting that love must belong to an ontological quest for oneness with the Absolute's all-embracing love of itself, idealists have always given a preferential status to a single type of object. Realists have sometimes committed the same mistake, as when Freudians define love as "nothing but" aim-inhibited desire for either mother or a sexual goal. We move beyond these constrictive modes of thought by denying that erotic love, for instance, can be reduced to either a devious search for God or a craving to become one with all of nature.

Reductivism of a different sort underlies the attack that some radical feminists have launched against love between the sexes. Feminists frequently distinguish between love as a present possibility and love as a hope for the future. Theorists such as Shulamith Firestone and Elizabeth Rapaport argue that authentic love between men and women cannot exist under the conditions of inequality that prevail in the world as we currently know it. They nevertheless believe that love becomes a viable option once equalization between the sexes finally occurs. It is this optimistic belief that feminists like Ti-Grace Atkinson reject. Atkinson claims that love between man and woman is inherently impossible. Even if male dominance were wholly eradicated, she would say, the most one could expect is the eventual forging of cooperative bonds different from love—relationships of friends or comrades but not of lovers.

It is Atkinson's mode of reasoning that seems to me particularly reductivistic. The view of the more moderate feminists mainly consists in generalizations about the circumstances under which love may possibly occur. They emphasize the importance of equality for there to be authentic love between man and woman, and they note that as yet mankind has failed to satisfy this prerequisite. Far from doubting that love between the sexes can exist, Firestone merely suggests that inequality prevents love from being anything more than a falling in love where lovers finally drag each other down. Unlike Firestone, Atkinson treats all romantic love as if it were reducible to falling in love at its worst.

In suggesting that heterosexual love is a confused idea that deserves no place in feminist aspirations, Atkinson makes a crucial distinction between friendship and love. The former, she says, is "a rational relationship which requires the participation of two parties to the mutual satisfaction of both parties." Love she considers incompatible with friendship: "'Love' can be felt by one party; it is unilateral by nature, and, combined with its relational character, it is thus rendered contradictory and irrational." But Atkinson gives us no reason to believe that love must be defined as unilateral. Is it *incapable* of being mutually satisfying? And is it particularly hazardous for women?

Thinking like a recruiting agent for the feminist cause, Atkinson addresses herself to the condition of women whose political activism may be undermined by sexual love. She assumes that a woman who loves a member of the oppressive class to which all men belong is thereby providing aid and comfort to the enemy. Even if this were true, however, Atkinson would only have shown that love creates special problems for women. But her thesis is much more extensive than that. She argues that love involves the attempt of the powerless to fuse with the powerful. And it is true that this attempt is sometimes made. Nor is she wrong to think that women have often loved men in the hope of sharing with them values that society has regularly assigned to males rather than females. What she ignores is the equally important fact that men love women for similar reasons: they wish to participate in the values females possess. Though males have dominated them unjustly, women who elicit love are not as powerless as Atkinson believes. The ability to experience reciprocal love has always been one of the greatest strengths of women as well as men. Atkinson cannot justify her assertion that love is inherently unilateral, and neither can she defend her conclusion about its being "contradictory and irrational."

Atkinson's theory is reductivistic in two respects: first, in treating all kinds of heterosexual love as if they were the same as falling in love; and second, by interpreting love as always an impassioned possessiveness inconsistent with friendship. These ways of thinking about love are not uniquely modern, or limited to radical feminism. In the eighteenth century, both Rousseau and Mary Wollstonecraft made similar assumptions about the incompatibility of love and friendship, though neither reached conclusions as extreme as Atkinson's. In *A Vindication of the Rights of Woman,* where Wollstonecraft castigates Rousseau for denigrating women as inferior creatures designed to please men, she nevertheless makes statements about love and friendship that resemble much of what he had said. Depicting friendship as "the most sublime of all affections, because it is founded on principle, and cemented by time," she maintains that the opposite must be said of love. She denies that sexual love can be constant; and she is certain that it must always be short-lived. She concludes that "the most holy band of society is friendship," which may exist once the feverish passion of love is succeeded by the "security of marriage" but cannot occur within love itself.

From its post-Romantic perspective, the feminism of contemporary theorists such as Atkinson returns to the pre-Romantic rationalism of Rousseau and Wollstonecraft. The faith in marriage as the appropriate context for heterosexual friendship has disappeared, and the radical feminists may be naive in believing that extramarital friendship with the male is any more likely than reciprocal love. But what remains constant, I think, is the fundamental mistake of believing that sexual love must always be a kind of falling in love. Neither Wollstonecraft nor Atkinson, on the one hand, nor Rousseau on the other, seems willing to allow the possibility that love can have dimensions of a significantly different sort.

Firestone's feminism goes a long way toward making up this deficiency. Firestone begins with a distinction between love and the conditions under which it is able to exist. She thinks that by its nature love is the self's attempt to "enrich itself through the absorption of another being." Love is dangerous for both participants, she remarks, because it involves vulnerability on one's own part and can destroy the other in the act of incorporating him. When it consists of "mutual exchange," however, love is not destructive. On the contrary, if it occurred between equals love would succeed as the enriching of both lovers—"each enlarging himself through the other: instead of being one, locked in the cell of himself with only his own experience and view, he could participate in the existence of another."

I have difficulty in understanding what Firestone means by "incorporation" or "absorption of another being." Is she merely referring to participation in someone's life, or is she too relying on the concept of merging? When she argues that love between the sexes can realize itself only if it involves mutual exchange, she seems to discard any vestiges of a belief in fusion. She describes falling in love as a search for merging that cannot succeed. Her distinction between love and falling in love specifically relates the latter to inequality resulting from male dominance as it now exists. It follows that the love that usually occurs "in our present society" does not indicate the nature of love itself. As long as the sexes are not equal in their social worth, she says, they cannot truly love one another. They can only fall in love, which means trying to absorb each other in an emotionally unstable and ultimately invidious relationship that manifests their inequality instead of eliminating it.

Leaving aside the question of whether falling in love is necessarily as harmful as Firestone thinks, one may well agree that happy or successful love depends on equality in the sense of reciprocal bestowal of value, mutual concern for the welfare of the other, and joint realization that this requires maximum opportunity for self-development in all respects. A belief in such equality was the basis of Shelley's feminism and that of others in the nineteenth century who saw no possibility of satisfactory love between male and female if they were merely master and slave, oppressor and victim. Stendhal advocated the education of women because without it they could not share their lovers' intellectual pursuits. Various Romantics urged an equalization of rights and privileges on the grounds that this would provide women with the feeling of self-respect essential for an adequate love life. The problem that still remains is whether love in our unregenerate state can facilitate the desired equalization or whether love cannot even exist—except as a pathological falling in love—until equality has been achieved.

In taking the latter point of view, Firestone neglects some of the major elements in her own ideas about love. For if love is indeed a mutual exchange, a sharing of selves through which the lovers participate in each other's being, it thereby overcomes various inequalities that might have separated them previously. That, in fact, has been the history of love in the Western world. The medieval lady, submerged in a political system that deprived her of the right to choose a husband, could rectify this injustice by finding a lover who would cherish her. Whether or not she ended up on a pedestal of poetic adulation, she could feel that her lack of power in society was counterbalanced and possibly outweighed by her access to the fulfillment that love itself provides. Romantic love in the nineteenth century extended this equalizing pattern to all women regardless of their birth or wealth.

On independent grounds one can and should condemn the many ways in which women have been denied their rights as human beings as well as their freedom to develop individual talents. One may also argue that the equalization that courtly and Romantic love provided some women merely masked the extreme inequality to which the vast majority have been subjected throughout Western culture. Overall it may even be the case that sexual love has done more to undermine than to strengthen the cause of woman's liberation. Women have often identified with the aggressor and acquiesced in their social enslavement for reasons of love. Radical feminists are justifiably sensitive to these evils. But they ignore the possibility that a woman's love for a man can be a liberating experience, while a man's love for a woman may convince him that neither she nor any other member of her sex should be treated as an inferior creature.

Firestone insists that male dominance makes it virtually impossible for men to love women in the present. I am forced to use the word "virtually" by the vacillation in her language. In one place she asserts that "men can't love." But in the next sentence she modifies this by saying only that they "have difficulty loving." The second formulation seems reasonable, since love is difficult for everyone. But Firestone means something further, and more interesting, than that. She believes that the state of inequality between the sexes limits men to falling in love, when they love at all, and that what passes for love in their case usually comes down to idealization in the sense of overestimation. Men glorify specific women, she thinks, as a personal compensation for their propensity to subjugate and misuse all other women. Though the beloved may submit, even reciprocate, in order to benefit from the intimate association with a male, she eventually realizes the futility of hoping to satisfy through any such relationship her healthy need to love.

The suggestion that only women can truly love is defended by some feminists as an inference from the idea that all love repeats the mother's love for her children. Apart from the implausibility of this belief, which I discussed in the previous chapter, I see no reason to think that women are uniquely equipped to love another person or that men—even in our sexist society—experience nothing but falling in love. Women idealize men in every sense that men idealize women. Firestone finds profound differences between men and women in terms of their varying attitudes toward sex. She claims that men confuse love and sex in a way that leads them to believe that they love a woman when they merely desire her sexually. As a result, she says, men have no conception of what love, even nonsexual love, is really like.

In rejecting this partisan view, we need not deny that men and women differ considerably in their experience of love. Firestone mentions Beauvoir and Reik as authorities who hold that sexual love does not mean the same thing for men and women. If she had been writing more recently, she could also have cited comparable statements by scientific investigators such as Trivers, Donald Symons, and Carol Gilligan. Since the sexes differ so greatly in their hormonal chemistry as well as in their prevalent social conditioning, it would be surprising if they had an identical phenomenology of either love or sex. This much need not be questioned.

In recent years women have begun to examine their femininity in studies that were hardly possible when science and philosophy were disciplines to which only men had access. These new and extremely promising contributions will not be furthered, however, by ideological assumptions that only women are able to love properly. Though it is true that men often think they love when they only lust, a comparable confusion occurs among women. Particularly when they were reared to believe that it was indecent or immoral to be sexually demanding, women frequently fell in love under the compulsion of libidinal urges. To this extent, their situation was parallel to the one that Firestone ascribes to men.

The fact that men have wanted to rule society, and that women have acquiesced in this, has certainly added to the differences in their attitudes. Without being inherently better or worse in their capacity for love, men in the Western world have often been encouraged to hide their inclinations toward tenderness or emotionality. But they have also found occasions for expressing them—if not with their wives, at least with their mistresses or, more chastely, with their daughters. Though men may dominate women as a whole while singling out an exceptional female who can even become a goddess to them, they also experience the joy of bestowing value gratuitously. That is a human faculty which is not limited to either sex.

In their special tie to the child that once was a part of themselves, mothers make a unique bestowal. They enjoy a kind of love that men cannot duplicate, even when they approximate it as loving fathers or mother surrogates. But mother's love is not the paradigm of sexual love. A man's relationship with a woman may reflect the love he did or did not receive from his mother, just as a woman's relationship with a man may indicate her feelings about her own mother's love (as well as her father's). Everything in this situation points to the likelihood that sexual love is significantly different for men and women. And yet we cannot conclude that either variety is healthier, more authentic, or more likely to succeed. Darwin once suggested that women are capable of a *greater* tenderness than men. In view of the role that nurturance plays in female biology, he may well have been right. But love is more than just a feeling, and a great quantity of tenderness is not essential for every kind of love. Even if men are biologically at a disadvantage in this respect, they surmount their deficiency through the imaginative bestowal of value. Nature has given them a different access to love, not necessarily an inferior one.

❋

The oldest reductivism is the one that couches its approach to love in the language of objectivistic ontology. In recent years the most intriguing effort of this kind appears in the writings of Paul Tillich. He insists that the concept of love can be explained only by analysis of its "ontological roots." Ontology itself he defines in terms of questions such as these: "What does it mean *to be*? What are the structures, common to everything that is, to everything that participates in being?" He considers it undeniable that being is a unity, that it is one and therefore that it must have a structure or texture of its own underlying the diversity of everything that exists and has some particularized being. In formulating an ontology of love, Tillich argues that only in its fundamental relation to being can love be understood. The kernel of his theory occurs in the following passage:

> Life is being in actuality and love is the moving power of life. In these two sentences the ontological nature of love is expressed. They say that being is not actual without the love which drives everything that is towards everything else that is. In man's experience of love the nature of life becomes manifest. Love is the drive towards the unity of the separated. Reunion presupposes separation of that which belongs essentially together. It would, however, be wrong to give to separation the same ontological ultimacy as to reunion. For separation presupposes an original unity. Unity embraces itself and separation, just as being comprises itself and non-being. It is impossible to unite that which is *essentially* separated.

Much of this is trivially true. But the implications of what Tillich intends are not trivial and they may not be true. To say that life is being in actuality can mean only that living things exist. To say that love is the moving power of life must mean that love motivates everything that lives. The first of these statements is not worth contesting. The problematic character of the second one becomes evident when the moving power of love is analyzed into the elements of original unity, separation, and ultimate reunion. This ontological analysis was originally given by Hegel in the fragment on love that I discussed in the second volume. Tillich develops Hegel's intimations, extending them in new directions and showing how this kind of ontology can answer basic questions in theology as well as philosophy.

Before considering these further issues, however, we must continue to raise doubts about the ontological approach itself. There is no love without a search for unity. In the unity which is accomplished love the elements that were previously separated lose their independent condition inasmuch as they have become united. But none of this implies that these unified elements belong, essentially and by their nature, to a unity that logically precedes them. Tillich makes this incredible assumption because he wishes to distinguish between how things exist and how they must be essentially. He sees mere existence, at least in human life, as an estrangement from its essential being. And since "estrangement presupposes original oneness," the unity of love must always be a reunion. But what justification can there be for asserting a fundamental alienation between essence and existence? Though these are not the same, there is nothing in either that can lead one to conclude that existence implies estrangement from essence. On the contrary, the being of anything reveals itself in how it actually exists. If we choose to say that ultimate being is the totality of everything, we shall have to make sense of that statement by offering indications of how it all makes a unity. And even if we can do so, how could we justify the belief that this unity is the oneness of love? That is what Tillich maintains. He thinks that love belongs to the ontological structure of being itself. As far as I can see, his dogma is fanciful wish-fulfillment. It lacks logical coherence as well as empirical confirmation.

As another way of formulating this criticism, we can examine Tillich's doctrine through his ideas about nonbeing. He says that "non-being is the negation of being within being itself." He realizes that his language is metaphorical, but he finds it useful for expressing his intuition that finitude entails nonbeing and yet also derives from a more ultimate being which precedes nonbeing. He asserts that in all things there must be a "prevalence" of being over nonbeing. Since being is presumably infinite, he claims that everything finite shows forth the presence of the infinite. When Tillich asks himself for the grounds of his belief, however, he unequivocally ascribes them to what he calls an act of "courage, and that in faith which is courage."

This admission on Tillich's part seems to me ruinous: it undermines the objectivism built into his ontology of love. For courage is not a necessary condition for being. It comes *into* being only as man —which is to say particular individuals such as Tillich himself—

makes the relevant affirmation. To say that being has precedence over nonbeing is to bestow exceptional importance on the former in a way that is not objectively required. It amounts to what I have been calling an idealization, a focusing of one's attention, the expression of a personal preference. It is therefore explicable only as one among other types of love.

Since Tillich directs his ontology toward problems that are theological as well as philosophical, his approach has immediate consequences for the branch of Christianity that he wishes to defend. Lutheranism has traditionally maintained that human nature as it exists in the world is inevitably estranged from its own essential being, which derives from the infinite God with whom it seeks to reunite. Though Protestant and Catholic denominations differ in their emphasis upon one or another aspect of the doctrine, they all agree substantially with this much of Tillich's ontology. My criticisms are not addressed to the contents of such beliefs. As non-verifiable idealizations, they express religious feelings and attitudes that can neither be proved nor disproved. They give no justification for an ontology of love rooted in the structure of being itself. If they are defensible, it is only as creative devices for the imagination of people who wish to bestow value in the manner of Christian idealization.

Tillich's ontology of love differs from earlier theology in his constant attempt to incorporate the ideas of non-Christian thinkers such as Spinoza and Nietzsche. He accepts their identification of being with the "dynamic self-affirmation of life." What Nietzsche means by the will to power, Tillich says, must be interpreted as ultimate being dialectically separating itself from itself and then returning to itself in the reunion which is love. This surely goes beyond Nietzsche, but I do not think it distorts his message. On the contrary, it helps us to understand his concept of amor fati. For if the self-affirmation of the will to power includes this dialectic of love, one can see how acceptance of all reality could lead to a love for it regardless of how horrible that reality might be. This way of reading Nietzsche reinforces one's inclination to see him as a follower of Hegel. In effect, Tillich synthesizes Nietzsche's thinking with contemporary versions of radical Protestantism that are ultimately based on Hegel's philosophy.

Nietzsche's influence on Tillich also appears in Tillich's rejection of Christian ideas about love being sacrificial. As a self-affirmation seeking reunion with the power of being, love cannot be self-destructive. Tillich takes this to mean not only that man uses love to overcome nonbeing, but also that the more of nonbeing he experiences in himself the more of being he will attain. "The more conquered separation there is the more power there is. The process in which the separated is reunited is love. The more reuniting love there is, the more conquered non-being there is, the more power of being there is."

Tillich links these ideas to Luther's conception of sinful man seeking redemption, but they also reflect Nietzsche's attack on that much of Christianity which idealizes weakness and self-rejection. At the same time Tillich differs from Nietzsche. In his insistence upon nonbeing as itself an element in the process of love striving for reunion, he evinces a kind of compassion that one rarely finds in Nietzsche. Tillich wishes to overcome negation or despair but he empathizes with those who feel it. His thinking may be finally unacceptable, as I think it is, but in part at least it exhorts us to compassionate love of a sort that Shakespeare articulates in *Measure for Measure*. Pleading for mercy toward the man who has wronged her, Mariana remarks: "They say, best men are moulded out of faults;/And, for the most, become much more the better/For being a little bad."

Shakespeare speaks as a moralist. He is not doing ontology, and he limits his reformatory faith to men who are only "a little bad." Tillich's view is more extreme. For him, as for Luther, mankind must be considered depraved in its earthly existence. That is what causes the estrangement which makes love both possible and necessary. Similarly, Tillich denies that love can be understood as just an ethical or an emotional phenomenon. Love is not merely ethical, he states, since it cannot be commanded. And neither will he treat it as simply an emotion or psychological attitude. For love requires more than just a phenomenological explanation. He thinks that only his kind of ontology can provide an adequate analysis.

As a final attempt to show that Tillich is mistaken in his approach, I need only consider his concept of "self-acceptance." Discussing what might constitute a nonselfish love of self, Tillich speaks of self-acceptance as "the affirmation of oneself in the way in which one is affirmed by God." The God referred to is not, however, the God of theism. Tillich holds that absolute faith transcends the theistic God, who must be deemed a being among others and therefore not being-itself. As against Eastern religions or Western mysticism that interpret union with divinity as a merging that dissolves the human spirit, Tillich retains theism's orthodox insistence upon a person-to-person encounter with a God whose being must always remain independent. But in transcending theism, Tillich identifies this deity as the "God above God" that he has been describing as being-itself. The ultimate actualization of love is therefore a participation in absolute being which leaves the individual intact and unsubmerged. In this kind of union, Tillich states, the self "receives itself back." It undergoes a strengthening rather than a loss of its "courage to be," which Tillich defines as "the courage to accept oneself as accepted in spite of being unacceptable."

I find this statement utterly incomprehensible. I can understand why Tillich thinks all mankind is unacceptable. That is merely a restatement of his notion about the estrangement which belongs to finite being. For traditional Christian reasons Tillich could also have maintained that unacceptable humanity is redeemed through the love of God, and in one place he does say: "In the loving person-to-person relationship Christianity manifests its superiority to any other religious tradition." But if self-acceptance and the courage to be transcend theistic religion, as Tillich maintains, the God above God is not a person. He (it?) can neither accept or reject, affirm or refuse to affirm. Being can only be. As the Clown in *Twelfth Night* says: "That that is, is." For the purposes of ontological discourse, being-itself may be considered the "ground" or "root" of all particular beings, and possibly we can make sense of such philosophical metaphors. But they give no sanction for personifying a category of analysis which has been defined as transcending personality. We may accept ourselves if we feel that we are fulfilling our nature or remaining in touch with our own reality, but this is always a feeling on *our* part. It belongs to our being as persons. Since being-itself is not a person, it can never be imagined as that which does the accepting, as that which has accepted us or could accept anything under any circumstances. One might argue that our being derives from being-itself. But even so, we are not *affirmed* by it in any sense analogous to an affirmation of oneself.

To the extent that my criticism is valid, we give up the need to formulate anything like Tillich's ontology of love. Under optimal conditions men and women may possibly reach a peak in their affective achievement—a summit of serenity or of consummatory splendor—that registers as a feeling of love toward everything. In their wonder and gratitude for this experience, they may also feel that they have been favored by being-itself. Certainly they are being sustained by cosmic forces beyond themselves, as we all are at every moment in our existence. But though their love depends on and profits from the world at large, it must always be produced by their own powers of bestowal. Love is a creation that human beings make, even when they project it upon being-itself.

The reductivism which motivates a desire for objectivistic ontology also occurs in the assumption that one or another love-object can be fundamental for love in general. Whether that object was the Platonic Good or the Judaeo-Christian God or the post-Freudian Mother, it was considered the magnet that drew all love to itself. It was idealized as the ultimate, though sometimes unknown, goal of the human search for love. Despite complications in Plato's own philosophy, the supreme love-object was also thought to originate love from within itself and thus to serve as the source of every other love. In various ways throughout this trilogy I have been arguing against these massive presuppositions. I am now in position to propose a pluralistic alternative.

Once we focus upon the diversified character of the objects that human beings love, we see how variegated are the different relationships. With no pretensions about completeness or absolute rigor in my enumeration, I need only list the following as characteristically distinct kinds of love: love of self, of mankind, of nature, of God, of mother or father, of children, of tribe or nation, of sweetheart or spouse or sexual idol, of material possessions, of food or drink, of action and repose, of sports, of hobbies or engrossing pursuits, of justice, of science, of truth, of beauty, and so on endlessly. Each variety of love, involving its special object, has its own phenomenology, its own iridescence within the spectrum that delimits human experience.

To be studied adequately, every type requires a separate analysis. From one to the other, their ingredients will often have little or nothing in common. Even in the comparison between love of mother and love of sweetheart or spouse, where the overlap may be quite significant, the essential differences must never be ignored. As I have suggested in this and the previous chapter, there is much that can be said for the idea that a man's love for a woman may be causally related to aspects of his previous love for his mother. But since the progression from love of mother to love of wife passes through stages of development that involve separation as well as infantile security, autonomy as well as regression, the later love can never be wholly explained in terms of the earlier. Neither can be reduced to the other, though both may best be understood within a vision of human reality that recognizes their dynamic interconnection.

Something similar must be said about all the other objects of love that I have listed. They can be ordered in alternate ways that reveal some relation between one or another of them. To express a chosen perspective of our own, we can arrange them in whatever pattern is meaningful to us. But there is no reason to treat any of them as metaphysically ultimate in the traditional sense. To think that all loves can be reduced to a single type restricts our comprehension instead of expanding it.

However we choose to analyze the many loves, we have to realize that the first one on my list is different from all the rest. The love of self has been so challenging to philosophers because it includes ambiguities of a peculiar sort. Ordinarily we do not love ourselves in exactly the same sense in which we love others. This does happen in those rare pathologies where a psyche dotes upon itself as if it incorporated two different persons. That was the original psychiatric use of the word "narcissism." It hews closely to the myth of Narcissus, who treated his own image as if it were another self. In states of extreme vanity something comparable, though greatly diminished, may occur. When Freud appropriated the term "narcissism," he applied it to a much more common phenomenon— the love of oneself not as a separate person but as the one who does the loving. Whether or not Freud was correct in thinking that loving others is just a circuitous way of loving oneself, he rightly perceived that normally one does not love oneself in the same sense that one loves other people.

On the other hand, bestowal and appraisal function in the love of self much as they do in the love of others. Though fully aware that our love is reflexive, we often bestow value upon ourselves; and to some extent this is similar to bestowing value upon another person. We also appraise ourselves. That too is not very different from appraising someone else. And if we are capable of love, will we not tolerate our own inadequacies as we do with others whom we love?

If this were all we meant by love of self, however, it would amount to little more than egoism. Instead of bestowing value upon other people, we would merely bestow it upon ourselves. Freud's economic theory, with its suggestion that the more love we expend outside the less remains to be directed inward, is probably based on the assumption that love is just a matter of rerouting the same bestowal. What Freud neglects is the sense in which love of self involves something more, namely *self-assurance* or *self-confidence*. When that exists, we overcome doubts or anxieties that might have hampered us. We allow ourselves to enjoy whatever we are doing. We scorn the ever-present possibility of failure and orient our being toward victory and success. Unless we love ourselves in *this* sense, bestow value upon our existence in this buoyant manner, we will scarcely have the heart to love ourselves in any other way. In our insecure condition we may selfishly seek to possess goods that ordinarily buttress our self-esteem. But that tactic does not work. Mere possessiveness will not create the love of self, and it reveals why love of self cannot be reduced to selfishness. Rousseau recognized as much when he distinguished amour de soi from amour-propre. Amour de soi, love of self, expresses confidence and assurance that makes selfishness unnecessary. Amour-propre is the selfishness of one who does not really love himself. It is a compensation for the self-assurance one does not have but desperately desires.

Self-confidence appears in one's behavior as secure and radiant self-affirmation. When Aristotle praised the "magnanimous man," he had in mind one who loved himself in this fashion. The magnanimous man is not necessarily a person who gives all his money to the poor, but in everything he does he evinces a generosity of spirit. When Spinoza said that all creatures seek to continue in their being and Nietzsche claimed that the will to power is ultimate in reality, they were treating self-affirmation as a universal principle. Their conception is poetic in the manner of metaphysics, and it makes us wonder whether anyone can live *without* self-love. Nevertheless it does account for the resentment of those whose lack of confidence has prevented them from fulfilling their nature as they would have liked.

By interpreting love of self as self-affirmation, we also see the wisdom in the psychiatric (and Hasidic) insistence that no one can love another unless he loves himself. Indeed, can one have love of any sort without a fundamental love of self? I think not. If only because the bestowing of value is a gratuitous act involving self-affirmation without which there could be no imaginative creativity, self-love would seem to be a necessary condition for every other love. Even when love becomes a form of submissiveness, the element of bestowal indicates that some degree of self-love is also present.

The different kinds of love, doubtless more numerous than my haphazard list may have suggested, are not generally reducible to one another even if analysis can reveal that they are interwoven in multifarious designs. Since I am not here giving the requisite analyses, I offer this generalization only as a working hypothesis. Even so, I may be able to show how my pluralistic approach supports what I suggested in the first volume when I distinguished between love of ideals, love of things, and love of persons.

These three categories cut across all particular kinds of love. Any love-object may fall within one or another of the rubrics, and some involve all three at once. When the nineteenth-century Romantics devoted themselves to a love of nature, they seemed to yearn for it as simultaneously a material object, an ideal goal, and a supervening mystical personification. For them nature was a field of force, the outcome of laws that scientists could investigate, but also it was a perfect oneness to which human beings belonged and with which they might commune—as if with another person—through feeling as well as reason. This aspect of Romantic love is evident in the nature poetry, landscape painting, and descriptive music of the period. Nature was portrayed as a physical reality that one might relish through the senses much as one could enjoy the pleasures of eating, drinking, and sexual activity. Yet nature as a thing to be loved coalesced with nature as the source of aesthetic completeness which disclosed an ideal purpose in the universe. Moreover, there was a personal bond between man and nature. In providing a permanent haven to his being, nature might allow man to stray from the home within her bosom but she faithfully remained as a parent who would always welcome his return. In loving nature, man was loving something like an infinite and eternal consciousness whose spiritual aspirations were not entirely different from his own.

I have chosen the Romantic love of nature as my example because romanticism represents man's greatest idealization, thus far, of love directed toward nature conceived as thing, ideal, and person coextensively. The traditional idea of a love of God lends itself to a similar analysis except for the fact that so much in this symbolism is nonempirical. God is defined as being outside of time and space. He is not a thing or material object, but he is the ultimate power, the ruling force in everything. He is not an ideal like goodness or beauty but he is the goal of man's desiring, and all ideals—including the ideal of love itself—belong to his essence. He is not a person like any seen on earth, but he has a personal relationship with human beings and serves as the epitome of spirituality in them. The varieties of religious faith illustrate the different ways in which God is thought to be lovable under the categories of person, ideal, and thing.

The difficulties in religious love dominated my discussion in the first volume. The problems inherent in a Romantic or quasi-Romantic love of nature were studied in the second volume and the beginnings of this one. A fuller analysis of sexual love, and all the

435

other loves, would reveal comparable dangers in any attempt to combine the love of person, thing, and ideal. Nevertheless, these hazards can be overcome. At its best, when it succeeds, sexual love harmonizes all three modes of loving someone else. The object of our possessive drive is then a man or woman who not only stimulates in us the pursuit of moral and aesthetic ideals but also appears as their living embodiment.

Platonistic philosophies misunderstand the nature of this incarnation. They think the beloved can only symbolize or represent ideals, and so they fail to see how sexual love may also be a love of persons that involves an acceptance of the other as he is, as he happens to be in the imperfect reality of ordinary existence. It is one of the facts of life, at least as human beings experience it, that we love people who seem beautiful or otherwise worthy of esteem. If we love them as persons, however, we love them as more than just the manifestations of beauty or goodness. We love them for themselves, which includes their beauty and their goodness. Loving people as persons is wholly compatible with loving them as things. Rather than destroying our capacity for a love of persons, as Kant thought, sexual instinct gives it a material base, a secure and suitable habitat within physical nature. When love is a mutuality of reciprocating interests, it enables men and women to respond to one another with a combined love of person, ideal, and thing. Such love prefigures human society at its most humane and life-enhancing.

I do not wish to speculate about the ramifications of a perfect community of love. Mankind has suffered greatly from philosophical dreams of utopia. The awakening has always been rude, and the consequences often catastrophic. No one kind of love will satisfy all our needs on all occasions. We require friends as well as lovers in the sexual sense. Where our lovers are also our friends, we may want to rank that above all other friendships. For the oneness we have then established will be able to satisfy a larger network of emotional and intellectual needs. Where ordinary friends enjoy each other's company and care about one another's welfare, those who unite sexual love and friendship create a bond that can support them in additional areas of life. But even this consummation, devoutly to be wished, must not be treated as an absolute. There will always be those who find a higher good in the love of mankind or in some purely spiritual love, define it as they may in accordance with their local faith.

No one can decide for anyone else. In each case, both advocate and critic will express their own particular hopes for love. These differ authentically from person to person. But they are not all equally valid. Religious belief has frequently been predicated upon gross illusion, just as scientific dogmas have often concealed underlying ignorance and moral dedication has legitimized insidious bigotry. In a pluralistic universe there are no easy answers.

Conclusion
The Search
For Harmonization

I~N The Preceding Chapter~ I
analyzed the concept of sexual love, suggested a distinction between falling in love, being in love, and staying in love, and then
sketched developments in my thinking about appraisal and bestowal, merging, and the various objects of love. Previous chapters
discussed twentieth-century ideas about love in the context of the
earlier volumes in my trilogy. Now we need only see how the systematic and historical approaches fit together.

If we limit ourselves to bestowal, the great event in the history of
thinking about love is the conceptualization of agapē. That idea
arises in the Old Testament, flourishes in the New Testament,
makes an accommodation with Greek philosophy in the caritas-
synthesis of the Middle Ages, renews its theological purity in
Luther's theology, and becomes a dominating element in much of
courtly, Romantic, and post-Romantic theory. But whether we accept the concept of agapē as it was intended by the religious tradition or subject it to the reinterpretation of a contemporary such as
myself, its emphasis upon mere bestowal might encourage us to
assume that true love must be gratuitous in the manner of falling in
love. God descends, mysteriously and for no reason that human
beings can fathom; self-sacrifice, the giving or even loss of oneself,
is idealized as it occurs in divinity as well as in man; people who love
one another are seen as helpless vehicles of a compelling energy
that uses them for ends beyond their own petty interests. Love is

438

envisaged as something that *befalls* both lover and beloved. They do not choose their destiny. It chooses them.

As I have described it, falling in love involves more than this alone since it often includes attitudes—such as the search for an ego ideal—that manifest what Plato calls eros. If I am right in thinking that the concept of eros is an idealization of appraisal, falling in love would have to be explained as both appraisal and bestowal. Nevertheless, that kind of love does not usually give both components the same importance: the very idea of falling bespeaks submission or self-abnegation that is more likely to result from bestowal than from appraisal. By reaffirming the role of appraisiveness, our theory avoids the limitations of a falling in love that manifests uncontrolled bestowals. We perceive that love is a choice of one's being by means of judgments and decisions that influence emotional response. It is self-correcting through appraisal as well as creative through bestowal. When directed toward another person, it can lead to a sharing of selves for which both parties are responsible. Even falling in love is not wholly unwilled. It is more than just a chance event that happens to some lucky (or unlucky) individual.

I offer this brief analysis as a tool for understanding the history of ideas about love as well as the nature of love itself. It may also help to harmonize realist and idealist attitudes. Though theorists in the Western world generally formulated their distinctions somewhat differently, we would be proceeding on a bias if we assumed that concepts of courtly love, Romantic love, or the realist attacks on them were only concerned about falling in love. Philosophy of love in the West often tried to integrate the three types of love within a unified perspective. Because of their orientation toward natural and mutual benefits, concepts of courtly and Romantic love continually sought for an accommodation with married love. The bond that I call staying in love endures by combining values of friendship and emotional intimacy that were idealized in courtly and Romantic love. Under favorable circumstances, staying in love becomes increasingly more secure and more gratifying, even when sexual intensity declines. Much of courtly and Romantic love cannot encompass this, but they elucidate stages of a trajectory that culminates in progressive oneness between husband and wife.

What I refer to as being in love is itself a kind of harmonization between falling in love and staying in love, between feverish yearning and more or less permanent union. Being in love depends on the successful cooperation of bestowal and appraisal, both serving as reinforcing partners. It is a goal that idealist and realist philosophies have accepted, though not uniformly, as foundational to human happiness.

But then, one might ask, does this mean that being in love is the *basic* concept of love in the Western world? Reading the history of love as a long and unfinished search for harmonizations of the sort I have mentioned, am I not assuming that being in love—which unites appraisal and bestowal and mediates between falling in love and staying in love—points us toward the ideal goal for which our civilization (and possibly all of mankind) has been seeking? And if we accept my analysis of sexual love as a combination of benevolent concern, libidinal impulse, and amorous emotion, will we not conclude that being in love satisfies these conditions more completely than either staying in love or falling in love? For staying in love may be accompanied by diminished sexuality, and falling in love may include only a modicum of benevolence.

Some people will indeed find it plausible to define sexual love as a striving toward being in love. They may even wish to reduce religious love, and in general most other varieties of love, to some aspect of being in love. But this solution goes against my pluralistic grain. I feel that it narrows historical reality in an indefensible manner and overly simplifies the diversity of experience. No reductivism, however gentle, can do justice to the disparate, pliant, and normally confused character of human affect—both as it occurs in practice and as philosophers have theorized about it. In trying to carry out the rigorous and detailed analyses that are required, let us never lose sight of this eternal, though possibly obvious, truth.

Bertrand Russell said: "The good life is one inspired by love and guided by knowledge." What the world needs now is not only love but also greater knowledge about the nature of love, in all its complexity.

Notes

p. 5   *l.26*   On this, see J. Richard Udry, *The Social Context of Marriage*, 3d ed. (Philadelphia: J. B. Lippincott, 1974), pp. 131–51; Hugo G. Beigel, "Romantic Love," in *The Practice of Love*, ed. Ashley Montagu (Englewood Cliffs: Prentice-Hall, 1975), pp. 136–49; William J. Goode, *The Family* (Englewood Cliffs: Prentice-Hall, 1964); and Robert F. Winch, *The Modern Family*, rev. ed. (New York: Holt, Rinehart and Winston, 1963).

p. 5   *l.29*   Robert Brain, *Friends and Lovers* (New York: Basic Books, 1976), p. 247. For a more balanced view, cf. Stanton Peele with Archie Brodsky, *Love and Addiction* (London: Abacus, 1977), particularly pp. 241–68.

p. 6   *l.13*   Bertrand Russell, *Marriage and Morals* (New York: Horace Liveright, 1929), p. 74.

p. 7   *l.4*   See "The Concept of Romantic Love" and "Benign Romanticism: Kant, Schlegel, Hegel, Shelley, Byron," in *The Nature of Love: Courtly and Romantic*, pp. 283–302 and 376–431.

p. 14   *l.29*   On this, see my book *Mozart and Beethoven: The Concept of Love in Their Operas* (Baltimore: The Johns Hopkins University Press, 1977), pp. 118–52.

p. 17   *l.17*   *The Republic of Plato*, trans. Francis Macdonald Cornford (New York: Oxford University Press, 1941), p. 208.

p. 32   *l.27*   Sigmund Freud, *On Creativity and the Unconscious* (New York: Harper Torchbooks, 1958), p. 177. For a variant translation, see note for p. 123 *l.4* below.

p. 35   *l.3*   On this, see two essays of mine on the Don Juan myth: "The Shadow of Dom Juan in Molière," in *MLN* 85 (December 1970): 838–57; "Molière's Dom Juan," *The Hudson Review* 24 (Autumn 1971): 447–60. See also my book *Mozart and Beethoven: The Concept of Love in Their Operas*, pp. 24–73 and passim.

p. 40   *l.10*   Søren Kierkegaard, *Either/Or*, trans. Walter Lowrie, rev. and augmented Howard A. Johnson, vol. 2 (Garden City: Anchor Books, 1959), p. 249.

p. 44 *l.28 Tagebüche,* 1:195. For a slightly different translation, see *The Journals of Kierkegaard,* trans. and sel. Alexander Dru (New York: Harper Torchbooks, 1959), p. 86.

p. 45 *l.13* Søren Kierkegaard, *Concluding Unscientific Postscript,* trans. David F. Swenson, completed and ed. Walter Lowrie (Princeton: Princeton University Press, 1944), p. 261.

p. 47 *l.4* Søren Kierkegaard, *Works of Love,* trans. David F. Swenson and Lillian Marvin Swenson (London: Oxford University Press, 1946), p. 114.

p. 48 *l.15* "Diary of the Seducer," in *Either/Or,* 1:437.

p. 48 *l.16* "The Other Dancing Song," in *Thus Spake Zarathustra,* pt. 3. My translation.

p. 48 *l.18 Either/Or,* 1:364.

p. 48 *l.25* Ibid., pp. 372–73.

p. 48 *l.37* Ibid., p. 356.

p. 50 *l.6* Leo Tolstoy, *Recollections & Essays,* trans. Aylmer Maude (London: Oxford University Press, 1937), pp. 3–4.

p. 50 *l.30* Karl Stern, *The Flight from Woman* (New York: Farrar, Straus and Giroux, 1965), p. 181.

p. 53 *l.13* Quoted in Ruth Crego Benson, *Women in Tolstoy: The Ideal and the Erotic* (Urbana: University of Illinois Press, 1973), p. 26.

p. 54 *l.8* Leo Tolstoy, *War and Peace,* trans. Louise and Aylmer Maude (New York: W. W. Norton, 1966), pp. 1282–83.

p. 55 *l.6* Leo Tolstoy, "Epilogue to *The Kreutzer Sonata,*" in *Death of Ivan Ilich, Dramatic Works, The Kreutzer Sonata, by Count Lev N. Tolstoy,* trans. Leo Wiener (New York: AMS Press, 1968), p. 423. For a more recent translation, see "Postface to *The Kreutzer Sonata,*" in Leo Tolstoy, *The Kreutzer Sonata and Other Stories,* trans. David McDuff (New York: Penguin Books, 1985), pp. 267–82.

p. 56 *l.2* See *The Nature of Love: Courtly and Romantic,* p. 313.

p. 57 *l.3* Leo Tolstoy, *What Is Art? and Essays on Art,* trans. Aylmer Maude (London: Oxford University Press, 1930), p. 240.

p. 57 *l.24* See Leo Tolstoy, *Confession,* trans. David Patterson (New York: W. W. Norton, 1983).

p. 57 *l.29* See Paul Boyer, *Chez Tolstoï: Entretiens à Iasnaïa Poliana* (Paris: Institut d'Etudes Slaves de l'Université de Paris, 1950), pp. 40, 77–78.

p. 57 *l.32* See *The Nature of Love: Courtly and Romantic,* pp. 333–34.

p. 58 *l.3* Renato Poggioli, "A Portrait of Tolstoy as Alceste," in *The Phoenix and the Spider: A Book of Essays about Some Russian Writers and Their View of the Self* (Cambridge: Harvard University Press, 1957), p. 97.

p. 58 *l.9* See Isaiah Berlin, *Russian Thinkers* (New York: Viking, 1978), p. 56; see also Boyer, *Chez Tolstoï,* p. 40.

p. 58 *l.25* "On the Relation Between the Sexes," in *Death of Ivan Ilich, Dramatic Works, The Kreutzer Sonata,* p. 453.

p. 59 *l.24* Leo Tolstoy, *Anna Karenina,* trans. L. and A. Maude (New York: W. W. Norton, 1970), p. 136.

p. 60 *l.9* Thomas Mann, "Goethe and Tolstoy," in *Essays by Thomas Mann*, trans. H. T. Lowe-Porter (New York: Vintage Books, 1957), p. 122.

p. 61 *l.4* Quoted in Poggioli, *The Phoenix and the Spider*, p. 101.

p. 62 *l.6* *What Is Art? and Essays on Art*, p. 100.

p. 62 *l.15* Quoted in Henri Troyat, *Tolstoy*, trans. Nancy Amphoux (New York: Dell, 1967), p. 497.

p. 63 *l.9* "On the Relation Between the Sexes," in *The Death of Ivan Ilich, Dramatic Works, The Kreutzer Sonata*, p. 473.

p. 63 *l.33* *Essays by Thomas Mann*, p. 155.

p. 63 *l.37* For references to Schopenhauer, see *Confession*, p. 43ff.

p. 64 *l.18* Leo Tolstoy, *The Kreutzer Sonata*, trans. Aylmer Maude, in *The Death of Ivan Ilych and Other Stories* (New York: New American Library, 1960), p. 178.

p. 65 *l.5* Quoted in Troyat, *Tolstoy*, p. 477.

p. 65 *l.14* On this, see Karl Löwith, *From Hegel to Nietzsche: The Revolution in Nineteenth-Century Thought*, trans. David E. Green (New York: Holt Rinehart and Winston, 1964), p. 367.

p. 67 *l.24* Richard Wagner, *My Life*, vol. 1 (New York: Dodd, Mead, 1911), p. 522.

p. 68 *l.6* Ludwig Feuerbach, *The Essence of Christianity*, ed. and abridged E. Graham Waring and F. W. Strothmann (New York: Frederick Ungar, 1957), p. 63.

p. 68 *l.31* Quoted in Erich Fromm, "Foreword," in Karl Marx, *Early Writings*, trans. and ed. T. B. Bottomore (New York: McGraw-Hill, 1964), p. vi.

p. 68 *l.36* *The Essential Marx*, trans. Anna Bostock, ed. Ernst Fischer in collaboration with Franz Marek (New York: Herder and Herder, 1970), p. 26. See also Frederick Engels, *Ludwig Feuerbach and the Outcome of Classical German Philosophy* (New York: International Publishers, 1941), pp. 33–36, 95.

p. 69 *l.7* Frederick Engels, *The Origin of the Family, Private Property and the State* (New York: International Publishers, 1942), pp. 40–74.

p. 71 *l.5* Friedrich Nietzsche, *The Will to Power*, trans. Walter Kaufmann and R. J. Hollingdale, ed. Walter Kaufmann (New York: Vintage Books, 1968), pp. 505–6.

p. 72 *l.17* See, for instance, Walter Kaufmann, *Hegel: Reinterpretation, Texts, and Commentary* (Garden City: Doubleday, 1965), pp. 258–59.

p. 73 *l.32* See *The Nature of Love: Courtly and Romantic*, p. 475ff.

p. 74 *l.19* Friedrich Nietzsche, *Beyond Good and Evil: Prelude to a Philosophy of the Future*, trans. Walter Kaufmann (New York: Vintage Books, 1966), p. 230.

p. 74 *l.23* Ibid., p. 205.

p. 76 *l.23* See Karl Jaspers, *Nietzsche: An Introduction to the Understanding of His Philosophical Activity*, trans. Charles F. Wallraff and Frederick J. Schmitz (Tucson: The University of Arizona Press, 1965), pp. 80–87.

p. 77 *l.13* Friedrich Nietzsche, *On the Genealogy of Morals*, in *On the Gene-*

alogy of Morals and Ecce Homo, trans. Walter Kaufmann and R. J. Hollingdale (New York: Vintage Books, 1967), p. 106.

p. 77   *l.23*   Ibid., p. 102.

p. 77   *l.32*   Ibid., p. 108.

p. 79   *l.23*   Friedrich Nietzsche, *Ecce Homo,* in *On the Genealogy of Morals and Ecce Homo,* p. 258.

p. 83   *l.14*   Friedrich Nietzsche, *The Gay Science,* trans. Walter Kaufmann (New York: Vintage Books, 1974), p. 274.

p. 83   *l.31*   On this, see Lawrence J. Hatab, *Nietzsche and Eternal Recurrence: The Redemption of Time and Becoming* (Washington: University Press of America, 1978), pp. 93–116; Martin Heidegger, *Nietzsche,* vol. 2: *The Eternal Recurrence of the Same,* trans. David Farrell Krell (San Francisco: Harper and Row, 1984); and Richard Schacht, *Nietzsche* (London: Routledge & Kegan Paul, 1983), pp. 253–66.

p. 84   *l.18*   *The Twilight of the Idols,* in *A Nietzsche Reader,* trans. R. J. Hollingdale (Harmondsworth: Penguin, 1977), p. 163.

p. 84   *l.26*   Ibid., p. 164.

p. 85   *l.16*   Friedrich Nietzsche, *The Case of Wagner,* in *The Birth of Tragedy and The Case of Wagner,* trans. Walter Kaufmann (New York: Vintage Books, 1967), pp. 158–59.

p. 85   *l.26*   Ibid., p. 59.

p. 85   *l.29*   *The Gay Science,* p. 89.

p. 86   *l.9*   Ibid., p. 319.

p. 86   *l.19*   Ibid.

p. 86   *l.37*   Ibid.

p. 87   *l.31*   *The Will to Power,* p. 387.

p. 88   *l.11*   Ibid., p. 388.

p. 88   *l.34*   Friedrich Nietzsche, *Thus Spoke Zarathustra,* trans. Walter Kaufmann (New York: Viking, 1966), p. 70.

p. 89   *l.12*   *The Gay Science,* p. 89.

p. 89   *l.22*   *The Will to Power,* p. 167.

p. 89   *l.24*   Ibid.

p. 89   *l.37*   *Thus Spoke Zarathustra,* p. 293.

p. 90   *l.12*   On this, see Walter Kaufmann, *Discovering the Mind: Freud versus Jung and Adler,* vol. 3 (New York: McGraw-Hill, 1980), pp. 100–103, 264–79. See also Bruce Mazlish, "Freud and Nietzsche," in *The Psychoanalytic Review* 55, no. 3 (1968): 360–75.

p. 90   *l.29*   *The Gay Science,* pp. 127–28.

p. 91   *l.5*   *The Will to Power,* p. 506.

p. 91   *l.16*   George Santayana, *The German Mind: A Philosophical Diagnosis* (New York: Thomas Y. Crowell, 1968), p. 135. Originally entitled *Egotism in German Philosophy.*

p. 91   *l.36*   Ibid., p. 119.

p. 92   *l.27*   Nietzsche, *On the Genealogy of Morals,* in *On the Genealogy of Morals and Ecce Homo,* p. 104. Italics deleted.

p. 92   *l.37*   Ibid., p. 105.

p. 93   *l.10*   *The Gay Science,* p. 262.

p. 93   *l.14*   *The Will to Power,* pp. 426–27.

p. 98 *l.3* On the question of translation, see Bruno Bettelheim, *Freud and Man's Soul* (New York: Knopf, 1983), p. 104ff. Bettelheim argues that Freud's term "Trieb" should always be translated as "drive" rather than "instinct."

p. 98 *l.7* Ernest Jones, M.D., *The Life and Work of Sigmund Freud* (New York: Basic Books, 1953–57), 2: 302–3; 3: 276–77.

p. 98 *l.26* Sigmund Freud, *Three Essays on the Theory of Sexuality*, trans. and rev. James Strachey (New York: Basic Books, 1962), p. xviii; in *The Standard Edition of the Complete Psychological Works of Sigmund Freud*, 7: 134. Freud's complete works are hereafter referred to as *SE*.

p. 99 *l.29* Sigmund Freud, *Group Psychology and the Analysis of the Ego*, trans. James Strachey (New York: Bantam Books, 1960), p. 30; in *SE*, 18:91.

p. 100 *l.22* Sigmund Freud, "The Most Prevalent Form of Degradation in Erotic Life," in *Collected Papers*, authorized trans. supervision Joan Riviere (New York: Basic Books, 1959), 4:204.

p. 100 *l.29* Ibid., p. 206.

p. 101 *l.22* Ibid., pp. 204–5.

p. 103 *l.6* Sigmund Freud, "The Libido Theory," in *Collected Papers*, ed. James Strachey (New York: Basic Books, 1959), 5:131.

p. 103 *l.8* *Group Psychology and the Analysis of the Ego*, p. 29; in *SE*, 18:90.

p. 103 *l.14* Sigmund Freud, *A General Introduction to Psychoanalysis*, trans. Joan Riviere (New York: Washington Square Press, 1960), p. 322.

p. 103 *l.17* *Three Essays on the Theory of Sexuality*, p. 83; in *SE*, 7:217.

p. 104 *l.22* Ibid., p. 42; in *SE*, 7:176.

p. 105 *l.23* *A General Introduction to Psychoanalysis*, p. 328.

p. 105 *l.33* *Group Psychology and the Analysis of the Ego*, p. 30; in *SE*, 18:91.

p. 106 *l.17* *A General Introduction to Psychoanalysis*, p. 332.

p. 108 *l.33* Ibid., pp. 332–33.

p. 110 *l.6* Ibid., p. 334.

p. 111 *l.31* Sigmund Freud, *Beyond the Pleasure Principle*, trans. James Strachey (New York: Bantam Books, 1959), p. 106n; in *SE*, 18:60n.

p. 111 *l.33* Ibid., p. 89; in *SE*, 18:50.

p. 112 *l.9* On this, see Philip Rieff, *Freud: The Mind of the Moralist* (Garden City: Anchor Books, 1961), p. 22.

p. 112 *l.13* *Beyond the Pleasure Principle*, p. 76; in *SE*, 18:41.

p. 112 *l.26* Rollo May, *Love and Will* (New York: W. W. Norton, 1969), p. 82.

p. 112 *l.31* Erich Fromm, *The Anatomy of Human Destructiveness* (Greenwich: Fawcett, 1973), p. 493.

p. 112 *l.35* Ibid., p. 496.

p. 113 *l.1* Ibid., p. 497.

p. 113 *l.7* Quoted in ibid., p. 503.

p. 113 *l.10* Ibid.

p. 113 *l.34* Quoted in Jones, *The Life and Work of Sigmund Freud*, 2:448.

p. 114 *l.9* *Group Psychology and the Analysis of the Ego*, pp. 41–42; in *SE*, 18:101.

p. 114   *l.33*   *Beyond the Pleasure Principle*, p. 88; in *SE*, 18:49–50.

p. 115   *l.14*   Sigmund Freud, "Instincts and Their Vicissitudes," in *SE*, 14:139.

p. 115   *l.29*   Ibid.For a discussion of this, see Douglas N. Morgan, *Love: Plato, The Bible, and Freud* (Englewood Cliffs: Prentice-Hall, 1964), pp. 143–45.

p. 116   *l.6*   *Beyond the Pleasure Principle*, p. 96; in *SE*, 18:37 (variant translation).

p. 116   *l.37*   Ibid., p. 24; in *SE*, 18:9.

p. 118   *l.3*   See Walter Kaufmann, *Discovering the Mind: Freud versus Adler and Jung*, pp. 264–78.

p. 118   *l.4*   Sigmund Freud, *Civilization and Its Discontents*, trans. James Strachey (New York: W. W. Norton, 1961), p. 69; in *SE*, 21:122.

p. 118   *l.8*   Sigmund Freud, "The Ego and the Id," in *A General Selection from the Works of Sigmund Freud*, ed. John Rickman, M.D. (Garden City: Anchor Books, 1957), p. 224; in *SE*, 19:41.

p. 118   *l.10*   Ibid.; ibid. in *SE* (variant translation).

p. 118   *l.30*   *Beyond the Pleasure Principle*, p. 108; in *SE*, 18:62.

p. 118   *l.34*   *Civilization and Its Discontents*, p. 66; in *SE*, 21:119.

p. 119   *l.8*   Jones, *The Life and Work of Sigmund Freud*, 2:320.

p. 119   *l.19*   *Beyond the Pleasure Principle*, p. 109; in *SE*, 18:63.

p. 119   *l.20*   "The Ego and the Id," in *SE*, 19:46.

p. 119   *l.22*   *Civilization and Its Discontents*, p. 66; in *SE*, 21:119.

p. 120   *l.14*   Fromm, *The Anatomy of Human Destructiveness*, p. 501n.

p. 120   *l.26*   *Civilization and Its Discontents*, p. 66; in *SE*, 21:119.

p. 121   *l.10*   George Santayana, "A Long Way Round to Nirvana; or Much Ado About Dying," in *Some Turns of Thought in Modern Philosophy: Five Essays* (New York: Charles Scribner's Sons, 1933).

p. 121   *l.20*   *Group Psychology and the Analysis of the Ego*, p. 41n; in *SE*, 18:101n.

p. 121   *l.27*   Ibid.; in *SE*, 18:101.

p. 122   *l.10*   *Civilization and Its Discontents*, p. 69; in *SE*, 21:122.

p. 122   *l.13*   Ibid.; ibid. in *SE*.

p. 123   *l.4*   This is the second of Freud's "Contributions to the Psychology of Love." As "The Most Prevalent Form of Degradation in Erotic Life" it appears in Sigmund Freud, *On Creativity and the Unconscious*, as well as in *Collected Papers*, vol. 4; as "On the Universal Tendency to Debasement in the Sphere of Love" it appears in *SE*, 11. In the latter, see p. 183.

p. 123   *l.16*   *Group Psychology and the Analysis of the Ego*, p. 55; in *SE*, 18:112.

p. 123   *l.24*   Theodor Reik, *A Psychologist Looks at Love*, in *Of Love and Lust* (New York: Farrar Straus and Cudahy, 1941), p. 16.

p. 123   *l.28*   Ibid., p. 19.

p. 123   *l.33*   Ibid., p. 20.

p. 124   *l.1*   Ibid., p. 22.

p. 124   *l.6*   Ibid.

p. 125   *l.12*   Ibid., p. 30.

p. 125   *l.20*   *Group Psychology and the Analysis of the Ego,* p. 54; in *SE,* 18:111.

p. 125   *l.26*   Ibid.; ibid. in *SE.*

p. 125   *l.31*   Ibid., p. 92; in *SE,* 18:139.

p. 126   *l.4*   Ibid., p. 30; in *SE,* 18:91 (variant translation).

p. 126   *l.13*   Ibid., p. 29; in *SE,* 18:90 (variant translation).

p. 126   *l.33*   Ibid., p. 91; in *SE,* 18:138–39.

p. 127   *l.11*   *Three Essays on the Theory of Sexuality,* p. 71; in *SE,* 7:205.

p. 127   *l.15*   Ibid.; ibid. in *SE.*

p. 127   *l.19*   My wording is a variant of William James' in *The Principles of Psychology* (New York: Dover, 1950), 1:347: "the Soul is an outbirth of that sort of philosophizing whose great maxim, according to Dr. Hodgson, is: 'Whatever you are *totally* ignorant of, assert to be the explanation of everything else.'"

p. 127   *l.28*   Ibid., p. 89; in *SE,* 7:223.

p. 128   *l.14*   Reik, *Of Love and Lust,* p. 16.

p. 129   *l.6*   *Civilization and Its Discontents,* p. 64; in *SE,* 21:117.

p. 130   *l.17*   On this, see Vernon W. Grant, *The Psychology of Sexual Emotion: The Basis of Selective Attraction* (Westport: Greenwood, 1979), pp. 41–59; also his *Falling in Love: The Psychology of the Romantic Emotion* (New York: Springer, 1976), pp. 29–38. See also H. B. Levey, "A Critique of the Theory of Sublimation," *Psychiatry 2* (1939): 239–70.

p. 130   *l.24*   On this, see my chapter "The New Sexology," in *The Goals of Human Sexuality* (New York: W. W. Norton, 1973), pp. 13–26.

p. 131   *l.27*   On this, see Frank J. Sulloway, *Freud, Biologist of the Mind: Beyond the Psychoanalytic Legend* (New York: Basic Books, 1979), p. 259.

p. 132   *l.11*   Jones, *The Life and Work of Sigmund Freud,* 2:320.

p. 132   *l.23*   *Civilization and Its Discontents,* p. 11; in *SE,* 21:64.

p. 132   *l.36*   Ibid., p. 12;in *SE,* 21:65.

p. 133   *l.5*   Ibid., p. 13; in *SE,* 21:66.

p. 133   *l.7*   Ibid.; ibid. in *SE.*

p. 133   *l.22*   *A General Introduction to Psychoanalysis,* p. 323.

p. 134   *l.4*   *Group Psychology and the Analysis of the Ego,* p. 80; in *SE,* 18:130.

p. 134   *l.22*   Reik, *Of Love and Lust,* p. 27.

p. 136   *l.18*   "On Narcissism: An Introduction," in *A General Selection from the Works of Sigmund Freud,* pp. 120–21; in *SE,* 14:98–99 (variant translation).

p. 136   *l.33*   Ibid., p. 121; in *SE,* 14:100 (variant translation).

p. 137   *l.3*   See *The Nature of Love: Courtly and Romantic,* pp. 174–75.

p. 137   *l.26*   "On Narcissism: An Introduction," in *A General Selection from the Works of Sigmund Freud,* p. 112; in *SE,* 14:88.

p. 138   *l.8*   Ibid., p. 113; in *SE,* 14:88–89 (variant translation).

p. 138   *l.12*   Ibid., p. 114; in *SE,* 14:89 (variant translation).

p. 138   *l.37*   Ibid., p. 115; in *SE,* 14:91 (variant translation).

p. 139   *l.14*   *Group Psychology and the Analysis of the Ego,* p. 44; in *SE,* 18:103. My brackets.

p. 139   *l.17*   Ibid., p. 43; in *SE,* 18:102.

p. 139   *l.32*   Ibid., p. 47; in *SE*, 18:106.

p. 140   *l.6*   On this, see Arnold H. Modell, M.D., *Object Love and Reality* (New York: International Universities Press, 1968), pp. 145–55. See also Daniel Rancour-Laferriere, *Signs of the Flesh* (Berlin: Mouton de Gruyter, 1985), pp. 25–32 and passim; and Jean Florence, *L'identification dans la théorie freudienne* (Brussels: Faculté Universitaires Saint-Louis, 1978), particularly pp. 176–201. See also the discussion in Nancy Chodorow, *The Reproduction of Mothering: Psychoanalysis and the Sociology of Gender* (Berkeley: University of California Press, 1978), p. 81ff. and passim.

p. 140   *l.10*   "On Narcissism: An Introduction," in *A General Selection from the Works of Sigmund Freud*, p. 117; in *SE*, 14:94 (variant translation).

p. 140   *l.23*   Ibid., p. 116; ibid. in *SE* (variant translation). My italics.

p. 141   *l.13*   Ibid., p. 122; in *SE*, 14:101 (variant translation).

p. 142   *l.9*   See Franz Alexander, Introduction to Freud's *Group Psychology and the Analysis of the Ego*, pp. xiv-xvi.

p. 142   *l.29*   *Civilization and Its Discontents*, p. 55; in *SE*, 21:108.

p. 143   *l.1*   Ibid., p. 69; in *SE*, 21:122.

p. 143   *l.13*   Ibid., p. 55; in *SE*, 21:108.

p. 144   *l.11*   Ibid., p. 48; in *SE*, 21:101.

p. 144   *l.17*   Ibid., p. 49; in *SE*, 21:102.

p. 144   *l.21*   Ibid.; ibid. in *SE*.

p. 145   *l.11*   Ibid., p. 50; in *SE*, 21:103.

p. 145   *l.18*   Ibid., p. 59; in *SE*, 21:112.

p. 145   *l.35*   Ibid., p. 61; in *SE*, 21:114.

p. 148   *l.20*   Ibid., p. 55; in *SE*, 21:108.

p. 149   *l.15*   Herbert Marcuse, *Eros and Civilization* (New York: Vintage Books, 1955), p. 184.

p. 149   *l.22*   Ibid., p. 193.

p. 150   *l.9*   For an argument against Marcuse similar to mine, cf. Erich Fromm, *The Crisis of Psychoanalysis* (New York: Holt Rinehart and Winston, 1970), pp. 14–20.

p. 151   *l.8*   *A General Introduction to Psychoanalysis*, p. 425.

p. 151   *l.16*   *Civilization and Its Discontents*, p. 49; in *SE*, 21:102.

p. 151   *l.31*   Ibid.; ibid. in *SE*.

p. 152   *l.14*   Ibid., p. 56; in *SE*, 21:109.

p. 152   *l.21*   Ibid.; ibid. in *SE*.

p. 153   *l.6*   Ibid., p. 56–57; in *SE*, 21:109–10.

p. 153   *l.21*   Ibid., p. 57; in *SE*, 21:110.

p. 153   *l.32*   Ibid.; ibid. in *SE*.

p. 154   *l.14*   Ibid., p. 59; in *SE*, 21:112.

p. 154   *l.24*   Ibid., p. 63; in *SE*, 21:114.

p. 155   *l.1*   *Collected Papers*, 5:284.

p. 155   *l.8*   Fromm, *The Anatomy of Human Destructiveness*, p. 495.

p. 156   *l.22*   *Group Psychology and the Analysis of the Ego*, p. 56; in *SE*, 18:112.

p. 157   *l.6*   Act III, scene 2.

p. 157   *l.16*   In *The Goals of Human Sexuality*, pp. 13–26 and passim.

p. 159   *l.9*   Marcel Proust, *A la recherche du temps perdu*, ed. Pierre Clarac and André Ferré (Paris: Gallimard, 1954), 3:109. All quotations from this edition are in my translation.

p. 162   *l.26*   On this, see Roger Shattuck, *Marcel Proust* (New York: Viking, 1974), pp. 166–72; see also Joyce N. Megay, *Bergson et Proust: essai de mise au point de la question de l'influence de Bergson sur Proust* (Paris: J. Vrin, 1976), p. 17.

p. 163   *l.9*   Henri Bergson, *An Introduction to Metaphysics*, trans. T. E. Hulme (Indianapolis: Library of Liberal Arts, 1955), p. 21.

p. 163   *l.12*   Ibid.

p. 163   *l.18*   Ibid., pp. 22–24.

p. 163   *l.30*   Ibid., p. 24.

p. 163   *l.36*   Ibid. Italics deleted.

p. 164   *l.31*   Henri Bergson, *The Two Sources of Morality and Religion*, trans. R. Ashley Audra and Cloudesley Brereton (Notre Dame: University of Notre Dame Press, 1977), p. 43.

p. 165   *l.1*   Ibid., p. 40.

p. 166   *l.4*   Ibid., p. 42.

p. 166   *l.35*   Ibid., p. 39.

p. 167   *l.8*   Ibid., p. 220.

p. 167   *l.13*   Ibid., p. 99.

p. 167   *l.15*   Ibid., p. 233.

p. 167   *l.25*   See "Evolutionary Love," in *The Philosophy of Peirce*, ed. Justus Buchler (London: Routledge and Kegan Paul, 1940), pp. 361–74.

p. 167   *l.33*   Bergson, *The Two Sources of Morality and Religion*, pp. 255, 257.

p. 168   *l.29*   Floris Delattre, "Bergson et Proust: Accords et Dissonances," *Les Etudes Bergsoniennes* (Paris: Editions Albin Michel, 1948), 1:126. My translation.

p. 170   *l.16*   *A la recherche du temps perdu*, 1:156–57.

p. 171   *l.36*   Ibid., 1:154.

p. 172   *l.21*   Ibid., 1:15.

p. 173   *l.24*   Ibid., 3:95.

p. 174   *l.15*   Marcel Proust, *Jean Santeuil*, trans. Gerard Hopkins (New York: Simon and Schuster, 1956), p. 580.

p. 174   *l.34*   *A la recherche du temps perdu*, 1:610.

p. 175   *l.22*   Ibid., 2:695.

p. 175   *l.34*   Ibid., 1:196–97.

p. 176   *l.15*   Ibid., 1:4.

p. 177   *l.14*   *Jean Santeuil*, p. 581.

p. 178   *l.9*   *A la recherche du temps perdu*, 1:159.

p. 178   *l.25*   Ibid., 1:139.

p. 181   *l.7*   Ibid., 1:657.

p. 183   *l.11*   Ibid., 1:933.

p. 184   *l.3*   Ibid., 2:293.

p. 187   *l.19*   Ibid., 1:796.

p. 188   *l.3*   Ibid., 1:100.

p. 190   *l.3*   Ibid., 1:833.
p. 190   *l.10*   Ibid., 3:106.
p. 191   *1.4*   Ibid., 1:343.
p. 192   *l.30*   See my discussion of Stendhal in *The Nature of Love: Courtly and Romantic*, pp. 351–75, particularly pp. 368–69.
p. 193   *l.4*   *A la recherche du temps perdu*, 1:609.
p. 193   *l.32*   Ibid., 1:303.
p. 195   *l.2*   Marcel Proust, "The Death of Baldassare Silvande, Viscount of Sylvania," in *Pleasures and Days and Other Writings* (Garden City: Anchor Books, 1957).
p. 195   *l.5*   *A la recherche du temps perdu*, 3:907.
p. 196   *l.10*   Ibid., 3:450.
p. 196   *l.20*   Jean-Paul Sartre, *Being and Nothingness*, trans. Hazel E. Barnes (New York: Washington Square Books, 1953), p. 234.
p. 196   *l.31*   Quoted in ibid., p. 235.
p. 197   *l.16*   Ibid.
p. 198   *l.6*   Marcel Proust, *Swann's Way*, trans. C. K. Scott Moncrieff (New York: Modern Library, 1928), p. 535.
p. 199   *l.13*   On this, cf. Leo Bersani, *Marcel Proust: The Fictions of Life and of Art* (New York: Oxford University Press, 1965), pp. 105–11.
p. 199   *l.17*   J.-B. Boulanger, "Un cas d'inversion coupable: Marcel Proust," *L'Union Médicale du Canada* 80 (1951): 483–93; also quoted in J. E. Rivers, *Proust and the Art of Love: The Aesthetics of Sexuality in the Life, Times, and Art of Marcel Proust* (New York: Columbia University Press, 1980), p. 18.
p. 201   *l.31*   José Ortega y Gasset, "Time, Distance, and Form in Proust," trans. Irving Singer, *The Hudson Review* (Winter 1959): 509. Reprinted in *The Hudson Review Anthology*, ed. Frederick Morgan (New York: Vintage Books, 1961), p. 394.
p. 202   *l.8*   See José Ortega y Gasset, *On Love: Aspects of a Single Theme*, trans. Toby Talbot (New York: New American Library, 1957), particularly pp. 7–18.
p. 204   *l.32*   *A la recherche du temps perdu*, 1: 746.
p. 207   *l.6*   Ibid., 1:402.
p. 207   *l.20*   Ibid., 1:84.
p. 208   *l.24*   On this, see A. E. Pilkington, *Bergson and His Influence: A Reassessment* (Cambridge: Cambridge University Press, 1976), pp. 146–77; Megay, *Bergson et Proust: essai de mise au point de la question de l'influence de Bergson sur Proust;* Shattuck, *Marcel Proust*, pp. 140–45; Delattre, "Bergson et Proust: Accords et Dissonances." See also the chapter on Proust and Bergson in Georges Poulet, *L'espace Proustien* (Paris: Gallimard, 1963), pp. 137–77; Etienne Burnet, "Marcel Proust et le Bergsonisme," in *Essences* (Paris: Editions Seheur, 1929), pp. 165–252; and Sybil de Souza, *La philosophie de Marcel Proust* (Paris: Editions Rieder, 1939), pp. 49–61.
p. 210   *l.19*   *A la recherche du temps perdu*, 3:873.
p. 211   *l.11*   Ibid., 3:878–79.
p. 212   *l.2*   George Santayana, "Proust on Essences," in *Essays in Literary*

Criticism by George Santayana, ed. Irving Singer (New York: Scribner's, 1956), p. 241.

p. 213 *l.2* Santayana quotes from Marcel Proust, *The Past Recaptured,* trans. Frederick A. Blossom (New York: Modern Library, 1932), pp. 196–204. This quotation appears on p. 243 of *Essays in Literary Criticism by George Santayana.*

p. 213 *l.14* *Essays in Literary Criticism by George Santayana,* p. 243.

p. 213 *l.18* Ibid., p. 244.

p. 214 *l.6* Ibid., p. 243.

p. 214 *l.11* Ibid., pp. 243–44.

p. 214 *l.24* *A la recherche du temps perdu,* 1:879.

p. 214 *l.30* On this, see also Van Meter Ames, *Proust and Santayana: The Aesthetic Way of Life* (Chicago: Willett, Clark, 1937), pp. 67–71.

p. 215 *l.19* *A la recherche du temps perdu,* 3:877–78.

p. 216 *l.12* *Jean Santeuil,* p. 597.

p. 217 *l.10* *A la recherche du temps perdu,* 3:905.

p. 217 *l.12* Ibid., 3:907.

p. 217 *l.20* Quoted in *The Nature of Love: Courtly and Romantic,* p. 370.

p. 218 *l.1* Sigmund Freud, *Leonardo da Vinci: A Study in Psychosexuality,* trans. A. A. Brill (New York: Random House, 1947), pp. 42–43. Wording slightly altered.

p. 219 *l.18* D. H. Lawrence, "A Propos of *Lady Chatterley's Lover,*" in *Sex, Literature, and Censorship,* ed. Harry T. Moore (New York: Twayne, 1953), p. 104.

p. 220 *l.29* On Luther, see my discussion in *The Nature of Love: Plato to Luther,* pp. 312–42. On Milton, see my discussion in *The Nature of Love: Courtly and Romantic,* pp. 241–56.

p. 220 *l.34* D. H. Lawrence, ". . . . Love was Once a Little Boy," in *Reflections on the Death of a Porcupine and Other Essays* (Bloomington: Indiana University Press, 1963), p. 176, pp. 170–71.

p. 221 *l.25* D. H. Lawrence, "Walt Whitman," in *Selected Literary Criticism,* ed. Anthony Beal (New York: Viking, 1966), p. 397.

p. 221 *l.36* Ibid., p. 399.

p. 222 *l.10* Ibid.

p. 223 *l.2* D. H. Lawrence, "Love," in *Selected Essays* (Harmondsworth: Penguin Books, 1950), p. 29.

p. 223 *l.10* D. H. Lawrence, *Women in Love* (New York: Viking, 1920), p. 137.

p. 223 *l.17* Ibid.

p. 223 *l.28* Ibid., p. 258.

p. 224 *l.12* D. H. Lawrence, *The Rainbow* (New York: Viking, 1961), p. 165.

p. 224 *l.14* Ibid., p. 167.

p. 224 *l.17* Ibid., p. 234.

p. 224 *l.24* Ibid., p. 473.

p. 224 *l.27* Ibid., pp. 475, 493.

p. 225 *l.6* D. H. Lawrence, *The First Lady Chatterley* (Berne: Phoenix Publishing, n.d.), p. 293.

p. 226 *l.25* *Reflections on the Death of a Porcupine and Other Essays,* pp. 176–77.

p. 227 *l.3* Ibid., p. 177.

p. 227 *l.7* *Women in Love,* p. 139.

p. 227 *l.35* *Sex, Literature, and Censorship,* pp. 117–18.

p. 228 *l.1* Ibid., p. 118.

p. 228 *l.6* Ibid.

p. 229 *l.22* D. H. Lawrence, *The Man Who Died,* in *St. Mawr and The Man Who Died* (New York: Vintage Books, 1960), p. 184.

p. 229 *l.29* Ibid., p. 207.

p. 229 *l.33* Ibid., p. 211.

p. 230 *l.27* D. H. Lawrence, *Kangaroo* (Harmondsworth: Penguin Books, 1923), p. 220.

p. 231 *l.4* *Sex, Literature, and Censorship,* p. 92.

p. 231 *l.9* Ibid., p. 120.

p. 231 *l.30* *The First Lady Chatterley,* p. 5. On Lawrence's Puritanism, cf. also Eugene Goodheart, *The Utopian Vision of D. H. Lawrence* (Chicago: University of Chicago Press, 1963), p. 162ff.

p. 232 *l.19* Quoted in *Sex, Literature, and Censorship,* p. 78.

p. 233 *l.27* Quoted in F. R. Leavis, *Thoughts, Words and Creativity: Art and Thought in Lawrence* (New York: Oxford University Press, 1976), p. 23.

p. 234 *l.12* D. H. Lawrence, *The Plumed Serpent* (New York: Knopf, 1966), p. 422.

p. 235 *l.3* John Carey, "D. H. Lawrence's Doctrine," in *D. H. Lawrence: Novelist, Poet, Prophet,* ed. Stephen Spender (New York: Harper and Row, 1973), p. 124.

p. 235 *l.18* *Sex, Literature, and Censorship,* p. 104.

p. 235 *l.24* *Kangaroo,* p. 188.

p. 236 *l.1* *Sex, Literature, and Censorship,* p. 111.

p. 236 *l.6* Ibid., p. 107.

p. 236 *l.15* *Reflections on the Death of a Porcupine and Other Essays,* p. 184.

p. 236 *l.27* Preface to *The Grand Inquisitor,* in *Selected Literary Criticism,* p. 235.

p. 236 *l.34* "Love," in *Selected Essays,* p. 30.

p. 237 *l.2* Ibid.

p. 237 *l.4* *Kangaroo,* p. 224.

p. 237 *l.7* "The Novel," in *Reflections on the Death of a Porcupine and Other Essays,* p. 110.

p. 237 *l.10* On this, see Walter Lacher, "David-Herbert Lawrence," in *L'amour et le divin* (Geneva: Perret-Gentil, 1961), pp. 63–102.

p. 238 *l.7* D. H. Lawrence, *Fantasia of the Unconscious,* in *Psychoanalysis and the Unconscious and Fantasia of the Unconscious* (New York: Viking, 1960), p. 135.

p. 238 *l.10* Quoted in Carey, "D. H. Lawrence's Doctrine," in *D. H. Lawrence: Novelist, Poet, Prophet,* p. 126.

p. 238 *l.14* *Psychoanalysis and the Unconscious and Fantasia of the Unconscious,* p. 135.

p. 238 *l.29* Kate Millett, *Sexual Politics* (Garden City: Doubleday, 1970), pp. 237–93.

p. 238 *l.31* *Reflections on the Death of a Porcupine and Other Essays*, p. 184.

p. 239 *l.5* Millett, *Sexual Politics*, p. 238.

p. 239 *l.8* Norman Mailer, *The Prisoner of Sex* (London: Sphere Books, 1971), p. 155.

p. 239 *l.21* *Women in Love*, p. viii.

p. 239 *l.29* Bernard Shaw, *Sixteen Self Sketches* (London: Constable, 1949), p. 178.

p. 240 *l.3* *Sex, Literature, and Censorship*, p. 104.

p. 240 *l.19* Bernard Shaw, *Candida*, Act III.

p. 240 *l.29* Quoted in Anthony Matthews Gibbs, *Shaw* (Edinburgh: Oliver and Boyd, 1969), p. 86.

p. 240 *l.31* *Sex, Literature, and Censorship*, p. 73.

p. 241 *l.7* Bernard Shaw, Preface to *Three Plays for Puritans*, in *Complete Plays*, vol. 3 (New York: Dodd, Mead, 1962), p. xliii.

p. 242 *l.3* *Sixteen Self Sketches*, p. 176.

p. 242 *l.11* Ibid., p. 177.

p. 242 *l.19* Ibid., p. 176.

p. 242 *l.28* On this, see Graham Hough, *The Dark Sun: A Study of D. H. Lawrence* (New York: Capricorn Books, 1956), p. 232.

p. 243 *l.4* *Sixteen Self Sketches*, p. 125.

p. 243 *l.16* Bernard Shaw, Preface to *Getting Married*, in *The Doctor's Dilemma, Getting Married, and The Shewing-Up of Blanco Posnet* (New York: Brentano's, 1911), p. 161.

p. 243 *l.20* *Sixteen Self Sketches*, p. 198.

p. 243 *l.27* Ibid., p. 178.

p. 244 *l.10* Eric Russell Bentley, *Bernard Shaw* (Norfolk: New Directions, 1947), p. 50.

p. 246 *l.25* Bernard Shaw, *Collected Letters, 1898–1910*, ed. Dan H. Laurence (New York: Dodd, Mead, 1972), p. 858.

p. 246 *l.31* Bernard Shaw, "Address, March, 1907," quoted in Archibald Henderson, *George Bernard Shaw: His Life and Works* (London: Hurst and Blackett, 1911), p. 152.

p. 247 *l.13* Bernard Shaw, *Collected Letters, 1874–1897*, ed. Dan H. Laurence (London: Max Reinhardt, 1965), p. 427.

p. 247 *l.33* Quoted in Alfred Turco, *Shaw's Moral Vision: The Self and Salvation* (Ithaca: Cornell University Press, 1967), p. 41.

p. 248 *l.6* *The Doctor's Dilemma, Getting Married, and The Shewing-Up of Blanco Posnet*, pp. 191–92.

p. 248 *l.9* Ibid., p. 192.

p. 248 *l.17* Ibid., p. 262.

p. 248 *l.28* Ibid., p. 134.

p. 248 *l.30* Ibid.

p. 248 *l.35* Ibid.

p. 249 *l.9* Bernard Shaw, A Foreword to the Popular Edition of *Man and Superman*, in *Complete Plays with Prefaces* (New York: Dodd, Mead, 1962), 3:748.

Notes

p. 250   *l.3*   Bernard Shaw, *Man and Superman: A Comedy and a Philosophy,* Act III.
p. 251   *l.12*   Ibid.
p. 251   *l.22*   Ibid.
p. 253   *l.14*   Bernard Shaw, "Program Note Don Juan in Hell," in *Complete Plays with Prefaces,* 3:746.
p. 253   *l.32*   Bernard Shaw, "Epistle Dedicatory to Arthur Bingham Walkley," in *Man and Superman: A Comedy and a Philosophy* (New York: Brentano's, 1905), pp. xxxi–xxxii.
p. 254   I read an earlier version of this chapter to the Santayana Society in December 1986. I am grateful for various comments and criticisms that I received, and for additional references provided by David Wapinsky.
p. 255   *l.7*   *The German Mind: A Philosophical Diagnosis,* p. 119.
p. 255   *l.37*   George Santayana, *The Sense of Beauty* (New York: Charles Scribner's Sons, 1936), p. 46.
p. 256   *l.10*   Ibid., p. 47.
p. 256   *l.14*   Ibid.
p. 256   *l.17*   Ibid., p. 48. See also Santayana's discussion of Stendhal's *De l'Amour* in George Santayana, *Persons and Places,* ed. William G. Holzberger and Herman J. Saatkamp, Jr. (Cambridge: The MIT Press, 1986), pp. 428–29.
p. 256   *l.28*   Ibid.
p. 257   *l.3*   *Some Turns of Thought in Modern Philosophy: Five Essays,* p. 92.
p. 257   *l.8*   Ibid., p. 98.
p. 257   *l.13*   Ibid., p. 99.
p. 257   *l.22*   George Santayana, *Reason in Society* (New York: Dover, 1980), p. 11.
p. 257   *l.32*   Ibid., p. 12.
p. 258   *l.2*   Ibid., p. 15.
p. 258   *l.6*   Ibid., p. 14.
p. 258   *l.10*   Ibid., p. 16.
p. 258   *l.11*   Ibid., p. 21.
p. 258   *l.21*   On this, see James on instinct, in *The Principles of Psychology,* 2:383–441.
p. 259   *l.14*   *Reason in Society,* p. 9.
p. 259   *l.21*   Ibid.
p. 260   *l.25*   George Santayana, *The Realm of Spirit,* in *Realms of Being* (New York: Charles Scribner's Sons, 1942), p. 569.
p. 260   *l.29*   Ibid., p. 572.
p. 260   *l.31*   Ibid.
p. 261   *l.1*   Ibid., p. 549.
p. 261   *l.4*   Ibid., p. 636.
p. 261   *l.22*   Ibid., p. 572.
p. 263   *l.9*   Ibid., p. 575.
p. 263   *l.17*   Ibid., p. 548.
p. 263   *l.21*   *Reason in Society,* p. 33.
p. 263   *l.23*   Ibid., p. 31.
p. 263   *l.33*   *The Realm of Spirit,* in *Realms of Being,* p. 641.

p. 264   *l.8*   Ibid.
p. 264   *l.22*   Ibid., p. 642.
p. 265   *l.1*   Ibid., p. 669.
p. 265   *l.4*   Ibid.
p. 265   *l.16*   See *The Nature of Love: Plato to Luther*, pp. 26–38.
p. 265   *l.22*   *Reason in Society*, p. 31. See also *Persons and Places* (p. 429), where Santayana says that love is "a rapture in adoration which seems to me its perfection. It presupposes the total abdication of physical, social or egotistical claims."
p. 266   *l.7*   See *The Nature of Love: Plato to Luther*, p. 39ff.
p. 266   *l.28*   For James' remark, see *The Selected Letters of William James*, ed. Elizabeth Hardwick (New York: Farrar, Straus and Cudahy, 1961), p. 183. For Santayana's comment on James' remark, see George Santayana, "On My Friendly Critics," in *Soliloquies in England and Later Soliloquies* (Ann Arbor: University of Michigan Press, 1967), pp. 247–48. See also Timothy L. S. Sprigge, *Santayana: An Examination of His Philosophy* (London: Routledge & Kegan Paul, 1974), p. 225.
p. 267   *l.18*   "Platonic Love in Some Italian Poets," in *Essays in Literary Criticism by George Santayana*, p. 99.
p. 268   *l.4*   On this, see Daniel Cory, *Santayana: The Later Years, A Portrait with Letters* (New York: George Braziller, 1963), pp. 40–41; John McCormick, *George Santayana: A Biography* (New York: Alfred A. Knopf, 1987).
p. 268   *l.12*   *Persons and Places*, p. 428. Italics deleted from first sentence.
p. 268   *l.14*   *The Realm of Essence*, in *Realms of Being*, p. 16.
p. 268   *l.23*   Ibid.
p. 268   *l.24*   Santayana's kinship to Proust is also evident in his discussion of "the illusion and revelation of the grand passion." He emphasizes the "madness in this devotion" but also remarks: "And yet what soul that has ever known a great love would wish not to have known it?" (*The Realm of Spirit*, in *Realms of Being*, pp. 687–88).
p. 268   *l.26*   *Obiter Scripta: Lectures, Essays and Reviews by George Santayana*, ed. Justus Buchler and Benjamin Schwartz (New York: Charles Scribner's Sons, 1936), pp. 80–81.
p. 268   *l.31*   Ibid., p. 81.
p. 268   *l.35*   *The Realm of Spirit*, in *Realms of Being*, p. 782.
p. 269   *l.1*   Ibid., p. 820.
p. 269   *l.12*   Ibid., p. 821.
p. 269   *l.25*   Ibid., p. 686.
p. 269   *l.34*   Ibid.
p. 270   *l.8*   Ibid., p. 687
p. 270   *l.11*   Ibid., p. 691.
p. 271   *l.16*   Donald C. Williams.
p. 271   *l.37*   George Santayana, *Dialogues in Limbo* (New York: Scribner's, 1925), p. 155.
p. 272   *l.5*   Ibid.
p. 272   *l.12*   Ibid.
p. 272   *l.19*   Ibid., p. 139.

Notes

p. 272 *l.23* Ibid., pp. 156–57.
p. 272 *l.30* Ibid., p. 158.
p. 273 *l.9* *The Realm of Spirit*, in *Realms of Being*, p. 792.
p. 273 *l.20* George Santayana, *Platonism and the Spiritual Life*, in *Winds of Doctrine and Platonism and the Spiritual Life* (Gloucester: Peter Smith, 1971), pp. 310–11.
p. 274 *l.8* For further discussion of Santayana on charity and religious love in general, see *The Nature of Love: Plato to Luther*, pp. 334–35, 358–59, and passim. See also George Santayana, *Dominations and Powers: Reflections on Liberty, Society, and Government* (New York: Charles Scribner's Sons, 1954), pp. 366–70.
p. 275 *l.5* *The Realm of Spirit*, in *Realms of Being*, p. 773.
p. 275 *l.15* Ibid., p. 807.
p. 275 *l.28* Ibid., p. 825.
p. 275 *l.36* Ibid.
p. 277 *l.22* "Friendships," in *Soliloquies in England and Later Soliloquies*, p. 55.
p. 277 *l.24* Ibid., pp. 55–56, 58.
p. 277 *l.28* *Reason in Society*, p. 148.
p. 277 *l.31* Ibid., p. 156.
p. 278 *l.26* George Santayana, "Friendship," in *The Birth of Reason and Other Essays*, ed. Daniel Cory (New York: Columbia University Press, 1968), pp. 80–81.
p. 278 *l.36* Ibid.
p. 279 *l.5* Ibid., p. 82.
p. 279 *l.33* Ibid., pp. 81, 85.
p. 280 *l.2* Ibid., p. 88.
p. 280 *l.13* For a discussion of Santayana's pluralistic moral philosophy, see my book *Santayana's Aesthetics: A Critical Introduction* (Westport: Greenwood Press, 1973), pp. 201–22.
p. 282 *l.9* "Interview with Jean-Paul Sartre," in *The Philosophy of Jean-Paul Sartre*, ed. Paul Arthur Schilpp (La Salle: Open Court, 1981), p. 13.
p. 282 *l.22* Quoted in Leo Fretz, "An Interview with Jean-Paul Sartre," in *Jean-Paul Sartre: Contemporary Approaches to His Philosophy*, ed. Hugh J. Silverman and Frederick A. Elliston (Pittsburgh: Duquesne University Press, 1980), p. 239.
p. 285 *l.21* *Being and Nothingness*, pp. 723–24.
p. 285 *l.26* Ibid., p. 724.
p. 285 *l.36* Nietzsche, *Thus Spake Zarathustra*, pt. 2, "Upon the Blessed Isles."
p. 286 *l.3* Ibid., pt. 3, "The Other Dancing Song."
p. 286 *l.19* Jean-Paul Sartre, *Nausea*, trans. Lloyd Alexander (New York: New Directions, 1964), p. 176.
p. 286 *l.31* *Being and Nothingness*, p. 784.
p. 287 *l.2* Ibid.
p. 287 *l.5* Ibid., p. 792.
p. 287 *l.24* Ibid., p. 798.
p. 287 *l.26* Ibid., p. 534n.

p. 291   *l.28*   For additional criticism of Sartre on the look, see Margaret Whitford, *Merleau-Ponty's Critique of Sartre's Philosophy* (Lexington: French Forum, 1982), p. 98ff.

p. 291   *l.36*   *Being and Nothingness*, p. 475.

p. 292   *l.1*   Simone de Beauvoir, *Adieux: A Farewell to Sartre*, trans. Patrick O'Brian (New York: Pantheon, 1984), p. 148.

p. 292   *l.9*   *Being and Nothingness*, p. 475.

p. 292   *l.22*   On this continuity of thought, see Pauline Newman, *Marcel Proust et l'Existentialisme* (Paris: Nouvelles Editions Latines, 1952).

p. 292   *l.35*   *Being and Nothingness*, p. 475.

p. 292   *l.37*   Ibid.

p. 293   *l.24*   On this, see Thomas C. Anderson, *The Foundation and Structure of Sartrean Ethics* (Lawrence: The Regents Press of Kansas, 1979), p. 39.

p. 294   *l.37*   *Being and Nothingness*, p. 478. See also Sartre's review "Denis de Rougemont: *L'amour et l'occident*," in *Situations*, I (Paris: Gallimard, 1947), p. 69. Sartre there says: "To desire [another person] . . . is to want to attain through the flesh, on the flesh, a consciousness—that 'divine absence' of which Valéry speaks." My translation.

p. 295   *l.15*   Ibid., p. 479.

p. 295   *l.25*   Ibid., p. 480.

p. 295   *l.35*   Ibid., p. 481. Italics omitted.

p. 296   *l.2*   Ibid., p. 483.

p. 296   *l.3*   Ibid., p. 484.

p. 296   *l.5*   Ibid., pp. 483–84.

p. 297   *l.1*   Ibid., p. 489.

p. 297   *l.31*   Ibid., p. 488.

p. 297   *l.32*   Ibid.

p. 297   *l.34*   Ibid., p. 484.

p. 297   *l.34*   Ibid., p. 489.

p. 298   *l.20*   Ibid., p. 484.

p. 300   *l.8*   Ibid., p. 493.

p. 301   *l.4*   Ibid., p. 505.

p. 301   *l.6*   Ibid., p. 506.

p. 301   *l.12*   Ibid.

p. 301   *l.18*   Ibid., p. 508.

p. 302   *l.8*   Ibid., p. 515.

p. 302   *l.14*   Ibid., p. 516.

p. 302   *l.20*   Ibid., p. 517.

p. 302   *l.30*   Ibid., p. 524.

p. 303   *l.19*   On this, see the following essays in *The Philosophy of Sex: Contemporary Readings*, ed. Alan Soble (Totowa: Littlefield, Adams, 1980): Nathan Oaklander, "Sartre on Sex," pp. 190–206; Robert Solomon, "Sexual Paradigms," pp. 89–98; Thomas Nagel, "Sexual Perversion," pp. 76–88. See also Roger Scruton, *Sexual Desire: A Moral Philosophy of the Erotic* (New York: The Free Press, 1986), pp. 120–25.

p. 306   *l.21*   On this, see Robert C. Solomon, "Sartre on Emotions," in *The Philosophy of Jean-Paul Sartre*, ed. Schilpp, p. 213f.

p. 306   *l.32*   *Being and Nothingness*, p. 327.

p. 307   *l.13*   Ibid., p. 333.

p. 307   *l.19*   Ibid.

p. 308   *l.16*   Ibid., p. 537.

p. 308   *l.20*   Ibid.

p. 308   *l.29*   Ibid., p. 547.

p. 308   *l.37*   Ibid., p. 555.

p. 309   *l.7*   Ibid., p. 554.

p. 309   *l.16*   On this, see Anderson, *The Foundation and Structure of Sartrean Ethics*, pp. 69–75.

p. 309   *l.21*   On this, see Paul Ramsey, "Jean-Paul Sartre: Sex in Being," in *Nine Modern Moralists* (Englewood Cliffs: Prentice-Hall, 1962), particularly p. 104.

p. 310   *l.5*   *Jean-Paul Sartre: Contemporary Approaches to His Philosophy*, ed. Silverman and Elliston, p. 239.

p. 310   *l.12*   Jean-Paul Sartre, *L'Existentialisme est un humanisme* (Paris: Nagel, 1958), p. 83. My translation. This essay appears as "Existentialism Is a Humanism," trans. Philip Mairet, in *Existentialism from Dostoevsky to Sartre*, ed. Walter Kaufmann (New York: New American Library, 1975), pp. 345–69.

p. 310   *l.22*   *Being and Nothingness*, p. 531.

p. 312   *l.5*   Simone de Beauvoir, *The Ethics of Ambiguity*, trans. Bernard Frechtman (New York: Philosophical Library, 1948), p. 72.

p. 312   *l.13*   Ibid., p. 135.

p. 313   *l.10*   Simone de Beauvoir, *The Second Sex*, trans. and ed. H. M. Parshley (Toronto: Bantam Books, 1961), pp. 613–14.

p. 313   *l.28*   Ibid., p. 614.

p. 314   *l.36*   Ibid., p. 615.

p. 315   *l.19*   Ibid., p. 628.

p. 316   *l.2*   Ibid., p. 629.

p. 316   *l.8*   Ibid., p. 689.

p. 316   *l.11*   Ibid., p. 688.

p. 316   *l.17*   Ibid., p. 445.

p. 316   *l.23*   Simone de Beauvoir, *La Force de l'âge* (Paris: Gallimard, 1960); quoted in Robert D. Cottrell, *Simone de Beauvoir* (New York: Ungar, 1975), p. 21.

p. 316   *l.25*   Simone de Beauvoir, *La Force des choses*, vol. 1 (Paris: Gallimard, 1963); quoted in Cottrell, *Simone de Beauvoir*, p. 91.

p. 316   *l.30*   On this, see Jean Leighton, *Simone de Beauvoir on Women* (Rutherford: Fairleigh Dickinson University Press, 1975), pp. 102–4.

p. 317   *l.21*   Jean-Paul Sartre, *Anti-Semite and Jew*, trans. George J. Becker (New York: Grove Press, 1962), p. 90.

p. 318   *l.6*   See Iris Murdoch, *Sartre: Romantic Rationalist* (New Haven: Yale University Press, 1959); Mary Warnock, *The Philosophy of Sartre* (London: Hutchinson University Library, 1965); Richard Bernstein, *Praxis and Action* (Philadelphia: University of Pennsylvania Press, 1971); Anderson, *The Foundation and Structure of Sartrean Ethics*.

p. 319   *l.1*   Jean-Paul Sartre, *Cahiers pour une morale* (Paris: Gallimard, 1983), p. 490. All quoted passages from this book are in my translation.

p. 319   *l.9*   Ibid., p. 430.
p. 320   *l.7*   Ibid., p. 493.
p. 320   *l.19*   Ibid., p. 516.
p. 320   *l.23*   Ibid., pp. 516–17.
p. 321   *l.1*   Ibid., p. 517.
p. 321   *l.13*   Ibid., p. 197.
p. 321   *l.19*   Ibid., pp. 523–24.
p. 322   *l.1*   Ibid., p. 124.
p. 322   *l.16*   Jean-Paul Sartre, *L'idiot de la famille* (Paris: Gallimard, 1971), 2:1274. My translation.
p. 323   *l.10*   *Jean-Paul Sartre: Contemporary Approaches to His Philosophy*, ed. Silverman and Elliston, p. 238.
p. 324   *l.4*   *Cahiers pour une morale*, p. 16.
p. 324   *l.30*   *Being and Nothingness*, p. 329.
p. 325   *l.4*   On this, see Sartre's comments in *Jean-Paul Sartre: Contemporary Approaches to His Philosophy*, pp. 236–37.
p. 325   *l.19*   Jean-Paul Sartre, *Critique of Dialectical Reason, 1: Theory of Practical Ensembles,* trans. Alan Sheridan-Smith, ed. Jonathan Ree (London: NLB, 1976), p. 436.
p. 325   *l.24*   Ibid., p. 437.
p. 325   *l.28*   Ibid., p. 438.
p. 326   *l.8*   Jean-Paul Sartre, *Life/Situations: Essays Written and Spoken,* trans. Paul Auster and Lydia Davis (New York: Pantheon Books, 1977), p. 66.
p. 326   *l.9*   Ibid., pp. 9, 13.
p. 326   *l.12*   Ibid., p. 13.
p. 326   *l.15*   Ibid.
p. 326   *l.18*   Ibid., p. 11.
p. 327   *l.6*   *Being and Nothingness*, pp. 478–79.
p. 327   *l.14*   On this, see Joseph H. McMahon, *Humans Being: The World of Jean-Paul Sartre* (New Haven: Yale University Press, 1976), p. 249.
p. 328   *l.19*   Jean-Paul Sartre, *Les jeux sont faits* (Paris: Nagel, 1968), p. 93. My translation.
p. 329   *l.9*   Jean-Paul Sartre, *The Devil and the Good Lord* (New York: Vintage Books, 1960), p. 145.
p. 329   *l.12*   Ibid., p. 133.
p. 329   *l.17*   Jean-Paul Sartre, *Saint Genet: Actor and Martyr,* trans. Bernard Frechtman (New York: George Braziller, 1963), p. 532.
p. 329   *l.22*   Ibid.
p. 329   *l.32*   *The Devil and the Good Lord*, p. 149.
p. 329   *l.33*   Ibid., p. 146.
p. 330   *l.2*   *The Nature of Love: Courtly and Romantic*, pp. 296–97.
p. 330   *l.3*   *The Devil and the Good Lord*, p. 112.
p. 330   *l.13*   On this, see Marie-Denise Boros Azzi, "Representation of Character in Sartre's Drama, Fiction, and Biography," in *The Philosophy of Jean-Paul Sartre*, ed. Schilpp, p. 460.
p. 331   *l.29*   Karl Jaspers, *Philosophie*, 1:55, trans. Marga Franck and Arthur Newton in cooperation with Eva Reinitz Gossman and Maurice

Friedman, in *The Worlds of Existentialism,* ed. Maurice Friedman (New York: Random House, 1964), p. 202.

p. 331   *l.35*   Karl Jaspers, *Psychologie der Weltanschauungen,* p. 124, trans. Marga Franck and Arthur Newton in cooperation with Eva Reinitz Gossman and Maurice Friedman, in ibid.

p. 332   *l.3*   Maurice Merleau-Ponty, *The Phenomenology of Perception,* trans. Colin Smith (London: Routledge and Kegan Paul, 1962), p. 354.

p. 332   *l.18*   Quoted in Martin Buber, *Between Man and Man* (New York: Macmillan, 1967), p. 221.

p. 332   *l.37*   Ibid., p. 211n.

p. 333   *l.7*   Martin Buber, *I and Thou,* 2d ed., trans. Ronald Gregor Smith (New York: Charles Scribner's Sons, 1958), pp. 27–28, 25.

p. 333   *l.34*   Ibid., p. 7.

p. 333   *l.35*   Ibid., p. 8.

p. 335   *l.7*   Buber, *Between Man and Man,* pp. 175–76. Comma added.

p. 335   *l.16*   Ibid., p. 176.

p. 335   *l.21*   Buber, *I and Thou,* p. 10.

p. 336   *l.7*   Ibid., p. 15.

p. 336   *l.8*   Ibid.

p. 336   *l.22*   Ibid., p. 17.

p. 337   *l.17*   *Between Man and Man,* pp. 173–75; and *The Writings of Martin Buber,* sel. and ed. Will Herberg (New York: New American Library, 1974), pp. 306–14.

p. 337   *l.19*   *Between Man and Man,* pp. 51–52.

p. 337   *l.29*   Ibid., p. 52.

p. 338   *l.3*   Ibid., p. 61.

p. 338   *l.7*   *I and Thou,* p. 106.

p. 338   *l.27*   Martin Buber, *Hasidism* (New York: Philosophical Library, 1948), p. 157.

p. 339   *l.7*   Gabriel Marcel, "I and Thou," in *The Worlds of Existentialism,* p. 213. See also Gabriel Marcel, "I and Thou," in *The Philosophy of Martin Buber,* ed. Paul Arthur Schilpp and Maurice Friedman (La Salle: Open Court, 1967), pp. 41–48.

p. 339   *l.16*   Ibid.

p. 339   *l.26*   For Marcel on Royce, see Gabriel Marcel, *Royce's Metaphysics,* trans. Virginia and Gordon Ringer (Chicago: Regnery, 1956). For Royce on fidelity, see *The Philosophy of Loyalty,* in *The Basic Writings of Josiah Royce,* ed. John J. McDermott (Chicago: University of Chicago Press, 1969), 2:855–1013. See also Kenneth T. Gallagher, *The Philosophy of Gabriel Marcel* (New York: Fordham University Press, 1962), pp. 66–81.

p. 340   *l.1*   See Paul E. Pfuetze, *The Social Self* (New York: Bookman, 1954), p. 164.

p. 340   *l.11*   Quoted in Jacques Choron, *Death and Western Thought* (New York: Collier Books, 1963), p. 258. See also Gabriel Marcel, *The Mystery of Being,* vol. 2: *Faith and Reality,* trans. René Hague (Chicago: Henry Regnery, 1951), 2:61.

p. 340   *l.17*   Marcel, *The Mystery of Being,* 2:62. See also his *The Existential Background of Human Dignity* (Cambridge: Harvard University Press, 1963), p. 74.

p. 340 *l.33* Gabriel Marcel, *Being and Having: An Existentialist Diary* (New York: Harper and Row, 1965), p. 135. See also Sam Keen, "The Development of the Idea of Being in Marcel's Thought," in *The Philosophy of Gabriel Marcel,* ed. Paul Arthur Schilpp and Lewis Edwin Hahn (La Salle: Open Court, 1984), particularly pp. 108–18.

p. 341 *l.5* *The Existential Background of Human Dignity,* p. 74; *The Philosophy of Gabriel Marcel,* ed. Schilpp and Hahn, p. 113. Italics deleted.

p. 341 *l.20* Quoted in Gallagher, *The Philosophy of Gabriel Marcel,* p. 81.

p. 341 *l.32* Murdoch, *Sartre: Romantic Rationalist;* Marjorie Grene, *Sartre* (New York: New Viewpoints, 1973). See also Ramsey, *Nine Modern Moralists,* pp. 103–5; and Suzanne Lilar, *A propos de Sartre et de l'amour* (Paris: Grasset, 1967), p. 251 and pp. 229–45. Lilar's book, written long before the publication of the *Cahiers pour une morale,* detects an evolution in Sartre's thought from a "séparatiste" philosophy to one that is "essentiellement reliante" ("basically unifying").

p. 341 *l.37* Robert C. Solomon, *Love: Emotion, Myth and Metaphor* (New York: Anchor Press, 1981), p. 276.

p. 342 *l.5* Ibid., p. 277. Comma added.

p. 342 *l.12* For another promising approach, see Hazel E. Barnes, *An Existentialist Ethics* (New York: Knopf, 1967), pp. 318–75.

p. 347 *l.4* Solomon, *Love: Emotion, Myth and Metaphor,* p. 88.

p. 347 *l.8* Howard L. Miller and Paul S. Siegel, *Loving: A Psychological Approach* (New York: John Wiley and Sons, 1972), p. 5.

p. 347 *l.30* John Bowlby, *Attachment* (New York: Basic Books, 1969), p. 364.

p. 347 *l.32* Ibid., p. 363.

p. 348 *l.6* Ibid., pp. 361–78, particularly pp. 364–65.

p. 348 *l.16* Quoted in ibid., p. 372.

p. 348 *l.20* Quoted in ibid., p. 371. See also Chodorow, *The Reproduction of Mothering,* pp. 62–73.

p. 349 *l.18* Harry F. Harlow, *Learning to Love* (New York: Jason Aronson, 1974), p. 28.

p. 349 *l.22* James, *The Principles of Psychology,* 2:551n.

p. 350 *l.16* On this, see Bowlby, *Attachment,* p. 166n.

p. 350 *l.20* Harlow, *Learning to Love,* p. 2.

p. 351 *l.7* Ibid., pp. 2–3.

p. 351 *l.17* Ibid., p. 3.

p. 352 *l.4* Ibid., p. 48.

p. 352 *l.17* On this, see Melvin Konner, *The Tangled Wing: Biological Constraints on the Human Spirit* (New York: Holt, Rinehart and Winston, 1982), p. 300.

p. 353 *l.9* Melanie Klein, "Love, Guilt and Reparation," in Melanie Klein and Joan Riviere, *Love, Hate and Reparation* (New York, W. W. Norton, 1964), pp. 57–119.

p. 354 *l.7* Ibid., p. 66.

p. 354 *l.9* Ibid.

p. 355 *l.19* Ibid., pp. 86–87.

p. 356 *l.34* Konrad Lorenz, *On Aggression,* trans. Marjorie Kerr Wilson (New York: Harcourt, Brace and World, 1966), p. 216.

p. 357   *l.35*   Irenäus Eibl-Eibesfeldt, *Love and Hate: The Natural History of Behavior Patterns*, trans. Geoffrey Strachan (New York: Holt, Rinehart and Winston, 1971), p. 128.

p. 358   *l.17*   Cf. Rancour-Laferriere, *Signs of the Flesh*, p. 20.

p. 358   *l.18*   Robert Trivers, *Social Evolution* (Menlo Park: Benjamin/Cummings, 1985), p. 456.

p. 360   *l.37*   Edward O. Wilson, *On Human Nature* (Cambridge: Harvard University Press, 1978), p. 157.

p. 361   *l.34*   Ralph Linton, *The Study of Man: An Introduction* (New York: Appleton-Century, 1936), p. 175; quoted in William N. Stephens, *The Family in Cross-Cultural Perspective* (New York: Holt, Rinehart and Winston, 1963), p. 201.

p. 362   *l.36*   Philip Slater, *The Pursuit of Loneliness: American Culture at the Breaking Point*, rev. ed. (Boston: Beacon Press, 1976), p. 93.

p. 363   *l.17*   On this, see "Two Systems of Sexual Mores," in my book *The Goals of Human Sexuality*, pp. 105–24.

p. 363   *l.23*   On this, see Udry, *The Social Context of Marriage*, pp. 140–42; Stephens, *The Family in Cross-Cultural Perspective*, pp. 206–7; Grant, *Falling in Love: The Psychology of the Romantic Emotion*, pp. 32–38.

p. 363   *l.32*   See Bronislaw Malinowski, *The Sexual Life of Savages in Northwest Melanesia* (New York: Liveright, 1929).

p. 363   *l.34*   Margaret Mead, *Coming of Age in Samoa* (New York: William Morrow, 1928), p. 105. See also Stephens, *The Family in Cross-Cultural Perspective*, p. 205; and Grant, *Falling in Love: The Psychology of the Romantic Emotion*, pp. 35–38.

p. 364   *l.19*   William J. Goode, "The Theoretical Importance of Love," in *The Practice of Love*, ed. Ashley Montagu, p. 135.

p. 364   *l.28*   On this, see Kenneth S. Pope et al., *On Love and Loving: An Invitation to Social Psychology* (New York: Holt, Rinehart and Winston, 1973); Praxedis Mayr von Baldegg, "Romantic Love: Psychological Theory and Late Adolescent Experience," Ph.D. diss., School of Education, Boston University, 1982; Winch, *The Modern Family*.

p. 365   *l.5*   Goode, "The Theoretical Importance of Love," in *The Practice of Love*, ed. Montagu, pp. 127–28. Italics omitted. See also Goode, *The Family*, pp. 39–40.

p. 365   *l.27*   See Sydney L. W. Mellen, *The Evolution of Love* (Oxford: W. H. Freeman, 1981), p. 106ff., pp. 136–41. See also Richard D. Alexander, *Darwinism and Human Affairs* (Seattle: University of Washington Press, 1979), pp. 123–24; and Rancour-Laferriere, *Signs of the Flesh*, p. 151.

p. 366   *l.25*   Rancour-Laferriere, *Signs of the Flesh*, p. 198.

p. 367   *l.31*   For a related discussion, see Grant, *Falling in Love: The Psychology of the Romantic Emotion*, pp. 9–10.

p. 371   *l.10*   See Winch, *The Modern Family*, pp. 630–35.

p. 371   *l.14*   Robert Brain, *Friends and Lovers*, p. 222.

p. 371   *l.15*   Ibid., pp. 133, 243.

p. 371   *l.19*   Ibid., p. 245.

p. 371   *l.25*   Philip Slater, *The Pursuit of Loneliness*, p. 93.

p. 372   *l.5*   Herman R. Lantz and Eloise C. Snyder, *Marriage: An Examination of the Man-Woman Relationship*, 2d ed. (New York: John Wiley and Sons, 1969), pp. 129–31.

p. 372   *l.34*   Vernon W. Grant, "Love, Sexual," in *The Encyclopedia of Sexual Behavior*, ed. Albert Ellis and Albert Abarbanal (New York: Jason Aronson, 1973), p. 646.

p. 373   *l.9*   Ibid., pp. 646–47.

p. 373   *l.25*   Grant, *Falling in Love: The Psychology of the Romantic Emotion*, p. 39. See also his *The Psychology of Sexual Emotion: The Basis of Selective Attraction*, pp. 1–41 and passim.

p. 380   *l.17*   Elaine Walster and G. William Walster, *A New Look at Love* (Reading: Addison-Wesley, 1978), p. 9.

p. 380   *l.21*   Ibid., p. 2.

p. 380   *l.25*   Ibid., pp. 2, 9.

p. 385   *l.2*   Francesco Alberoni, *Falling in Love* (New York: Random House, 1983), p. 69.

p. 385   *l.8*   Ibid., p. 32.

p. 388   *l.37*   See Ortega y Gasset, *On Love: Aspects of a Single Theme*, pp. 19–78. See also my discussion of Ortega's views on Stendhal, in *The Nature of Love: Courtly and Romantic*, pp. 363–66, and in my essay "Ortega on Love," *The Hudson Review* 11 (Spring 1959): 145–54.

p. 389   *l.8*   On this, see *The Nature of Love: Courtly and Romantic*, pp. 273–76.

p. 392   *l.8*   Winch, *The Modern Family*, p. 579.

p. 392   *l.26*   On this, see Rancour-Laferriere, *Signs of the Flesh*, pp. 144–45. See also Bernard I. Murstein, "Critique of Models of Dyadic Attraction," in *Theories of Attraction and Love*, ed. Bernard I. Murstein (New York: Springer, 1971), pp. 19–20.

p. 395   *l.22*   Sonnet 116.

p. 397   *l.18*   John McTaggart Ellis McTaggart, *The Nature of Existence*, ed. C. D. Broad (Cambridge: Cambridge University Press, 1927), 2: 151.

p. 397   *l.32*   Ibid., p. 152.

p. 397   *l.36*   Ibid.

p. 398   *l.5*   Ibid., p. 153.

p. 398   *l.7*   Ibid.

p. 398   *l.14*   Ibid., p. 154.

p. 401   *l.2*   Ibid.

p. 401   *l.28*   On McTaggart's philosophy of love, see Scruton, *Sexual Desire: A Moral Philosophy of the Erotic*, pp. 232–33. See also P. T. Geach, *Truth, Love and Immortality: An Introduction to McTaggart's Philosophy* (Berkeley: University of California Press, 1979), pp. 165–74.

p. 401   *l.33*   Russell Vannoy, *Sex without Love: A Philosophical Exploration* (Buffalo: Prometheus, 1980), p. 195. He refers to *The Nature of Love: Plato to Luther*, 1st ed. (New York: Random House, 1966), p. 13.

p. 402   *l.5*   Ibid.

p. 402   *l.26*   Ibid., p. 194.

p. 402   *l.32*   Ibid., p. 197.

p. 403   *l.23*   Ibid., p. 193.

p. 403   *l.25*   Ibid.

p. 404   *l.2*   Ibid., p. 195.

p. 404   *l.31*   Ibid., p. 197.

p. 405   *l.16*   Wallace Stevens, "Poetry Is a Destructive Force," in *The Collected Poems of Wallace Stevens* (New York: Knopf, 1971), p. 192.

p. 405   *l.30*   Christina Robb, "Modern Romance," *The Boston Globe Magazine* (February 9, 1986): 57.

p. 406   *l.25*   Book VIII, chap. 5.

p. 408   *l.28*   Silvano Arieti, M.D., and James A. Arieti, Ph.D., *Love Can Be Found: A Guide to the Most Desired and Most Elusive Emotion* (New York: Harcourt Brace Jovanovich, 1977), p. 92.

p. 409   *l.5*   Act V, scene 1.

p. 409   *l.27*   Solomon, *Love: Emotion, Myth and Metaphor*, p. 268. Cf. Sartre's remark that love seeks "a union which, by its nature, it rejects." (*Situations*, I, p. 69. My translation.)

p. 409   *l.35*   Ibid., pp. 268–69.

p. 410   *l.36*   Ibid., p. 269.

p. 411   *l.19*   Scruton, *Sexual Desire: A Moral Philosophy of the Erotic*, p. 230.

p. 415   *l.1*   *Pride and Prejudice*, chap. 25.

p. 415   *l.2*   *A la recherche du temps perdu*, 1:399–400.

p. 416   *l.1*   Arthur D. Colman, M.D., and Libby Lee Colman, Ph.D., *Love and Ecstasy* (New York: Continuum, 1975), p. 3. Italics deleted.

p. 418   *l.8*   Erich Fromm, *The Art of Loving* (New York: Harper Colophon Books, 1962), p. 46.

p. 418   *l.20*   For another psychiatric interpretation of love as fusion, particularly in relation to Freud's concept of identification, see Willard Gaylin, M.D., *Rediscovering Love* (New York: Viking, 1986), pp. 98–116.

p. 418   *l.21*   Fromm, *The Art of Loving*, p. 55.

p. 419   *l.12*   Shulamith Firestone, *The Dialectic of Sex* (New York: William Morrow, 1970); Elizabeth Rapaport, "On the Future of Love: Rousseau and the Radical Feminists," in *Philosophy of Sex: Contemporary Readings*, ed. Soble, pp. 369–88. See also Constantina Safilios-Rothschild, *Love, Sex, and Sex Roles* (Englewood Cliffs: Prentice-Hall, 1977); Caroline Whitbeck, "Love, Knowledge and Transformation," *Women's Studies International Forum* 7, no. 5: 393–405; and Robert C. Solomon, "Love and Feminism," adapted from Solomon, *Love: Emotion, Myth and Metaphor*, in *Philosophy and Sex*, ed. Robert Baker and Frederick Elliston (Buffalo: Prometheus Books, 1984), pp. 53–70.

p. 419   *l.20*   Ti-Grace Atkinson, "Radical Feminism and Love," in *Amazon Odyssey* (New York: Links Books, 1974), pp. 41–45; extracted in *Feminist Frameworks: Alternative Theoretical Accounts of the Relations Between Women and Men*, ed. Alison M. Jaggar and Paula Rothenberg Struhl (New York: McGraw-Hill, 1978), pp. 301–3.

p. 419   *l.34*   Ibid., p. 44.

p. 421   *l.1*   Mary Wollstonecraft, *A Vindication of the Rights of Woman: With Strictures on Political and Moral Subjects* (New York: Source Book Press, 1971), p. 94.

p. 421   *l.5*   Ibid., pp. 42, 43.

p. 421 *l.24* Firestone, *The Dialectic of Sex*, p. 144.

p. 421 *l.30* Ibid., p. 145.

p. 423 *l.24* Ibid., p. 153. Italics omitted.

p. 424 *l.19* See Trivers, *Social Evolution*, p. 214; Donald Symons, *The Evolution of Human Sexuality* (New York: Oxford University Press, 1979), pp. 219–20; Carol Gilligan, *In a Different Voice: Psychological Theory and Women's Development* (Cambridge: Harvard University Press, 1982), passim. See also two essays by Carol Gilligan: "The Conquistador and the Dark Continent: Reflections on the Psychology of Love," *Daedalus* 113, no. 3 (Summer 1984): 75–95; and "Remapping the Moral Domain: New Images of the Self in Relationship," in *Reconstructing Individualism: Autonomy, Individuality, and the Self in Western Thought*, ed. Thomas C. Heller et al. (Stanford: Stanford University Press, 1986), pp. 237–52. See also Terry Smith Hatkoff and Thomas E. Lasswell, "Male-Female Similarities and Differences in Conceptualizing Love," in *Love and Attraction*, ed. Mark and Glenn Wilson (Oxford: Pergamon Press, 1979), pp. 221–27.

p. 425 *l.21* Cited in Rancour-Laferriere, *Signs of the Flesh*, p. 196.

p. 425 *l.32* Paul Tillich, *Love, Power and Justice: Ontological Analyses and Ethical Applications* (New York: Oxford University Press, 1954), p. 18.

p. 425 *l.33* Ibid., p. 19.

p. 426 *l.8* Ibid., p. 25.

p. 426 *l.28* See *The Nature of Love: Courtly and Romantic*, p. 399ff.

p. 427 *l.24* Tillich, *Love, Power and Justice*, p. 38.

p. 427 *l.32* Ibid., p. 39.

p. 428 *l.26* Ibid., p. 36.

p. 429 *l.6* Ibid., pp. 48–49.

p. 429 *l.22* Act V, scene 1.

p. 429 *l.35* See also Paul Tillich, *Perspectives on 19th and 20th Century Protestant Theology*, ed. Carl E. Braaten (New York: Harper and Row, 1967), p. 105, where Tillich remarks: "You cannot say that love *is* emotion. Love has an element of emotion in it and very much so, but it is not an emotion. It is a reunion, as I would call it, of separated entities that belong to each other eternally. This experience cannot be identified with the personal reaction which we call feeling."

p. 430 *l.1* Tillich, *Love, Power and Justice*, p. 34.

p. 430 *l.10* Paul Tillich, *The Courage to Be* (New Haven: Yale University Press, 1953), p. 186.

p. 430 *l.14* Ibid., p. 188.

p. 430 *l.15* Ibid., p. 164.

p. 430 *l.22* *Love, Power and Justice*, p. 27.

p. 430 *l.28* Act IV, scene 2.

p. 433 *l.5* See my discussion above, pp. 133–39.

p. 440 *l.35* Bertrand Russell, "What I Believe," in *Why I Am Not a Christian and Other Essays on Religion and Related Subjects*, ed. Paul Edwards (New York: Simon and Schuster, 1957), p. 56. Italics deleted. See also Paul Grimley Kuntz, *Bertrand Russell* (Boston: Twayne, 1986), p. 107f.

Index

Abelard, 34
Agapē, 13, 15, 26, 46, 167, 220, 236–37, 247, 273, 391–92, 402, 438
Aggression, 34, 86, 100, 116ff., 145–46, 155, 184, 315, 346, 356–57, 377
Alberoni, Francesco, 384–85, 463
Alexander, Franz, 448
Alexander, Richard D., 462
Altruism, 139, 150–51, 244, 346, 357–61, 373, 380, 411
Ames, Van Meter, 451
Amor fati. *See* Cosmic love
Anderson, Thomas C:, 457–58
Andreas Capellanus, 17, 87, 186
Anthropological concepts, 5, 361, 363–64, 371–72
Appraisal, xii, 128, 137–38, 142, 157–58, 216, 323, 370, 390–406, 433, 438–40
Aquinas, Thomas, St., 9
Arieti, Silvano and James A., 464
Aristotle, 18, 89, 131, 281, 346, 396, 434
Atkinson, Ti-Grace, 419–21, 464
Augustine, St., 72, 396
Austen, Jane, 415, 464
Autonomy, 409–11, 413–14, 432
Azzi, Marie-Denise Boros, 459

Babbitt, Irving, 19
Bain, Alexander, 349
Balint, Alice, 348
Balint, Michael, 348
Balzac, 316
Barnes, Hazel E., 461
Bate, Walter Jackson, xiii
Baudelaire, 191
Beauvoir, Simone de, xi, 281, 291, 311–17, 424, 457–58
Beethoven, 14, 61, 441
Beigel, Hugo G., 441
Being in love, 370, 383–90, 406, 409–11, 415–17, 438–40
Being, love of, 321, 430–31
Benson, Ruth Crego, 442
Bentley, Eric Russell, 453
Bergson, Henri, xi, 112, 162–70, 205–6, 208–9, 211, 219, 237, 243, 245, 247, 257, 261, 334, 360, 449–50
Berkeley, 159
Berlin, Isaiah, 442
Bernard, Claude, 159
Bernstein, Richard, 458
Bersani, Leo, 450
Bestowal, xii, 110, 128, 136, 138, 142, 157–58, 216–17, 298–99, 317, 323, 360, 370, 374, 380, 390–406, 408, 411, 416, 422,

Bestowal (*continued*)
425, 428, 431, 433–34, 438–
40
Bettelheim, Bruno, 445
Bizet, 85
Boccaccio, 36
Boulanger, J.-B., 450
Bowlby, John, 348, 358, 366, 461
Boyer, Paul, 442
Bradley, F. H., 339
Brain, Robert, 371–72, 441, 462
Brodsky, Archie, 441
Browning, 274
Brunner, Emil, 340
Buber, Martin, xi, 68, 281–82,
293–94, 332–39, 341–42, 460
Burnet, Etienne, 450
Byron, 441

Calvin, 219
Carey, John, 452
Caritas, 23, 222, 230, 272–74, 280,
312, 438
Chodorow, Nancy, 448, 461
Choron, Jacques, 460
Christian concepts of love, 4, 9,
12–15, 17–18, 23, 25–26, 31–
32, 34, 38–49, 55–57, 67–68,
71–74, 79, 82–85, 89, 152–54,
167, 222–23, 227, 230, 236–37,
259, 271–75, 285, 293, 312, 318,
336–37, 346, 371, 384, 402, 406,
428–31, 438
Colman, Arthur D. and Libby Lee,
464
Compassion, 18, 64, 73–74, 78, 90,
157, 273–76, 375, 429
Comte, Auguste, 69
Copernicus, 243
Cory, Daniel, 268, 455
Cosmic love, 70–71, 75–76, 79–
83, 102–3, 143, 162, 167, 228,
263–65, 271, 274–75, 418, 428,
431, 435
Cottrell, Robert D., 458
Courtly love, x, 4, 9–31, 35–36,
175, 346, 422–23, 438–39

Crystallization, 58, 186–87, 192,
201, 256, 380

Dante, 9, 12, 21, 36, 397
Darwin, 75, 112, 167, 249, 358
Delattre, Floris, 449–50
De Rougemont, Denis, 19, 34, 362,
371
Descartes, 20, 159
Don Juan legend, 34–35, 39, 244–
45, 249–53, 404–5, 441
Don Juan personality, 48, 64, 231,
355
Dostoyevsky, 62, 67, 236

Eckhart, 236
Eibl-Eibesfeldt, Irenäus, 357–58,
366, 462
Einstein, 154, 243
Engelhardt, Herbert, xiii
Engels, Frederick, 67–69, 443
Eros, 97–100, 111–16, 118–22,
142–43, 148–49, 154–55, 273,
396, 439
Essences, 196, 210–14, 261–63
Essentialism, 130–32, 157, 389
Ethological theory, xi, 345, 356–58
Existentialism, xi, 94, 281–342,
346

Fairness, 411
Falling in love, 202, 370, 383–90,
406–10, 415–17, 419–24, 438–
40
Family love, 54, 114, 124, 126,
204–5, 242, 278, 350, 353–54,
361, 378, 382
Father, love for, 366–68, 431
Father's love, 138–39, 278, 350,
353, 357–58, 365–69, 413, 425,
431
Fechner, G. T., 117
Feeling, love as, xii, 57, 78–79, 90,
93, 100–102, 132, 151, 155,
161–74, 176, 178, 196, 199, 203,
206, 210, 216, 244, 336, 341,

353, 360, 380–82, 411, 416–17, 425, 428–29, 431, 434–35
Feminist concepts, xi, 12–13, 64, 238–39, 252–53, 312–17, 346–47, 368, 418–25
Feuerbach, Ludwig, 67–69, 73, 77, 443
Fichte, 187
Ficino, 17, 137, 259, 267, 285, 354, 413
Fidelity, 14, 22–24, 51, 235, 240, 255, 315–16, 339–41, 348, 363–64
Firestone, Shulamith, 419, 421–25, 464–65
Flaubert, 159, 322–23
Florence, Jean, 448
Francis, St., 18, 144, 151
Fretz, Leo, 456
Freud, xi–xii, 3, 32, 90, 97–162, 190, 218–19, 236, 242, 256–57, 259, 287, 293, 298, 301–2, 345, 347–48, 352–53, 355–56, 362, 371, 378, 384, 387, 396, 415, 418–19, 431, 433, 441, 445–48, 451
Friendship, 76, 89, 114, 126, 144, 204–5, 225, 235, 248–49, 269, 277–80, 316, 325, 327, 330–31, 350–51, 356–57, 373, 380–82, 419–21, 436, 439
Fromm, Erich, 112–13, 120, 155, 418–19, 443, 445–46, 448, 464
Frustration, 22–24, 145, 180, 256–57, 267, 353, 357, 383, 403
Fusion. *See* Merging

Gallagher, Kenneth T., 460–61
Gandhi, 62
Gaylin, Willard, 464
Geach, P. T., 463
Genet, Jean, 282, 297, 308, 329
Gibbs, Anthony Matthews, 453
Gilbert, W. S., 247
Gilligan, Carol, 424, 465
Goethe, 16, 274
Goode, William J., 364–65, 441, 462

Goodheart, Eugene, 452
Gorky, Maxim, 60–61
Grant, Vernon W., 372–76, 447, 462–63
Grene, Marjorie, 341, 461

Hagstrum, Jean H., xiii
Harlow, Harry F., 349–53, 358, 461
Hatab, Lawrence J., 444
Hatkoff, Terry Smith, 465
Hatred, 30, 85, 114–16, 119–20, 153, 184, 194, 218, 300, 317, 329, 336, 346, 353–57, 367, 386
Hegel, ix, 16, 35, 40–41, 45, 62–63, 67, 69, 72–73, 77, 79, 112, 167, 246–47, 306, 321, 339, 418, 426, 428, 441
Heidegger, 281, 306–7, 331, 334–35, 337, 444
Henderson, Archibald, 453
Hobbes, 120
Hodgson, S. H., 447
Homosexuality, 199–201, 204, 226, 239, 267–68, 351
Horney, Karen, 353
Hough, Graham, 453
Humanity, love of, 56–57, 67–69, 76, 78, 91, 126, 143, 153–56, 166–69, 260, 271–72, 337–38, 360–61, 369, 418, 431, 437
Hume, 101, 159
Husserl, 281, 306

Ibsen, 247, 253
Idealist concepts, 6, 8, 12, 20, 24, 26–27, 29, 31, 33, 61, 66, 69, 85, 102, 150–51, 154, 159, 162, 168, 185–86, 207, 249, 261–63, 303–4, 312, 333, 339, 342, 346, 360, 401, 418, 439–40
Idealization, xii, 15, 17, 30–32, 34–35, 47, 51, 58, 61, 110–11, 140, 157, 199, 227, 239, 243, 248, 254, 265, 314, 321, 370, 374, 380, 400, 423–24, 428, 435, 439

Ideals, love of, 80, 141, 216, 247, 258–60, 263–69, 360, 434–37
Interdependence, 306–11, 325–27, 381, 412–16

James, Henry, xi, 172
James, William, 258, 266–67, 299, 332–33, 349, 447, 454–55, 461
Jaspers, Karl, 76, 331–32, 443, 459–60
Jealousy, 51–52, 193–200, 204, 216, 279, 363–64, 373, 375, 381
Jewish concepts of love, 12, 34, 43–44, 152–54, 293, 336–37, 431, 434, 438
Jones, Ernest, 98, 119, 132, 445–47
Joyce, James, 231, 353
Jung, 112

Kant, 43, 46, 82–83, 86–87, 92, 101, 297, 312, 354, 369–70, 413–14, 436, 441
Kaufmann, Walter, 443–44, 446
Keats, 4
Keen, Sam, 461
Kierkegaard, xi, 38–50, 65–66, 70, 76, 86, 337, 441–42
Kinsey, 234, 376
Klein, Melanie, 353–56, 366–67, 461
Konner, Melvin, 461
Kuntz, Paul Grimley, 465

Lacher, Walter, 452
Lafayette, Madame de, 388–89
Lantz, Herman R., 463
La Rochefoucauld, 405
Lasswell, Thomas E., 465
Lawrence, D. H., xi, 32, 219–40, 242–43, 248, 329, 394, 406, 451–52
Lawrence, Frieda, 231
Leavis, F. R., 452
Leighton, Jean, 458
Leonardo da Vinci, 218
Levey, H. B., 447

Liebestod, 31, 117, 221, 257
Lilar, Suzanne, 461
Linton, Ralph, 361–62, 462
Lorenz, Konrad, 348, 356–58, 461
Love-objects, 17, 101–2, 105, 123–24, 133–42, 177–82, 185, 188–92, 313–14, 347–49, 366–68, 430–38
Lovesickness, 30
Löwith, Karl, 443
Lucretius, 8, 30, 196, 258, 406
Luther, 25–26, 31, 45–46, 73, 219–20, 230, 236, 247, 428–30, 438, 451

McCormick, John, 455
Macksey, Richard A., xiii
McMahon, Joseph H., 459
McTaggart, J. M. E., 397–401, 463
Mailer, Norman, 238–39, 453
Malinowski, Bronislaw, 462
Mann, Thomas, 60, 63, 91, 443
Marcel, Gabriel, xi, 281–82, 293–94, 339–42, 460–61
Marcuse, Herbert, 148–50, 448
Marital passion, 379–83
Marriage and marital love, 4–7, 28–29, 31–34, 39–40, 42–43, 46–47, 49–56, 59, 69, 87–89, 114, 123, 133, 144, 156, 190, 200, 204–5, 216–17, 220, 235–36, 239–40, 248–49, 251, 260, 269–70, 277–79, 315–16, 337–38, 341, 354, 363–64, 366–68, 370–72, 378–83, 395, 413, 421–23, 431–32, 439–40
Marx Brothers, 247
Marx, Karl, 67–69, 145, 316, 324, 362, 443
Matasy, Katherine, xiii
May, Rollo, 112–13, 445
Mayr von Baldegg, Praxedis, 462
Mazlish, Bruce, 444
Mead, Margaret, 363–64, 462
Megay, Joyce N., 449–50
Mellen, Sydney L. W., 365–66, 462
Memory, 208–10, 212–13

Merging, 8, 14–20, 26, 30, 32, 118, 120, 132–34, 163, 183, 185, 193, 203, 207, 216, 219–23, 226–27, 275–76, 293–301, 307–9, 316, 322, 324, 326, 329–32, 335, 338, 342, 370, 406–18, 421–22, 430, 438
Merleau-Ponty, Maurice, 331–32, 460
Mill, John Stuart, 67, 196
Miller, Howard L., 461
Millett, Kate, 238–39, 453
Milton, 5, 219–20, 230–31, 451
Modell, Arnold H., 448
Molière, 34, 250, 441
Montagu, Ashley, 441
Montaigne, 6, 87, 200, 380
Morgan, Douglas N., 446
Moslem concepts of love, 12, 293
Mother, love for, 104, 122, 127, 139, 171, 190, 199, 350–55, 366–68, 413, 419, 431–32
Mother's love, 138–39, 203–5, 215, 248–49, 278, 291, 350, 352–53, 357–59, 365–69, 413, 418, 424–25
Mozart, 34, 39, 250, 441
Murdoch, Iris, 341, 458, 461
Murstein, Bernard I., 463

Nagel, Thomas, 457
Nature, love of, 60–61, 165, 171, 183, 251–52, 256, 338, 418–19, 431, 434–35
Neoplatonism, 4, 13, 17, 21, 220, 258–60, 267–68, 285
Newman, Pauline, 457
Newton, 243
Nietzsche, xi, 32, 65–94, 48, 117–18, 194, 223, 246–47, 253, 274, 276, 281, 285–86, 356, 428–29, 442–44, 456

Oaklander, Nathan, 457
Object-love, 135–42, 150–51, 348–49

Oneness, 4, 14, 23, 27, 87, 132–34, 143, 150, 183, 220, 269, 275–79, 293, 297, 301, 307–9, 311, 322–23, 325–26, 328–32, 334–35, 410, 414, 416, 418, 426–27, 436
Ortega y Gasset, José, 201–2, 385, 387–88, 450, 463
Ovid, 186

Parental love. *See* Mother's love; Father's love
Pascal, 45, 67, 293
Paul, St., 126
Peele, Stanton, 441
Peirce, C. S., 167, 449
Perkins, Moreland, xiii
Persons, love of, 46, 140–41, 162, 165, 168, 171, 177, 181–96, 201–3, 205–7, 215–18, 220–31, 251–52, 256, 265–70, 272, 275–80, 291, 294–300, 319–33, 335–36, 338–42, 350, 372–76, 387–88, 390–401, 403–6, 417–18, 424, 430, 432–39
Petrarch, 21
Pfuetze, Paul E., 460
Pilkington, A. E., 450
Plato, 8–9, 12–13, 16–17, 20–21, 28, 42, 60, 80, 99, 111–12, 126, 133, 141, 157, 173, 190, 211–12, 225, 233, 242, 254, 258–63, 266–68, 270–71, 273–74, 281, 303–4, 316–17, 346, 396, 406, 418, 431, 436, 439, 441
Plotinus, 263, 268, 285
Pluralism, x, 129, 132, 248, 278–79, 376, 388–90, 417, 431, 434–37, 440
Poggioli, Renato, 57, 442–43
Pope, Kenneth S., 462
Poulet, Georges, 450
Promiscuity, 22, 24
Proust, xi, 159–219, 268, 275, 292–94, 296, 313, 415, 449–51, 455, 464
Psychiatric concepts of love, xi, 94, 97–158, 160–61, 171, 345, 352–

Psychiatric concepts (*continued*)
56, 366–68, 370, 408–9, 418–
19, 432–34
Psychological concepts, xi, 345,
347–48, 350, 356, 364, 379, 392
Puritan concepts, 31–32, 219–53

Ramsey, Paul, 458, 461
Rancour-Laferriere, Daniel, 366–
67, 448, 462–63, 465
Rapaport, Elizabeth, 429, 464
Realist concepts, 6, 8, 26–27, 31–
33, 156, 158–59, 168, 207, 211,
214, 216, 219, 247, 276, 282,
339, 341, 346, 353, 415, 418,
439–40
Reik, Theodor, 123–25, 128, 134,
384, 424, 446–47
Religious love, 8, 25, 28, 35, 49,
56–57, 60–61, 69, 151–55, 157,
166–69, 205, 220, 229–30, 237,
293–94, 332, 335–37, 339–41,
369, 418–19, 428–31, 435, 437
Rieff, Philip, 445
Rivers, J. E., 450
Robb, Christina, 464
Rolland, Romain, 132
Romantic concepts of love, x, xii,
4, 6–7, 10–12, 14–20, 23–34,
46–47, 55, 61, 65–66, 69, 88,
93–94, 115, 117, 132, 143–44,
156, 159–63, 186–87, 191, 194,
199, 216, 221–23, 227, 230,
235–36, 241–42, 255, 257, 263,
274, 285, 294, 297, 304, 313,
319, 323, 328, 346, 353, 370–71,
377, 379, 387, 410, 416, 421–23,
434–35, 438–39
Romantic love, xii, 3–7, 40, 63,
123–25, 166, 220–21, 240–41,
342, 346, 350–52, 361–68, 370–
75, 384, 410, 419
Romantic passion, 379–83
Rousseau, 24, 57–58, 60, 62, 66,
69, 76, 165, 201–2, 216–17, 233,
328, 330, 406, 412, 415, 420–21,
433
Royce, Josiah, 255, 339, 460

Russell, Bertrand, 6–7, 233, 440–
41, 465

Sade, 30, 75, 353, 404
Safilios-Rothschild, Constantina,
464
Santayana, xi–xii, 78, 80, 91, 121,
157, 212–14, 216, 254–80, 396,
444, 446, 450–51, 454–56
Sartre, xi, 48–49, 196–98, 281–
311, 313, 316–331, 334–35,
339, 341–42, 410–12, 450, 456–
59, 464
Schacht, Richard, 444
Schiller, 129
Schlegel, Friedrich, 4, 7, 94, 143–
44, 441
Schopenhauer, 8, 18, 52–53, 63–
64, 69, 71–74, 76–79, 85–88,
91–93, 98, 102, 114–15, 121,
196, 215, 243, 246–47, 249, 251,
254–55, 263, 274, 281, 443
Schweitzer, Albert, 18
Scruton, Roger, 411, 457, 463–64
Self-love, 83, 126, 134–37, 139–
40, 201–2, 337, 418, 428–34
Sensuous vs. passionate, 234–35,
239, 375–78
Sexuality, 8–12, 31–33, 36, 50,
52–56, 59–61, 84–89, 92–93,
97ff., 161–62, 165, 170–71,
173–79, 187, 189, 219, 221, 224,
228–40, 242–45, 249–51, 255–
60, 268–69, 300–306, 347–48,
350, 362–63, 365, 368–78, 391,
418, 424, 435–36, 439–40
Sexual love, 3ff., 8–12, 31, 34, 47,
55–56, 58–59, 60, 69, 83–94,
100ff., 166, 168, 177–96, 202–6,
215–18, 225–27, 230, 237, 243,
257–60, 268–69, 278–79, 292–
300, 312–17, 319–24, 328–30,
336, 350–52, 354–56, 361, 365–
90, 418–25, 431–32, 435–36,
440
Shakespeare, 157, 195, 234, 251,
395, 406, 409, 429–30, 448,
463–65

Sharing of self, 409–12, 413, 422, 439

Shattuck, Roger, 449–50

Shaw, G. B., xi, 32, 219–20, 238–53, 453–54

Shelley, 4, 7, 94, 186, 253, 406, 441

Siegel, Paul S., 461

Singer, Josephine Fisk, xiii

Slater, Philip, 362–63, 371–72, 462

Snyder, Eloise C., 463

Sociobiological concepts, xi, 345, 358–61, 366

Sociological concepts, 5, 27–28, 346, 361–65, 371–72, 388

Solomon, Robert C., xiii, 341–42, 409–11, 457, 461, 464

Souza, Sybil de, 450

Spinoza, 23, 79, 156, 159, 275, 428, 434

Sprigge, Timothy L. S., 455

Stages of love, historical, 35–37

Stages of love, psychological, 41, 49, 64, 177–85, 191–92, 346, 348–56, 432, 440

Starr, Mimi, xiii

Staying in love, 370, 383–90, 406, 411–17, 438–40

Stendhal, 4, 24, 58–59, 92–94, 159, 186–87, 191–92, 195, 201–2, 207, 217, 253, 256, 379–80, 385, 388, 415, 450, 454, 463

Stephens, William N., 462

Stern, Karl, 442

Sterne, Lawrence, 406, 464

Stevens, Wallace, 405, 464

Stopes, Marie, 233

Sublimation, 90, 92, 103, 129–30, 132, 259–60, 383

Sulloway, Frank J., 447

Suttie, T. D., 125

Symons, Donald, 424, 465

Tenderness, xii, 100–101, 127, 158, 184, 193, 197, 199–200, 215, 224, 229, 238, 321, 375, 381, 416, 425

Theological approaches, xi, 9, 15, 25–26, 46–48, 51, 79, 219–20, 222, 229–31, 236–37, 239, 245–46, 272–73, 336–41, 418, 425–31, 435, 438

Things, love of, 162, 215, 265–67, 401, 431, 434–36

Tillich, Paul, 340, 425–31, 465

Tirso de Molina, 34, 250

Tolstoy, xi, 32, 49–66, 70, 102, 389, 442–43

Toynbee, Arnold, 35

Transparency, 326, 335, 413–15

Tristan legend, 11, 15, 18, 20, 34–36, 175, 227, 240

Trivers, Robert, 358, 424, 462, 465

Troyat, Henri, 443

Turco, Alfred, 453

Udry, J. Richard, 441, 462

Vannoy, Russell, 401–6, 463–64

Voltaire, 58, 66

Wagner, 11–12, 67, 69, 73–74, 85, 117, 162, 221, 227, 240, 257, 443

Walster, Elaine and G. William, 380–81, 463

Wapinsky, David, 454

Warnock, Mary, 458

Wedding, concept of, 370, 406, 415

Weil, Simone, 337

Whitbeck, Caroline, 464

Whitford, Margaret, 457

Whitman, Walt, 18, 221–22, 237, 274

Williams, Donald C., 455

Wilson, Edward O., 358, 360, 462

Winch, Robert F., 441, 461–63

Wollstonecraft, Mary, 420–21, 464

Zola, Emile, 8, 159